Two Arabs, a Berber, and a Jew

Two Arabs, a Berber, and a Jew

Entangled Lives in Morocco

LAWRENCE ROSEN

The University of Chicago Press
Chicago and London

Lawrence Rosen is the William Nelson Cromwell Professor of Anthropology at Princeton University and adjunct professor of law at Columbia Law School. He is the author of many books, including *Bargaining for Reality, The Culture of Islam,* and *Varieties of Muslim Experience,* all also published by the University of Chicago Press.

The University of Chicago Press, Chicago 60637
The University of Chicago Press, Ltd., London
© 2016 by The University of Chicago
All rights reserved. Published 2016.

25 24 23 22 21 20 19 18 17 16   1 2 3 4 5

ISBN-13: 978-0-226-31734-2 (cloth)
ISBN-13: 978-0-226-31748-9 (paper)
ISBN-13: 978-0-226-31751-9 (e-book)
DOI: 10.7208/chicago/9780226317519.001.0001

Library of Congress Cataloging-in-Publication Data

Rosen, Lawrence, 1941– author.
   Two Arabs, a Berber, and a Jew : entangled lives in Morocco / Lawrence Rosen.
      pages ; cm
   Includes bibliographical references and index.
   ISBN 978-0-226-31734-2 (cloth : alk. paper) — ISBN 978-0-226-31748-9 (pbk. : alk. paper) — ISBN 978-0-226-31751-9 (ebook)   1. Morocco— Intellectual life—21st century.   2. Morocco—Social life and customs— 21st century.   3. Berbers—Morocco.   4. Arabs—Morocco.   5. Jews— Morocco.   I. Title.
   DT325.5.R67 2015
   306.0964—dc23

                                                                  201504459

♾ This paper meets the requirements of ANSI/NISO Z39.48–1992 (Permanence of Paper).

For Clifford Geertz and Hildred Storey Geertz
Teachers, colleagues, friends

Has there come upon man a while of time when he was a thing unremembered?
QURAN 76:1

I will [tell] the story as I go along of small cities no less than of great. Most of those which were great once are small today; and those which in my own lifetime have grown to greatness were small enough in the old days.

HERODOTUS

From now on I'll describe the cities to you, the Khan said. In your journeys you will see if they exist.

ITALO CALVINO, *Invisible Cities*

Therefore, I decided with the help of God to blacken these pages with what I saw and heard during this voyage, be it clear or obscure. For I am but a woodgatherer of the night, the one who lags behind, a horse who is out of the race. You should not judge me too harshly, for I am only doing it as a reminder to myself, and to inform others who may ask me from among my fellow countrymen. Let the masters of composition and rhetoric excuse me, and let the burden of the men of metaphor and allusion be lifted from me. I beseech God to cover my mistakes.

Disorienting Encounters: Travels of a Moroccan Scholar in France in 1845–1846: The Voyage of Muḥammad aṣ-Ṣaffār

Sefrou, 1972

Sefrou, 2008

CONTENTS

Prologue: A World of Difference

A child's among you takin' notes,
and faith he'll print it.

—Robert Burns

You would hardly believe how difficult it is to place a figure alone on a canvas
and to concentrate all the interest on this single and universal figure and still
keep it living and real.

—Edouard Manet

Ordinary people have intellectual lives. They may never have written a
book; they may never even have read one. But their lives are rich in ideas,
constantly fashioned and revised, elaborated and rearranged. Just as no
one speaks exactly the same sentences as anyone else, and rarely the same
sentence twice, so, too, the act of daily living comprises an ongoing re-
creation of the means by which we capture experience and make it our
own, a capacity that is of the very essence of our species.

To be an intellectual in this sense is not to be equally knowledgeable
or wise in all domains of life. Who among us has not met a person justly
recognized for his or her accomplishments in one field but who, when the
conversation turns to other matters, appears, in these unfamiliar places, to
confirm Carl Sandburg's quip that "an expert is just a damn fool a long way
from home"? But when we *are* at home we are all masters of certain ideas,
whether in their unreflective application, their rearrangement to fit our current needs, or the newly revealed possibilities through which we make our
situations conform to our images of them. Thought, it has been said, is
extrinsic, not intrinsic—something fashioned not in the "secret grotto of

the mind" but worked over in the enactment of our shared conceptualizations. Like every human endeavor, thought may be performed with brilliant aplomb or mind-numbing regularity, but it is always pursued with and through the concepts we share with others, and thus rejoins, at one extreme, our most private of attributions and, at the other, our most embedded of associations.

To attend to the intellectual lives of ordinary people is also a central tenet of the practice of anthropology. We anthropologists may, as Clifford Geertz noted, see ourselves as the miniaturists of the social sciences, intrusive seekers who attempt, by "painting on Lilliputian canvases with what we take to be delicate strokes, to find in the little what eludes us in the large, to stumble on general truths while sorting through special cases." Or we may view ourselves as the ultimate arbiters of human sensibility, limping up, like the devil in the Kipling poem, to explain it all over again. Either way, that which is ordinary remains the centerpiece of the anthropologist's subject matter and professional ethos. Such a focus may carry with it the possibility for boundless self-importance or, properly proportioned, a responsibility to make the extraordinary lives of ordinary people comprehensible in terms both scientific and human.

Rarely is the burden of this responsibility greater than when it involves trying to offset stereotypes or when, as one novelist put it, we are trying to avoid "the most banal of human faults—the failure to imagine the life of another." Anthropology, as a discipline, has reason to be justly proud of its accomplishments. We have demonstrated, for example, contrary to the common opinion of its day, that race has no bearing on intelligence, societal complexity, or cultural accomplishment; we have shown that, contrary to then-current colonial attitudes, nonliterate peoples have systems of legal theory worthy of the name of jurisprudence or religious schemas entitled to comparison with any established theology. And if, at times, anthropologists have fallen prey to obscurantism or self-congratulation, they never have to go far, if only they remain attentive, to hear people expressing a life of ideas that challenges all our abilities for comprehension and translation. Where settled images have formed about people from another culture, the need to convey the range of intellectual lives is especially compelling. And there are few places where this is more pressing than in our understanding of the cultures of the Middle East.

Nearly one of every four people on the planet today is an adherent of the Muslim faith. The variation is, of course, enormous, but it is precisely that—variation on themes that do possess a high degree of commonality, particularly within linguistic communities such as that comprising the speakers of Arabic. Regrettably, Western images of the Muslim world are far less varied. Mention the Middle East to most people in the West, and visions of terrorism or gender discrimination, ruthless punishments or Machiavellian politics have a way of leaping to the fore. What is lost in the process is not simply the range of variation but the lives of ordinary men and women, lives of far greater intellectual richness than the reduction to simple stereotypes can ever embrace. It is to the conveyance of this intellectual life that anthropology owes much of its raison d'être; it is in the representation of this life of other minds that each anthropologist finds a large measure of personal and professional purpose.

Like all scholars and writers, anthropologists are beset by metaphors. If it is better to think of the heart as a pump than as a furnace or the eye as a receptor than as a beacon, one can hope that the choice of metaphors is, if not actually revelatory, at least (as Samuel Butler said) "the least misleading thing we have." And if one were to choose a metaphor as an entry point to thinking about Arab societies quite generally, it might be that of the marketplace. For not only is the economy built around constant hawking and haggling, but so too in many respects is social life. It is in this realm of relationships that men (and to a varying extent, women) must forge networks of dependents in order to secure themselves in a world perceived as dangerous and uncertain. And just as there are regularities in the marketplace, there are standards of appropriate engagement in social life. It is in this environment that each of the people I will describe must be placed. And it is in this environment that any ethnographer must make choices about his or her own relationships with the people concerned and how to represent them in a form the Western reader can find approachable.

How one goes about such a task has many solutions. For me, I will simply say that I regard the anthropologist's role in this regard as rather like that of one of the characters in a short story by Paul Theroux who describes himself as "an unrepentant eavesdropper" who finds "anonymity a consolation." The bounds of my "eavesdropping" have, for the most part, been set by the conventions of my trade and personal embarrassment. My quest has been for regularities and ranges of variation, not for idiosyncrasy. Through decades of conversation and decades of note-taking I have doubtless come to embody Lévi-Strauss's droll comment that "if this is escape I am one of escape's bureaucrats." But there is also my own discomfort at intruding beyond the point of individual ease—mine and theirs—that has precluded too great a search for the intimate history of each of the people I will describe here. I have, in this respect, tended to assume, as Emily Dickinson cautioned, that their ideal reader, like hers, might be one who "permits a comfortable intimacy and yet lets the innermost Me remain behind its veil."

Indeed, through all the years of intense inquiry there have also been moments of simply settling back among these friends, letting the slight linguistic haze through which most anthropologists operate close around me, reveling in the feel of their presence, the cadence and sonorities of their words. There were also, perhaps, times when I, like many anthropologists, have inadvertently mimicked that "free-floating attention" that Freud commended, in which, wandering between that which could be understood from the contextual and that which could only be grasped in the passing moment, I could sense my friends' meaning more from its intensity than its reason. At such moments I could understand, too, what that wisest of guides to ethnographic observation, Frédéric Chopin, meant when he said, while stranded among the Scottish gentry during a concert tour, that he was spending his time "watching them speak and listening to them drink."

Indeed, with the exception of a few texts, I never recorded the conversations I overheard or in which I took part. To do so, I believe, risks too much reliance on the recording device rather than attending to the uncertainties that need clarification at that very moment. It can also mean giving up that wondrous sense of losing oneself in the luxury of the conversation itself. This also accounts, in part, for my not using quotation marks around the statements of the people represented here: even long after, I hear their voices with utter clarity—in many instances their exact words—yet the themes they pursued and the flow of our conversations have also become interwoven over the years. Since what they have to say depends in no small part on what I have to say, perhaps it is best not to pretend to an unprovable precision.

But why, one may ask, should they have talked to me in the first place—why not just ignore a stranger who, like some oversized child, had to be taught everything from scratch? There are various possible answers. Hermann Hesse spoke of the "intimate disclosure to the perfect stranger," that revelation we can more easily make to someone who, being outside the repercussions of our ongoing relations, can be taken into one's confidence precisely because he or she does not quite count. Did they share their ideas with me because they wanted to test their own account against my response to it? Was it because they were as eager to embellish their own standing through our mutual contact as they were to use my inquiries to proudly display their own ideas? Or could it even be that through what one poet called the "unreflective revelation of the obvious" they could state the self-evident, and by doing so, make it so? Through many years and many encounters the answers still elude me, even as their words and acts blur the boundaries of our enterprise. Perhaps, in the end, all that can be said is that they talked to me because I listened. They talked to me because we were friends. They talked to me because they wanted to be remembered.

This book is not, then, a set of individual biographies. There are many admirable instances in the anthropological literature of scholars who have attempted a full statement of an informant's life, whether ostensibly in that person's own words (Paul Radin's *The Autobiography of a Winnebago Indian*) or in a highly edited presentation thereof (Oscar Lewis's *The Children of Sanchez*). Those who have studied Morocco seem especially prone to such biographical accounts, no doubt because this is a society in which the force of personality figures so prominently, a society in which capturing the terms of discussion is vital to controlling the outcome of actions. To do full justice to those who figure here it would, then, be indispensable to present a far more complete picture of their words and deeds. But because the goal here is a bit different, it is important to indicate the boundaries of this book.

It is not false modesty to say that I do not have either the detailed knowledge of these people's lives—their deepest emotions, their most intimate acts—or the requisite literary skills for telling such a story. Moreover, I am not intent on showing their responses to all of the most current political questions that they and their society face. It is the deeper background of such intellectual lives that is often lost in the literature. History—particularly political history—can be written from the top down or the bottom up. One can envision people's lives as so oriented by what happens at the level of national development as to render all of their endeavors a function of state action or, starting the other way round, see the state as floating above the beliefs and emotions of daily life in a way that renders the two largely disconnected. In this work neither of these orientations is ignored or governing. But if the intersection appears intermittent, it is in part because a view from below may serve as a brake on an overly state-directed view of events, just as a view that ignores the intersection with national events would suggest a false dichotomy in their lives.

My concern, then, is with the ideas these people expressed in my presence. To the extent that I can place these ideas in their national context and in their personal histories, I do so, on the one hand, with the emphases they gave to the relation of Morocco's larger course and their personal lives and, on the other, with full and unapologetic awareness of the limitations of my own knowledge and respect for their privacy. Thus I hope that, without unduly confusing my assessments with their presentations, each of our voices will be clear even if, at the point where their ideas and my captivation have been joined, to some degree the separation remains, for me at least, blessedly indistinct.

They are, in every way I know, the most extraordinary of ordinary people. In his own way each is a man of the world, yet their conceptions of that world and how a man operates within it are, notwithstanding many superficial similarities, not the same as those encountered in other cultures and other times. Indeed to Westerners these men may seem remarkably familiar, navigating their relationships in ways that appear quite similar to our own. At other moments, their assumptions about human nature and human qualities, their vision of time or the attribution of intentions and responsibility may appear to be offset just a few degrees from our own, and as the distance grows, the divergence may take one farther away than initially appeared likely. In each feature, then, a careful eye to the unique and the characteristic, the similar and the critically different must always be kept in view.

There is Haj Hamed Britel, the enthralling elderly raconteur who, during his years in Sefrou and in one of the nation's coastal cities, saw his nation change from a near-medieval monarchy of the late nineteenth century to a modernizing nation of the late twentieth, a man who has been a participant-observer in many of its struggles for continuity in the face of outside provocation. Through his cornucopian knowledge one sees the assumptions about history and humanity that continue to inform the view of events that many Moroccans, Arabs, and fellow Muslims carry with them into the world that affects us all.

There is Yaghnik Driss, by origin from Fez, the engaging, humorous teacher of small children, devoted lover of his faith, husband, father, and object of his pet dogs' adoration. He embraces Islam with imagination and verve, thus giving the lie to any view of the faith as stagnant, uncreative, or oppressive. In his delightful storytelling, unpretentious moralizing, and eclectic philosophizing, one encounters a man of enormous charm, the perfect guide to the religion of tolerance that Islam incorporates despite domestic extremes and foreign stereotypes.

There is Hussein ou Muhammad Qadir, the savvy and insightful Berber entrepreneur whose pride in his language and culture meld seamlessly with his attachment to the joys of operating in a wider marketplace of goods and people. In him, and in his entire settlement, the flow of information passes with remarkable finesse, and the openness to ideas and experiences is writ deep in his ease of movement and his keen sense of just what political animals humans really are.

And there is Shimon Benizri, the kindly Jewish cloth dealer, meek in the finest sense of the word, devoted to his family and totally at home, first in his rural community and later in town, in a country that has always had a set of relations to his people that escapes easy judgment. In him one sees not only the history of the Jews of Morocco but why it is in no sense a contradiction to refer to him and them as "Arab Jews."

And there are the women—forceful, articulate, informed, and wise. The wives of each of the men described here will be referred to at times, and I was able to get to know them and their daughters to some extent. Describing the intellectual lives of these women is less easy for me, though, for the simple reason that it was more difficult, initially as a single man, to speak alone and in detail with them, and virtually impossible to follow them through many domains of their lives. Fortunately, others—both scholars and women writers from North Africa and elsewhere—have given us a host of portraits of Moroccan women that need to be read alongside accounts like my own. In doing so one will see that these women have intellectual lives no less sophisticated and involved than those of the men and that they are undoubtedly playing a crucial role in the changes their society is currently undergoing.

After decades of work in North Africa I could, of course, have chosen to present the intellectual lives of many other people I have come to know. There is the liberal academic, so deeply committed to his country's well-being that he gave up a career in the West to teach, direct, and render in Arabic his own insights as a scientist and patriot; there is the young woman making both a career and a family life as she oversees the distribution of food and medicine to impoverished farmers and herders deep in the Middle Atlas Mountains; there is the veteran of the French forces in Indochina who welcomed me to his circle of friends, all of whom shared with me their understanding of places and times that affected our interrelated lives; there is the illiterate gardener, named for the mother who never revealed his father's identity, who always spoke with such dignity, and who, on a trip to a saintly shrine, feared entering the sacred precincts because, he said, some of the misdeeds committed in the course of his life rendered him unworthy to be in the saint's presence; there is the old man who lived in a cave in the nearby hills and talked with naive grace about the way new inventions might disrupt the way people think and relate to one another; there is the dutiful daughter who chafed at wearing a veil but was not afraid to acknowledge why her respect for the generation of elders to whom she was attached would be hurt if, while her husband was away, her immodesty were taken to imply any sense of personal disrespect. I have left out so many, even though they populate my own thoughts at every turn. But short of yet another recitation of the Five Pillars of Islam or a tedious rendering of the ways in which one regime has followed another, how can we understand the world these people have made and its impact on our own without attending, in all humility, to the ideas of at least a few of those who have so strikingly become entwined with one's own life and imagination?

The four men who form the centerpiece of this book did not really know one another: Haj Hamed had met Yaghnik briefly; the others met only once or twice when I happened over the years to introduce them. Yet they all interacted regularly with people like each other. More important— and this is a central theme of this book—each of them revels in the differences they collectively represent. This orientation is deeply writ in Moroccan and Muslim culture: "Difference is a blessing," said the Prophet. "A difference is not a distinction," he said. "Had God so willed He could have made us all the same," says the Quran itself. Without in any way romanticizing such variation, all of those discussed here share a culture in which difference is vital, in which the diversity of their inclinations and connections is seen as enlivening their range of social possibilities. How, individually and as a society, they have structured such differences into their culture forms a large part of their intellectual biographies and is indispensable to an understanding of how, for them, difference forms a basis for linkage rather than a fault line of separation.

If these four men do not know one another personally, they share a setting that is not only a physical space but the source of their nurturance. It is the terrain for all that has gone into the relationships they individually negotiate and the guidelines by which they collectively enact their personalities and choices. Sefrou, as their place, is experienced differently and indeed differentially by each, yet all recognize it as vital to who they are. Located fifteen miles south of Fez on the edge of the Middle Atlas Mountains, it has grown from a small city of 3,000 (half of them Jewish) before the turn of the twentieth century, to some 25,000 when I arrived in the mid-1960s, to some 80,000 at present. Even in its early years it had all the characteristics of an urban center. For the Haj, notwithstanding many years living on the coast, it is truly a city, with all the institutions and amenities of cities of far greater scale; to Yaghnik, it is his home town of Fez scaled down but with the qualities and problems that are typical of the nation at large; to Hussein it is the market center for him and his fellow tribesmen, a proprietary attachment embraced in their reference to it (usually with the French term) as "our *village*"; and to Shimon Benizri it was the economic and communal center for those Jews like himself who were scattered across the tribal hinterland and who collected in the town at various times of the year and periods in their own lives.

Sefrou has a very long history and has been the object of many travelers' admiration. Visitors over the centuries have referred to it as an oasis, "a small Jerusalem," a haven perched on the cusp of mountain and plain. Because it lies between massif and lowland, along a key route from the Sahara to Fez and beyond, it has also been caught up in fights of historic import. Chronicles thus speak of how Yusuf ben Tashfin massacred opponents in the city in 1063; how in 1736 the sultan Muhammad ben Ismail, furious at the protection the Berbers of the region had given his rebellious brother, killed many of the town's inhabitants and took their heads to Fez; or how, during the course of another Berber revolt in 1811, tribesmen surrounded an army sent against them and pillaged the whole region. But no less common are the glowing terms in which those who came through Sefrou described its peaceful setting.

Indeed, travelers have for a dozen centuries never failed to remark on the beauty of Sefrou and their own regret in departing from it. Al Idrissi, writing in the twelfth century, speaks of Sefrou as "a small and secluded but civilized town, where there are not many markets. Its inhabitants are for the most part agriculturalists, who cultivate a quantity of cereals; there are also a large number of large and small cattle. The waters of the land are sweet and abundant." Collette visited Sefrou in the 1920s and described it as "Paradise on earth, rather as we picture it, if we picture it as oriental and populous and confined. Sefrou is a patch of fertile, humid earth, alive with the gurgle of water. The pomegranate grove flames, the cherry swells, the fig tree has the odor of milk, the grass yields its juices as we bruise it. . . . The eyes and teeth of the young Jews gleam. . . . A place so amiable makes man amiable." And Edward Westermarck, a Finnish anthropologist who worked extensively among the Berber tribes of the Sefrou region starting in 1899, wrote in the summer of 1910 (when temperatures of 125 degrees were recorded by the geographer Dr. Félix W. Weisgerber) of his journey up from Fez:

> "We took our way along the caravan route [which] passes through tracts of land overgrown with palmetto, spindle-trees, and gorse, and by little villages stationed like outposts here and there. . . . A few hundred yards from where the road leaves the mountains, the little town lies on either side of the river, nestling amongst gardens, where the cherry-tree flourishes better than any other place in Morocco, side by side with oranges, pomegranates, and olives. The situation is delightful, and, thanks to the streams that pour down the

mountains and are brought into the fields, the country is fresh and green even in the heat of summer." [After a stay of four weeks he wrote of his departure:] "Farewell, you splendid town, I shall never see you again, for you have given me all I wanted of you!"

For each of them, as for so many others, transient contact with the city leaves a vivid impression, an indelible trace of memory; for those whose entire lives are tied up with it, those memories inform present and future acts no less than past encounters. It was Marcel Proust who said, "The one divine thing man does is to remember." But even if memory plays tricks on us, it does not do so randomly. In studying what these people told me about their city, their tribe, their lives, I could attempt, at every point, to find other sources to confirm what they recall; I could hedge each of their utterances with uncertainty as to their accuracy. I could even excuse myself if I prove to be a poor historian by pleading that I am no historian at all. And I am certainly willing to convert a potential failing into a possible virtue by transforming my lack of knowledge into naive open-mindedness in the way Lytton Strachey noted in the preface to *Eminent Victorians* when he said, "Ignorance is the first requisite of the historian—ignorance, which simplifies and clarifies, which selects and omits, with a placid perfection unattainable by the highest art."

The truth is that I have often been able to verify the recollections of these men and women from independent sources or found their stories and accounts present in the collective memories or published literature on Morocco and other parts of the Muslim world. But even where independent confirmation has not been possible, it is the nature, the structure, the logic of their thoughts that is most important to this enterprise; attending to how they construct their world and not just whether everyone does it similarly or with equal attention to extraneous "facts" is not the sole basis for finding merit in their accounts.

Anthropology is indeed a science—of the irreducibly personal and the indisputably characteristic, of aspects and foundations, expressions and implications, ineradicable trivialities and evanescent truths, perduring instances of verbal wrestling and transcendent moments of quiet apprehension. It is also handmaiden to the humanities, seeking the patterns in our multifarious capabilities, ferreting out the insights and fictions of our attributes, discerning the commonalities of our culture-bearing species no less than the characteristic peculiarities of our individuality, and reaching beyond the instrumentality of one another's existence to forge that most unusual of relationships—a lifelong friendship that spans a cultural divide.

It is not an unmediated gap. There have been moments when I have felt as though I ought to apologize to these friends for fear, as one Muslim poet might have me say to them, that "my memory keeps getting in the way of your history." But it would, in truth, be hypocritical of me to do so, since I take no small pleasure, after so many years, in sensing that our histories and our memories have become enmeshed. All I can offer to these extraordinarily ordinary people who have given me so much is my limited ability as chronicler and my extravagant capacity for admiration and to ask of them—as Muslims and Jews are both commended by their faiths to ask of one another during their most sacred days:

allahu ma-_gh_afir lana اللّٰهُمَّ غَفِرِ لَنا
ani m'vakesh mechila אני מבקש מחלה

Through our mutual forgiveness
may we be granted forgiveness in our turn.

Committed to Memory:
Haj Hamed Britel
235 Qla'a

Haj Hamed Britel

In memory each of us is an artist: each of us creates.

—Patricia Hampl

I can never remember things I did not understand in the first place.

—Amy Tan

From the hillside above the city of Sefrou, alongside the saintly shrine of Sidi ʿAli Bouseghine, it is just possible, in the quiet of the early morning, to imagine Morocco as it was a little over a century ago—before there was a single paved road, before most people had ever seen a European, before electricity or artificial light or the sound of the internal combustion engine. There, with the wind that slopes down the escarpment of the Middle Atlas Mountains carrying away the smell of diesel and the noise of motorized traffic, much of contemporary life seems to dissipate, and the contours of the land seem to bear witness to an earlier form of human imprint. At such a moment, in the slanting morning light, you can often see the glimmer of the river as it cuts through the town, discern the outline of the walls of the old city, and describe the limits of the irrigated gardens before they were overrun by urban expansion. And if, as the sun climbs steadily in the distance, you follow the rim of the hills, past the pilgrims' hotel and the site of the old French fort, past the gravel diggings and restive goats, to peer down the edge of the hillside, you will also see, nestled along the river, the backs of its multistoried houses forming an ancient wall, its narrow

Sefrou with the Qlaʿa in foreground

streets intermittently visible, the small enclave known as the Qlaʿa. Urban in its own right, yet with one eye cast toward its rural hinterland, the Qlaʿa, when I first saw it in the mid-1960s, had, notwithstanding the many years he worked in the coastal city of Safi, been the home—or at least the home base—for more than seventy years of Haj Hamed ben Muhammad Britel.

We met over lunch at the home of Clifford and Hildred Geertz, with whom I overlapped a couple of months at the beginning of my fieldwork. They had heard from one of the Haj's distant relatives that he was particularly knowledgeable about the history of Sefrou and, by virtue of his many years living in one of the coastal cities, of Morocco as a whole. I can picture him perfectly that first day, for though I had only been in Morocco a short time and was still groping for my way in Arabic, I was instantly smitten with the Haj's boyish enthusiasm, the extraordinary warmth of his slightly sardonic smile, and the way he casually scattered cigarette ash as he gestured his way through a lively story. When, some time later, I began to work with him and to know him, it was as if I had received the gift of a grandfather I had never known as a man.

We began to meet every few days at his home in the Qlaʿa. I would make my way up the narrow streets to the ancient house at number 235, where he and his wife, the Haja, and their daughter-in-law and her children lived. Like all such houses, its interior was totally hidden from the street, its windows set so that neighbors could not see inside, its doorway giving no real clue of what lay within. The arrangement was typical and wonderfully spacious: on the ground floor a sitting room with kitchen, several small side rooms, and what may truly be called a "water closet," since the toilet consisted of a slippery platform for one's feet, a hole in the center, and a running stream beneath. Upstairs, behind the balustrade, another series of rooms surrounded the central clerestory, while above all was the flat roof where the women could gather unobserved.

To the side of the main room, however, was the Haj's favorite place, a long narrow room with wool-stuffed settees along each side and a grated window at the end looking out toward a small garden and the edge of the enclave wall. There, in the midafternoon, the Haj and I would meet to sip sweet mint tea, listen to the doves nestled in their cage cooing the hours of the prayers, and talk of the Haj's life and of his times.

There was upon a time, until there was, a world that exists not—and really does.

—Opening to Moroccan stories

I was born, the Haj said, in the last years of the reign of the sultan Moulay al-Hassan—in fact I saw him with my own eyes when he came to Sefrou. With my prompting questions we had begun, as most novice anthropologists are wont, with the Haj's life history, but already my thoughts were racing ahead of his words. He couldn't really remember seeing the sultan, I thought: Hassan died in the early summer of 1894, and the Haj, who, like many Moroccans, is not certain of his exact birth date, but from whose account appeared to have been born around 1892–93 and would still have been an infant at the time. Was he mixed up about the dates? The timing, however, fit: worried that disorder in the desert oases might justify further incursion from French-controlled Algeria, the sultan did pass by Sefrou with an army and entourage of thirty thousand at the end of June 1893, when Dr. Louis Linares, a European accompanying him, described the city as having "large well-cultivated gardens watered by numerous irrigation canals that produce fruits and vegetables in abundance that are then taken to be sold in Fez." Had the Haj perhaps been held up to see the last of the truly traditional precolonial sultans as the monarch made one of his unending tours of the country trying to hold together those powers of command and taxation that were soon to devolve into the hands of the Europeans? Other than saying that the sultan looked very drawn, the Haj could not describe the monarch, but Pierre Loti, who saw him while visiting Morocco in 1889, gave a classically Orientalist account of the sultan:

> Assuredly he is not cruel; with those kind, melancholy eyes of his he could not be so; in the just exercise of his divine power he sometimes punishes severely, but, it is said, he likes much better to pardon. He is a priest and warrior, and he is both to excess; penetrate, as might be a prophet, with his celestial mission, chaste in the midst of his seraglio, faithful in the most rigorous religious observances and fanatical by heredity, he seeks to model himself as far as possible on Mohammed. One may read all this, indeed, in his eyes, in his handsome countenance, in his majestically upright carriage. Such as he is, we cannot hope, in our epoch. Either to understand or to judge him; but, such as he is, he is beyond all question grand and imposing. . . . He betrays an indefinable shyness, almost timidity, which gives his personality a singular and altogether unexpected charm.

In a book published in 1897, another traveler, the Italian Edmondo de Amicis, was equally taken with the sultan, whom he described as

Sultan Hassan I

the handsomest, most attractive young man who ever won an odalisque's heart. He was tall, active, with large, soft eyes, a fine aquiline nose, dark, oval face, and a short, black beard. His expression was at once noble and melancholy. . . . His graceful bearing, his expression, half-melancholy, half-smiling; his subdued, even voice, sounding like the murmur of a brook; in short his entire appearance and manner had a something ingenuous and feminine, and yet, at the same time, a solemnity that aroused instinctive admiration as well as profound respect.

Perhaps this was the man the Haj saw, even if he might not have described him in this fashion. There was, of course, an alternative. If he had not actually seen the sultan, had the Haj only been told about him and, as many of us do, was he recalling a striking moment related so often by family members that it seemed to be part of his own recollection? Indeed, could I trust the Haj's memory, especially if, as I assumed must happen, it was going to conflict at some point with one or another Moroccan or Western source? And yet, to my continuing amazement and delight, this was to be both the first and the last moment I was to doubt the Haj's accounts. In subsequent years I spent innumerable hours interviewing dozens of others, reading scores of documents and histories, and pouring over hundreds of pages of field notes for inconsistencies in any of the Haj's descriptions, but as in that first example, in every instance, the Haj's commitment to our task, his highly circumstantial accounts, his readiness to admit when he did not know something (or when he had the story from others), and his own distinction between facts and interpretations made him as remarkable a resource on local history as he was master of its telling. Although I have had many occasions in my work as an anthropologist, whether in Morocco or elsewhere, to wonder if I was getting something right or if I was simply encountering different people's interpretations of events, I never failed to confirm, if there were other ways available, a single thing the Haj ever told me.

That last year of Hassan's reign, when the Haj may have seen him pass, was a truly noteworthy moment in Moroccan history—the end of an era that stretched back, in its overall design, to the seventeenth century and the very beginnings of what is now the oldest continuous dynasty in the Arab world. It was a country without a single paved road or bridge, a time of impending European domination, chaotic tribal fissures, and growing strains in a world on the edge of change. But even though the tumultuous events of that era were soon to embroil the Haj, growing up in the 1890s was clearly a time of boyhood adventures and memories.

When I was a small boy, with just a long curl of hair growing on my shaved head (so Allah could have yanked me up to heaven had I died) and still wearing a ring in my right ear (as boys then did before "entering the mosque" at the age of about seven), I was tutored by a very learned and powerful teacher, a *fqi*. It was in the early afternoon, when we had retired to the side room, and the Haj, leaning toward me on one of the banquette pillows, was warming to the task, the ever-present cigarette and sweet mint tea the indispensable accompaniment to his tale. This teacher, said the Haj, was so powerful he even had power over the *jnun*, the invisible creatures of the netherworld. He wrote out magical phrases for people and was a Sufi mystic and magician of great force. The fqi had no children of his own and he took a special interest in me, treating me as if I were his own son. One day—it was a Wednesday—this fqi told me that we were going to have a very special lesson. He told me to follow him, and we climbed to the roof of his house, locking the door behind us so we were sure to be alone.

The fqi then told me that two events had recently occurred. He said that not long ago he had given his daughter in marriage to a particular man, but one of the suitors who had failed to win her hand was now using black magic against her in an attempt to break up her marriage. Indeed, the failed suitor had himself gone to another fqi, who had prepared a magic formula that led the bride to try to run back to her parents' house. The two mothers of the couple, the fqi told me, had come to him and given him a nice present in the hope that he could undo the magic that was being worked on the girl. The fqi was, however, not certain which of the suitors was working the magic or, if magic was being worked, of what type it was. And then there was the second event: the fqi had left his shoes outside a doorway, and when he returned they were gone. The fqi was not sure who had taken them. He then told me that we were now going to find out the truth about both of these situations.

The fqi first made a fire and prepared tea. He lit some incense and chanted a number of phrases from the Quran. He then told me several things I was to say at the right moment and that after each I was to ask about the problem of the married couple and the whereabouts of the fqi's slippers. Now give me your right hand, said the fqi. I held out my hand and the fqi took some ink. First he wrote the name of Allah many times on my hand, after which he drew a line in such a way as to form a square. Then he took another dab of ink and let it drop into the center of this square.

Now look into your palm, said the fqi. As I gazed into my palm, the square slowly changed into a mirror. At first it was a blurred image, but then as it cleared I was able to see my own face staring back at me from my palm. The vision clouded, and as it cleared once again, the mirror became a window, a window into the realm of the genies. In fact, what I saw was the court of the sultan of the jnun. The whole atmosphere was frantic, with fire and smoke and lots of boiling pots. An enormous bull was being sacrificed, and the women were all preparing a meal of couscous. But the women were very strange: they had one breast in front and another attached to their backs. And then, the sultan of the genies arrived, with loud music and banners flying. The sultan himself was red in color, but he was dressed all in white and riding a beautiful horse. A golden chair was placed in front of his tent, and as the fqi urged me I repeated the phrases of greeting and respect and told the sultan of the jnun how we were trying to prevent the breakup of the young couple's marriage and how the fqi's slippers had come to be missing.

Again the vision grew blurred, but as the clouds withdrew, I saw a man holding a slip of paper on which were written magical words. I recognized the man as one of the girl's frustrated suitors, and I cried out to the fqi the man's name and all that I saw. One more time the vision clouded, and I saw, when the picture was once again clear, the nephew of the fqi, Lahsen, slipping up to a doorway and taking a pair of shoes left by the threshold. I cried out: Oh, there's your nephew Lahsen, and he's taking your shoes, he's taking your shoes! As I continued to watch, the scene changed and I saw a great meal being served to the sultan of the jnun and his entourage, and then I watched as they packed their tents and slowly departed. After that the picture changed back into a mirror and finally faded away altogether.

From this powerful magic my teacher was able to determine who had bewitched his daughter and who had taken his shoes, and to write out for each an appropriate magical formula. The couple was never again bothered, and they had many children, and the man who coveted the young bride gave up his attempt to have her for himself. And that very evening, the Haj concluded with a knowing smile, the missing slippers were returned to the fqi.

Khiyyar.

Such was Haj Hamed's wondrous *Arabian Nights* tale, rendered with all of the characteristic flourishes I was to come to recognize in his way of telling: the leaning forward and the intense gaze punctuating the story for effect, the trail of cigarette ash a memento of the passing tale, and—perhaps most notably—the dramatic pause followed by the breathy release of his favorite coda, *khiyyar*, a term that means not just that something is "okay" or "all right" but carries the root implications of "something to wonder at," "something out of the ordinary," something truly "beneficent." As the years passed, I was to find many other accounts in which an Arab wizard uses a magic square of ink in one's palm to gain a window into the world of the jnun, but none that I read had the delight of watching the Haj take the story straight to the heart of his listener.

If those early years seemed quite adventurous it was, perhaps, for more reasons than those of boyish enthusiasm. The insecurity of the broader Moroccan order and the uncertainty of the times to come were, in fact, replicated in small—both in their characteristic features and in their flaws—in the city and region of the Haj's upbringing and in the ensuing course of his own life.

Sefrou in the last decade of the nineteenth century was a small walled city with a population of some four thousand, half of whom were Jewish. Legend has it that in the ninth century Moulay Idris II, who refounded Fez, declared as he passed through the region that he was leaving the *city* of Sefrou for the *village* of Fez—just the sort of assertion that bolsters the Sefrouis' claim to ancient urbanity and underscores the intercity rivalry common throughout the country. Sefrou is also crucially located. Fifteen miles south of Fez, it is one of a series of towns lying along the base of the Middle Atlas Mountains where streams bubble up and irrigate a network of gardens that offer both the appearance of an oasis and the reality of a local agricultural base and central market for the tribes of the region. At the time

The Qla'a

of the Haj's boyhood the city was still contained entirely within its walls, the gates closed each night and patrolled against thieves and invaders. The Haj's quarter, the Qla'a, also presented its exterior house walls as a common defense, but in many respects this enclave, set apart by a short distance, faced as much to the countryside at its rear as to Sefrou, and many of its inhabitants did business with the nearby tribesmen as well as managing extensive garden lands that rose above and alongside those of Sefrou proper.

Morocco in the 1890s was—as in so many respects it remains to this day—a land upon which, by the sheer force of personality, men sought to forge the alliances that would grant them a measure of worldly security and with it the sense that, for a while at least, others would not fail to recognize the traces of their passing. In such a world, where the institutions of monarchy or saintly descent, legal claim or moral sanction were thoroughly suffused by the way they could be molded to a set of relationships, it is perhaps unsurprising that, in the coolness of his guest room, his bare feet tucked under his bloused trousers, his cigarettes at the ready, it was to the figures of that age and their ways of making themselves known that, over the course of weeks and months, the Haj effortlessly turned our attention.

Not a path of events—a maze of personalities.

—Barry Unsworth, *Losing Nelson*

You're never really done for as long as you've got a good story—and someone to tell it to.

—Alessandro Baricco, *Novecento*

In those days, said the Haj, sultans tried to rule through local administrators, called *caid*s, as well as by showing their own presence by moving among their royal cities—Fez, Marrakech, Meknes, and Rabat in particular—and the tribal regions that were frequently beyond their regular control. Often, too, these local caids were enormously powerful—even a potential threat to the sultan—and one of these was the most important man in the Sefrou region in the years surrounding the turn of the century, Caid Omar al-Youssi.

In the period before Caid Omar's ascendance to power at the turn of the century, the Haj continued, the Sefrou region was actually ruled by two caids, both of them Berbers, appointed by Sultan Sidi Muhammad shortly before his death in 1873: Caid Omar's father, Muhammad ou Taleb, and a man named Haj Bougrine l-Helliwi. Both caids lived in Sefrou; in fact their houses abutted one another. Bougrine came from a very tight-knit tribal subdivision (or "fraction") of the Ait Youssi tribe—the main tribe of the Sefrou hinterland—a group called the Ait Helli, who (as a document I read from the French military archives also asserted) sometimes portrayed themselves as Arabs rather than Berbers. Omar's father, Muhammad, from the Buhadu fraction of the Ait Youssi, was an ambitious man who wanted to control all of the Ait Youssi territory. He told the sultan a number of lies about Haj Bougrine, and the sultan, believing him, had Bougrine taken to the coast, where he was thrown in jail. The sultan also scattered Bougrine's family and did nothing to prevent Muhammad ou Taleb from tearing down Bougrine's house in Sefrou and another that he maintained at the rural shrine of the tribal saint, Sidi Lahsen Lyoussi. Bougrine's tribal supporters responded to these acts by refusing to accede to Muhammad's authority, uniting instead under the command of a great descendant of the Prophet in a line of local saints, one Sidi Muhammad Larbi Derqawi, whose forbearers originated down near the Sahara and who had a number of green-turbaned followers in this area.

When the Ait Helli rose under Derqawi, the Haj continued, Muhammad ou Taleb went to the sultan and told him that Derqawi wanted to become sultan of the whole Saharan region. This was hardly the first time the tribes of the region had resisted the central authority: only a few years earlier, in 1884, with the help of some French military advisers, Caid Muhammad had been sent into the mountains to pacify rebellious tribesmen. Give me the horses and men now, said Muhammad ou Taleb, and I will bring this Derqawi in. The sultan responded by giving Caid Omar's father some troops from Fez—but not so many that Muhammad might himself prove unfaithful to the sultan. With these forces at his command Muhammad set out to defeat the rebellious Ait Helli, leaving his son, Omar, who was at that time his father's representative (_khalifa_), in charge of things back in Sefrou.

Muhammad and his men went up to a place high in the Middle Atlas Mountains called Tit n'Ourmes where, in the winter of 1891, they encountered the forces of the Ait Helli. But Muhammad and his men managed to get themselves trapped in the redoubt there, and the Ait Helli set the entire place on fire, burning all those within to death. Upon the death of his father, Omar convinced the sultan to provide him with an army from Fez that he took up into the mountains, where he defeated Derqawi's forces and chased the survivors back to their Saharan strongholds.

As he spoke, the Haj's account rang a bell. I recalled that Dr. Linares, who chronicled the sultan's passage through the Middle Atlas in 1893, also noted how close Caid Muhammad was to the sultan, how distracted the Bougrine family was by the downfall of their leader, and how even a few years later followers of Derqawi came into the sultan's camp and told Linares they would not hesitate to go against the sultan himself in the future for having enabled Caid Muhammad to wage war against their spiritual leader. Since alliances shift with breathtaking rapidity in this part of the world and the length of memory is often a function of current impact rather than enduring enmity or nostalgia, if the followers of Derqawi harbored resentment for the past, it was unlikely to have been divorced from their persisting concerns. Linares even mentions that during that 1893 expedition, when the Haj may actually have seen Sultan Moulay al-Hassan, Omar returned to destroy the remnants of the fortification where his father died. On that occasion he was gravely wounded in an encounter with tribesmen but succeeded in exacting the fines levied on the resisters for killing his father and rejecting the caid sent by the sultan to rule over them. Later, looking back at his account, I saw that Linares reported how at one point Omar attacked some tribesmen who had not participated in his father's murder. Under Berber custom Omar was obliged to pay blood money for those he mistakenly killed, a sum (as Linares drolly notes) that he would be sure to extort back as soon as the sultan's retinue left the area.

As I listened to the Haj's account of these events, I was beginning to get a feel not just for the substance of his concerns but for the way he told his stories of the past and where the distinctive emphases in his narrative were occurring. The Haj had begun his account at a crucial moment in Moroccan history, and it is no wonder that for men of his generation it should have made such an enduring impact on their memory. Morocco at that time consisted of a central government, or *makhzen*, which usually controlled the major cities of the country, whereas in much of the countryside the regime was hard pressed to maintain its authority. Eugene Aubin (the nom de plume of Eugene Descos, a French diplomat) wrote in 1903 about the style of royal military expeditions in the following terms:

> War in Morocco is a very peculiar thing. To reduce a restless tribe, the Makhzen is accustomed to quarter on the doomed territory a *mahalla* [military expedition], which conscientiously sets itself to devour it. While the army is engaged in ruining the country in this way, and occasionally indulging in quite harmless amusements, several Shorfa [descendants of the Prophet or a local saint], summoned by the Makhzen, as enjoying a real local influence, have an interview with other Shorfa requisitioned by the tribe, and enter into a series of negotiations, with the purpose of destroying the

cohesion of the turbulent clans. When everything is practically settled, the conditions of submission suggested or bought, and the country completely ruined, the *mehalla* resolves upon decisive action. It performs a *souga*, that is to say, an offensive reconnaissance which enables it to capture several villages, and cut off the heads of a few unsuspecting peasants. These glorious spoils are the sign and symbol of triumph, and will be carried through all the Imperial cities. Thereafter the *mahalla* retires with the pleasant consciousness of a duty done and a task completed. . . . The result was to demonstrate, and that very quickly, the permanent characteristic of Moroccan warfare, in which the actions fought are never intended to gain any strategic result, but simply to influence the course of negotiations.

Often, then, the monarch had to engage in a delicate game of using intermediaries to play tribes and regions off against one another and hold the country together by sheer force of personality. As Aubin noted, the sultan's right-hand man, or vizier, was "the statesman on whom devolves the formidable duty of fomenting the tribal jealousies in order to secure the supremacy of the Makhzen." Indeed, as Abdellah Hammoudi has pointed out, the king's ministers often fueled divisions in order that the monarch could demonstrate one aspect of his legitimacy by playing the role of spiritually potent and worldly consequent intermediary. During the Haj's infancy, as throughout Moulay al-Hassan's reign (1873–94), the sultan had to move about the realm trying to enforce his taxation and administrative powers. Local dynamics included fissiparous tribal attachments and religious zealots who would emerge full bore from the periphery attempting to replicate what the existing dynasty itself had managed since its inception to accomplish—the combination of religious legitimacy with personal power and notable descent.

But there was also something odd about the Haj's telling—or perhaps my way of grasping it. As I listened, his story was not always strictly chronological, and it was through my own questioning that I often had to get information that filled in what seemed to me to be gaps. The Haj never failed to provide chronology when I sought it: he understood perfectly my need for a story that moved inexorably through time. But when left to his own telling, his emphasis frequently lay elsewhere. Three elements, it was becoming clear, were key to the Haj's way of relating the past: the centrality of the culturally defined person, the idea of time as personalized involvement, and the deep-seated ambivalence that, as I was later to appreciate, accompanies virtually all Moroccan approaches to power.

It has been said that for the Arabs history is biography. But it is biography told somewhat differently than in the West. Like other Moroccans, the

Haj was incredibly circumstantial, each name and place figuring so prominently that, as I began to grasp more about how people and events are understood generally, it was obvious that credibility rested on detailed knowledge of these situated personalities. But why, I thought, doesn't he describe
what each person looked like or tell me something about their age, the
sound of their voices, their mannerisms or expressions—the things I would
take as indicative of their "personalities," particularly if he was to emphasize their individual distinctiveness rather than impersonal social and economic forces? Why not the sort of description of bearing and gesture that
Loti had given of the sultan Hassan I? And why did the Haj not always rely
on chronology as his organizing theme without my prompting? At the risk
of falling into a well of detail or being set adrift in a story that seemed to
lack an overarching emphasis on "before" and "after," I had to focus on
how the Haj was ordering things no less than on their actual content.

Left to his own devices, I began to see, the Haj was more disposed to
speak in terms of situated individuals whose actions could only appear
comprehensible if the interplay of circumstance and attachments were
made clear. His was indeed "not a path of events, but a maze of personalities." Constantly pressed to retell his story in the style of my own culture—
where time reveals the truth of persons—I had to be careful about the way
I was translating the Haj's account into one that would make sense to me
and not bore those to whom I relayed it. As a result, I had to catch myself
up at moments and recall the emphases the Haj gave as he set about rendering history in his own fashion.

Time, for example, had a different quality than I was accustomed to. For
the Haj, as for his compatriots, time may be thought of as a set of person-
moments, actions by particular individuals who are themselves so situated
in a network of interpersonal attachments that the critical issue is less what
each was "like" than what the impact was on the ever-widening circle of relationships affected by those actions. A "big man" who has a larger network
of ties has a more significant effect on others' relationships than a man of
less import, but his style of building alliances is much the same as that of
lesser figures, notwithstanding the enormous differences in scope. So for
the Haj the story would be incomplete without indicating each person's
relationships. As a result, I had to keep track of an extraordinary range of
people and their interconnections if I were to understand who, in his sense
of what constitutes history and identity, they were.

Similarly, events would not always be related in chronological order because the crucial question is whether an act has continuing effects or is no
longer relevant to later occurrences. Thus the Haj might use a term that

translates as "very early on" (*zaman*) as opposed to one that seemed to mean "recently" (*bekri*) but would then apply it to events that were, in fact, closer in time to a later occurrence than those denominated as recent. The logic, I began to see, was dependent on the continuing effect in later relations. Thus an event that was actually long ago but highly relevant to contemporary ties may be denominated as "recent," and a recent one that has no continuing effect may be referred to as "long ago." Yet for me to grasp his account I had to assemble the story in the style of my own culture while remaining sensitive to his own choice of emphasis.

Time and person perception are conjoined, too, inasmuch as Arabic, like other Semitic languages, does not have a present tense. For Moroccans things that exist—that "are"—constitute aspects of a person or a thing, so that knowledge does not so much possess an independent existence as it is incorporated, embodied, at any instant as an attribute of some *one*. Human nature is not a central concern for the Haj, notwithstanding his belief that humans are largely, if quite variably, composed of reason and passion, nor is history the linear unfolding of some inherent or divine plan. Rather than chase human nature into its recesses and force it to give up its secrets (as many Western scientists, philosophers, and poets would have), humankind is to be understood as set loose in the world, and human qualities are to be discerned not simply by what is intrinsic to them but by the effects they have on people's relationships. Time and person are interwoven as qualities of the individual, not as ineluctable forces. To say, as Arabs do, that "when the times are just, one day is for me and one day is against me" is a statement not of the inevitable course of history but of the contingent quality of time as part of one's identity and personal relationships. "Men resemble their times more than they do their fathers," say the Arabs: it is not time that reveals persons but persons who create the times and thus characterize time itself.

A related feature of the Haj's way of telling had to do with the idea of causation. For him causation was always traced to some sentient being—to God, a person, an animal, or a spirit; things do not so much make things happen. Of course he knew that heating water made it boil and that without food life could not be sustained, but that sort of causation does not fully describe the course of human history. Rather, what mattered for the Haj was who did what and, when it came to determining a believable account, who was telling the story. And the "who" was not just an isolated personality but, again, someone so embedded in a network of attachments, so much an actor whose deeds affected others' networks, that one could literally identify him and decide whether to place confidence in his account by virtue of his associations.

To be credible, then, one has to have one's own relationships altered by an action's effects. Thus the Haj would sometimes mention whom he got the story from. Occasionally he even supplied the chain of relaters in much the same way that accounts of the Prophet's acts and utterances are made believable by those face-to-face linkages to his companions, linkages that were vital, in turn, to the authority attached to the collected Traditions of the Messenger (*ḥadith*), which stand second only to the Quran as guides to proper human conduct. Just as in court, where, in the past, one had to be certified as a "reliable witness" by others who swore to one's embeddedness in society, so, too, the Haj traced causation to not only sentient beings but to those whose worldly consequences made them (in the Arab idiom) men of "word." It is as true for Moroccans, then, as Michael Gilsenen has said of the Lebanese, that lying and truth are not mere abstractions but are the "subjective property of a particular speaker whose language conforms to reality." In a sense, to put the matter somewhat differently, it is the person who makes the story believable, not the other way around. And part of the Haj's role as a reliable witness to history thus lay in his claim that the events he related were vouched for by the effect the men whose acts he described had on him. Similarly, when I saw during my work in the local courts that sometimes a man of consequence was held to a higher standard than one with a very small sphere of relationships, I could understand how this precept did not violate a principle of treating equals equally because, from the Moroccans' perspective, a man with a broader network has a greater impact on others and should, therefore, be held to more rigorous expectations.

Something else also seemed rather curious: at no time had the Haj actually described Omar or, for that matter, any of the other characters who figured in his accounts. By contrast, I recalled Aubin's description of Omar, following a lunch the writer had with him in 1903: "This warlike chief, whose body is covered with wounds . . . has become stout, and his full face, framed in its red beard, gives him a very pacific air." I have never found a photograph of him, so one day I asked the Haj explicitly: What was Omar like? What did he look like? How did he comport himself? Oh, replied the Haj quickly, he was a big, heavy-set man with very white skin, a heavy beard, and very light-colored hair, almost blond. He had great authority, "a single word." In those days you could leave money lying on the street and no one would dare to touch it because Omar would throw you in one of his three prisons if you did.

Again, the Haj had shifted quickly away from my inquiry about appearance to an emphasis on relational consequence. When I asked if there were any photographs of Omar, the Haj said he knew of none, but the very idea seemed to him rather irrelevant. One notices, too, that Muslims do not constantly comment on the ordinary appearance of others, whether sacred or mundane, and do not treat pictures as windows into an individual's character. This is not because of any clear prohibition on images in Islam: images—even of the Prophet—were not unknown from the earliest times and may still be found in some parts of the Muslim world. As perhaps I should by then have realized, the physical aspects of a man were relevant for the Haj only as they immediately played into an assessment of his impact on the world of other men. I had to follow his lead, therefore, and not assume, as my culture would, that I can tell something of a man's "character" from his visage, much less his portrait. I had to see through his eyes how the Haj composed his view of the man—of any man—by his associations and his impact, something no form of still life, no photograph or portrait, could be expected to embrace.

Returning to the main line of his story, the Haj said that following his defeat of the Ait Helli and the avenging of his father's death, Caid Omar set about consolidating his power in both the countryside and the city. When another leader of the Ait Helli fraction set himself up in Sefrou as a rival to Omar late in 1901, the city was split into rival camps where (as Aubin put it) "for three months a fusillade went on from the top of the minarets and the terraces of the houses" before Omar emerged victorious and his adversary was forced to take sanctuary in the shrine of Moulay Idris in Fez. As the sole power in the region, Omar now had control over a key trade route.

Indeed, Sefrou, in Omar's day, was a vital economic center for the region, and one reason the tribes regarded Sefrou as so important was because of the caravan trade that passed through the town. These caravans began at the pre-Saharan oasis of Erfoud, said the Haj, unlike those that went to Marrakech all the way from Senegal. They consisted of mules, donkeys, and a few horses—perhaps as many as a hundred; camels were not used because of the hilly terrain and the fact that water is not a problem along that route. At Erfoud a verbal agreement would be made with a representative from the confederation that controlled safe passage of the caravan through their territory. After the agreement was announced publicly, word was passed along the route to the tribal groups to ensure against any attack during the ten days it took to get over the Middle Atlas Mountains. The caravans carried dates, goat and sheep skins, and ingredients used for tanning, perfume, and the preparations of a body for burial. There was even one woman, Lalla Tekfa from the Ait Seghoushen d-Sidi ʿAli who, with the support of her tight-knit clan, used to give her protection to caravans that carried wood and charcoal from the Middle Atlas forests in the later period of disorder following Caid Omar's death. Such women could be very strong, said the Haj: during the Protectorate some women even took up arms in the northern mountains when their men fell or were away. In the case of Lalla Tekfa her *handira* (a bedspread-like personal wrap) would be draped over the lead animal of a caravan, and no one dared to touch those under its protection.

I knew that long before the French Protectorate began in 1912, Sefrou was the central marketplace for the nearby tribal fractions, some people spending two days on the road bringing their herds in for sale. Indeed, the Sefrou market was off limits to all disputing during the market days of Wednesday through Friday, said the Haj. But how, I asked, was the peace of the market organized? There is a very serious custom, the Haj said, a form of the ʿar, an act (sometimes translated by Western scholars as a "conditional curse") used to compel human or saintly intervention and whose violation will bring God's punishment for sure. Representatives of various tribal fractions would meet and exchange their turbans (*tʿatau rezuz*), agreeing, for example, to free passage along various routes or to secure a general peace. If someone broke the arrangement, he would be heavily fined, and if his kinsmen wouldn't help pay it, he might be killed, any fine being split among the other groups. It was so serious that if two enemies saw one another in town, they would simply turn aside from one another. If someone did cause a fight, his own tribe or fraction would usually punish him, and if for some reason they didn't, the others would. Looking at me very intensely the Haj repeated: This kind of ʿar is really, really very serious indeed.

But when Caid Omar came to power, he dissolved one such tribal agreement and generally abolished all collective gatherings (sing. *jemaʿa*), extending his own rule far up into the Middle Atlas. He alone assured the sanctuary of the city, the general peace of the countryside, and the safe passage of traders on the basis of his own power. Dissolving the agreement also may have been intended to keep the tribes from coalescing into a viable opposition, though with the additional power he could draw on from the sultan's forces he had little to fear from a united front against him.

The late nineteenth century in the Sefrou area was, as the Haj was leading me to see, something of a microcosm of the country as a whole: local big men compounded their own networks of obligation with whatever official status, religious claim, or purported descent they could assert, their local impact being as variable as their ambitions. In a sense the polity resembled nothing so much, to borrow Clifford Geertz's analogy, as larger and smaller constellations. The sultan's configuration was larger and more involuted than that of a local power figure or family head, but the dynamics of creating obligational bonds were not all that different. Debts would be formed, networks would be cumulated, and alliances had to be constantly serviced and called into action in order to demonstrate their continuing viability. Patrons must be ready to activate their networks at short notice, such that, as Ernest Gellner put it, a big man may even "strike a match to see if it will work when the day comes, or he may wish to show his opponents what good matches he has." A local big man might even mimic the entourage of a sultan. Omar's retinue, for example, included a steward who managed his grain; a market overseer who handled his flocks and set prices (for everything from meat, oil, and honey to bread and doughnuts); scholars who attended on his transactions and rituals; and the holy man who sat with him in life and who, in death, was denominated a saint and buried on the grounds of the caid's palace. The potency of such constellations, of course, depended on the man at the center for their success, and that was certainly true for Caid Omar.

It was only a few years into Omar's own reign, the Haj continued, that the sultan Moulay al-Hassan I died (in 1894) and disorder broke out in the country. It was, I knew, quite common that when a sultan died, a period of chaos would ensue. But chaos always has a cultural design: it is rarely the war of all against all. Whether it is the Ranters in seventeenth-century Britain or the Bolsheviks in Russia in 1917, black ghetto disturbances following the death of Martin Luther King, massacres in Indonesia in the 1960s, or the anarchy of post-Saddam Iraq, there is usually a pattern to social disorder. In Morocco the death of a sultan was like the reshuffling of a deck of cards, where the mechanisms and resources for alliance formation were being tested, confirmed, and reconfigured. At such moments the Jewish quarter would often be plundered or tribal alliances recast. The Arabic word for such generalized moments of disorder is *fitna*, and it was to this crucial concept that the Haj had recourse when describing the death of the sultan.

Fitna, I deduced from what the Haj said, is the breaking apart of the bonds of obligation that people have formed and thus risks the potential breakdown of the entire "community of believers." Some Moroccans see society as held together by a series of knots, like those on a loom, that are stronger than any single strand, such that the gaps that open up, like the differences among men, actually contribute to the strengthening of the whole. To others fitna may be more like pulling the plug on an electrical system held together by that running imbalance of pluses and minuses that constitutes a network of interpersonal debts. Yet for all its threatening aspects, fitna also holds out the opportunity to reshape ties, to level prior arrangements so that new opportunities will arise to test claimed or emergent alliances. In such a system it is uncertainty that creates relationships, whereas certainty yields inflexibility, a belief that may account for the Arab saying that "certitude divides, uncertainty unites." It could as well have been the Haj, then, as Henry Adams who said that "chaos often breeds life." So, in that wonderful way in which an Arabic word may simultaneously embrace a meaning and its opposite, it is not surprising that "fitna" means not only "chaos" and "disorder" but also "allure," "temptation," and "fascination."

To understand such moments, and Moroccan political culture more generally, the Haj had thus begun to initiate me into the plethora of details that, from his perspective, could alone lead me to join in his vision of history. He early on had me memorize the location of each bakery, mosque, and bath in the city's quarters, every gate, irrigation canal, religious brotherhood, and saint's shrine, in order for me to grasp, I think, that any space is defined by the relationships formed through it and that the places of human relationship would be meaningless if I could not give them their proper names. Seeing Sefrou as a terrain of associations—whose individual names were part of the struggle for their definition—was a process we were to take up many times and through a number of interruptions as the years of our working together passed.

The tents of the sultan are never folded.

Choose the course to safety, even if it twists and turns.

—Moroccan sayings

I had been away from Sefrou for several years, but it was with a child's eagerness that I immediately headed to one of his usual hangouts, the store of his relative Youssef on the main street of the "new" city, to find the Haj. There, seated where he could see the passing world, a cigarette at the ready, quite unchanged, sat my old friend. As I approached, he broke into a smile that only broadened when I bent to kiss his hand, a sign of respect, he knew, not of submission. Do you have a car? was the first thing he said, and before I knew it, we were off to the mountains to visit his friends, with questions and stories flying. That evening, as we sat up late at the home of

Sheikh Driss Amzian, a member of a Berber tribal fraction known in past days as mediators and experts on Berber customary law, the Haj, readily picked up the thread of our inquiry.

When the sultan was away or weak or challenged, even a territory as close as Sefrou was to one of his capitals could be recalcitrant, if not anarchic. With Sheikh Driss and the men who wandered in for the evening nodding in agreement, the Haj had settled on the banquette and, lighting a cigarette, turned to the story. Once, when I was about ten there was so much disorder that my father and I were held up by bandits as we were making our way back from Fez to the Qla'a. They stole all our money and clothes, except for our underwear. In those days, if no strong caid could control the tribes of a region, chaos could occur at any time. That is why, for the Sefrou region, you have to understand why Caid Omar al-Youssi—and even his father before him—were such important men, especially when a sultan died.

Indeed, said the Haj, when the sultan died (in June 1894), there was a small war between Sefrou and the settlement of Bhalil that lies on the hillside just down the road to Fez. Before the new sultan could grab hold of things, the people from Bhalil descended on Sefrou, demanding that the gate be opened so they could ransack the Jewish quarter. The Jews were attacked elsewhere in Morocco, but here the Sefrouis refused to open the gates—refused (as we say) to let them "eat" the Jews—and told the Bhalulis to go back where they came from.

The Bhalulis then made the mistake of breaking into some of the gardens, wrecking fences, injuring trees, and stealing crops. The really big blunder was that in one garden they killed a boy from the Meghrawi family. The next morning the Sefrouis massed their forces, said the Haj, and with a huge number of Ait Youssi tribesmen—who have always regarded Sefrou as their *"village"* (here the Haj used the French term) and will defend any invasion of it from outsiders—stormed Bhalil and killed a large number of people. When the fighting ceased, a special sacrifice of a bull, which is traditionally made at the end of all wars between Muslims, was offered as a kind of guarantee that God would punish anyone who broke the peace. The central government also made the people of Bhalil pay a large fine for having gone into dissidence. Until Caid Omar gained full control of the city three years later, no Bhalulis came into Sefrou at all.

It was in this period that Omar began to add to his power in the countryside and consolidated his hold over the city of Sefrou as well. He did so mainly by bribing some of the sultan's ministers who, after the death of

Caid Omar's palace

the sultan and for the next half dozen years, dominated his teenaged son and successor, Moulay Abdelaziz. Omar even convinced the new king to make him pasha of the city as well. He built his *riad*, a huge palatial residence with its own gate, where the municipal offices and reception room are now. Naturally, the Haj continued, there were those who objected to a Berber ruling an Arab town, but people did appreciate that under his tight control there was a lot more security than there had been. Of course a lot of Omar's strength came from the way he used his dependents to advantage. For a time he relied on his brother, a hard man named Mimoun, as his representative in their home territory, but this brother died early on, and his other brother, Muhammad ou Rahu, engaged in so much whoring that he "dirtied the caid's face." Omar—a rather puritanical man—finally locked him in his house until he too died.

Like any big man Caid Omar also used connections through his family to extend his reach. He married one of his daughters, Khaduj, to the sultan Moulay Abdelaziz, and a second to a brother of Tehami al-Glawi (one of the great caids and kingmakers of the High Atlas Mountains in the south). When that brother died, Tehami himself "inherited" her. But Omar was also hedging his bets, said the Haj smiling. He was a firm supporter of Sultan Moulay Abdelaziz against those who wanted to replace him with one of his siblings, Moulay Hafid or Moulay Muhammad. But since it was yet another of Tehami's brothers, Madani al-Glawi, who was later instrumental in making Moulay Hafid the sultan in the early years of the French Protectorate, it is clear that by placing one daughter in each camp Omar was taking no chances.

When I asked about the caid's own wives, the Haj quickly responded that Omar had one wife, Maryam, who was from his tribal fraction, as well as several others, including a Jewish convert—but, said the Haj, I don't know anything about them. The Haj did, however, acknowledge that legendary figures were often said to have had four wives, one of them ideally being a *cherifa* (the descendant of a saint or the Prophet), another a Berber, a third a Negro, and the fourth a Jew. Legally, the Haj continued, a man was not supposed to have more than four wives, but in fact a rich or powerful man could have as many as he wanted. What he would do is after taking his fourth wife he would take a Negro concubine (*khedama*), and then he could take an additional four wives. The slave acted as a sort of separator, and the fiction was that the big man had no more than four in any one group of wives although he may have many more at the same time. Even King Hassan II is said to have taken more than four wives as a way of building up his alliances.

As for Caid Omar, he formed some alliances through marriage but he mainly relied on the men he paid to keep order. He had men without number, said the Haj, and he kept them under very tight control. At times he would even gather them all together and publicly marry them off to the local prostitutes. He also had some slaves, including three or four slave women he inherited from his father, along with many slave concubines that he had bought. All of the slaves were black, and they were brought from south of the Sahara to be sold in Fez. There was never a slave market in Sefrou, he said. The one in Fez was closed down under French pressure in 1905, though the Haj acknowledged that, as I had read, some slavery continued informally into the early 1920s, with abduction and covert sales replacing open markets. At the turn of the century slaves were not terribly expensive to purchase, he added—and I later found a letter from an American missionary of the period who said they could be purchased for as little as forty dollars. But maintaining them for a lifetime could be costly, so only the rich ever had slaves. The men were used mainly for gardening work, while the women were used for housework.

Omar could be quite brutal, too. The Haj said that on one occasion he killed a slave after he had sent him three times to fetch mint for his tea and each time the slave sniffed the bouquet of mint before bringing it to the caid. A few well-to-do people in Sefrou also owned slaves in those days. In fact, the Haj noted, one of my kinsman owned two female slaves and the two husbands he bought for them; several others—including the man who later became pasha under the French—married their slaves. (Aubin, I recalled, had noted that black female slaves could move about more freely than free white women and could, in theory, compel a master to sell them to another by taking sanctuary in a shrine.) In any event, said the Haj, when Omar came to power, people stopped buying slaves, and those who had them only kept their older ones. Since slaves were a sign of some wealth, no one wanted the caid to think he was well-off because the caid would only tax each of them the more heavily. So slavery itself passed out of existence.

There was something in the way the Haj spoke about slaves—the way he seemed to shrug and look down—that prompted me, sometime later when we had returned to his home and were sitting alone in his side room, to hesitantly ask: Did you ever own slaves? The Haj reached for another cigarette and without looking directly at me quietly replied, yes. In the silence that followed I recalled that slavery was, of course, condoned in sacred text. The passage I later looked up says: "We have exalted some of them above others in degrees, that some of them may take others in subjection" (Sura 43:31). I knew, too, that slavery in Muslim lands had largely been stopped by Europeans and that the king of Saudi Arabia ended the practice in his country when he bought up all of the remaining slaves, freed them, and forbade further sales.

Moreover, I appreciated that this was one of those moments when a Quranic precept comes into conflict with changing social practice, and, as in any faith, a sincere believer may be forced to choose between inerrant scripturalism and a form of interpretation that requires criteria of consistency if the world is not to be rent by a flood of uncertainty bordering on unbelief. In this regard the Haj, as far as I had ever been able to tell, was, like many others in Morocco, what might be called a scriptural realist: he takes the Quran literally but is not unwilling to find a way to maintain that commitment while facing the practicality of trying to apply each of its propositions. Theologians had long debated the issue of literalism, some arguing that as the primal cause of all things, God's word was not subject to interpretation; others (like the patron saint of the Ait Youssi tribe) argued that rational inquiry into the state of the natural world allowed metaphorical extensions: inasmuch as God had provided man with an array of alternatives, it is his obligation to sort through them. In some sense, then, the Haj's implicit approach fit Clifford Geertz's characterization of scripturalism as a process in which "Islam becomes a justification for moder-

Slave children, early twentieth century

nity without itself actually becoming modern." Like the belief in jnun for Muslims, Mary's virginity for Christians, or the unconsumed burning bush for Jews, there always comes a moment, even for literalists, when one must decide just how literal one is really going to be without falling into unending doubt. In the Haj's case, the issue of slavery may have posed such a test.

When I moved down to the coastal city of Safi—in about 1908–9—slaves were still being auctioned there, the Haj said, his gaze still downcast. (Aubin helped me imagine the scene, for he had described the slave market of Marrakech only a few years before: "Those that I saw put up for sale were old and withered, and the bidding was slack. Careless bystanders felt the arms, the legs, and the breasts of the Negresses, or even examined their teeth. In short, it was a deplorable sight.") But by the time I began living in Safi, the Haj continued, the trade had been reduced to the sale of kidnapped black children; no adults were being sold. The boys, used only for physical labor, were usually about six or seven years old and could be bought for ten to fifteen rials, while girls (who were about ten years old) cost as much as sixty rials because a girl could be a cook, servant, concubine, or wife. In those days one rial could buy eight kilos of mutton or ten chickens, and just one-tenth of a rial got you five loaves of bread. I was working as a notary in the court most of that time, earning two-tenths of a rial for every document registered in the court, and we listed a great many each year. So with the money I was earning I bought four boys and two girls. But I sold them soon after—the boys to people in Safi, the girls to someone from Fez. I was doing it just to turn a quick profit. I was young and crazy, said the Haj, sadly shaking his head, his voice barely audible: I should have known that the children had been kidnapped and that it was wrong. If shame and remorse have a face, it was in the look the Haj bore at that moment, and though I should perhaps have been thinking of the children, the truth is that it was to the Haj's sadness that I found myself drawn. Later I sought to reflect on what such times must have been like for him generally.

In all of his descriptions of Moroccan social life in the years just before the onset of the French Protectorate in 1912, the Haj was describing a pattern that was—and still is—vital to much of Moroccan social and political organization. Not everyone had enforcers and slaves, much less the ability to get the sultan's direct attention. Rather it was the resources, the process, the accumulation of allies that possesses such a recognizable pattern. Whether it was a family head with his close relatives and neighbors, a Caid Omar maintaining his own palace and miniature court, or the sultan himself, each constellation of associates was at once a world to itself and a threat to any other. Since the legitimate exercise of power in this kind of system involves calling up one's supposed allies at times to be sure they will respond as needed, since one is only as good as one's last performance and must constantly justify one's power by proof of its effectiveness, and since anyone who can put together a still larger and more responsive network is recognized ipso facto as the legitimate possessor of whatever power usually accompanies the position, the threat of a challenger waiting in the wings or charging up from the periphery necessitated constant servicing of one's network or risk of its dissolution. Moreover, as the Haj was quick to imply, whether for Caid Omar or a sultan, it is very difficult to pass one's power to another, even a son, since these networks of obligation are intensely personal and do not automatically survive the death of their central figure intact. As the Moroccans say, "Three days after a man's death, his property divided, his dependents scattered, a man ceases to exist."

But so long as Omar did hold sway, his version of this pattern was typical. To pay for his miniature court and maintain his finances, Omar was always looking for revenue, said the Haj. Whether for the caid or the sultan, taxation lay at the heart of the regimes' powers and failings. Already in the mid-nineteenth century—when assistance for the Algerians led to the defeat of Moroccan forces at the Battle of Isly (1844), and again in the winter of 1859–60 when Spain inserted itself along the northern coast through its victory at the Battle of Tetouan—Morocco was burdened with loans from European banks to pay its war indemnities, a process that in turn led to still further taxation of the populace. I had read that under the sultan Sidi Mohammed IV (1859–73) the traditional taxes on livestock and produce that were affirmed as legitimate by religious scholars had already proven insufficient for the regime's needs and actually undercut the forced loyalty of those from whom the sultan would commonly take assets and then return other favors. For a time the sultan was able to institute special duties, but this not only alienated urban merchants who found them onerous but exacerbated the very sort of local rebelliousness that Caid Omar sought to control in the 1890s. When borrowing from Europeans began in earnest and the sultan turned to the religious scholars for further support of his new taxes, these latter figures began to withhold their consent. By 1873, when Moulay al-Hassan came to the throne, the special-duty taxes were abandoned in favor of a new agricultural tax, which was, in turn, resented by those who had previously never had to pay taxes and by the local officials whose tax farming was now to be handled by the government directly.

The local implications of these national policies were quickly noted by the Haj. Caids used to get their income from taxes, he said, but after some of those taxes fell into disfavor, they had to get their income from bribes. There is a story people tell of how a Berber once saw a poor man whose clothes were in tatters but who said he was a descendant of the Prophet, a *cherif*. If you are a cherif, said the Berber, your clothes should not be so poor. It is the same with a caid, said the Haj: if he says he really is a caid he has to look the part; how else would you know that he is really a man of "force"? And the only way to do that was to get money however he could. Thus Omar began to dominate control over the caravansaries in Sefrou and, through them, the whole chain of trade passing to Fez. He convinced the sultan to withdraw permission from a rival, an urban Arab descendant of the Prophet who manufactured bullets, and forced the man out of town. Most important, from the Haj's perspective, once he became pasha of Sefrou as well as caid of the Ait Youssi tribe, Omar began to grab land from people in Sefrou. He was even willing to abuse the local scholars and judges to accomplish this.

To understand what occurred, the Haj said, you have to know that, prior to the Protectorate, judges (*qadis*) were chosen by the sultan. A man named Ben Abdelwahad Dwiri was sent by the sultan from Fez to be the qadi in the early days of Caid Omar's tenure as pasha of Sefrou. This was the period during which Omar was doing most of his land grabbing. He used to have people dragged into the office of the court notaries and force them to sign over their land in front of these official witnesses. But Dwiri refused to go along with this practice and even condemned it as sinful. Soon after, in the dead of night, a group of respected Sefroui religious scholars (*ulama*) came to Dwiri's house and told him that he must get out of Sefrou immediately because his life was in danger. Initially Dwiri refused to go, but they begged and pleaded with him until they finally convinced him that Omar intended to kill him. That same night, said the Haj, they sneaked the qadi out of the Lalla Sitti Messaouda gate, the small one at the back of the city, where they got him onto a waiting mule and sent him on his way.

Omar then chose a local cherif from an important family, Moulay Abdesslam ben Khiyi al-Adlouni, to be qadi and got the minister in charge of such matters to obtain the sultan's formal approval of his appointment. Moulay Abdesslam was more amenable to the caid's manipulations. But the ulama still were not. They went to Moulay Abdesslam and told him that he too must not record any bad land transfers for the caid, or God would punish him. When Omar learned of the ulamas' opposition, the Haj continued, he sent his guards to take four of them into custody: my cousin Taleb Muhammad ben Abdelwahad Shawi Britel, Moulay 'Ali l-Adel al-Alaoui, Sidi Muhammad ben 'Ali al-Alaoui, and Haj Abdallah Jebli. Each of them was tied with his hands behind his back, his feet bare, his head uncovered, and his mouth stuffed with hot peppers, and all four were linked with a rope tied around their necks. They were then paraded through the town, the guards beating them as they went, and subjecting them to every kind of indignity. Thereafter they were thrown into prison, where all but the last of them died. Two other Sefroui ulama, Moulay Tadli al-Alaoui and

Haj Muhammad Bouzidi, went to Omar and castigated him for this outrageous deed. They, too, were subjected to the same punishment and soon after died in prison. After this, there were never again any ulama in Sefrou.

When I asked what Omar's jails were like, the Haj said that he was never inside one of them, but he knew they were dreadful. I had some idea, though, from an account by the illustrator and artist George Montbard, who visited one of the sultan's jails in Fez in 1893 and wrote:

> In the middle of [the main prison door] an aperture about the size of a man's head has been cut, in the shape of a heart, with the point downwards. It is through this hole that the prisoners are allowed to see their relatives and friends, and receive from them the food that the Sultan, absorbed in the duties of the haram, is always forgetting to dole out to them. It is by this door that the prisoners enter and their dead bodies are brought out. On presenting a written order from the Pasha, the warder showed us into the cells on the ground floor, where the ragged prisoners, some of them in fetters, appear to bear their sad fate with philosophic calm. They live on donations, and what their families and friends bring them. Those who have no one to take an interest in them die of starvation, or nearly so, unless they devote themselves to manufacturing trifles of rushwork . . . the sale of which brings them in a few coppers to buy a little food.
>
> The upper story is of frightful aspect. Under deep vaults lit by one pale gleam of light filtered through a hole, prisoners in rags, infested with vermin, are chained to massive square pillars. Iron collars are fastened round their necks, and rings riveted round their ankles, and when these phantoms with livid flesh, emaciated features, make a movement, their heavy chains clank with a sinister sound.
>
> In the ground among the filth, exsanguinous bodies, lean as skeletons, are stretched. They lay as rigid as corpses, and foul, hairy black rats career over their bare limbs.

Thinking later about the Haj's account of the imprisonment and death of the city's most notable scholars, I was struck by how little this event registered in the accounts of others in Sefrou to whom I repeated it. Indeed I could find no one outside of the Haj's own generation who had even heard of it. Why, I wondered, is there not a monument to these brave men, why no annual celebration marking their resistance to the depredations of the local tyrant? Why am I the one who feels the need to record the names of these men? Perhaps it is connected to the fact that, as everyone was quick to point out, in Omar's day there was peace and order: you could (as many told me) leave money on the ground, and no one would touch it for fear of the caid's punishment. Tyranny, they repeated like a chant, is preferable to chaos. Perhaps, too, in a system where legitimacy arises from the construction of a network of obligations it was also true that to some extend Omar, like so many "big men" before and after him, rendered others complicit in many of his deeds so that acceptance of his actions would be less separable than if the powerful figure claimed to rule solely by divine right. Unlike the Western practice, no plaques or markers, no holidays or special prayers would then be appropriate to memorialize such events. Rather, memory, as the Haj so often exemplified, was once again being separated into two main categories—those events that have continuing force in the relationships of people at the present time and those that do not. The former are kept alive by word of mouth, whereas the latter are set in the attic of memory and may only be dredged up by the reminiscence of contemporaries or the inquiry of the stray anthropologist.

Once again chronology was playing no significant role in the recollection of the ulamas' demise. A recent event that no longer plays a role in everyday relationships, as I had already seen, will often be marked as "bygone," "ancient," or "departed" and be largely ignored, while a more distant event in time that continues to have relational force will be designated with a word that means "prior," "preceding," or "foregoing" and be recalled as appropriate. How events are categorized, then, becomes an intriguing marker of the perception of current affairs. But absent their impact on continuing relationships and notwithstanding my own view that the men who were murdered by Omar were local and national heroes—and certainly they were admired by the Haj—there was no collective memory or any established cultural vessel in which to pour such a collective memory. Given the focus on current relationships, history becomes neither an unbroken stream of events nor proof in this world of historical necessity, but an array of human connections whose currency alone controls their recollection.

Indeed, if there was a category into which the memory of such men could repose it was in a counterbalancing occurrence that could be said to right the situation and render it complete. Thus the Haj referred to the much later loss of the land grabbed by Omar when the French, in turn, took most of it away from Omar's son, Caid Muhammad. For the Haj and his fellow Moroccans, the key concept then is not so much memorializing as it is "justice"—justice in the sense of equivalence rather than exact identity of that which needs to be measured, justice in the sense of something appropriate to the person and the time, justice as a balance in the sense that, as Moroccans say, "The hand of a free man is a scale," and justice in-

99. - SEFROU (Maroc)
Visite d'un Télégraphiste français
aux fils du Caïd Omar

Edit. Niddam et Assouline, Fez (Maroc)

Caïd Muhammad with French engineer

scribed in subsequent relationships, itself the surest form of memorialization. For all my desire that memory should be made permanent in a statue or a celebratory event, I could grasp what the Haj seemed to imply, a vision of memory as less certain of permanence or instruction if embodied in a material form than if it is incorporated in living relationships. It is there, in the effect on the course of relationships whose just elements are mankind's responsibility—those unenumerated powers that the Quran calls the "Rights of Man" as opposed to the "Rights (or Limits) of God" that mankind should not overstep—that their value and their meaning may continue to live. Absent that impact events disappear: the past is irrelevant; what was once has departed.

The Haj drew me back to that earlier world, too, when he noted that there were a few people who were able to avoid Omar's depredations. Until an international conference that took place after the First World War abolished the practice, there were a number of people in Morocco under the direct protection of a foreign power. The process had gathered momentum in the mid-nineteenth century after the previously mentioned defeat of Moroccan forces at the hands of the French and Spaniards resulted in heavy indemnities the Moroccan government tried in part to recapture through taxation of its citizens. However, a protégé (in Arabic, *hemmayya*, one who is "borne along" or "carried") was exempt from paying any taxes whatsoever to the sultan, caids, pashas, or their subalterns. Instead they paid taxes to the consul of the nation that had issued them their documents of protection. The protection accorded a man also extended to his close family (including brothers and their wives). In Fez there were consuls from France, England, Spain, Italy, Germany, and other nations that the consuls for these countries might also represent. Whenever someone like Caid Omar gave a protégé trouble, the man's consul would intervene on his behalf, said the Haj, and although the sultan's courts had the right to judge such a protégé, in fact the intervention of the consul was usually enough to get the matter smoothed over or dismissed.

The powers of protection were, however, not the same from all countries. France was especially forceful, said the Haj: if a protégé was thrown in jail the consul himself would come up from Fez and get him out. The protégés of France were the only ones whom Caid Omar was careful to leave alone, although on at least one occasion he threw a man named Haj ben Bisa of Sefrou in jail when the latter refused to sell the caid his land. The consul put pressure on Omar, got the man out of jail, and later rewarded the caid for his "cooperation" by arranging a four-hundred-odd-hectare royal land grant. Becoming a protégé of a given country was a fairly easy task, the Haj said, calling only for a small gift of money to the consulate and a feeling on the part of the consul that the applicant was worth protecting. Many of those who obtained protection were traders. But there were also a number of Jews who were protégés of France. Several additional families were made protégés of the English; they had a special flag they flew from the tops of their houses in times of disorder. In the same way, said the Haj, when Caid Omar was grabbing land, the Ouled ben Khadira family and my cousin Abdelwahad Shawi Britel (who was a notary, not a businessman, but wanted to avoid the special tax, or na'iba, applied three times per year and used partly to support the sultan's troops stationed with local officials like Omar) became protégés of Italy in the hope of keeping their property from being taken by the caid.

But Omar may have gone too far. About seven years later, said the Haj, the sultan and his ministers, aware that Caid Omar had been building up quite a significant base of personal power in this region, summoned him to Marrakech, where the sultan kept him for about two years to cool off and to remind him of his subservience. Here is what happened, said the Haj, moving to the edge of the banquette and clearly warming to the story, and how it led to the strained relations between his people in the Qla'a and the Sefrouis.

Omar's land grab had put a huge burden on the people of both the Qla'a and those of Sefrou. When the situation had become quite intolerable to everyone, a plan was hatched. It was agreed that ten men from each of the five quarters of Sefrou (the Qlaʿa being counted as one of them) would journey to Fez, where they would take sanctuary in the shrine of Moulay Abdallah. From there they would send a letter to the sultan, who was in Marrakech specifying the caid's misdeeds and stating that it was not proper for a Berber to be ruling over an Arab city. They would then wait for the sultan to act, while remaining in the inviolable precincts of the shrine. However, on the morning appointed for their rendezvous at the main gate leading to Fez, the representatives from the four Sefrou quarters failed to show up without telling the Qlaʿa contingent. The Qlaʿaouis, however, remained true to their word and went on to Fez, where they did indeed take sanctuary in the shrine.

When Omar learned of their deed, he seized all of the property of those ten Qlaʿaouis. The Qlaʿaouis remained in Fez a while and then went on to Tangiers, where there was an assistant (*khalifa*) of the sultan. They made an ʿar sacrifice at the door of this khalifa, who then forwarded their letter to the monarch. Shortly after receiving this complaint the sultan ordered Caid Omar to Marrakech, where he remained for about two years. Upon returning from "exile," Omar gathered together at his palace representatives from the various Ait Youssi tribal fractions, leading figures from the Jewish community, and representatives of the quarters of Sefrou and the Qlaʿa. After dinner he began to berate the Sefrouis. He told them that they were women, and Jews, and so on and so forth, and that they didn't have the courage of the Qlaʿaouis. For despite the fact that the men of the Qlaʿa had acted against him, Omar showed his complete disdain for the cowardly Sefrouis and expressed his admiration for anyone who acted like a man. He then turned to the Ait Youssi tribesmen and told them to judge these Sefrouis, for he would not even deign to pass judgment on them. During the period of almost two years during which the Qlaʿa representatives were away in Fez and Tangiers, they had made an arrangement with a Jew from Fez to lend them money to live on. The Ait Youssi judges now ruled that the Sefrouis must pay this Jew the sum borrowed plus the accumulated interest. The total sum was quite large, and it was a rather heavy punishment for those Sefrouis involved.

I also have to tell you about something else that happened at that time, the Haj added. Of the ten Qla'aouis who went off to Fez and Tangiers, three returned to the Qlaʿa a short while later. They took sanctuary in a religious brotherhood lodge (*zawia*) in the Qlaʿa, and everyone kept their presence secret. But one man, Hadou Alla, saw that bread was being baked in the public oven and taken into the zawia regularly. He thus discovered that the three men were back in the quarter and informed Caid Omar of their presence. The caid then broke the sanctuary of the zawia, arrested the men, and had them severely beaten and thrown in jail. This treachery was not the direct fault of any one man from Sefrou, but the events were blamed on the cowardice of all the Sefrouis involved because of the confiscation of the property of the ten Qlaoui representatives and the violation of the sanctuary of their zawia. The Sefrouis had also turned against the Qla'aouis because of the fine that had been exacted from them. Sometime later Hadou Alla and all of his family except one son died natural deaths—proof, said the Haj, of the great power of sanctuary in a shrine and the punishment from God that awaits anyone who violates its protection. Recalling a proverb, the Haj concluded: "He who escapes a small runoff may still be destroyed by the flood."

The Haj was not the only one to testify to these events. Later I found a communication from a missionary named J. P. Welliver writing on March 19, 1901, from Fez, who reported:

> Omar had been summoned to appear at court more than once, but had refused to go, and being a Berber and backed by a section of a powerful Berber tribe, had probably supposed he would never have to answer such summons. Recently, however, the Sultan appointed his successor, but the new Kaid, being a member of a rival branch of the same tribe, was not recognized by the people, nor by Omar. Soon, however, a large body of troops was sent to bring the refractory Kaid Omar to court, and finding himself confronted by the inevitable he left at once for Morocco City [Marrakech], preferring to go of his own accord rather than to be taken a prisoner.

Shortly after Omar left for the court, the Haj continued, an incident took place that led to a period of disorder and dissidence within the city itself. A fraction from the Ait Helli tribe, the Beni Alaham of Marmousha, came to Sheikh M'barek, who served in Omar's absence, sacrificed an animal at his door, and made the following request: Because of earlier fights with Caid Omar, the Beni Alaham had been barred by the caid from entering the marketplace at Sefrou. Now the grain stocks of the fraction were quite low and the people wanted Sheikh M'barek to intercede on their behalf and obtain permission for them to enter the marketplace the following week to trade. With Caid Omar in Marrakech, Sheikh M'barek went to Caid Omar's khalifa at that time in Sefrou, Moulay Larbi al-Adluni, to request permission for the tribesmen to enter the market that week. The people would be under his, Sheikh M'barek's, protection: "I will be responsible for their good conduct," he told the khalifa.

Moulay Larbi agreed to allow the tribesmen to enter the market in peace. So on Wednesday, the Beni Alaham entered Sefrou and sold a great number of their flocks. On Thursday they purchased grain and other necessities and amenities. On Friday, however, when they went to the caravansary to get their mules and prepare to leave the city, they found that Moulay Larbi had locked it up and refused to give them their animals. When Sheikh M'barek learned of this development, he went to Moulay Larbi and demanded to know why the khalifa was acting in this way. Moulay Larbi gave no explanation but simply refused to release the animals, saying that they now belonged to him. On Friday afternoon, Moulay Larbi mounted his horse and rode to the mosque for prayers. Along the way, Sheikh M'barek stopped him, kissed the hem of his garment, and asked him to be a reasonable and honorable man and release the country people's mules and belongings. Moulay Larbi brushed him aside and proceeded on to the mosque. Having been twice refused, and bound by his word to protect the country people, Sheikh M'barek then had word sent out to the tribes in the countryside. Later that afternoon, as Moulay Larbi was returning from the mosque, he and a nephew of Caid Bougrine were killed by assassins. That night the tribes entered the city through the Beni M'dreg gate. The forces under Sheikh M'barek and his tribal allies took control of the quarters of Chebbak, Casbah, and the Jewish quarter (*mellah*), while Caid Omar's sons and assistants maintained control of the Taksebt and Zemghila quarters. For "forty days" (an aphoristic number, by which the Haj may have meant "for a considerable time") there was general *siba* (disorder, rebelliousness) in the town and the internal gates at Merba', Taksebt, and Chebbak remained closed. The people from the Qla'a were sympathetic to M'barek's side and still went to market through the gate that he kept open in the area that he controlled. After some forty days a main body of the sultan's troops arrived and forced the tribesmen out of the city. And within the year Omar had bribed some of the sultan's ministers at Marrakech and gotten permission to return to his duties as caid of the Ait Youssi and pasha of Sefrou.

Listening to this account I could see that the Haj's story was pointing up a key aspect of the political order of the day, namely, the sultan's dependence on others. For all his claims as a descendant of the Prophet Muhammad in the line of the ruling dynasty, the sultan, like any other powerful figure, was only as good as his last performance: he had to justify his power in no small part by the effectiveness of his acts. And while it is true that

Moroccans frequently attribute the success of a monarch to that spiritual electricity, or *baraka*, which he may embody, even this feature is neither inheritable nor incontestable. The French and postindependence monarchy built up the concept of institutionalized *baraka* as a prop to the legitimacy of the sultans they backed, whereas popular conceptions were always more mixed, requiring constant demonstration that the power was indeed in its claimant and not in some contender. And in the late nineteenth to early twentieth century contenders were indeed plentiful.

Perhaps the most colorful pretender in this period was Jilali ibn Idris al-Zarhuni al-Yusufi, a man popularly known as Bouhamara, "the one who rides on a she-donkey." Operating mostly in the northern mountains and intermittently claiming to be one of the older brothers of the ruling sultan, he escaped capture, even from an expedition led against him by Caid Omar. Indeed, in late 1902 and early 1903, when Eugene Aubin was following events on the ground, tribes of the region were constantly extorting money from the sultan and raiding both the countryside and Fez, notwithstanding promises, often betrayed, of support in attacking the pretender. True, it was Omar who saved the sultan when the regime was threatened by riotous tribesmen after the rout of December 1902. However, Omar, "dragging his unwilling troops after him on an ineffective reconnaissance," was no more successful than two other expeditions that were sent to suppress the pretender, who put his finger on the weakness of many attacks led against him when he noted: "These people would be dangerous if they had a single commander to lead them. But each column has its own leader; it is a flock of hens with no cock."

Ultimately Bouhamara was only able to engage in sporadic attacks in the northern part of Morocco, his efforts perhaps being sustained more by his contacts with Europeans than by any enduring following. Compromise with Bouhamara was perhaps less attractive than with other great lords to the sultan, however, by virtue of the pretender's claim to be Moulay M'hammad, the sultan's brother, who was actually kept under close quarters in the royal palace at this time. When Bouhamara was finally subdued by a unified royal force in the summer of 1909, he was sent back to Fez and kept on public display in a cage until he died. Since pretenders and saintly-lineage descendants throughout Moroccan history have not only come roaring up out of the country's margins—sometimes to initiate whole new dynasties—no sultan could fail to recognize that any opponent who, in addition to proving himself through the fabrication of a network of allies, trenches on the sultan's genealogical legitimacy could be a dangerous symbolic threat. Whether, as some argue, Bouhamara was never a serious chal-

Bouhamara in cage

lenge or was a symptom of the competing economic and political forces of the moment, given the contentious nature of legitimacy at various moments in Moroccan history, sultans understood that the possible threat from such individuals could be ignored only at one's peril.

Caid Omar continued to rule until his death in the late spring of 1904. The cause of his death, said the Haj, revolves around the following incident. In the early part of the century there were several descendants of the Prophet (sing. *cherif*, pl. *chorfa*) living in the Sefrou vicinity who were regarded by people almost as living saints. One of these was Sidi Hamed ben Abdeljebar l-Wazani, who people also referred to as *wali Allah*, or representative of God. He came from Skoura, well up in the Middle Atlas Mountains, and lived for a brief while in the Qla'a before settling in Sefrou. He was unquestionably the most important cherif among the Sefrouis, Ait Youssi, and nearby Beni Warrain tribes at this time and had (the Haj emphasized) great spiritual power (*baraka bezzaf 'ad*). He was often called on to arbitrate disputes between tribal fractions as well as between individuals. But on this particular occasion Abdeljebar and Caid Omar clashed head on. I'll tell you the story, said the Haj.

One night a thief from Bhalil sneaked into Sefrou by way of the river and looted several homes and stores. The caid's guards caught the man, and Omar ordered him taken to the prison. Along the way, the prisoner and his guards passed the house of Abdeljebar. The thief cried out to the holy man to grant him sanctuary, and Sidi Abdeljebar, for whatever reason he may have had, granted it to him. One of the guards hurriedly returned to the caid to ask whether they should indeed hand the prisoner over to the cherif. Omar told them to ignore Abdeljebar and his proffered sanctuary and to take the prisoner to jail as ordered. The line between these two powerful figures was now drawn.

Fearing that the caid might move against Abdeljebar, some of the Ait Youssi tribesmen hurried him out of town to safety. Learning of the affront to their holy man—and no doubt having plenty of other reasons for wanting a fight with the caid—a huge number of tribesmen assembled around Abdeljebar at the Middle Atlas settlement of Skoura. Caid Omar, in turn, gathered some soldiers from Fez and a number of Ait Youssi who, said the Haj, were under his thumb and so highly fractionated that they could not refuse the caid's orders, however reluctant on this particular occasion they may have been to follow them. The assembled company met the forces of Abdeljebar at Tazouta, where Caid Omar died in the very first volley. Who exactly was it who killed him? No one knows, said the Haj. Some say it was a man from his own side. Others say that it was Caid Bougrine who finally got his revenge and that he killed Omar with a silver bullet because all other kinds of bullets would just slough off the caid like rain. But in the volley of shots no one could tell for sure. The only thing that mattered at that moment was that Caid Omar was dead.

After Omar's death there was indeed a period of *siba,* or "civil disorder," which usually implies a struggle for the redistribution of power. But this did not happen within the walls of Sefrou itself. Instead, said the Haj, what happened was that people from all over the region descended on the grain storehouse (*mers*) that Caid Omar had built at the quarry near where the river that later cuts through Sefrou falls over the Cascades. They tore down the walls of the warehouse, killed one another fighting for possession of the stores, and carted off everything they could. In this period there were a number of hard years of famine in Morocco. Indeed, as it would turn out, half of all the years during the last quarter century leading up to the establishment of the French Protectorate in 1912 were years of severe drought, infestations of locusts, and intermittent epidemics. The weather pattern of the period 1878–84 in particular was responsible for severe shortages of food that affected the whole of North Africa and much of Europe . Such moments were regarded as similar to those occasions when a sultan died and disorder threatened the land. In this instance, said the Haj, the government sent troops up from Fez, gathered up what grain they could, and packed it off to Fez. The troops themselves remained quartered in Sefrou for some time. As people entered the city, they had to surrender their weapons to the soldiers and got them back only when they left. There was famine in much of Morocco during the year Omar died, said the Haj: we called it 'am smida, the year of semolina, from the hard wheat people had to use to make bread.

In the countryside, however, it was siba between the Ait Youssi and the Beni Warrain tribes. These two groups had fought on and off for as long as anyone could remember. During Omar's time, however, this and all other fights in the area stretching all the way back over the Middle Atlas Mountains were brought to a halt. The fighting that now broke out was nevertheless sporadic. When an Ait Youssi lookout saw a party of Beni Warrain coming, he would warn his fellow tribesmen by lighting a signal fire or waving a ḥaik (a woman's cloak, but also a man's garment at that time, though of course not worn over his face). Women would even go out on the battlefield and throw henna dye on any man who ran from the enemy. Before a battle began or even during the course of the fighting, one or more descendants of the Prophet or a saint might intervene to terminate the fight. They usually brought with them some object—a flag, a book that belonged to the saint, or, in the case of the main saint of the Ait Youssi, Sidi Lahsen Lyoussi, the coverlet (kswa) from his tomb symbolizing the 'ar (the obligation whose violation could result in divine punishment)—which they thrust on both sides. But even that was only effective for a while; the fighting continued until the arrival of the French.

As I reflected on the Haj's account, in all its extraordinary detail and color, I could also see that there was another implied theory of history that went with it, a view that to him was so obvious as to require no separate articulation. His view was not quite that of an Arab Thucydides, seeing men as naturally repelled by any claim of superiority, yet there was always the focus on the force of personality being neither linked to social background alone nor capable of being passed intact to one's successors. Similarly, his was not quite the view of the Arab historiographer Ibn Khaldun (1332–1406), a vision of the cycles of tribal solidarity arising either from within the marginal regions where the tribes thrived or from within a distressed urban environment only to dissipate as the exercise of power and the sloth that accompanied success undercut that very cohesion. Instead, the Haj stressed the importance of an individual's asel, a term that implies not only a person's "origins" in a geographic sense but that peopled space wherein one's customary ways of forming ties and the repertoire of relational possibilities associated with that group supply the foundation upon which an individual can fashion an intensely personal network of consequence. His explanation thus rested on the deep-seated belief that men are creatures not of fate but of that combination of effort and circumstance that reveals not a divine plan but a divinely implanted capacity to explore the world that God has given us. It was not surprising, then, that on one occasion he reminded me of the tradition (*hadith*) in which a Bedouin, having ridden up to the tent of the Prophet asks whether, in descending from his mount to learn of the new religion, he should trust to Allah that his camel will not run away or should instead tie his camel down, and receives from the Prophet the reply: "Trust to Allah—and tie your camel down!"

As for Morocco as a whole, the Haj also made clear that he always regarded the country as one entity, notwithstanding the differences of region, language, wealth, or identity as Berber, Arab, or Jew. It was never for the Haj or his compatriots exactly a question of national identity in the contemporary political sense but of a more or less definable zone within which the game could go forth. It was as if everyone was involved in the same set of circumstances and rules, and it was this singular, uniting pursuit that made all the difference, a vision of a country as a common terrain of engagement rather than of simple geographical boundaries or immutable sovereignty, a territory defined more by the people engaged than the structures applied. The sources of authority, the style of attaining legitimate power, and the shared orientation within Islam were all elements in a coherent view of the state as a fact, however much its representatives and its policies could remain in contention. The Haj's view, then, was one that Clifford Geertz was later to encapsulate when he wrote: "Not quite an anarchy and not quite a polity, the Moroccan state had, with its endemic particularism, just enough reality to persist." It was, for the Haj and his fellow players, an approach that would soon receive its severest test in the years leading up to and through the establishment of the French Protectorate over Morocco.

There is no blessing in a woman who travels, or in a man who does not.

—Arabic saying

A man in motion has a chance.

—Norman Mailer

Once again work and life had prevented my return to Sefrou for several years. When I did return, though, it was as if I had never been away. I made my way up through the ancient gateway and tangled streets of the Qla'a to that altogether familiar doorway at number 235, where the greetings from the Haj's wife, his daughter-in-law, and grandchildren were as warm as ever. The Haj came out of his side room, chided me gently for my absence, and with barely a pause we set to. It was good to be back in the Haj's home, but as the spring weather was so fine, more often than not in those days we retired to his nearby garden to continue our discussions.

Between Fez and Sefrou lies the Sais plain, a territory that, in earlier times, was, like so much of central Morocco, more readily controlled by the sultan than were the mountains but still required his intermittent presence to assert dominion. And it was at the edge of the Sais plain, just as one comes upon the outskirts of Sefrou, that the Haj owned a garden of several hectares. The gardener was a fellow named Omar who was himself rather elderly, someone who, with his weepy eyes and curious expression, looked as if he had just been abruptly awakened. There was also the donkey, who wandered about eating whatever it pleased. When I asked the Haj if the donkey was not destroying some of his produce, he gave me that characteristic Moroccan smile one writer described as suggesting you had just asked how babies are made. He then explained that the donkey was quite old, that he had always worked hard, and for his "retirement" the animal had the run of the garden. Animals are not like people, said the Haj, pointing out the donkey's graying muzzle: we age from the outside in, whereas animals age from the inside out, which is why, even though they may appear

Haj and author in garden, 1967

Haj in garden, 1967

unchanged, one day they just fall over and die. You have to share with the animals, he also reminded me, which is why whenever we eat outside we should throw at least some food on the ground for the birds, the insects, and the other animals.

It was there, too, on those balmy afternoons, that we would spread a blanket on the ground and the Haj would wander about for a time, checking on his favorite fruit trees, or just strolling, his hands clutched behind, one entwining the thumb of the other, muttering to each tree his approval or nodding heavenward in private conversation. It had been some time since my last visit, so, as the Haj made his rounds of the garden, I collected the questions that had occurred to me in the interim and settled in to wait my chance to ask the Haj about the years surrounding the arrival of the French.

There was, however, something in particular that had preyed on my mind during my absence, and when the moment seemed right, I broached the topic. On several occasions in our work I had asked the Haj about the years leading up to the arrival of the French in Morocco and his own activities at that time. He kept skirting the issue. He even hinted at one time that there was something shameful about his own actions in those days, and not feeling comfortable probing too closely, I never pushed him on the subject. But this time, when I gently worked my way around to those pre-Protectorate days, the Haj, on his own, told me the full story.

This all took place, he said, in the early spring of 1907, after the sultan Moulay Abdelaziz had given the French permission to build a port at Casablanca. The site involved a lot of dredging work. Labor disputes exacerbated relationships with the local population. In addition, a lot of sand and stone was needed from land in the area to complete work on the harbor. The region near Casa is called the Chaouia, and the people who live there, said the Haj with clear disdain, are just plain "crazy." They said that the French were taking their land away, literally digging it up and carting it off. About five to six hundred people, led by a number of religious notables, *ulama*, had gone on foot and horseback from the Fez area to help the Chaouia people. I was still young but well aware of things (*nadi*), so I joined those going off to confront the French.

We traveled down to Fez, where we were joined by groups from elsewhere in the region, and then moved on to Meknes. At Meknes, Muhammad al-Kittani, a cherif and head of an important religious brotherhood who some saw as a pretender to the throne, tried to talk us out of fighting the French. He believed the coming of the French was inevitable, something he saw from his books. He was also an enemy of the sultan, who he thought was in league with the French, but could not get support to become sultan himself because many people didn't accept his claim to be a direct descendant of the Prophet in the alternative line of the Idrissi. None of our local caids went with us, but it was at Meknes that we linked up with the famous Berber warrior Moha ou Hamou al-Zayyani, of the Zaen tribal confederation. We didn't engage in any fighting. In fact, Zayyani was talked out of fighting when a woman from one of the Chaouia groups came to him at night and said to him: "Do you think all of us here in the Chaouia are going to become Christians? Go back to your own areas; we will not become Christians, have no fear." It was also said that the Chaouia people were in league with the French and were planning to spring a trap on us. And so we left—that finished it.

This last statement seemed terribly abrupt. I could picture the Haj, hardly out of boyhood, eager for adventure and, with that typically Moroccan yearning encapsulated in such sayings as "movement is a blessing" and "every absence increases prestige," wanting to know more of his world, wanting to feel that he was moving to effect in it. I knew from accounts of the Chaouia incursion that matters were quite fluid at this moment in Moroccan history. In 1902 a European had been killed in Fez, and the populace was incensed when the sultan broke the sanctuary of the holy shrine of the city's patron saint Moulay Idris to capture the culprit. Two years later, in 1904, France signed secret accords with Britain and Spain as part of the Entente Cordiale. Included in the accords was the French promise not to "obstruct" British actions in Egypt, in return for which the British promised to allow the French to "preserve order . . . and provide assistance" in Morocco. Crop failures in 1905–6 brought many people to the coast to receive aid from Europe, but their dependence only fueled anger at outside influence over the sultan. By 1907 a rebel in the north was capturing Western hostages for ransom while the murder of a French doctor in Marrakech prompted colonial incursion from the Algerian border and further pressures on the sultan to accept European loans. Fear that the Europeans would take Moroccan lands for their own colonists was widespread; indeed, between 1907 and 1912 the French (often assisted by native troops) were to seize over 115 square miles of native lands in the Chaouia region alone. When the Haj said the Chaouia people thought the French were literally carting off their soil, though, they may have been referring to the fact that, in the course of excavating the harbor at Casablanca, the work was very close to a Muslim cemetery and, believing the French digging constituted desecration of a Muslim burial site, the people of the area killed nine European laborers, an act that, in turn, prompted the French bombardment of Casablanca early in August of that year.

But that still did not seem to explain why the Haj, otherwise so garrulous, had cut off his own story so abruptly. It was only after a long pause that the Haj began to speak about what had made him so hesitant to tell me about this moment in his life.

As we made our way back home, he said quietly, we ran short of supplies—so we wound up stealing things from people all along the way. We were not thieves, but we were hungry and thirsty, and our clothes were not clean. As he spoke these words, he looked down, reached resignedly for another cigarette, and looked visibly sad. Neither then nor later did I probe for details: the Haj had drawn into himself and having no place there I could only rest silent and wonder. Perhaps, thinking of those days, when (to borrow a phrase) he and his companions were "witnessing history without the clarity of hindsight or narrative," he could once again feel, in a moment of such personal and national confusion, that, in an idiom of our own, "it was like peering through a windshield lashed with rain." Perhaps, too, the Haj was not merely summoning a feeling or an image but, in the original sense of the word, *remembering*, inasmuch as our word for that process, that emotion, comes from a root meaning "to pass back through the heart." Clearly, from his manner and his words, the Haj, even though in his teens at the time and always a man for whom the moral, the religious, the practical, and the necessary are inextricably entwined, felt either deeply conflicted about his conduct or simply ashamed. Like his admission of having bought slave children, it was not to be the last occasion when he admitted to a situation of ambiguous regret.

Just outside the southern gate of the old part of Sefrou, down a few steps into a darkened chamber, was the workshop of two brothers who were weavers of cloth. Often, in the late afternoon, when the heat of the day was beginning to pass and the nap that followed a noonday meal was over, the Haj and I would make our way down to the weavers, and with the warmhearted brothers listening avidly, the sound of the shuttle and foot pedal somehow in sync with the tempo of the tale, they would follow the conversation, interjecting queries of their own, as the Haj led us back through this period in the history of their town.

It was there, one day, that I asked the Haj: When did you first have contact with a Christian? He said that the first Christian he saw was a missionary. There were two English "lady doctors" in Sefrou. They lived by themselves in the Chebbak quarter and gave people vaccinations (*jedri*). The Haj clearly respected their efforts; indeed he noted that Moroccans were quick to take to a variety of Western medical and scientific practices. But, he added with mild disgust, I did not like what they had to say about religion. They said Jesus was the son of God, but the Quran says God has no minister or representative: He alone has all the power in His hands.

I actually recognized who these missionaries were from the archives I had been reading. Missionaries had first arrived in Sefrou in 1893. They came from two separate groups, the British North Africa Mission and another then known as the Gospel Missionary Union of Kansas. Indeed, as late as the mid-1960s one elderly woman from the latter mission could still be seen in the town. I had read the publications of the British missionaries, and years ago I had even flown out to Kansas to see the Americans' records. It was strange to be greeted at the airport by a fellow midwesterner speaking fluent colloquial Moroccan Arabic and stranger still to have been put up overnight upstairs in the retired missionaries' home, where, memorably, they were gracious enough to pray for my dissertation over dinner. I learned from letters and publications in their archives that the people the Haj was referring to—and whose names he remembered quite clearly— were undoubtedly two Britons, S. M. Denison and Margaret Mellett, who had established an outpost in Sefrou in 1893 (and reported on outbreaks of cholera and smallpox there through the rest of the century). They were joined by the American missionaries, particularly Victor Swanson, by the mid-1890s. Later, I came across these American missionaries' accounts of their first contacts with the Moroccans and recognized that their guide was none other than the granduncle of my Berber friend Hussein ou Muham- mad Qadir (the subject of a later chapter). Things came full circle when, many years later, during a long night of storytelling with others in a guest room on the Sais plain, one of the men who had grown up in Sefrou and attended the missionaries' school jumped up on the banquette and began singing "Jesus Loves Us, Every One" in Arabic. Of course, he added with a smile, I was only there for the candy they gave us!

But if the presence of the missionaries was the Haj's first sighting of Christians, his first real contact with Europeans did not come until his late teens when, in a pattern that was not all that unusual in its day and was, in a modified fashion, to be practiced much later in his own life, the Haj was taken into the home of a very important family and moved to the coastal city of Safi, where he was to spend most of the next twenty-one years.

It was the custom in those days, said the Haj, to bring teachers to live in the royal household while teaching the sultan's sons. During his reign the sultan Moulay al-Hassan brought one of these teachers to Fez, where he was the neighbor of my maternal aunt. This man's name was Si Beder- dine Ouriagli. A second teacher of the sultan's sons was named Si Tehami Ababou. The sultan hired them to instruct several of his sons—Moulay Ab- delaziz (his successor), Moulay Zein (later promoted as sultan by some dissidents), Moulay Youssef (who was sultan under the French from 1912 to 1927), and Moulay Boubker. Both tutors were intelligent and well ed- ucated, the Haj continued, but whereas Si Bederdine was somewhat thin and timorous, Si Tehami was assertive and especially rigorous in training the sultan's offspring. Later, when Moulay Hafid came to the throne, the new sultan appointed his brother Youssef as his deputy and Si Tehami as a minister. Although Si Bederdine spent these years working his extensive landholdings, the two tutors remained very close. In fact, they each married the other's sister, and the sultan attended the wedding celebrations. When Moulay Hafid abdicated, his successor Moulay Youssef made Si Tehami his private secretary (hajib, chamberlain)—a key post, indeed a very intimate one, because he controlled all access to the sultan—and appointed Si Be-derdine as the *qadi* (judge) of Safi.

One day, said the Haj, while I was visiting my aunt in Fez, her husband introduced me to their neighbor, this man Si Bederdine. He had just received his posting to Safi, took a liking to me, and asked me to come help in his court. My father was already dead and the position so favorable it was immediately arranged for me to accept. That was how I wound up in Safi.

As the Haj spoke, I tried to remember what I knew about Safi in the early twentieth century. Located some 120 miles south of Casablanca, the city had a long history of European contact and trade. The Portuguese had established themselves in the city for more than fifty years beginning late in the fifteenth century and built a castle that remains to this day. Writing in 1903, Aubin had described it as "the most beautiful city on the Moroccan coast," populated by some ten thousand souls, of whom fifteen hundred were Jews, but difficult as a port owing to a treacherous bar and surf. Although Aubin offered statistics showing it handled rather little commerce, the Haj disagreed. Safi, he said, was a very important town when I lived there because it was the main port for the entire area south of Morocco, especially Marrakech. Agadir didn't exist, Casablanca was not yet a

Haj (*left*) in Safi, ca. 1930

real harbor, Essaouira was tiny and unimportant, and El Jedida counted for little. As the main port for Marrakech, Safi had also long served as a place from which European ambassadors and traders established contacts with the country. It was in Safi that the Haj picked up his smattering of a few foreign phrases that, quite unexpectedly, he would occasionally throw into one of his stories.

In Safi, said the Haj, I worked in the court as an *adul* (notary). Whenever a piece of land was transferred, for example, the fee was divided between the qadi, and the two notaries needed to validate and record the transaction. I also served as the qadi's administrative representative in his absence. The qadi held court in his home. He was a totally honest man: if anyone offered him money, he would go up to the second floor and tell me that he would not come down again until the man offering the bribe had left. Of course, it was also true that Si Bederdine was a very rich man; he inherited lots of land and built up a considerable fortune on his own.

Throughout the time I was in Safi, I also kept in touch with Si Tehami Ababou, now the royal chamberlain. Indeed, on two occasions during his reign the sultan Moulay Youssef came to Safi with his whole court, and on those occasions he was, of course, accompanied by Si Tehami. A lot of work went into preparing for the royal visits, especially for the ceremony welcoming him with milk and dates. At one point the sultan even asked for the hand of Si Tehami's daughter in marriage to one of the sultan's sons. But we have a saying: "If you marry a king, it is the same as death." Why? Because the wife of a sultan may not be seen by others—even rarely, if at all, by her own family—and she may not leave his palace until she is carried to the grave. Si Tehami did not want to lose all contact with his daughter, even though it meant marriage into the royal family, so he graciously turned down the sultan's offer.

Meanwhile Si Tehami grew very rich. Today in your country, said the Haj, public officials are all paid from the Treasury, but in Morocco at that time an official made his money from people coming to him and asking him to help them get something done and then paying the official for his help. The sultan did not give Si Tehami land outright, the way he did some others. Instead, Si Tehami was able to buy land cheaply, and it was to these lands he turned in his later years after Moulay Youssef died in 1927. Really, he retired because he wanted the late sultan's son Idris to succeed to the throne, but the grand vizier Muhammad El Mokri—with whom he always fought—along with the French succeeded in choosing Muhammad V, who was very young and whom they thought they could control.

It was in 1911, when I was about eighteen and had been in Safi only a couple of years, that I married Khadija bent Moulay l-'Abes, herself from Safi, whom we all call the Haja. Of course she didn't use that title then, but only after we made the pilgrimage to Mecca in 1957. I had been living in a house owned by Si Bederdine, but after I got married, we moved into a connecting part of his official residence. The property was actually owned by the pious endowment (*ḥabus*), but later I convinced them to sell it to me outright, though I always call it Si Bederdine's house.

Through the years in Safi I still visited Sefrou and Fez from time to time—it depended on my work and how quiet the countryside in between was at that moment. Si Tehami was a rough but likable man, and I remained close to him—and especially his kindly wife—and I always stayed at their home in Fez as I made my way up from the coast. Sometimes the trip began at Marrakech, where I often visited. Between Marrakech and Safi there were only three tribes, and none of them was "difficult," the Haj noted. If everything went well, that part of the trip could be made in three days and two nights. Porters had to carry us on their backs to or from the boat, just as they did with goods being brought in or out. From Safi to Sefrou it first took two days on a steamboat to Casablanca, where we rented donkeys for the two-day trip to Rabat, and then five more to Fez.

Talk of travel between Safi and Sefrou came up, too, when I was having tea once with the Haj and his wife. The Haja, already well into her eighties

Passengers carried to shore in Safi

The Haja

and tucked up on a banquette, laughed when recalling how she and the Haj rode mules all the way up from Rabat during those years. As she sat there, all her bits of colorful clothing and pillows gathered round her, she said: Now this is just the way I arranged myself on the mule, my legs tucked up like this, my things to either side. Later, when she stood to go into the other room to rest, I saw she was completely bent over, as if that posture on the mule and banquette had become fixed, her natural state.

Morocco was, however, in particular turmoil in the years immediately surrounding the Haj's arrival in Safi. At the very end of 1907, following the indecisive events in the Chaouia in the early spring of that year, a crowd of forty thousand urbanites and tribesmen rallied in Fez to demand that the sultan's brother Moulay Hafid be declared sultan in place of his brother Abdelaziz. A few days later the formal proclamation was made, the expectation being that the new sultan would strenuously oppose the French, to whom the sultan Moulay Abdelaziz was increasingly turning for financial support. Abdelaziz was often seen by Moroccans as a rather immature person, noted more for the Western toys he accumulated at his palace than for his approach to national preservation. Samuel Levy Bensusan, traveling in Morocco in 1904 and writing in the Orientalist style of the day, relates how a well-connected "Moorish gentleman, full of the dignity that would seem to be the birthright of his race, a keen if resigned observer of the tragic-

Sultan Abdelaziz on bicycle

comedy of his country's politics," told the author, apropos of the bicycles, automobiles, cameras, and mechanical toys sold to the sultan:

> Christians came to the Court Elevated by Allah, and said to my Lord Abd-el-Aziz, "Be as the Sultan of the West." And they brought him their abominations, the wheeled things that fall if left alone, but support a man who mounts them, as I suppose, in the name of Shaitan [Satan]; the picture boxes that multiply images of True Believers and, being as the work of painters, are wisely forbidden by the Far Seeing Book; carriages drawn by invisible djinoon [genies], who scream and struggle in their fiery prison but must stay and work, small sprites that dance and sing. The Christians knew my Lord was but a young man, and so they brought these things, and Abd-el-Aziz gave them of the country's riches, and conversed with them familiarly, as though they had been of a house of a Grand Shareef.

But while he could be characterized by Aubin as "the sultan of universal confusion" and "a slave of the most extravagant caprices," Moulay Abdelaziz may not have been as great a fool as others made him out to be. It is true that he did make some serious mistakes. In particular, he had removed the key figures in the older patronage system and thus lost the support of those who benefited from it. As historian C. R. Pennell has said: "The source of legitimate patronage had gone and what was left was the form of the old system, a simulacrum of Moulay Hassan's policies, and the use of force, which became a weapon of weakness, not of strength." Troops had come from part of the south, many to side with Hafid, who opposed his brother's reliance on the French, others to ally themselves with the sultan and the French, who after the events at Casablanca and border incursions from Algeria now had some fifteen thousand troops in the country. For a time, the French and these latter troops assisted the sultan's move to Fez in an attempt to reassert his authority. As in 1904, when the French had first tried to impose a protectorate (only to provoke the Algeciras conference that presaged the divided zones of influence among the European powers throughout much of Africa), another attempt was made at imposing such a mandate. But matters were by no means entirely within the control of the French. Abdelaziz, who appeared willing to grant France's request in exchange for support against his brother, later had to be hastily moved out of Fez for his own safety. Bensusan translates his Moroccan informant's summary of the sultan's actions leading up to this moment in the following, rather biblical, tone:

> In the beginning of the season of change the French were angry. "All men shall pay an equal tax throughout my land," said the King of the Age, and the Bashador [ambassador] of the French said, "Our protected subject shall not yield even a handful of green corn to the gatherer." Now when the people saw that the tax-gatherers did not travel as they were wont to travel, armed and ready to kill, they hardened their hearts and said, "We will pay no taxes at all, for these men cannot overcome us." So the tribute was not yielded, and the French Bashador said to the Sultan, "Thou seest that these people will not pay, but we out of our abundant wealth will give all the money that is needed. Only sign these writings that set forth our right to the money that is brought by Nazarenes [Christians—i.e., Europeans] to the seaports, and everything will be well."
>
> So the Sultan set his seal upon all that was brought before him, and the French sent gold to his treasury and more French traders came to his Court, and my Lord gave them the money that had come to him from their country, for more of the foolish and wicked things they brought. Then he left Marrakesh and went to Fez; and the Rogui [pretender to the throne], Bu Hamara, rose up and waged war against him.

Indeed, this was a moment when all of Morocco was in turmoil. The pretender Bouhamara was still at Aioun Sidi Meluk (in the northern mountains, near Taza) in open revolt, and the Algerian border was anything but secure. By the late summer of 1907 the ulama of Marrakech had joined in declaring Moulay Hafid sultan, to which, as we have seen, was added a similar proclamation from the ulama of Fez the following January. Like Moulay Abdelaziz, Hafid had to garner internal support at the same time he had to compose the finances of his realm and keep the European powers at bay. The French had not seen the uprising of the Hafidists coming. As Edmund Burke III shows, the French thought of Morocco as an isolated backwater, trapped in a time warp, a museum of cultural survivals, where Islam and politics, religious brotherhoods and calcified urban elites reinforced a convenient view of the country as one in which cultural stasis drove internal politics. In fact multiple and contending forces, by no means isolated from the surrounding world, were running fiercely through the country. At every turn, though, Morocco's control over its own fate was slipping away. Through most of 1908 the monarchy remained in contention, but in mid-August, in what may have been a case of internal betrayal by some of Abdelaziz's ostensible supporters, Moulay Hafid led an army he had raised in Marrakech into the battle at Oued Oum er-Rebia where he defeated his brother. Two days later Abdelaziz abdicated. But this victory hardly settled the chaos that continued to rend the country.

The response during this turbulent period within the Sefrou area was not unexpected. In this area, said the Haj, the Ait Seghoushen tribesmen, who are mainly descendants of the Prophet in the (nonruling) Idrissi line and very honorable men—"their words do not just fall on the ground"— rose under one Moulay M'hamed Seghoulni. They took firm control of the mountains around Tichoukt and were not pacified until many years later by the French. There was no overt violence at this moment around Sefrou, the Haj added, but there was a desire on everyone's part to ensure the safety of the Sefrou marketplace by reinstituting the agreement that had been voided some years earlier by Caid Omar. So five important men (one from each quarter of the city) were chosen, and they in turn picked a man named Lahcen Kermouch to be their leader. When it is unclear who is actually the sultan, the Haj explained, localities may choose someone to act as their momentary leader. This temporary chief is called the *sheikh r-rbi'a* because the latter term, which means "springtime," suggests that his tenure will be like the hoped-for beneficence that lies between the harsher periods of winter and summer. In Sefrou, Kermouch was chosen when the quarter representatives met in the watchtower over the main gate to Fez and exchanged turbans, each man giving his to another, who then took it home and hid it. If one of the men should later violate the agreement, the others would come to his house, find the hidden turban, and dye it a very dark color as a sign of his betrayal. Dyeing the head covering, the Haj concluded, is a very grave form of the 'ar and will surely result in God's curse on the traitor. For four years (1904–8), until the sultan appointed one Caid Bouchereb, the city was kept reasonably peaceful by these local men, but no one really had full control of the situation.

On their side the Berbers also chose two men as temporary war chiefs. These two sheikhs and a large number of their respective supporters, said the Haj, then met in Sefrou at the garden where Bel Haj's café—the one where we often have breakfast—now stands. They solemnly agreed (with another exchange of turbans) to make Sefrou a sanctuary from all fighting and freely open to all groups. This was a temporary agreement, not an alliance or confederation in any sense, and was later rendered irrelevant by the coming of the new power, the French.

This was a moment of many contending forces, said the Haj. There was in Fez at the time that the sultan Moulay Hafid was in residence that same important Idrissi cherif named Muhammad ben Abdelkebir al-Kittani, who had been at the events in the Chaouia in 1907. Kittani had significant attachments to the Sefrou region and the Middle Atlas more widely. (His father, I was later to learn, had been called upon to mediate the dispute between the people of Bhalil, where their brotherhood had a substantial following, and the residents of Sefrou following the war between the two that the Haj had described earlier; indeed he helped the people of Bhalil seek forgiveness from the sultan for their actions at that time.) Now, according to the Haj, many people thought the younger Kittani was indeed hopeful of overthrowing the Alawite dynasty and replacing it with the alternative Idrissi line of descent headed by himself. Earlier on, Kittani had supported the rise of Moulay Hafid to the throne. Locally, he had even gotten the Bhalil people—perhaps grateful for his father's earlier mediation on their behalf—to send fifty mules to Meknes in support of Moulay Hafid's efforts to displace Moulay Abdelaziz from the throne. But later the sultan felt threatened by the religious brotherhood Kittani headed and the influence he exercised with the artisans and rabble of Fez who were to play so significant a role in deposing Abdelaziz.

Kittani had further alienated himself from the sultan in other ways. Although the Haj did not mention it, in 1909 Kittani was among a small group who had supported the replacement of the absolute monarchy with an Ottoman-style constitution, one in which a consultative assembly of religious scholars (like himself, no doubt) would share power—a proposal, however, that never gained traction. As European goods had flooded into the country undermining local crafts, Kittani had become an important voice not only against the monarch's association with the foreigners but an enemy of the newly emergent merchants who benefited from the European trade. Tea, which had been introduced into Morocco in the seventeenth century, gained widespread use. More important, Moroccans took their tea with such huge amounts of sugar that, notwithstanding failed attempts to produce it locally, dependence on its import became a major factor in the national economy. Kittani forbade the use of tea and sugar, as did an opinion (*fatwa*) of a number of Islamic law scholars whose influence the sultan had tried to limit, in part because they claimed the processing of sugar abroad involved the use of pig's blood.

Afraid that the sultan might imprison or kill him and wanting to consolidate his tribal backing, Kittani, in March 1909, finally fled the city of Fez for the Beni M'tir tribal territory in the Middle Atlas Mountains back of Sefrou, around El Hajeb. Entering their territory and partaking of their sanctuary—even though he made no sacrifice—constituted a form of that supernaturally sanctioned form of conditional curse, or 'ar, said the Haj: Indeed any sanctuary (*mezreg*) is a form of the 'ar, even if it doesn't include a sacrifice. The sultan, however, enlisted one fraction of the Beni M'tir to betray the pretender, and not long afterward he was caught. They brought him and his father to Fez, said the Haj, where the two were imprisoned and where, soon after, the sultan had Muhammad Kittani flogged to death. The other fractions of the Beni M'tir, infuriated by the sultan's deed, rose up against the monarch's forces at El Hajeb. But then, the Haj added with a smile, the Beni M'tir have always had a reputation for going off half-cocked: Their nickname is *ibli itir*, which implies that they are like genies that go flying around wildly, because they were always rising up against sultans or caids or whomever. In the first battle, however, the Beni M'tir were victorious. They blocked up the numerous water sources in that area, used their horsemen (against the sultan's unmounted army) to maneuver the soldiers into a position below the dammed waters, and at the right moment broke the sultan's forces altogether by releasing a tremendous torrent of water on them and then riding down those who tried to flee. The sultan countered by sending in army units from all over the area to crush the localized Beni M'tir revolt. But this victory did not ensure peace. Roads were often cut, access to markets disrupted, and eventually the tribes from all over the Fez region congregated on the Sais plain and prepared to attack Fez and murder the sultan.

Native troops who fought with French

The tribes, said the Haj, had no one in particular that they favored for sultan; their rising stemmed (in its immediate cause) from the sultan's violation of the sanctuary given his enemy by the Beni M'tir. In fact, the sultan had breached this kind of sanctuary before, some said under pressure from the French, which is why people said of the sultan, "You have dirtied my face." Confronted with an imminent attack on Fez by the combined forces of the Middle Atlas tribes, the sultan asked the ulama of Fez if it was permissible to seek assistance from the French. The scholars said that under the circumstances what would have been forbidden was now permitted. So the sultan turned to France for military help, which ultimately led to his signing the Protectorate agreement. Local tribesmen were also recruited to the French side. Already in 1908 some 1,200 tribesmen had been enlisted to assist the French in countering threats to the sultan, a number that would grow to 10,000 before resistance was fully quashed nationwide in 1934. Indeed, estimates of the number of Moroccan troops (variously recruited as *goumiers*, *Spahis*, or *tirailleurs*) who died fighting for the French between 1907 and 1922 run from 12,000 to 22,000, and far more were never credited with saving France during the first and second world wars. However much the tribesmen were incensed at the sultan's breach of the sanctuary they had granted al-Kittani, the Haj was quick to note, the real cause for the Protectorate was the fact that the sultan's treasury was depleted. Still, the Haj emphasized, the violation of the 'ar was not merely

Moha N'Hamousha, 1967

a contributing factor to the formation of the French Protectorate but a significant cause in and of itself because it showed the sultan had no shame and was now just a tool of the French.

The Haj's account, though not inaccurate, was fleshed out when the opportunity arose to interview a number of other elderly men in the Middle Atlas who had actually participated in the events surrounding the capture of Kittani and the tribes' later attack on several of the royal cities. Edmund Burke III and I had even interviewed Mohand N'Hamousha, then aged ninety-six, who had been a member of the Kittani brotherhood and at whose doorstep, he told us, Kittani did make a sacrifice as he sought help in escaping the sultan's troops. Mohand, who went on to confront the sultan in the days leading up to the Protectorate and to retreat to the mountains, where he fought the French for seven years before eventually accepting a post under the Protectorate, was not among those who betrayed Kittani. Like the Haj he cited names and places in great detail and was obviously saddened as he recounted the friends he lost to the withering cannon fire and privations attendant on his struggle against this external domination. No doubt he shared the lament, collected by Arsène Roux during the period of World War I, in which a tribal poet of Mohand's region says: "The Makhzen is no more! The Christians strut about with total impunity. Cry for the fate of our cities: Fez, Meknes, Agourai, Sefrou, and Tabadout! Surely the Christians are the cause of our fall! Fez and Meknes are lost, not to mention Sefrou and Casablanca. Can one not make the crow of the mountains white?"

In this lead-up to the Protectorate men like Mohand and the tribes of the Fez-Meknes region had become increasingly disturbed by the reliance of the sultan on the French. By the early part of the century more than ten thousand Europeans were settled in Morocco. One sign that the country's finances were slipping out of its government's control was the fact that the local currency lost 90 percent of its value and much of the country's trade was being conducted in European currencies. Casablanca, where most Europeans congregated, was growing rapidly: from roughly 1,000 Europeans in 1907 it grew to 20,000 foreigners by around 1912 and to over 30,000 Europeans in the next two years, along with a similar number of Muslims (plus 9,000 Jews). Between 1910 and 1912, with the French banks essentially in control of the government's finances, foreign trade (as the historians I was reading pointed out) had doubled, and in 1911–12 alone the trade deficit grew twentyfold. The French military undertook to reform the sultan's army, while government "advisers" began to dole out large parts of the government to the great caids of the south and their allies. Increasingly the sultan relied on the French, and increasingly, his resources having been depleted battling Bouhamara and his other enemies, funds were unavailable for any independent endeavors.

Early in 1911 the Beni M'tir (Aith Ndhir), furious at the execution of one of their fellow tribesmen by the French and more broadly by the sultan's complicity with the foreigners, gathered with other tribal groups to attack Fez. The notables of Fez and Sefrou both proclaimed another of the sultan's brothers, Moulay Zein, as monarch in place of Moulay Hafid. By April 1911 the American missionary Victor Swanson was writing from Sefrou: "I think Morocco has never been in a worse condition, at least not in modern times. The tribes of the interior, both Arabs and Berbers, are agreed in a general rebellion against the Sultan and his government. Here in Sifru I am shut in, scarcely getting outside of the house. The people of Sifru try to keep up a kind of peace with the tribes around, so that their cattle and fields may not be molested. The poor Jews are terrified. Just how long this state of things will continue no one knows."

Further challenges to the sultan surfaced. In addition to other cities proclaiming as sultan the monarch's brother, various tribesmen of the Fez region were demanding a wide range of changes in the system of taxation, military service, and approval of local administrators. When they did descend on Fez to confront Moulay Hafid, I asked the Haj, how were these various groups of Ait Youssi and other tribes organized? The Haj's judgment was sharp and negative. Not all of the Ait Youssi took part in this confrontation, and those who did participate were simply thieves (_khettafa_; _ravisseurs_ in one French dictionary's translation), people who had no land of their own. They participated as individuals and not even as tribal fractions, much less as a whole confederation. Those who had land and better sense didn't get involved. The fighters who did participate had exchanged turbans among the various groupings to form a temporary alliance, he continued, but beyond that they simply were not organized. It was a case of everyone for himself, he said—a _dula bla rais_—a "nation" without a chief.

Pursuing his own interpretation, I asked the Haj if there was some special reason that accounted for the poverty of so many at this particular time. At first the Haj mentioned the stock response that God gives in various proportions to each man, but he then repeated that crops had fared poorly in much of the region throughout the preceding years. When I asked about the burden of taxes, he said that the only direct imperial taxes were entry fees to markets. Taxes may only have been a few percent of the value of things owned or brought to market, but it was what the caids took in addition and the way taxes kept changing that hurt. It was the

khers, the tax paid on festive occasions—a good part of which got no farther than the local caid—and the general depredations of these caids that
had so impoverished a lot of people. Like another tax, called the *na'iba*,
or *firda*, the tax at festivals was not a tax recognized by the Quran, and
its imposition occasioned frequent revolts, especially in the countryside.
Sultan Moulay Abdelaziz had tried applying a "modern" general tax on
everyone, but opposition from the wealthy, coupled with the local caids
doubling it so they could take a share, estranged all sectors of society. Indeed, when Moulay Hafid came to the throne, he had imposed severe taxes
on the tanners of Fez—who had rioted on previous occasions, especially
in 1873, when burdened with taxes most regarded as un-Islamic—and the
new sultan had further alienated the tribes of the Fez region with similar
levies. Moreover, in 1911 the government had fallen in France, and control
by the metropole over its own forces operating in Morocco was lax, such
that troops may have provoked matters on their own. By 1911, then, all of
these forces pushed the tribes into open revolt against the sultan and his
French supporters.

A large force of French troops, combined with the many Moroccan soldiers who were already employed by them, moved on Fez. In the name of
rescuing Europeans stranded in the city, a French column occupied Fez in
May, while other troops took Meknes and Rabat soon after. It was in the

Generals Moinier and Dalbiez leading column to Fez

spring of 1911, said the Haj, with the French established in Fez, that the tribes from the region gathered at Sefrou's northern gate and the next day (May 25, according to the records I later consulted) set off toward Fez to fight the French. The French, intent on controlling the road across the Sais plain between Fez and the Middle Atlas routes to the Sahara, were armed with machine guns and, having met the tribesmen on the way, succeeded in driving them back. There was a second encounter early the following day (June 5), by which time the French, under the command of General Moinier, had pushed their way almost to Bhalil. Lieutenant Colonel (later General) Gouraud wrote of the battle: "The Moroccans showed real courage: truly they were brave; . . . charging at a gallop . . . under a hail of bullets. . . . Honors for the day go to the *goums* [the native forces fighting with the French]." In keeping with custom, which was as well known to the French as it was to the Muslims, the caid of Bhalil came out to the road and sacrificed a bull as a sign of his people's desire to end the fighting. The French acknowledged this 'ar, but, said the Haj, the caid's own son began sniping at the French soon afterward from his perch in a tree. The French thought that it was the father who had put him up to it, that the Bhalulis were not sincere in their desire for peace and might even be laying a trap, so they proceeded to attack Bhalil, resulting in casualties on both sides.

However, the French did not come all the way up to Sefrou at this mo-

French troops enter Sefrou

Fort Prioux overlooking Sefrou

ment, noted the Haj: they turned off to the countryside instead. Getting a grip on the rural disorder was their first priority. With the Moroccan government so weak, the French had to overcome serious threats in the south and the possibility of a link-up between tribesmen from the Middle Atlas and those of an Islamicist rebel known as El Hiba, who had been trying to move his troops north and was not defeated until the end of August.

Although the French had veered away from Sefrou earlier in 1911, the Haj continued, by that fall they returned (entering the city on September 3). Sefrou escaped any damage, however, because it gave up without a fight. It was Ramadan, and the cannon that signaled the end of the night and the beginning of the day's fast at first reminded Gouraud of the resistance they had encountered at Bhalil the previous spring. Gouraud describes how five hundred troopers in full uniform, mainly native Moroccan and Senegalese, entered the city. "The whole population is on the terraces and in the streets," he wrote, "the Jews in colorful clusters and even a few Muslim women, among them one very pretty, unveiled. We sound our trumpets: preceded [by] its reputation for power and generosity, the army of France, without a shot fired, enters Sefrou. Our entry could very easily have been delayed, because of the dense surrounding gardens, and the rocky outcropping that have greatly contributed to securing the city to the Berber horsemen." Pulling a white handkerchief from his pocket and waving it in the air, the Haj explained that at the suggestion of the pasha's right-hand man a white flag was waved from a tall house and the ramparts.

That is how the city surrendered. You may have heard that the surrender was signaled by waving the white flag from the top of one of the mosques or at the suggestion of a missionary living in Sefrou at the time (a story I had indeed heard from others), but everyone knew perfectly well how you showed surrender to the French, and those accounts are not how it happened.

Once the French arrived in Sefrou, said the Haj, they bought the hill-top overlooking the city, called Jbel Sidi ʿAli Benziyan, from the three or four Qlaʿa families that owned it and proceeded to build their stronghold, Fort Prioux, there. It was a man named Sidi Rahu, the son of a great *cherif,* who had a house in the Qlaʿa and who was himself a man of great spiri-tual power, who attempted to dislodge the French. I knew a bit about Sidi Rahu. I had seen French reports from the period noting that the battle at Fort Prioux took place during some three weeks beginning December 14, 1911, but I did not know some of the local details. I had heard, too, Mo-hand N'Hamousha's account of being present at this battle. After Sidi Rahu had attacked the fort at night and been driven away, the Haj explained, the French came down to Sidi Rahu's family house in the Qlaʿa, completely demolished it and carted away the elaborately carved wooden door and frames, which they later incorporated in the structure of the fort. People who do not know think the French destroyed the house because of Sidi Rahu's rebelliousness, but actually after his father, Mimoun, died, Sidi Rahu left the house in the care of a man named Youssi ben Ali ej-Jeleb, who was

French sortie returns to Sefrou, January 4, 1912

in the habit of bringing whores to the house and having orgies there. It was for that reason the French tore it down. Even though his family was now dispersed, Sidi Rahu, who many people believed inherited his father's considerable spiritual powers (*baraka*), continued his fight against the French.

As I listened to him, I could see that the Haj had a high regard for Sidi Rahu, in part because this man and his fraction-mates had been involved in the fight at Fez and continued their resistance for a number of years thereafter. But others I spoke with regarded Sidi Rahu's clan, the Ait Arfa, as very bad people. One man even said that Rahu wanted to become "just like Caid Omar" and set himself up as the ruler—here he used the word for a pretender to the throne, no less—of the whole Ait Youssi area. He also likened him to Bouhamara in this respect, referring to him as being *miuwui*, which means "insurgent, rebellious, factious, dissident, anarchist, and violent." The Haj was not unaware of such views. He said that Sidi Rahu only used force against neutral or pro-French locals in order to get them to supply him with food and materials. It's true that on one occasion he got some people from the nearby settlement of Senhadja to go to the market in Sefrou to buy goods for his forces, he added, and that Sidi Rahu threatened to burn their village if the Senhadjis refused. A spy informed on the Senhadjis, and the French rounded them all up when they entered the city. The French then lined them up against the wall by Bab Merba' and executed them. One of the Senhadjis, said the Haj, managed to avoid being hit by ducking behind another man and then pretending to be dead. The French apparently didn't even deign to give the man a coup de grâce, so he survived.

The French were finally able to get the formal Treaty of Fez establishing the French Protectorate signed on March 30, 1912. But that hardly ended opposition. Two revolts occurred soon after in Fez. A mutiny by some of the Moroccan soldiers stationed in the city on April 17, 1912—precipitated by their French instructors' humiliating actions and a timely solar eclipse— led to the murder of a number of French residents, the killing of some Jews, and tremendous damage to their quarter. A French column of twenty thousand men (including many native troops, or *goum*) led by General Moinier (and apparently with no knowledge or approval from the metropole, itself disrupted by a government crisis) arrived on April 24 and, following a devastating bombardment, brought the city into submission, even as it further encouraged the resistance of tribal leaders in the region. In late May, General Lyautey having arrived in the country and tribesmen throughout much of the central interior having risen, the tribal warriors were again unsuccessful in attacking the enhanced French garrison in Fez. The tribesmen who threatened the city on this occasion were far better organized than they had been the previous year, and it was not until early summer, with the help of their modern weaponry, that the French were able to turn back the threat to Fez. The French now began to direct their attention to battles aimed at "pacifying" the entire countryside, a process that in some parts of the Moroccan south lasted more than twenty years.

The main resistance to the French in the mountains back of Sefrou, in the area called Tichoukt, the Haj continued, came not from Sidi Rahu but from a man named Moulay M'hamed, the strong man of the Ait Seghoushen d-Sidi 'Ali tribal fraction. When the French arrived in that area, Moulay M'hamed greeted them with a round of gunfire and was soon after joined by Sidi Rahu. On February 15, 1913, Gouraud, remaining behind in Fez—which he described as still restive following the events of the previous spring—sent a sizable force with artillery to an area outside of Sefrou

General Lyautey

called Mezdgha Jorf after Sidi Rahu and some seven to eight hundred of his fighters had pillaged and burned a settlement of the Oulad el-Haj. In a three-hour battle on the morning of the February 19 Rahu and his associates were routed. "The local French battalion [led by an officer named] Prokos is superb," wrote Gouraud, "the Senegalese less so."

As the months of fighting wore on, Sidi Rahu finally agreed to a peace arrangement with the French. The French had tried repeatedly to bribe both him and Moulay M'hamed but never succeeded in doing so, said the Haj. Sidi Rahu made an honorable peace settlement with the French; he was not a sellout. He returned to his home at Annonceur, taking with him what Ait Youssi tribesmen were left at Tichoukt, and he died there. He had received no grain or gifts from the French—would not accept them—and this, the Haj emphasized, was proof of the man's honorableness.

Moulay M'hamed was not willing to make any settlement, the Haj continued. At this point no less a figure than General Lyautey himself arrived on the scene. Hubert Lyautey had taken over as the first resident-general of the newly formed Protectorate. He was always sparing of his own troops, employing local Moroccan forces when he could, unlike the Spanish, who suffered tens of thousands of casualties in their zone to the north. But while Lyautey, who could never resist a maxim, asserted that the proper procedure was to "show force in order not to have to use it," he certainly was not above applying crushing military power and modern weaponry when he felt the need. He did not rely on force alone, though. He also used sagacious recruitment of the notables of Fez and calculated amnesties to initiate what he hoped would be a form of efficient control, his aim being to create an administration with a very different tone and set of consequences than the French involvement in Tunisia and, most especially, Algeria. He even gave a speech in 1916, saying: "It is absolutely necessary to set aside all prejudice and insensitive behavior, symbolized by the expression '*sale bicot*' (dirty wog), applied wholesale to all Moroccans, an expression so profoundly shocking and dangerous because those to whom it is addressed realize only too well that it implies a contempt and a menace which leaves a bitterness that nothing can efface."

In this instance, said the Haj, Lyautey sent word to Moulay M'hamed via a courier that he would guarantee the latter's safety if he would meet with the general. The two did meet at Tagzout and agreed that Moulay M'hamed would come with the general to the sultan Moulay Youssef, while Lyautey's soldiers would be left surrounded by the warring tribesmen as a guarantee against their leader's safe return. (This may have been around the same time that Lyautey was described in a document I had read as having visited Sefrou on November 8, 1916.) Moulay M'hamed then proceeded with Lyautey to Rabat, where he met with the sultan and through the monarch arranged a settlement with the French. However, when Moulay M'hamed returned to his tribe, the latter would have nothing to do with this peace treaty.

As a sign of his good intentions, Moulay M'hamed had already sent several of his wives and children to live in Sefrou (in a house given them in the Taksebt quarter by the French), said the Haj, and the children were going to the French school that had been started there. When the tribesmen renewed their fighting against the French, the latter took Moulay M'hamed's two grown sons to Rabat, where they were placed in what the Haj described as a tower dungeon. These two sons, however, managed to escape by fabricating a rope from some of their garments and lowered themselves to the ground. As soon as their escape was discovered, word was sent to all the caids of the area to be on the lookout for them and to return them immediately to Rabat if they were apprehended. When an illiterate sheikh of Zaer received this message, he sent it with a messenger to the mosque to have someone there decipher it for him. The man to whom the messenger handed the letter turned out to be none other than one of the escaped prisoners. He told the messenger that this was an order for the sheikh to assemble his troops and proceed to a rendezvous with other royal troops at a place directly opposite from the path the brothers intended to take in making their own escape. The brothers then made their way via Tadla and Zaen to the Beni M'guild who, as allies of the Ait Seghoushen, got them safely through Guigou to their home. When they arrived there, they found their father very ill, and when he died, the latter's paternal nephew, one Said ou Mohand, became the leader. He too fought hard against the French. One of his favorite tricks was to place a grenade in a cone of solid sugar, which was then sold to the French by a Jew. When, in one instance, the thing went off and killed several French soldiers, the Jew (an innocent party to all this) ran away, and, said the Haj with a smile, if he is still alive, he is probably still running.

Finally, however, Said made a settlement with the French and was himself appointed caid of that area. They really had no choice but to make a settlement, the Haj was quick to add: their grain supplies had long since run out, and they were denied access to the markets. The weather up in those mountains is bad enough, but without grain their situation was desperate. They held out a long time on the most meager of supplies, but with all the rest of Morocco fallen and their resources almost exhausted, they were forced to make a settlement while they could still get decent terms.

A pattern was clearly taking shape not only in the Haj's account of the contact with the French but in the accounts of many others with whom I have discussed this period. Physical resistance around Sefrou remained sporadic. On October 10, 1919, the American missionary Victor Swanson wrote from Sefrou: "The Berbers southeast of Sefrou are still in a fighting mood and quite often make raids down on peaceful villages. Just yesterday they came down within an hour's distance of Sefrou and carried off all the livestock the poor people possessed. There was some fighting and several were killed on both sides." And Jacques Berque, writing about this same moment, recalled how "two warriors captured at Sefrou were taken before the investigating officer: 'If I let you go, what will you do?' 'We shall kill you.' A sign is given to the huge guardsman. They leave. Two shots ring out."

Yet whatever their opinion of one or another sultan, whatever their urban or rural resistance to foreign incursion, at some point—starved, harassed, and technologically overpowered—even many of the leading fighters had no other choice but to give up, many of them taking positions in the new colonial administration. Writing about events in 1922, a French officer, Captain Pierre Valerie, noted that the Ait Youssi had already been in contact with the French for quite some time and that while other groups merely engaged in a symbolic show of force (*un baroud d'honneur*), the Ait Youssi initially engaged in a fierce battle on March 29. But by April 26, the French having penetrated their territory completely, the resisters sacrificed a bull as a sign of submission and that evening surrendered their arms.

Given the power of the French and the conditions in the mountains, it is hardly surprising, then, that the Haj and others should feel it was no shame for those resisting colonial incursion to eventually surrender. Of course, not all of the fighters saw matters the same way at the time. Jonathan Wyrtzen has retrieved from the collection of poems gathered by Arsène Roux in 1914–18 from Middle Atlas fighters of the time a wonderful example. Two poets, one who had submitted and one who was still involved in the fight, challenge each other's decision. 'Abid, who has given in, teases 'Alla about the lack of supplies the latter will have available come winter: "Go then and graze on the *ifsi* plant, when the long rains fall, when the persistent rains come, nourish yourself with the grass of the gazelles," to which 'Alla, challenging the other's subservience, replies, "I have not, as you have, committed evil actions in order to merit punishment. But you, after having been struck, you return right back to him who struck you." 'Abid concludes, though, by pointing to the futility of 'Alla's resistance: "'Alla, did not the Christian break your jaw and pull out your teeth; that is the compensation of your jihad." Notwithstanding such repartee, perhaps Thomas Powers's

Sultan Hafid and French officers

phrase best fits the situation. Speaking of the American Indian wars he said: "Nothing works in a desperate situation quite like putting up one hell of a fight, and then knowing when to quit." Or perhaps George Orwell had it right when he said that the quickest way to end a war is to lose it.

Notwithstanding the great loss of life, particularly in the Spanish zone in the north, by the time I began interviewing people more than half a century after the beginning of the Protectorate and a decade after independence, the tone of remembrance was, quite strikingly, seldom one of anger or of regret. No doubt at some point there were many who, observing various occasions of French ineptitude, may have agreed with the sultan Moulay Hafid when, after the French forced his abdication in August 1912 and replaced him with the figurehead Moulay Youssef, he remarked to a Western writer: "Is not the wisdom of God manifest? . . . Has He not given intelligence even to a dog? A little less, it is true, than to the elephant. But a little more than He bestowed upon the French administration."

For the most part, however, there was, notwithstanding the insult to their independence, grudging yet genuine admiration for many aspects of the peace and development that accompanied the Protectorate. The French did improve health, said the Haj, and their technology was quickly appreciated. There had been postal service as early as 1894, while telegraph service was initiated in 1913. I remember, said the Haj, when they wanted to build the electricity-generating plant up by the waterfall. A French engineer set up a little machine in the marketplace and connected an electric light to it. Suddenly it began to rain—but the light did not go out. How could you not see the benefit? Jacques Berque, too, seemed to support the Haj's approach when he said about the Moroccans during these times that "a whole gamut of attitudes was displayed, from unfriendly reserve to good-natured complicity, without ever departing from a general background of protest."

In time, more than 400,000 Frenchmen were to come to Morocco, fully a quarter of them living in rural areas. In addition to the French farmers who had begun to populate the countryside around Sefrou, the number and variety of Europeans living in the city proper was to grow slowly from 140 in 1926 to 218 in 1931, 246 in 1936, 339 in 1941, 495 in 1947, and 710 in 1951–52, before declining to 337 in 1960 and just 73 in 1971. Notwithstanding its military and administrative domination, for most Moroccans the French administration was not regarded as excessively heavy-handed. Lyautey could famously praise those who did not stick mindlessly to the rules ("initiative is successful disobedience") while asserting, too, that one cannot build a country with the winners of good conduct prizes. (Lyautey was never a shrinking violet: In 1930 an interviewer asked how he would have dealt with Jesus if he had been Pontius Pilate. He replied that there was indeed an analogy in their situations but that he would have acted more quickly to eliminate the threat that Christ posed: "I would not have waited until He had infected the crowds of the capitol with his seditious poison. I would have had Him put before a firing squad in His home province.")

Despite Lyautey's desire to keep his administration small and relatively unobtrusive—in 1920 he stated that the Protectorate's governing concept was "oversight [*contrôle*] as opposed to direct administration"—the French approach to governance at home could not fail to pour over into the colonies, such that, by contrast to the British system of indirect rule through local institutions, the colonial administration in Morocco became unavoidably top-heavy. As Douglas Porch has said: "He claimed to be an enemy of bureaucracy, but under Lyautey Morocco became a bureaucrat's paradise: three times as many Frenchmen were employed to govern Morocco as Englishmen were used to rule India with forty times the population." It was a pattern that, in time, was to affect the Haj's choices as well.

If at noon the king declares that it is night, behold the stars.
Don't believe, but don't criticize.
If you find them worshipping a donkey, bring it some fodder.
A problem is solved when it gets tougher.

—Moroccan sayings

Haj Hamed reading *Arabian Nights*

Often, taking respite from the heat of the day in the coolness of his side room, the Haj would have me rest for a bit while he would huddle, bare feet tucked beneath his Turkish trousers, his felt cap set at a rakish angle, reading a large old book. From time to time in those early days I asked what he was reading, but on each occasion, with a boyish grin, he would put me off: It has some things in it that are a bit shameful, he would say, a bit risqué. It was only much later that he admitted it was a copy of the *Thousand and One Nights*.

After a proper midday siesta we would return to the Haj's account of the Protectorate years. Picking up the thread of our conversations, Haj Hamed described how, in the period 1908–26, he had continued to live and work in Safi. He kept in close touch with Sefrou, though, traveling back to visit family, checking on his holdings, and keeping tabs on the local situation, knowing that he was most likely to return to the city permanently at some point. Around 1926 the sultan asked Si Bederdine to move to Sidi Slimane as qadi, said the Haj, and for two years I worked with him there. At that point the older man returned to Fez and soon after fell ill and died. I had no interest in staying on in the Sidi Slimane court: the town was small and there wasn't enough work to maintain the sort of living I was able to make in Safi. So I came back to the Qla'a, began dealing in sheep, and with another man I went into a partnership on a small store selling tea, sugar, cooking oil, and the like. Later I was appointed as the head of the poorhouse—what you call (the Haj said, in one of his rare uses of French terms) the Société Bienfaisance, no? I still dealt in animals, mostly with Sheikh Driss, the man we visit up in the mountains; I tended my gardens and kept my interest in the store for another ten years.

I also took on the job of adviser (*mustashar*) at the local court. The French started this practice of having two such advisers who sat with the pasha and the French official (*controleur civile*) when the pasha was deciding civil cases. The qadi's court, which decided matters of personal status according to Islamic law, was quite separate, and there were no advisers attached to it. We had two pairs of advisers, all of whom were from Sefrou and knew the place and people very well. The other three were even

French and Moroccan notables

Alaoui chorfa, descendants of the Prophet in the line of the ruling family. We met on Tuesdays, would listen to the cases but say nothing during the hearing, and then talk to each other and the pasha about our view of the matters. Sefrou, of course, was such a small place then—some eighty-five hundred people, of whom half were Jewish—that everyone knew everyone else's business, and we paid a lot of attention to a person's reputation and background in our advice. But when things were not clear, an oath, sworn at one of the mosques on Friday, was the way cases were concluded.

During the majority of those years, the Haj said, the French administration in Sefrou was much the same as it was in other cities of the country that had been subdued. A French commandant was in charge of this whole region. Under him was a rural administrator, the *rais l-baladiya* (always a retired French army officer), and a government representative (*mendub l-makhzeni*) who was responsible for the city. This latter figure was, the Haj said, always dressed in civilian clothes but was often still actively in the army or recently had been. The Moroccan judicial and municipal officials were formally under him, but when one of them—Muslim or Jewish— argued that something was not in keeping with his religious law or local custom, the government representative usually gave them no argument. Relations between French and local authorities were almost always excellent. But there were abuses.

For example, on one of my visits to Sefrou in the early 1920s I had gone up to Guigou to see the father of Youssef, our storekeeper friend, whom I had not seen for some nine years. There was a French captain, whose name the Haj pronounced as "Doublewa," in charge of the area at that time. (The Haj says there are still some humorous songs about this man, who apparently used to ride down the street throwing out handfuls of small coins that he kept in his bulging pockets.) This Frenchman invited me to have tea with him. I was then engaged in trading at Safi and knew a great deal about the market there and the international trade carried on from that port. The Frenchman was impressed by my knowledge and asked me to remain at Guigou and do some trading there. He did not want the Jews to continue in their capacity as peddlers in the countryside and thought I could increase the prosperity of that area if we combined knowledge and connections. I declined the offer. The Frenchman then gave me the choice between remaining in Guigou as a trader and being thrown in the local jail. What could I do? He gave me a place to live and baggage animals, and for two years I traded in the hills. The roads were still "cut" by the tribes at times, but I knew people who helped me. I was only able to extricate myself from all this when the sultan Moulay Youssef, on a visit to Fez, was approached on my behalf by the pasha of Fez. The sultan in turn got the French to let me go back to Safi.

The pasha for Sefrou during most of this period—and later also as caid for a good part of the territory around Sefrou—was a man named Muhammad ben Allal Cheradi Lamuri. He was, said the Haj, a strong military figure and worked closely with the French representative until the "pacification" of the Middle Atlas countryside around 1926. This latter Frenchman was himself of military extraction, so he was much concerned with Lamuri's ability to help keep the countryside relatively quiet. But Lamuri was also a greedy man.

When Lamuri came to power, said the Haj, he bought land in the nearby area called Misra from its Sefroui owners. Actually, he forced them to sell for insignificant sums, for a mere "breath." He then used his office to compel people to work the land by corvée labor (which we call tuayza, the term local people use for any mutual help done without pay). All men from the entire Sefrou area were required to spend one or two days per year working Lamuri's lands. It all came to an end, though, around 1934 when one of Lamuri's aides struck a man who was doing corvée labor on one of the pasha's farms. The man was not severely injured, but he was bleeding a lot. People gathered from all around and accompanied the man into Sefrou, bringing him to the bureau, which at that time was located just inside Bab Taksebt. They showed the wounded man to the French commander, a captain named Matir, a very powerful and upright man. When Matir heard the story, he immediately stopped all corvée labor in the Sefrou area and saw that this was enforced. In fact, he used to ride out alone—a fact that marked him as a brave man, said the Haj—and would ask all the people he saw working if they were doing tuayza labor, and he would tell them that they must never again do any such work for Lamuri.

When, however, the French military representative was replaced by a civilian around 1931, the French began to realize that Lamuri was probably now a liability. Remember, said the Haj, that for quite some time Lamuri had arbitrarily threatened people with imprisonment as a means of extorting money and land from them. The French finally removed him a couple of years later as a result of the following incident: The rais l-baladiya, the head of the appointed city council, at that time was living a fast and loose life, particularly with a number of Jewish prostitutes. He was also taking bribes from many Jews, in return for which he got them various kinds of merchandise, including materials to fix up the Jewish quarter, the mellah. The Pasha Lamuri, the French commandant, and lesser French officers wrote to Rabat about the man's conduct and requested that he be removed.

The *rais* and his friend the qadi (who the Haj says was also living fast) wrote their own letter to Rabat. The government then decided that it was probably best to summarily remove all parties concerned from office, and that was the end of the pasha Lamuri.

Matters were somewhat more complicated when it came to dealing with the Berbers. Policy toward the Berbers had, I knew, vacillated over the course of French involvement in Morocco. But many of the contradictions came to a head when in 1930 the French tried to separate the Berbers from the Arabs by placing the former under their own customary laws (*'orf*) and the latter under Islamic law (*shari'a*). When the French first came, said the Haj, they spent several years learning Berber law and recording its practices and judgments. They then called in the fraction elders and asked each in turn by which law they wanted to be judged. In 1930 they proclaimed the Berber Dahir, which said that the judges of those tribal fractions who were Berbers but used shari'a law—like many of the Berber fractions living near Sefrou—now had to use Berber customary law or be thrown in jail. A special prayer (*latif*) was held in Fez to protest the measure, and the French did throw the judges from some recalcitrant groups in jail. But the Berbers living near Sefrou remained intransigent. The local commandant wrote to Rabat asking for instructions. Rabat wrote back that those Berber groups who had always used shari'a could continue to do so if they chose. After independence, of course, when the *'orf* was abolished altogether, said the Haj, there was no resistance to its demise. Most of its functions had been thoroughly undercut by the French pacification of tribal disputes and their displacement by judgments rendered by governmental officials.

I was in Safi, he continued, when the Berber Dahir was announced, and since Safi was not a Berber area, there was little reaction there. But in many other parts of the country, special prayers, like that in Fez I mentioned, were said in order to overturn this attempt by the French to divide and conquer Moroccans. In fact, the Haj insisted, the Berber Dahir played a significant role in having exactly the opposite result of what the French wanted—it brought people together in opposition to the colonial rule. By the time I returned to Sefrou, people were already openly talking about independence, he said. They knew that the sultan Muhammad V, who took over after his father died in 1927, had long held nationalist sympathies, and when the United States promised to help us gain independence after the Second World War, things began to heat up. (Here the Haj was referring to the meeting of Roosevelt and the sultan during the allied leaders' meeting at Casablanca in January 1943, where, many Moroccans believe, the president promised that the United States would return the favor of

Morocco having been the first nation to recognize American independence by urging the French to remove themselves after the war, a promise that, whether it actually occurred, many Moroccans of the Haj's generation continue to accept as fact.)

Also, said the Haj, during the Protectorate period, from 1932 until independence in 1956, I served on the municipal council. In Sefrou's case it was called a mixed municipal commission because there was one section with appointed French members and another that was subdivided between the Muslim and Jewish members, though mostly the whole Moroccan section would advise together unless it was something specific about the members' own communities. For much of that time (1944–53) the pasha was Si M'barek Bekkai, who later became the first prime minister of Morocco, just as the local administrator of the tribal region, Caid Lahsen Lyoussi, became the first minister of defense—so you can see how important a region this was.

But during most of those years, I gently suggested, you were, even if to a very limited degree, assisting the French administration, were you not? The Haj did not hesitate in his response. The French were the power at that time. Me, I stay close to the wall: I don't involve myself a lot in party politics. We have two sayings: "Cleave to the oppressor" (stay separate but close enough to know what he is doing) and "The ruler is the one doing the asking" (he is the one who needs you). Like many others in Sefrou, we gave money to the partisans of independence. In fact, the leader of the Independence Party (*Istiqlal*), Allal al-Fassi, had a lieutenant here, a man named Mezwar. When the French threw him in jail, his brother asked me to take care of the man's gardens here. Later, when Mezwar was hiding out in Meknes, I went down there and gave him some of the profits from his gardens plus some extra money for Istiqlal. We showed our opposition to France in other ways. For example, in 1944 we held a prayer, a *latif*, in which you ask God to turn things around, in that case that the French would be forced to leave Morocco as a result of the American landing. A *latif* is an extremely powerful prayer—God will not ignore it—and each of the religious scholars (*ulama*) of Fez who organized the prayer expressed his serious intent by spitting on the ground and rubbing the spittle into the earth with his foot. (Spitting on a potential successor is also one of the ways that spiritual power, baraka, may be transferred from one person to another, and the symbolism of transferring such power from the religious leaders to the land was a not insignificant ritual gesture.)

This pattern of working with the French was one I encountered time and time again in Morocco. From my conversations with the Haj and many others over the years, I have come away with the impression that for those of the Haj's generation the idea of "collaboration" applied only if someone acted in a way that directly harmed another Muslim. Working with the French was no worse than working with a bad Muslim government, and the overall proposition—contained in such sayings as "chaos [fitna] is worse than tyranny," that "it is worse to make a man live in chaos than to kill him," that (in the words of al-Ghazzali) "tyranny is preferable to anarchy," or indeed that (to quote one last phrasing) "the just infidel is preferable to the unjust Muslim"—seems to have taken precedence over blanket disapproval of ties with the French. As Jacques Berque put it, in their administration of Morocco the French acquired accomplices rather than collaborators. Faced with a wide array of French officials, Moroccans seem to have done what they always do—to judge a person by more than his most immediate aspect, even though that forms the baseline for initial assessment—and to have managed their own ambivalence, simultaneously noting the occupier's aggression and distinguishing (as Berque notes) among "things to be forgiven, admired or loved." The fact that the French administration left Islamic family law alone also appears to figure in the Haj's equation.

Interestingly, the attitude of the next generation to the Haj's cohort appears to have changed over time. Initially, many of them thought their fathers too accommodating to the French, too willing to forgo resistance once the military struggle ended. Over time, however, many of them have revised their view, now regarding the parental generation as having preserved a distinctive Moroccan cultural and national identity against the day when the younger generation could make a bolder move toward independence. This attitude shift, clear in the literary as well as political realm, in no way excused those whose actions went beyond mere acquiescence.

Indeed, when the boundary of harm to a Muslim was transgressed, the Haj did not hesitate to imply that retribution was justified. When independence came, he said, people in the Istiqlal party killed four caids in various parts of the country. All the other caids who had been against the king sought protection from Si Bekkai, who was then the prime minister. Bekkai kept the caids with him until the situation cooled off and then sent them off to house arrest in different cities for several years. But there were "executions," said the Haj: I witnessed some in Rabat. At that time, he continued, I was working in the city administration in Sefrou, mainly in charge of the orphanage and poorhouse, and like all other such local Moroccan appointees in this period just after the king's return to the country, I went down to Rabat to pay my respects to the monarch. There, in the palace itself (mechouar), with the gates barred, Istiqlal party members had lined

up a number of people they suspected of having been French sympathiz-
ers. The people they agreed were guilty of such collaboration were pulled
out of line and killed, mainly with pistol shots. It was the young men in
the Istiqlal party who did this, but I think some of them were paid by enemies of the victims involved to kill them on the pretense of collaboration. Everything was upside down in those days, and the sultan himself
was at first quite powerless to do anything—or at least he didn't act immediately. Shortly afterward, however, the sultan climbed to the roof of
the palace and told them to stop the killing, that he personally forgave all
those among the accused who were still alive.

Were any people in Sefrou killed during the period just before or after independence? I asked. The Haj said that a Sefrou Muslim named
Ben Khenafru, an ardent Istiqlal party man, tried to kill Boumediane
l-Meghrawi, who was the government-appointed head (*muqaddem*) of the
Chebbak quarter and a supporter of the French. Ben Khenafru took a shot
at l-Meghrawi one Friday after the latter left the mosque and was walking
down the main street of the Sidi Hamed Tadli quarter, but he missed him
and killed a friend of l-Meghrawi who was walking with him. This same
Ben Khenafru also took a shot at Si Abdelmoghit Zaki, deputy to the pasha, but only wounded him in the leg. Later, when the Istiqlal party itself
split, Ben Khenafru sided with the famous opposition leader Mehdi Ben
Barka (who was murdered by allies of King Hassan II years later) and was
himself shot down by Istiqlal party people somewhere between Zaer and
Oujda. One other person who was killed was a Jew whose name I can't
remember, he continued. During the struggle for independence the fighters for Istiqlal told people not to smoke any cigarettes because they either
came from France or brought profits to the French. In Fez children used to
fit razor blades into potatoes and throw them at anyone they saw smoking
cigarettes on the street. Cigarette dealers were also warned not to sell any of
their merchandise. The Sefrou Jew I just told you about? He continued to
sell cigarettes despite this warning and someone gunned him down in his
store because of it.

Most of the support for the independence movement from this area,
said the Haj, was financial. People in the city were too much under the
eyes of the French to do anything else, although some people did go off
to join the Army of Liberation. The Haj stressed the importance of the financial help given the movement by urban dwellers. He said, pointing to a
light fixture, that it is like electricity: one only sees the light, but the important factor is the electricity, which is invisible and travels in hidden underground cables. The money that supplied the movement was the electricity,

Si M'barek Bekkai, pasha of Sefrou

Assassination attempt on sultan in 1953

the real force, not just the light; the sabotage activities of the Army of Liberation were only its visible manifestation. From other sources, however, I later learned that in 1946 Istiqlal set up a network of shopkeepers in Sefrou and its nearby market towns, a network that was very helpful in later elections that favored the party.

The years leading up to national independence were, then, years in which the Haj, like many others, kept his opposition to French control close to his chest. His ideal throughout this period was the pasha Si M'barek Bekkai. Bekkai, a Berber from the Algerian border region who rose to the rank of colonel in the French army, having lost a leg while fighting for the French in 1940. He was, however, eventually dismissed from his post as pasha of Sefrou for refusing to sign a petition calling for the

Sultan Muhammad V

removal of Muhammad V as sultan. In August 1953, when the French banished Muhammad V and his family first to Corsica and then to Madagascar and replaced the monarch with the puppet sultan Muhammad ben Arafa, an attempt was made on the new sultan's life. Bekkai, an ardent monarchist, went into voluntary exile at the same time. But removal of Muhammad V only reinforced opposition to the Protectorate. Within two years numerous attacks took place against Europeans, while the Army of Liberation exercised increasing control of the countryside and strikes shut down many urban enterprises. When the sultan was returned to the country at the end of October 1955 and a treaty ending the Protectorate was signed the following spring, men like Bekkai, who had no formal political party attachment, found themselves in and out of government posts but stymied in their attempt to remove governors and administrators appointed solely on the basis of partisan connections. So, too, for the Haj and other "notables" of his generation, loyalty to the king and pride in national sovereignty was always tempered by wariness of party attachments and greater admiration for those who did not fit permanently into government posts than for those who did.

In his account of these years, once again the Haj's implicit view of history came through with clarity. His was not the view of history as directional or as revelatory of a divine plan, as it has been over the course of time for many Christians. His approach to events, as some scholars have said of Islam more generally, rested on the notion that in exercising one's imagination one may find its accord with reality. Seen from this perspective, one can sense how the vision of history fits with other Moroccan cultural forms, including art. Now the seemingly repetitious designs on the wall of a mosque are not mindless iteration but demonstrations that at every juncture alternative paths exist and choices must be made; now one can understand that the way tiles fit together so no two angles are precisely replicated mimics a world in which unique individuals encounter one another in situations that, however characteristic, are never exactly the same. If prayer, for the Haj, is that ritual reversal of the ordinary—when one stops the action of the world and relinquishes the mundane sense of individual maneuvering—and if, moreover, prayer requires an initial statement of intent to be valid, then each time I would watch the Haj pause in our conversations to say his five daily prayers, whether in the quiet of his garden or in the hurly-burly of a rural market, I felt privy to a sense of submission that for all its publicity was intensely private.

In Morocco, as historian Edmund Burke III neatly suggests, everything is intended except its consequences, if for no other reason than because, like the figuration in an enclosing arabesque, every instance presents a choice, a quality every man must exercise since at all times he is constantly among men who, despite seeming replication, are never precisely alike. The world of the Haj and his countrymen is one in which process clarifies moral ambiguity and the sheer joy of engaging difference is the very fulfillment of one's God-given capacities for reason and movement. In prayer, as in a variety of artistic and literary forms, what may, therefore, appear as mere duplication is instead conceived as the presentation of a decision—always with overtones of the moral—that no reasoning person can avoid. As a critic has said of a modern Sudanese novel, "Repetition can perform different functions simultaneously. . . . It suggests several possible outcomes for the story which may or may not materialize later on, thus presenting the reader with a choice. Just as it emphasizes similarities, repetition also insists upon disparities and contradictions. The reader is then forced to establish links between motifs or between larger elements in the novel and to calculate the likelihood of one alternative being realized as opposed to another."

I knew, too, that the Haj accepted the choices he had made in his life and that on that day when the winding sheet he wore while he circumambulated the holiest of places in Mecca would become his burial shroud, it was, in truth, with those choices alone that he would stand before his maker. It was in his familial life that I was to see many of those choices at work.

God has created us brothers but has given us separate purses.

—Turkish saying

Do business together as if we were strangers, and then you can chew me up as if we were brothers.

—Moroccan saying

I did not understand the meaning,
but my heart was grieved by it,
and I understood its grief.

—Arab poem

If anything occupies a central role for most Moroccans, it is surely the family. From the confines of a dwelling beyond which uncertainty and insecurity threaten to the dominance of males who are often confronted by strong women in a persistent pattern of mutual maneuvering, the family is at once haven and launching pad, resource and fallback, emotional foundation and emotional trial. For the Haj the life of his family has been one whose sheer admixture frustrates simple summation.

The Britels came from Andalusia, the Haj told me, some six hundred years ago when Jews and Muslims alike were expelled from Spain. Of the four main divisions of the family one group settled in the north at Tetouan, others on the coast at Salé, while our branch picked the Qla'a in Sefrou because it reminded them of Spain. It is really best that families are split up this way; otherwise they will eventually fight among themselves. When heirs have to share a house, for example, fights invariably break out until some members find a new residence. It can even happen with the best of intentions. We have a saying: "He bent to kiss his son and poked him in the eye." There needs to be one strong leader of a family, especially for handling decisions about property and marriages.

Perhaps the most contentious of the Haj's family ties was with his brothers. Together they shared a number of gardens, but, the Haj once said bitterly, my brothers were bad, they gave me nothing from the gardens, they ate everything themselves. I was angry, I wanted them to give me some. Don't take everything for yourselves, I said. Did you sue them? I asked. He smiled as one would at a child, and shaking his head simply said, No, they were my brothers. But the underlying bitterness was quite evident. He went on to tell me about a similar situation that arose following the death of his brother Bou Ali just three years earlier. The brother left $600 with the Haj to split among the deceased's children, but they fought so much among themselves that the Haj finally refused to give them the money until they gathered in front of a court notary to acknowledge receipt of the funds. They in turn sued the Haj for the distribution, so the Haj hired a Jewish lawyer from Fez to handle the matter in such a way that the Haj would not have to come face to face with the heirs again. Eventually, the lawyers on both sides agreed to the distribution and formalized the settlement before the requisite notaries.

Balanced against the difficulties with his brothers, though, was his enduring affection for his wife, the redoubtable Haja. The affection they felt for one another was palpable. Once, I teasingly asked the Haj about why he had never taken a second wife. He smiled and replied that a man with more than one wife is like a man who has to tend to the kind of well where a harnessed animal must constantly be coaxed to walk in circles to haul up the water, a process that means neither man nor beast ever has any rest. I am very attached to our friend Sheikh Driss, the man we visit in the moun-

Haj and family

tains, said the Haj, but he is crazy for having taken a second wife. He divorced his first wife after she had no children but later remarried her after
the second wife bore him children and the first wife's family pressured him
to take her back with no addition to the bridewealth and no written agreement. When the two wives didn't get along, he had to make separate cooking and sleeping places for each. The poor man has had no peace since!

If the Haj and Haja were content with their own marriage, the situations of their children were quite another matter. The couple had two sons
and two daughters. One of the sons was killed in a motorcycle accident,
having served, like thousands of others from the colonized countries of Africa, with the French forces in Southeast Asia. A daughter, already married

but childless, had also died as a young woman. The Haj had been careful, he thought, in selecting his children's spouses. In each case go-betweens helped negotiate the bridewealth payment, but unlike most others, the Haj does not like the possibility of recording with the court the "furnishings of the household" supplied by the bride's marital guardian, goods that would remain with her in the event of divorce or widowhood. When these things are not recorded, any added household items are presumed to belong to her, so the greater the accumulation, the greater the restraint on the husband's arbitrary power of unilateral divorce. The Haj also preferred mates for both his son and daughters from outside their own kin but from families well known to them. People often say it is best to marry a cousin, the Haj remarked, so property stays within the family. But when your father-in-law is also your paternal uncle, you may never be the authority in your own home. In the case of his son Tahar, the bride's family met the Haj's criteria of being from outside their own immediate kin group and of being nonargumentative, religious, and well respected. Regrettably, the problems that ensued have come from his son.

Tahar had, from the time I got to know the Haj in the mid-1960s, already worked for years in France. He drank a lot, came home yearly for a brief visit, and fled back to France, leaving behind his wife Habiba and their children, who lived with the Haj and the Haja. On the rare occasions when I saw him, he would dart in the room for a moment and then vanish, always there by his absence. To the Haj and the Haja, though, Habiba is more of a daughter than a daughter-in-law; they have loved her deeply, and she has always treated them with the utmost affection and respect. Until the 1980s she always wore a full-face veil and covering garment when leaving the house, out of concern (she would tell me) for the older people's sensibilities, even though she thought such veiling unnecessary. As her in-laws aged, Habiba, herself afflicted with a weakening heart condition, took care of the household and her own numerous children.

The Haj's surviving daughter, Zohara, was married to a highly educated man, who was to serve as a school principal and judge, but who was not always the easiest person to get along with. Tragedies abounded. When the Haj's sister and her husband died, the Haj took their twelve-year-old son into his house and raised him. When he grew up, the Haj paid his bridewealth, and for a year the young couple lived in his house. Later the nephew moved out, grew prosperous in the building supplies industry, and became, said the Haj, uppity and distant to the point where they barely spoke. The whole thing saddens me, said the Haj, because I thought of him as a son. The Haj also raised several orphaned children—at least one from an impoverished cherifian family, another when a close friend, on his deathbed, asked the Haj to take in his soon-to-be orphaned son. But these arrangements, too, did not always have happy results. There is no formal adoption in Islamic law, but the Haj raised the friend's boy and arranged and paid the bridewealth for his marriage. For whatever reason, however, the two never seemed to form a close tie. Once, a man entered Youssef's store while I was talking with the Haj, and when I later asked who it was, it came as a surprise to me that it was this man he had taken in, so frosty was their greeting.

Once, too, I recall the Haj saying that boys always leave their fathers. But I have stayed close to mine, I said. Ah, replied the Haj, smiling, but are you not here and your father far away? It was one of those moments when, as I was to see with many others, the idealized patriarchal system is put to a test. For while sons must initially be dependent on fathers and teachers and often endure a long period of a master-disciple relationship, they must at some point separate from these parental figures if they are to be able to forge ties of interdependency in their own names. As warm as the father-son relation is when a boy is young, it becomes far more formal and distant as the boy grows into manhood. If, for example, a man is in a café and his son enters, one of them will usually leave, it being shameful to be together in a venue where card playing, gossip, and strong language are common.

Even the Haj's grandchildren seem somewhat distant. One has taken brief jobs as far away as Libya, while others, struggling with unemployment, have drifted away. One of Zohara's sons left a wife and child behind in Morocco to try for a career as a singer and poet while living illegally in America, only to be run down and killed by a car while crossing a street late at night in Nevada. Unable to return the body to his hometown, Zohara came to the United States for the burial, and the photo I was sent of her son's grave in a foreign desert is one of the saddest I can recall. When I saw her in Fez a few years later, both son and husband having passed away, she was as gracious as ever, but much of the energy has dispersed. Habiba, the beloved daughter-in-law who had seven children and remained to care for the aging Haj and Haja, also had to cope with a daughter afflicted with Turner syndrome, an ailment that left the girl a stunted child well into her twenties. That the Haj should have experienced the tragic loss of two children and the virtual abandonment of his other son may not have been irrelevant to the way in which our work together allowed memory to fill a certain void. Perhaps for the Haj, as a novelist once said, "The sadness in this life created a space for memory."

Though I never sensed in all our conversations that he regarded Islam as a place of solace in the face of these disappointments, it was, however, clear that the Haj took great comfort in having made the pilgrimage to Mecca in 1957. He especially loved traveling through Switzerland and Egypt on his way to the holy sites, it being so vital to his sense of identity to be one who sees others' ways with his own eyes and returns to garner the prestige that comes from knowing others firsthand. When our conversations turned to issues of religion, the Haj expressed a viewpoint common among Moroccans, that he does not need others who profess greater purity to tell him he is less than a good Muslim. Indeed, his form of religion—which includes regular prayer and the fulfillment of all formal religious requirements—is also a form of immeasurable tolerance, a focus on persons, not their faith alone, and on the candor with which any man or woman approaches relations with others. It was therefore the Haj who one day said he had arranged for us to have coffee in a café with the remaining Jewish religious official in Sefrou, a man the Haj regarded as knowledgeable and wise. And it was the Haj who, at a rural market well up in the mountains, encountered a young Jewish sheep dealer, both men expressing, in private as well as in each other's company, the greatest of affection and admiration. Whatever else may be true of him, the Haj was a man of his culture and of his religion, and it was by observing these relations over many years that I learned to replace the stereotypes or romanticized talk of an Andalusian moment or Abrahamic commonalities with the far more subtle and admirable reality of the Haj's encounters with those who were socially and culturally distinct.

Fresh forever be the recollection of those days passed by,
with neighbors in whose company
our nights were festivals indeed.

—Ibn al-Farid

Six more years passed before I returned to Sefrou. I felt badly for not keeping in touch. Indeed it was with some foreboding that I made my way up that familiar road from Fez to Sefrou with a colleague from the university in Rabat. We drove slowly through the Sais plain, where I remembered the young Haj had been accosted, past the road that veers off to the hilltop they call Jbel Bina—"the hill that lies between us," the people in Sefrou and those in Bhalil—while, with his voice ringing in my own account, I told my companion the Haj's stories of how the Bhalil people warred against the Sefrouis after the death of a king and of how he fled homeward after the fiasco in the Chaouia in 1907, as if the stories had somehow become my own. As we approached Sefrou, I pointed out the Haj's garden, surrounded now by numerous villas, past the gaudy archway erected for a festival but left up year-round, and across the tiny bridge where the river makes its way down from the waterfall above the Qla'a and bisects the city on its way to the countryside below. As we rounded the bend onto the main street of the Ville Nouvelle, however, I had some inkling that all was not well. When I entered Youssef's store, he greeted me warmly. But he sensed my anxiety immediately and with great gentleness told me that the Haj had indeed passed away. The date, I later determined, was Saturday, April 29, 1982, known in the Muslim calendar as the twenty-fourth of Jumada II in the year 1402.

Memories flooded back from all the years we had worked together. I thought of that wonderful moment, as we met for breakfast at Bel Haj's café, when the Haj wagged his finger at me and, with a teasing smile, said: You Americans! What about us? I asked. You are always thinking about money, he said. What makes you say so? I inquired. How do you greet each other in the morning, he asked with a wry smile? You say (using his few words of English) "Good Money! Good Money!" I remembered, too, those moments when the Haj was deep in the details of his recollection. At such times names would pour forth in great profusion, a veritable cornucopia of identifiers and nicknames, dates and places, their very sonority, coupled with my growing familiarity, rendering them a magical chant: how in the days of Caid So-and-So, the son of So-and-So, whose head was the shape of a pear and whose garden was watered by such-and-such canal; how So-and-So, the six-fingered one, fought with another over the price of a donkey. On and on. It was more than memory that was at work. For Moroccans each habitation has a name, each man has a place, and every point of contact prompts notice of every other in a chain of hoped-for beneficence that only the association of sentient beings can bring forth.

I thought, too, of the time I encountered some American tourists in Marrakech who expressed concern because Moroccans, they opined, had nothing to do in the evenings if they lacked a television set and how, so contrary to my countrymen's expectations, I had stayed up with the Haj and others till the wee hours of the morning reveling in their showman-ship as they performed one story after another. I even thought of the time I realized that I only knew the city in the daytime, so I walked the streets all night long and was invited by the porters, seated on the ground around a small fire under the walls of the old city, to share the broken glass contain-ing coffee that passed from hand to hand, how I walked with the garbage collector and his mule through one neighborhood after another while he pointed out where the internal gates used to be closed to ward off marauders, and how in the predawn light a cook who had seen me in town asked if I wasn't the friend of that nice old man Haj Hamed Britel. That very quest for knowledge that is so central to Muslims was, I could see through all of that night, more than the mere collection of information, for in the variety of knowledge lay the bonds that held the Haj's world together as a place of reason—and as a site where, I always felt, he had held a place for me.

It was from Youssef, too, that I learned about the Haj's family and friends. He mentioned that Omar, the retired gardener we used to visit in his cave on our way up to the home of Sheikh Driss, had gone on the pilgrimage to Mecca. I was astounded. How could he possibly afford such a trip? I asked. No one knows for sure, said Youssef. Was it the Haj? I asked. One does not inquire of such a gift, said Youssef wistfully, but his quiet smile told me all I needed to know. I recalled, too, how I had initially thought the Haj rather penurious for the way he always seemed to let me pay for things, until, near the end of my first long stay in Morocco, he presented me with his collection of coins from the nineteenth century, and one of those beautiful, big, leather traditional wallets men wear under their djellabas, a gift he surely knew would always remind me of our shared involvement in his history.

Later that morning my colleague and I drove out the El Menzel road to the new cemetery where the Haj was buried. Muslim graves may or may not be marked, and after forty years a graveyard may be used for another purpose. As the old cemetery just outside the gate to Fez was soon to reach its allotted limit and be converted to another use, a new burial ground had been opened, one where people were simply laid to rest in the order in which they died. There were several *tolba* present at the graveyard, men who chant Quranic passages at a funeral or at the bidding of those visiting the grave of a loved one. I called them over and asked their help in locating the Haj's grave. After a bit of a search we found it. Like all the others it was marked by a simple headstone. Beneath his name was written an invocation and a passage from the Quran: "May God strengthen him with His all-encompassing mercy and make him reside in gardens. We belong to God and we return to Him." I asked the *tolba* if they would say a prayer for the Haj, and listening to their unembellished chant, fraught with the sonorities of life and the reality of death, I could not hold back the tears. I placed a few pebbles on the tombstone, explaining to the rapt *tolba* that it was the custom of my people to indicate in this fashion that a mourner had passed that way. The chanters smiled and moved on. Later, I asked my colleague

The Haj departs

the meaning of the words the *tolba* had sung. After several Quranic verses, he told me, they prayed for the soul of the Haj Hamed Britel—and then they prayed "for his friend who has come from far away."

I once asked the Haj how a man prays if he is unable to stand and bow. He said you pray with your eyes, closing them in turn for each of the three prostrations.

When I visited the Haja and Habiba some time after he passed away, I asked about the Haj's final days. They told me that he had not left the house for about a month but many people came to visit him. The doctor forbade him from smoking but everyone laughed at the way he hid cigarettes all over the house and bummed them from his grandsons and visitors. Sometimes at night he would speak of me and my wife and wonder where we were, would we return. Eventually he had grown weaker and weaker until finally he was confined to his bed. On Thursday someone from the family went to collect the payment that the French government still sent for the son who died having fought in Indochina. On Friday the Haj was mostly in bed. On Saturday morning they found him there: he had died quietly sometime in the night. Perhaps, it was thought, in the hour before dawn, as the sleepy muezzin made his climb to the top of the minaret, as the doves cooed the time of the first prayer, the Haj lowered his eyes once, twice, and then, closing them in final submission, he withdrew.

Khiyyar.

A Midmost Nation:
Yaghnik Driss

Yaghnik Driss

Thus we appointed you a midmost nation
That you might be witnesses to the people,
And that the Messenger might be a witness to you.

—Quran II: 137

We met in the garden of the Frenaie. A remnant of colonial Morocco, the
Frenaie was situated just outside of Sefrou on the road to Fez, and though
it advertised itself as a hotel and did, in fact, take in the odd European trying the less-traveled road, it existed mainly for its bar. There, with all the

provincial bonhomie its rotund French patron and his equally stout wife could muster, Muslims could slip unnoticed through the heavy foliage at the front gate and, at the risk of losing those potions the Quran has promised them in the hereafter, partake in relative seclusion of the prohibited "wines of earth."

I had been in Morocco for little more than a week and had settled at the Frenaie while looking for an apartment. Youssef, the local storekeeper who was working with me on my Arabic each noontime, had responded to my inquiry about an additional instructor by informing me that he was sending someone to the hotel that afternoon with whom I might study. His name, he said, is Yaghnik, which to an English speaker sounds closest when pronounced *ee-rah-neek*, though that middle consonant is really a guttural trill. In the bright and unusually warm sun of that early February day in 1966, I awaited my new teacher with some apprehension.

The car that swung quickly through the gate was a Renault Dauphine, tiny, encircling, and humorous. It was not at all like the more common Citroën Deux Chevaux, whose designers had worked out the car's ergonomics so that even if the driver lacked the requisite paunch or elevated chin, he would nevertheless be constrained to assume the pose of a typical French peasant on his way to market. By contrast, the man who popped from behind the wheel of the Dauphine was so round and sprightly it seemed as if the car itself had been molded around him.

I knew a bit about Yaghnik from our mutual friend: that he was in his early thirties, that he was a native of Fez, and that he lived with his wife and two small children in an apartment attached to the girls' grammar school of Sefrou, where he had taught for the past seven years. What I had not been told about was his energy, his inventiveness, his good humor, and most of all his uncanny ability to make almost any subject instantly accessible to the initiate. Indeed, as I came to realize in those early weeks of our work together—and as succeeding years have only reconfirmed—Yaghnik was, in every respect, an ideal teacher of young children, among whom I, a virtual beginner in Moroccan language and culture, surely had to be numbered. It was Yaghnik's special gift that he could always find a way to make you understand, always find some other words, always discover an analogy or metaphor to get his point across without diminishing its authenticity or force. I had loved every single one of my grammar school teachers; I just never thought I would have the chance to do it all over again.

But there was something else I had not been told about Yaghnik, something I only began to appreciate once I understood more about his culture and his religion—that Yaghnik is, as the Quran says, one of those people of the middle, a man deeply attached to Islam and all that it imports and, at the same time, no less attached to the "modern" world of people and things that accord with the powerfully inclusive religion conveyed by the Prophet Muhammad. For Yaghnik, much of this orientation was directly connected to his personal background and education.

Yaghnik was born in Fez during that period of the mid-1930s when the world was between two wars and Morocco was midway in the years of French colonial rule. His family is said to have originated in the Tafilelt, a thin strip of oases that reaches deep into the Sahara and has for centuries been a wellspring of Moroccan spiritual and commercial fervor. Except for noting that both he and his father were born in Fez, Yaghnik's genealogical reflections do not run very deep: he simply says that his family came from the south many generations ago. Unlike some of the eastern Arabs, most Moroccans are not overly concerned with the precise details of their genealogies. Those individuals who claim descent from the Prophet—particularly if it is in the line of the Alaoui dynasty that has held the throne since the seventeenth century—or those who trace their ties to one of the popular saints whose descendants share in the gifts brought to their predecessor's shrine are, however, naturally more concerned to assert detailed proof of their familial connections. Genealogical amnesia notwithstanding, in every respect Yaghnik, like his fellow countrymen, betrays no uncertainty as to his own identity. Instead, as I began to understand him, it became evident that, regardless of his family's background, Yaghnik is, above all, a Fassi, a man of Fez, a man of the ancient capital of Morocco.

For Moroccans the place from which one originates conveys much more than mere geography: it says a great deal about the customs one employs in dealing with others, the expectations one harbors about others, and that whole complex of everyday habits—from the smallest item of politesse to the implications of a turn of phrase for one's religious sensibilities— through which people orient themselves in the world. As in many other parts of the Arab world, these distinctions, symbolized in gesture, dress, accent, cuisine, and bearing, are exquisitely localized. Indeed, it is one of the reasons why it is said that the man who has traveled widely and knows the features of different populations gains in prestige, for he will know how others relate to one another and thus how, in an ever-widening array of places, a connection may be negotiated for the benefit of oneself and one's dependents. To know another's source of nurturance, whether it be from Fez, the mountains, or a given tribe, is thus to presuppose, as a point of departure for the formation of a personal relationship, important aspects of anyone's way of being in the world.

The people of Fez in particular think of themselves, and have traditionally been thought of by others, through a set of characteristics that, however inexact they may be as descriptions of any one person, form a baseline
for identification and an index of some of their city's central institutions.
Fez was founded in the latter part of the eighth century c.e. by Moulay Idris
I, who established Islam in Morocco. In the subsequent centuries Fez, with
its shrines and mosques, its academies, brotherhoods, and charitable foundations, has been strongly identified with the Islamic institutions of the
country. (To this day the people of Turkey call Morocco "Fez," and the sign
at the city limits welcomes visitors to "The Spiritual Capital of Morocco.")
To the Fassis this overall image bespeaks refinement, religiosity, and the
highest standards of those crafts—of leather, cloth, tile work, jewelry, and
the table—that are connected with learning, traditional deportment, and
elegant hospitality.

In the past, when transportation between urban centers was long and
dangerous, the pleasure taken in reaching the gates of a safe city and avail-
ing oneself of its baths, cafés, inns, and mosques, was enormous. No less
intense, however, was the sense of intercity rivalry. Each Moroccan city,
large or small, imagined itself more true to the essence of Islamic civilization; each professed that its inhabitants spoke a "purer" form of Arabic than any other, adhered more firmly to the true precepts of Islam, and
maintained an enviable plateau of civility and culture. Proverbs, songs, and
jokes convey this sense of rivalry. To this day the people of Sefrou chide
the Fassis, whom they tend to see as haughty and sanctimonious, by reminding them that, on his way to reestablish Fez, Moulay Idris II, the son
of its first founder, is reputed to have said, "I leave the *city* of Sefrou to go
to the *village* of Fez." And the Fassis return the slight, playing on various
words and sayings to suggest that the people of Sefrou have a rather shaky
attachment to the true spirit and precepts of Islam. On one matter at least
there is broad agreement: Fez has almost always been at the heart of whatever changes were afoot within Morocco, and this was certainly true of the
years when Yaghnik was growing up there. His description of those years
touched on all of these features.

Like all the other boys, he said, I began studying in the school attached
to the mosque when I was five years old. It was all repetition of passages
from the Quran, written on slates as a way of learning our letters and sacred
text at the same time. It was the beginning of my own memorization of the
Holy Quran. That early educational experience left its mark in many ways.
Over the next two years, particularly when we began working together in
the records of the local court, Yaghnik would joke about how, if I got things

wrong, one person would have to hold me on his shoulders while another beat the bare soles of my feet, just the way small boys are punished in the Quranic schools. At other times we would pass the doorway of one of these schools and, to the sounds of the rhythmic chanting of the children, Yaghnik would stop in his tracks, pick up on the beat, search till he found the passage in his memory, and then repeat it carefully before moving on, as if to assure himself it was still properly lodged where it belonged.

Eventually, he said, I began in the regular school system. It was still the years of the French Protectorate, and though the French established schools for the elite, I just went to the regular schools where everything was in Arabic. I studied all sorts of subjects: philosophy, astronomy, history, grammar, literature. I was close to getting the baccalaureate when the government changed the rules for finishing a degree. The officials were trying to limit the number of people getting the *bac*, something they have done repeatedly over the years. At that time what they did was require you to take a foreign language and to pass both written and oral tests for the diploma. I thought to myself: Well, that won't be so hard; I'll get through all the Arabic subjects first and then I'll get through the foreign language requirement. I could have studied any language, but I chose Spanish because the spelling is just the way things sound, not like French, where the writing and the pronunciation are so different. I passed the subjects in Arabic with no trouble, but I couldn't pass the foreign language. The new government *système* worked against me. It was like a dam, and I was on the side where things got stopped. I took the exam four times over the years and never passed it, so I never got the *bac*.

Although Yaghnik never passed the exam, he often uses French words mixed into his colloquial Moroccan Arabic. This is not pretentious. Like most Moroccans it is part of his personal history to have been exposed, in his case during the days of French colonial power, to elements of French language and culture, and often he uses such words (indicated here with italics) as a normal part of his speech. One is often struck, in Yaghnik's wonderful style of amalgamation, by his use of these French, or sometimes Spanish, words with an Arabic grammatical construction, such as the plural (*groupat*, for "groups") or, in one marvelous instance over dinner, by his combination of the French verb "to pass" and the Arabic suffixes for "it" and "to me" combined into a single word, *passer-ha-li*. If anything, Yaghnik is unusual among Moroccans for his lack of multilingual virtuosity; most Moroccans must control colloquial Arabic in addition to the very different modern literary Arabic (used in schools, the media, and in more classicized form in the Quran), French (or, more recently, English), and (if they are from such a background) their own dialect of Berber, itself completely unrelated to Arabic. The educational system has become Arabized for most subjects in recent years, but Yaghnik's Arabic education had more to do with nonelite, traditional status than with any antipathy to Western forms.

Eventually, Yaghnik continued, I transferred to another school, where I studied psychology and where I got a diploma that was sort of the equivalent of a baccalaureate. I also read a lot on my own. But mostly I attended the Qarawiyin, the great mosque-university in Fez founded in 859 C.E. Even when I was a student there, the Qarawiyin was not simply a place for studying the Quran, religious law, Islamic metaphysics, and grammar: we also had courses on world geography and history, science, and mathematics. There were two levels or degrees that you could get at the Qarawiyin— sort of like a baccalaureate and a full undergraduate BA. For my 'alim diploma, equivalent to that baccalaureate degree, I had to learn the entire Quran by heart and repeat it word for word in front of one of the teachers. It took me until I was twenty-six and had already been teaching school in Sefrou for a couple of years before I was able to do it.

Yaghnik's education both set and reflected the pattern of his approach to knowledge and to its practical involvement in the guidance of his life. He was not one of the tiny handful of his generation educated in Western-oriented universities. Indeed at independence in 1956 it is estimated there were only about forty such university graduates in the whole country— all of them men—and only six girls who had graduated from secondary school. Those who did get some higher education tended to obtain it through traditional schooling. When, however, Yaghnik attended the Qarawiyin, it was a place that was very much in transition. Anyone learned in the Quran could issue a certificate (*ijaza*) indicating that another was proficient in the Quran, so religious education was quite varied and decentralized. But as this form of voluntary, open education was giving way to a mixture of Western-inspired subjects and increasing government control over schools, the pattern of building a religious following was beginning to change. Ultimately Yaghnik obtained a somewhat modernized version of a classical Islamic education in the years surrounding the acquisition of national independence.

But he was far from being a somber religious type. He dressed in Western clothes, enjoyed films and languid afternoons at nearby hot springs, and found in Western psychology—which in Arabic is called *'ilm nafs*, the study of natural dispositions, or passions—a link between the Islamic portrayal of humanity's natural urges, channeled by the training of one's reasoning powers through study and wise mentoring, and the exciting world of everyday affairs. With his classmates he even acted in several plays by Shakespeare. However, unlike Muammar Qaddafi and various translators, students resisted the temptation to render the author's name as Sheikh al-Zubayr. (Qaddafi, incidentally, was not the first to claim that Shakespeare was actually an Arab Muslim living in England, though the Libyan strongman was perhaps unique in insisting the bard's true name was Sheikh Zubayr bin William!) Shakespeare does present some intriguing problems for Arabs. For example, there being no infinitive in Arabic with which to render "to be or not to be" that famous phrase is often translated as "either I or we," a revealing reflection of the emphasis in Arab cultures on the crucial role for identity of relationships rather than self-fashioning. Nor was Yaghnik's encounter with Shakespeare unique. Egypt's Gamal Abdel Nasser, as a sixteen-year-old in 1935, played the Roman dictator in a performance of *Julius Caesar*—described in the playbill as "the hero of popular liberation"—and when his postal clerk father saw his son about to be assassinated by Brutus, he jumped up from the audience to rescue him. Yaghnik and his colleagues did not, as did some in Shakespeare's own time, use the plays, however, to suggest that the sovereign may be no more than a player himself. For centuries Moroccans also allowed a student at the Qarawiyin, called "sultan" for that day, to command a favor from the real sultan. Eventually, however, King Hassan II abolished the tradition when one student-sultan, instead of asking for gifts to the poor, demanded political alterations.

Although in this period anticolonial sentiment was certainly rising, by his own admission Yaghnik was not especially active politically. Those Moroccans who were admitted to the French-run lycées often seem to have adopted a certain form of Cartesianism, dividing the world into discrete physical, mental, and spiritual realms without feeling that they had become the hypocrites of whom the Prophet and the Quran are so scathing. For Yaghnik, by comparison, the all-encompassing vision of the Quran was seen to comprehend everything from man's essential nature to the latest scientific discovery and thus to offer a view of the world that did not require strict compartmentalization or a sense of discrepant categories. Without intense self-conscious concern or travail he was already starting to find his own version of a middle way.

During the next two months we worked on my Arabic. Each lesson, though, was filled with content, as neither of us could stand grammar drills for very long. Where the storekeeper replicated his own education by the use of *dictées* and memorization, Yaghnik, ever the effusive grammar school instructor of an oversized elementary pupil, found ways to make himself easily understood as I pressed upon him my incipient anthropological inquiries. I had with me a copy of A. J. Arberry's fascinating translation of the Quran (entitled *The Quran Interpreted* in deference to the orthodox view of the Holy Book's inimitable and untranslatable nature), and often our discussions turned to matters of religion. By early April we began, quite effortlessly, to explore topics that one must often wait until much later in an anthropological study to explore, namely Yaghnik's rendition of the Islamic and Moroccan ideas about the nature of creation, the cosmos, and the ultimate destiny of mankind.

The Prophet said: "The Quran descended in five categories: The lawful, the unlawful, the obvious, the figurative, and the parables. Therefore, observe the lawful and forbid the unlawful, act upon the evident and believe in the figurative, and take the parables as examples."

—Abu Huraira, *in Baihaqi's collection*

In the beginning God was entirely alone. Yaghnik paused. He rocked gently as he silently rehearsed several Quranic verses but seemed to shake off each of them, like a baseball pitcher looking for the most appropriate signal from the catcher, until he settled on the one he wanted, and then, like a ship heeled to the best angle, moved unerringly ahead. At first the sun, the planets, and the earth were all conjoined in a single mass that gave the appearance of an immense cloud of smoke, he said. Then God proceeded to separate each of the stars and planets from one another. The earth was a relatively small, round body entirely covered by water. But God stretched it out: he made mountains, and where there had previously been clouds of smoke, he made flat land so that man would eventually be able to walk on it. In two days God created the whole earth, though the length of these "days" is not known to us. In the next four days God created all the things from which living forms gain their sustenance. Then in the next two days he created the seven heavens, each one of which has its own *programme*. It may take hundreds of years to get from one of these heavenly realms to another; we really don't know. The lowest of them is beyond anywhere that we can see or know. The earth and the sun and stars that we see are not part of these heavens. Even the astronauts can only go as far as the planets and the stars. Only the Prophet Muhammad has ever climbed through all the heavens, and this he did in a single night. Some say it was only his soul that made the journey; others say that it was his whole being. Even though the distance is vast, it is obviously possible to cover it in a single night. After all, couldn't I go up to the shrine overlooking Sefrou for a single night and wake up the next morning there while you, in the same time, had traveled all the way home to your parents in America?

Returning to a theme of clear importance to him, Yaghnik again stressed that in everything he did God had a purpose, a practical application, a *programme*. The moon, for example, was originally created with its own fire, like the sun. But God put out the moon's fire, Yaghnik said, and made it shine, like a great mirror, with the light of the sun, but only at night. This he did so man would know how to measure time, for each of the phases of the moon teaches us how to count and thus how to tell the hour, whether for work or prayer. That is also why the Muslim calendar is a lunar one. Indeed, the scientists tell us that the sun itself is losing its force and that one day it will die and with it everything on earth. Once again he searched his memory and, finding the passage he wanted (Sura 81:1–14), recited in Arabic, as I followed Arberry's rendition:

> When the sun shall be darkened,
> when the stars shall be thrown down,
> when the mountains shall be set moving,
> when the pregnant camels shall be neglected,
> when the savage beasts shall be mustered,
> when the seas shall be set boiling,
> when the souls shall be coupled,
> when the buried infant shall be asked
> for what sin she was slain,
> when the scrolls shall be unrolled,
> when heaven shall be stripped off,
> when Hell shall be set blazing,
> when Paradise shall be brought nigh,
> then shall a soul know what it has brought forth.

We have already seen some of the stars fall, Yaghnik continued. Don't you call them shooting stars? And when the time comes, the seven oceans will suffer earthquakes, and the hydrogen and oxygen that make up the water will be separated from each other, and all that will be left will be a glowing and a halo. Everything will break apart and be ruined, and all will be returned to nothing. That will be the Day of Judgment.

Until then even the stars in the sky will continue to have their special purpose. Actually there are two kinds of stars, he continued. The first are those that shine at night for the purpose of showing man the road, giving him something from which to tell directions. The other kind shoots out flames that incinerate devils. You see, early on God created the angels, whose purpose it is to carry out the orders of God. These orders are transferred from the highest level, God, through the angels and on down the line. The devils—the ones you sometimes call "genies" and we call *jnun* (sing. *jinn*)—eavesdrop on these conversations, stealing the words of God and working against him. The jnun, like people, can be good or bad, and some of them who are evil work secretly with people on earth: by listening in on the angels they can find out what God plans to do before it has been done. They then tell this to their allies on earth and by these predictions accomplish their evil designs. The jnun climb as high as they can in the heavenly spheres to eavesdrop on the angels but from time to time are incinerated, shot down by a star. When we see a "shooting star," we know that it is a jinn who has been burned up by one of the stars. Sometimes these devils form a ladder by climbing one on top of the other until the one at the top is high enough to pass the word back down the line to the one at the bottom, who records what is to happen in the future. The angels, however, protect themselves against this invasion of their privacy: one of them acts as a sort of policeman, and when he catches a jinn listening, he strikes him dead with a blast of fire, like that coming from a space rocket. So when you see a comet, you also know that this is really the blast used by the guardian angel to eradicate a snooping jinn.

I had thought the outline of Yaghnik's story of creation fairly straightforward up to this point. It was not until a later session, however, that he surprised me by saying that the first thing God created was not the earth or the angels or men but the Prophet Muhammad. The Prophet, he said, was created out of light and earth, but it was not until much later that he was given human form and placed on earth. Just as the Haj had not automatically moved to a physical description of Caid Omar or any of the distinctive characters who populate his memories, Yaghnik did not, either at this moment or any other, relate any accounts of the Prophet's physical appearance. Initially I assumed it was because Islam forbids representations of the human figure, but I was to learn that is not true. The only relevant passage in the Quran (Sura 3:49) actually refers to Jesus who, alone and by the grace of God, was permitted to create from clay the likeness of a bird and infuse it with life. Nor is there any clear prohibition on such representations attributed to the Prophet. To the contrary, he is said to have saved from destruction at least one bas-relief figure of Jesus and Mary in the sacred Ka'aba in Mecca and permitted other representations on fixed objects, like his wife A'ishah's pillow, as opposed to moving ones, like curtains, that might imply lifelike qualities. Persian, Mughal, Central Asian, and Turkish artists, in particular, did not hesitate to depict the Prophet, whether as instructor or transiting to heaven in a single night. A century or so after the Prophet's death, as Islamic practice and texts were solidifying, the fear of idolatry led to the widespread prohibition on human, as opposed to floral and animal, representations. The Prophet's face was then commonly veiled or the features erased, though some representations persisted.

Prophet Muhammad as youth

Iranian banner with Prophet's portrait

Verbal descriptions, related through chains of reliable witnesses back to those who knew him, painted a picture of the Prophet in terms that usually emphasized his humanity—indeed in many regards his ordinariness—by suggesting that he was not a person of extremes. Companions thus spoke of him as "neither tall nor short, neither very white nor very dark, his body not chubby, his face not round and heavy; he was not marred by a skinny body, a large stomach, or a small head; his beard was thick and his eyebrows finely arched and joined together." Nowadays, even in strict Islamic countries, pictures of political leaders are not only commonly displayed in dwellings, businesses, and street rallies, but even in Iran a popular picture, present in many homes and public gatherings, shows the Prophet as a youngster, his gown slipping off one shoulder, a flower behind his ear, and a look on his face that might appear less suggestive of agape than eros. Notwithstanding such visual exceptions, authoritative traditions (*ḥadith*) focus predominantly on the Prophet's acts, since following his practices (*sunna*)—whether in his style of prayer or in his habits of personal hygiene—should serve as guidelines for those who follow him. Unlike films, which Muslims commonly feel are more informative because they show a man interacting with others in the world, visual portrayals of contemporary figures are not played down primarily on religious grounds but simply because such portraits do not really tell you what you need to know about another's relationships and acts.

In Yaghnik's case the physical portrayal of others presents no problem. Not only does he have a photo of himself as a young man hanging in his living room, but he has no hesitation in approving of the placement in virtually every shop of a photo of the king. (Indeed, there are reported instances where the police have prodded shopkeepers who do not show such a picture to do so, the absence of a picture being one of the subtle ways Moroccans at times protest government actions.) For Yaghnik, as for others, a static representation of another is therefore not very interesting, as it tells one nothing about how a person deals with others, the preeminent form of information necessary to understand how that other person might interact with you.

Yaghnik's way of assessing persons by their actions more than their appearance was only one of the ways I had to adjust my thinking in order to grasp how he was explaining the Quran's version of creation and the place of humankind within it. That the basic outline was similar to the version in the Old Testament was only to be expected. It is a fundamental precept of Islam not only that the Quran is the exact word of God relayed through the angel Gabriel to his illiterate listener Muhammad but that the message he conveyed through earlier prophets, such as Moses and Jesus, has, from the Muslim perspective, been so distorted by their followers that only the Quranic account is to be trusted. Thus Jews and Christians, as People of the Book, are far ahead of unbelievers for having once possessed some portion of God's word, but they did not retain it intact. Indeed, much of the legitimacy of the Quran lies precisely in its "corrected" accounting of well-known biblical tales, and the Quran itself is largely devoid of stories not found in those earlier, flawed books.

It was not, however, the variation in the stories or the additional details about the jnun that made me vaguely uneasy but simply that the stories—if that was even the right word for them—were not being told the way stories "should" be told. As with the Haj's historical accounts, things were not necessarily in chronological order, and when particular Bible-like tales did begin to appear in Yaghnik's account, chronology was not the main ordering principle of the narrative. It was not just that Yaghnik, like most people, would wander down one set of associations and then recall himself to the main line of his story. Indeed, at first I wondered if this was a case, as several French novelists and filmmakers of the sixties had tried to enact, in which every story has a beginning, a middle, and an end—though not necessarily in that order. In fact, the Quran is simply arranged from longest to shortest chapter, and though small children may be taught the few stories first, the full recitation of the text follows that order. But that did not quite capture Yaghnik's style of narration either. Rather, it began to appear that, for Yaghnik, a "story" like that of creation did not require chronology as its keystone. Indeed, the more comfortable I became in Arabic, the less Yaghnik seemed to need to respond to the form of logic I may have been urging upon him so as to grasp each element of the story in the manner that made the most sense to me.

In this regard Yaghnik was, as I began to appreciate, actually being true to the style of the Quran itself, for the Quran does not use time as the predominant vehicle for revealing truth. Instead we are shown aspects of things, facets of people, angles of situations. We see the same things in various contexts. Thus elements of the creation story are retold numerous times, with the quality of God's rewards played up one time, his punishments another, the demonstration of human failings emphasized in one chapter, the legitimacy of the Prophet as the final recounter of truth in another. On his own—and, no doubt, in response to the way I often posed my questions of clarification—Yaghnik, ever the practical practitioner of the middle path, "translated" his accounts to me in ways that he, as a Muslim and as a "modernist," could accommodate himself to without self-conscious difficulty. The virtuosity lay not in what I first took to be charming references to astronauts and shooting stars—the Islamic equivalent of Sunday school analogies modeled for the beginner—but in his exploration of the facets of God's work rather than their unfolding in time. It was as if one might describe the truth of a diamond by describing its appearance as one turns it in the light, rather than by recounting its long history as compressed carbon. Early Islamic theologians had described time as a series of discontinuous instants, each of which was a discrete revelation and each of which calls for a decision by those to whom it is revealed to accept as true. The Quranic style of narration is, therefore, not a straightforward relating of a tale through time—the "modern" Western way of helping the true to appear obvious—but a reaffirmation of the situational quality of every feature of the divine order. Indeed, what may appear as mere repetition is not so much a vehicle for inviting interpretation as a means of avoiding chaos and demonstrating, as in so many other domains of Muslim cultural life, that the moral choice of acceptance occurs at every juncture of a life lived in the light of revelation.

Moreover, the explanations couched in terms of space flight and air travel that were so much a part of Yaghnik's own appealing style had a very literal aspect to them as well. To a believing Muslim the Quran is not simply conclusive of earlier prophetic accounts: it is also inclusive of that which has ever been or ever will be. It is thus very common for Muslims to point to a passage in the Quran that is said to predict space flight or prove, by citing particular verses, that some of the jnun are really good or bad germs or that antibiotics and evolution are not just later additions to the knowable but fully present in the text. When Yaghnik would make his "modernist" analogies, he was exercising his own imagination, but he was doing so in a very literalist way, for to him later developments are already inscribed in the Quran. As we sallied back and forth between his accounts and my queries, I was beginning to see how subtle the implications of our different ways of telling truth were. I was particularly curious about the re-lation of angels, jnun, and man, and the place these genies occupy in God's *programme*. It was not long before Yaghnik returned to the topic.

The angels are like men, said Yaghnik, in that they were created directly by God without the mediation of parents. They have no gender and, be-ing made of pure light, when they die they simply go out, like a light. The jnun, who were created after the angels but before man, are made of a smokeless fire. They are invisible, so their exact form is not known to us. If we could see them, they would probably look quite horrible to us, some with seven misshapen heads, others with eyes in the back of their skulls. But then the same is true of the angels, whose looks (if we could see them) would also be quite horrifying. As different as they are, the jnun are nevertheless like men in a great many ways. They live in their own in-visible world, but they eat and drink and pray and die just like men. This is how it came about:

Initially God created a kind of jinn who settled on the earth. But these jnun lived without any structure to their lives at all. They had no govern-ment, no courts, no order; everything was chaos (*fitna*). When God saw how wickedly they were acting, he killed all of them, all except one small boy jinn whom the angels asked God to save and allow to live with them in heaven, where they would teach him to pray to God and be good. God gave his assent, and for many years the boy lived among the angels and gave praise to God.

God, however, was not finished with his creations. He wanted, as part of his *programme*, to finish the world, to make it *complet*. Now, God all along could have created things instantly: if he had wanted to, he could simply have said "Be!" and it would have been done. But God did things step by step so that the angels and men would know that everything has to be part of a plan and done one thing at a time. Thus in his next step for creating the world, God gathered all the angels together and told them that in addi-tion to the angels he wanted to create a representative on earth to carry out his orders. The angels objected to this. They did not want there to be more evil things on earth as there had been when the jnun lived there. But God said, I know what will be.

First God created all the animals. He made them from earth, but he gave them souls, though animals' souls merely animate them, animals being neither good nor bad. You see, said Yaghnik, all of the things that God created have their own way of expressing recognition of God's unity and expressing their thanks to him for creating them. Flowers, trees, rocks—all have their way of praising God, though man does not know how they do it. On Judgment Day, God will allow those animals who have been kicked or bitten by other animals to kick or bite back the one who attacked them. Then God will turn them all into dust, since there is no heaven or hell for the animals, with the exception of a few special ones like Saint Joseph's donkey or the mule the Prophet rode. In the order of judgment the animals will come just before the unbelievers so the latter can see that they will suffer the same fate as animals if they do not recognize Muhammad as the capstone of God's prophets.

Having created all the animals, God now created the first man, Adam. He fashioned him out of the earth itself, as the Quran says, "of a clay like that of the potter." He made man beautiful, so that, as he told Adam, you will be decorous, shy, and shameful before me. Man, says the Quran, should take comfort from knowing that he has been made from earth and that he will be reconstituted from earth. There are no men made from metal so that they could outlive ordinary men: the robots that you in America or the people in China have made are not men. And so we know that nothing has been promised life beyond that which has been promised to man.

But clay alone was not life. God now breathed into Adam's body and gave him a soul—a soul that man himself can never comprehend. Breath, or *nafs*, is life itself, and all creatures—men, jnun, animals, and angels— have it. Some say it is the same as the soul, *ruḥ*. Others say that they must be different, since the Quran tells us we cannot know our own souls; if we did, we would lock them up and never die. If the *nafs* of angels is composed of light and the *nafs* of the jnun is composed of fire, then the *nafs* of man is composed of either breath or blood. Those who argue that *nafs* and *ruḥ* are separable point to fakirs who can hold their breath or be buried underground for many days yet not die. Others say that *nafs* and *ruḥ* leave the body at death simultaneously, as shown by the absence of breath, the bloodless look of the corpse, and the clear departure of the soul. Wherever it is situated, though, man's *nafs* is more than mere breath or blood. It is the vehicle that carries man's essential quality, the animator (in concert with the soul) of man's passions and drives and impulses.

The other thing God gave to Adam and his descendants was the power of reason, *ʿaqel*. Animals have almost no reason, though camels, dogs, and horses have some, and donkeys absolutely none, which is why we say of a particularly stupid man that he has the head of a donkey. The *ʿaqel* of the jnun is less well developed than that of man, but they are physically more powerful. This is proved by the fact that Solomon was able to rule over the jnun and, like some other men of great spiritual force, harness their physical power to construct things for him. Man's reason is what allows him to guide his passions, his *nafs*, into useful directions. But not everyone's *nafs* is the same. There are four basic elements that form a person's disposition, and as the amount of each varies, so does the result. If the element of earth is dominant, a person will be meek by nature; if fire predominates, the person will tend to be angry; if water is foremost, he will be cold to others; if air prevails, one tends toward gaiety, frivolity, and irresponsibility.

Only later, when I read more carefully in other Islamic sources, was I able to assess how characteristic and how distinctive Yaghnik's account was up to this point. There are a host of traditions, some rendered authoritative by favored scholars, and an even more bewildering variety of local folk versions of the creation story. For example, the idea that the angels are made of light does not derive from the Quran but from later commentaries, as does that of the jnun eavesdropping on them. Since so many of the passages concerning these matters in the Quran are allusive and connected to a variety of religious issues, it is easy to see why such variations should have found quite differential support. Moreover, orthodox Islam has always been very wary of the ecstatic and the overstated, and those who have felt a need for greater detail have had to fill in for themselves. Some, like Yaghnik, do so within the framework of traditional Sunni Islam, appreciating that so long as a practice or belief is not clearly antithetical to explicit provisions in the Quran, it lies within man's power to reason his way through such matters. Adherents of ecstatic sects, such as the various *sufi* orders, are often more extravagant, skirting and sometimes crossing the line the orthodox have prepared for them. One tenth-century account, drawn up after the sayings and actions of the Prophet had been collected—and itself clearly drawing on a wide range of earlier Near Eastern ideas—speaks in great detail of how God commanded the life force to enter at Adam's mouth, to move through his skull for two hundred years, and then slowly move through the rest of his body "right to the tips of his fingers—so that he could thereby actually record his own primeval state!" In an Egyptian version the angels object to the creation of mankind, with his feet of clay, because of his inevitable dishonesty:

> We are made out of pure light, our thoughts can be seen by everybody, we are all honest and pure minds. If, however, a thinking spirit is hidden between walls of flesh and bone, like an animal, he will have the desires of an animal but not its innocence since he can think and knows the difference between good and evil. His desires will enslave his brain and natural wishes will turn into greed, greed will cause jealousy, jealousy leads to hatred, hatred to violence. An animal kills out of need, men will kill out of greed.

Other influences and emphases were also readily apparent in Yaghnik's account. The classical categories of earth, air, water, and fire that had become amalgamated in Islamic thought—and preserved until Western scholars could recapture the ancient Greek sources through translations from the Arabic—bespeak a long history of contact between East and West. The account of Judgment Day as one in which a mistreated animal gets to inflict a similar punishment on his aggressor speaks to the concept that justice is always a balance and that chaos is a world without justice. And Yaghnik's constant emphasis on the practicality of every creation of Allah and every prescript in the Quran indicates that the touchstone of reality is not the ethereal world of a hereafter but the concrete effects that divine guidance offers for man in this life. Like early Muslim scholars, Yaghnik has, therefore, no problem with most of modern science. But whereas those early investigators did not make the transition to experimental studies— perhaps because advances in mathematics, optics, and medicine had been geared to their practical effects on human relationships and no clear connection to the ways people might relate to one another through abstract science was evident to them—Yaghnik understands why some Muslims place limits on such knowledge. Thus not only is it common for Muslims to accept a version of creationism, but when evolution is taught in the schools, it is usually said to apply only to lower animals and is not taught as applying to the human species.

Not only do visions of creation of the sort Yaghnik was describing pose the possibility of different substantive interpretations of sacred sources, but they can reflect highly localized and personal approaches, as became evident when Yaghnik resumed his account. Now, said God, I want to have an examination. It was the first examination in the world, just like in school. I want to examine the angels and Adam to see who is smarter. What was the test? God told Adam and the angels all the words there are in all the languages he created, and then he tested the ability of the angels and Adam to repeat all the words he told them. The angels could not remember any of the words, but Adam remembered every one of them and won the contest. Adam had been given a good mind, the sort with which he could invent televisions and automobiles. God implanted this ability in men, just as he put seeds in all the plants, so that the sons of Adam would always acknowledge that there is only one God and he is Allah.

After Adam won the contest, God ordered all the angels to bow down to man because of his superior knowledge. And all the angels did bow down, but not the one jinn whom the angels had saved from the first creatures of the earth. Why won't you acknowledge man? asked God. Because a jinn is made of fire, which burns earth and is therefore superior to earth, he replied. Then leave us, God commanded. And it was from that moment on that the jinn was known as Iblis, or Satan. Iblis, of course, blamed his expulsion on Adam and all mankind. So he said to God: Before I go will you grant me a single favor? Ask anything you want, God replied, except forgiveness, and I will grant it. Then let me live until the last man dies, said Iblis. Very well, said God, your wish is granted. And give me permission to go everywhere that man goes—in his world, in his house, in his blood—and never to be seen by him. Do as you will, said God, but do not deprive him of his knowledge of me: even if he wants to go to hell with you, he may go. Is that all? asked God. That is all, said Iblis. And he descended to earth.

Iblis traveled down from God, through all the seven heavens, to earth, and as he traveled, the angels destroyed the path behind him. God swore to give man knowledge to help him against Iblis. He settled Adam in a place called Eden, a place which is not on earth and the likes of which we do not know. But it must have had wonderful things. The trees in Eden must have grown upside down, their roots in the air and the fruit hanging so low that Adam could just reach up and take whatever he wanted. In Eden if you wanted to see your parents and they were somewhere else, you would have a kind of television that would let you see where they were at any time. Or you could call on a bird that would bring you whatever kind of food you wanted. There would be small children to wait on you, and the women would be different from the women on earth, more beautiful and made of a sort of sparkling glass, and they would never have to menstruate. There would be rivers with different kinds of drinks in them. There would be no day or night, no seasons (though fruits from all the seasons), no cold, and no heat. There would only be the light from the moon that would shine all the time. If everyone lived in such a place, they would just eat and drink and walk about—that is all. It is here that Adam lived alone.

In time God created Eve from Adam's left side. They loved each other and lived together happily in Eden. But God had set one condition for them: they must not eat the fruit of one particular tree in the garden. Satan came, though, in the blood of Adam and Eve and asked them if they liked the look of the forbidden fruit. If you want to live forever, he said (working through their thoughts), eat the fruit. Both of them ate the fruit at the same time. Instantly their clothes fell away from them, and the crowns and jewels that adorned them fell away. For the first time they had to go to the toilet. They looked at their nakedness, and they reached up into a tree and took down leaves to cover themselves. God came to them and said: What have you done? And they told him. And God said, I will forgive you, but you cannot live any longer in Eden. You have to live on the earth from which I created you. So Adam and Eve fell to earth, landing on Mount Arafat. And they lived there—Adam and Eve and Satan, always at odds with one another.

Once again, in Yaghnik's account I was confronted with a version that was simultaneously normative and one of a number of variations on the Adam and Eve story encountered in many parts of the Muslim world. Other variations speak of how, after the devil tempted Eve to eat from the forbidden tree, she left the Garden of Eden to meet a call of nature, of the way Adam followed, but they could not find each other, and of how Adam saved food for her but she did not reciprocate, which explains why women receive only half the inheritance men do. For Yaghnik, however, the story of Adam and Eve's fall is not taken as proof of mankind's evil tendencies. Like the whole line of prophets, Yaghnik explained, it was in Adam's nature to be without sin (ma'sum), to be incapable of doing anything forbidden (haram). In eating the proscribed fruit, Adam was simply forgetful, just as every prophet at some time committed an infraction by his own forgetfulness. Even Muhammad was briefly tempted to include several pagan gods, as you can see in the passages some call the Satanic Verses. Indeed, as I followed Yaghnik's account in my translation of the Quran, I noted that, in additional to being forgetful, human beings were also described as fretful, grudging, greedy, and proud. But Yaghnik sees these tendencies as capable of being superseded if only one recalls the sacred message and the advantage of one's God-given reason. For him, as for his fellow believers, it comes as no surprise, then, that the very name for humankind in Arabic is al-insan, the forgetful ones. And therein lies one of the main differences between man and God, said Yaghnik, for man forgets, and God does not.

On earth, Yaghnik continued, things were very different indeed for Adam and Eve. In Eden there was no such thing as blood or feces or urine. God's purpose in bringing these features into the life of humans—including women's menstruation—was to point up the difference between life on earth and a heavenly existence. Menstruation was not a punishment for Eve. Menstrual blood is dirty only because it stagnates in a woman's womb and becomes bad. Then if it flows back to a woman's heart it can kill her. That is why it has to be expelled. However, if it happens that the woman becomes pregnant, the blood remains good by virtue of being mixed with a man's sperm and flowing through the developing body of the baby. If a man has intercourse with a menstruating woman, her bad blood will make him sick. A man and his menstruating wife may, however, eat and drink together, and even share the same bed. During her period a woman may not enter a mosque, pray, study the Quran, or participate in certain parts of the pilgrimage; at the end of her cycle she must take the same ritual bath that a man gives himself after each occasion of sexual intercourse, the same bath an unbeliever takes when entering the faith and that a corpse must be given before burial. All of this, he said, was set in motion when Adam and Eve fell to earth.

Though it did, of course, include many familiar elements, Yaghnik's account of Adam and Eve was striking in several very important ways. As other scholars have noted, it was Adam's ability not just to memorize but to go beyond what God had taught him that made him initially so worthy in God's eyes. Indeed, one sees from the outset how crucial knowledge is in the Quranic vision of reality and why the word for knowledge is the second most frequently used word in the Quran after the name of God. The contrast to Western sacred texts is noteworthy: as Sir Mohammad Iqbal says, "The Old Testament curses the earth for Adam's act of disobedience, whereas the Quran mentions the Fall in order to indicate man's rise from a primitive state of instinctive appetite to the conscious possession of a free self, capable of doubt and disobedience." But perhaps most intriguing is the contrast in the role each text assigns to the figure of Eve.

The Quran never actually refers to Eve by name; it speaks of her only as Adam's spouse. Adam and Eve are referred to in the plural, as having been created from a single soul. Eve is not said to have been formed from a part of Adam's body (Sura 4:1 and 39:6), notwithstanding the version of later commentators to which Yaghnik gave voice. The Quran also never mentions the snake. Nor does it blame Eve for humanity's fall. Indeed, it is Adam who is twice cited as responsible for the loss of Eden (Sura 20:115 and 121). It was only in the second century after the Prophet's death, perhaps (some Western scholars speculate) as Islam felt strong enough to overwhelm surrounding religions by incorporating aspects of them, that commenters, as part of the process of tracing Prophetic wisdom through chains of reliable witnesses leading back to Muhammad's companions, adopted the view that there was a woman named Eve who was created from a crooked rib of Adam that can never be straightened and that menstruation and painful childbirth are punishments for her innate foolishness. Storytellers then began to elaborate. For al-Kisa'i, Eve "had seven hundred tresses studded with gems of chrysolite and incensed with musk, which formed a crown, and emitted a rustling sound. The serpent was shaped like a camel and, like the camel, could stand erect. She had a multicolored tail . . . a mane of pearl, hair of topaz, eyes like the planets Venus and Jupiter. [Satan speaks from its mouth, saying:] Hurry and eat before your husband Adam, for whoever eats first will have precedence over his companion." Afterward, Eve blames Satan, saying: "I never thought that anyone would swear by Thee if he were lying." "Depart now from Paradise, deceived forever henceforth," said God.

But, I asked Yaghnik, is the nature or disposition (*nafs*) of men and women the same? Yes, he answered, but it is not always distributed in the same proportions. It is all a matter of inclinations, leanings. Women have a tendency to be frivolous and to go astray. Their reasoning powers are often less developed, though that may be due to the fact that they do not get as much education and are not linked to good leaders so their reason could develop. It is much the same for children, who differ from adults because when they are born, their *nafs* is very large and their reason very small. That is why instruction and discipline from parents and teachers is so important if one is to gain control over one's *nafs*. That is why the Quran says that men have to be the *chauffeur* of women, Yaghnik's choice of the French term here being typical of his blending traditional and contemporary terminologies, since the passage (Sura 4:34) usually cited speaks of a husband as being the "leader, protector, or head" (*qawwam*) of the household.

Indeed, what is so striking about Yaghnik's account is that, for all his respect for the literature of the Prophetic Traditions and all his own storytelling embellishments, he follows the far more equalizing version of the Quran rather than the commonly accepted version that seeks to justify male superiority on the basis of creation itself, even though he does refer to Eve as created from Adam's rib. Nor does Yaghnik do so out of an ideology of textual literalism or as a conscious counter to those who read into sacred text an agenda about women they cannot read out of it. Rather, in his sincere respect for the intelligence of women—his wife, his daughters, his students in the girls' school—Yaghnik sees in the Quran a story of humankind, not of male versus female. In all its modesty Yaghnik's is a stunning example of a thoughtful middle way in a culture, even in its more benign forms, where women are generally regarded by men as prone to be foolish and lacking in self-control. Yaghnik's approach does not constitute an explicit intellectual counter to popular religious views, but it certainly demonstrates how one deeply believing Muslim embodies a significant alternative.

Picking up the thread of his story, Yaghnik now began to account for the way in which humankind came to propagate itself. After Adam and Eve had been on earth for some time, he said, they began to have many sets of twins, each set consisting of one male and one female, the children from different sets marrying one another. One of these sets contained Cain and his twin sister and another Abel and his twin sister. Cain should have married Abel's twin and vice versa, but Cain's twin was beautiful, and he wanted her for himself. Later, when both brothers went to make a sacrifice, God refused Cain's offering because of Cain's desire for his own sister. As a result, Cain became intensely jealous of Abel and killed him. He didn't know what to do with the body, so he carried it around on his back for some time. Then God sent down two angels in the form of ravens, and Cain watched as one of them killed the other and then buried his body in the earth. Cain now knew what to do with Abel's body and proceeded to bury it.

It was also at this time that the earth was repopulated with the jnun. Iblis is actually the "father" of the jnun. He had one leg that was masculine and one that was feminine and when they mixed he gave birth to the whole line of jnun. At first these offspring were all bad, like their father, but some of them heard the teachings of wise men and prophets—Abraham, David, Solomon, and others—and were converted from their evil ways. Others were converted by the Prophet Muhammad, which is why, in some traditions, a place is set aside in the mosque for the Muslim jnun to participate in the prayers. Those jnun who still remain bad can enter our bodies and distort the way we act. That is what happens when you see a close friend or relative acting in a very uncharacteristic way. The jinn has probably chosen to attack that person because he or she has inadvertently killed one of the jnun. Since they are invisible to us, this could happen just by swinging an ax normally or driving a car down the street. One female jinn, Aisha Qandaisha, is especially dangerous: she can take on the appearance of a human or an animal and may come to men at night, driving them insane with her sexuality and turning them into apostates. You can tell her, though, by her feet, which are like those of a goat. In general, jnun do not bother people whose reason has been developed, which is why ignorant people, especially country people, are most vulnerable to them. But you can always keep the jnun at bay by employing phrases that use the name of God or showing that you are devoted to God's ways.

Once again Yaghnik's version of creation had in it a wonderful mix of normative and idiosyncratic elements. When he spoke of the comparison of man to the angels, he inserted the story of a school examination—indeed, the sort of language examination with which he had so much trouble—as a way of accounting for man's innate superiority in this regard. Yaghnik's version might also seem to be consonant with the Old Testament emphasis on Adam's ability to give names to all things, but that particular act is not part of the Quranic account. The actual text (Sura 2:31) reads: "He [God] said, "Adam, tell them their names." And when Adam had told them their names, God said, "Did I not tell you I know the unseen things in the heavens and the earth?" Thus Adam was not given the power of creating names, only of conveying them. Nevertheless, speech is clearly of central importance to the Islamic conception of what sets man apart from other beings. For example, Solomon, who is invariably described as among the wisest of men, is distinguished by his ability to understand even the speech of birds (Sura 27:16). And certainly for Arabs mastery of language is vital, a person of significance being referred to as one who "has word," the capacity to capture the terms of an issue being as valuable as any material asset. Thus it is always the blend of innate disposition, learning, and control of language that informs Yaghnik's accounts, whether of a single person or in the course of divine creation.

For Yaghnik, unlike some other Muslims, Iblis's rejection of man occasions no special problem. To Yaghnik it is a straightforward emanation of his inherent nature that Satan would claim superiority over earth based on his composition as fire. As in all such matters Yaghnik sees Satan as having the free will to have done otherwise, but his natural disposition led him to reject God's command to pay obeisance to man. This is not for Yaghnik, or for other orthodox Muslims, a choice between worshipping God and worshipping man, a choice the great Persian mystic and "heretic" of the ninth and tenth centuries, Mansur Al-Hallaj, had taken as proof that Iblis was the preeminent monotheist, refusing to equate God's product with God himself. To the contrary, the orthodox Sunni position that Yaghnik expounds shows that when reasoning powers pretend to take precedence over submission to God's overt commands, no claim of inherent superiority can save one from destruction. Yet Iblis does strike a bargain with God, a bargain that, in Yaghnik's version, may also reveal something of his own culture. For the moment Iblis is granted the single favor he requested—to live until the last man dies—he pushes for yet another grant, to go everywhere with man unseen. To attempt all the traffic will bear, to seek even other favors when only one was initially allowed, to engage in a constant process of bargaining strikes a familiar chord in Arab culture, where one often encounters those who have the temerity (or the courage) even in the face of vastly superior power to test the limits of a bargain, in the certain knowledge that no relationship is without its capacity for constant revision or extension. Indeed, the Prophet himself is said to have bargained with God as to the requisite number of daily prayers, ultimately getting Him down from fifty to just five.

It is especially noteworthy, too, that in the Quranic view women are not the immediate cause of humanity's fall. Adam and Eve are jointly to be blamed for eating the forbidden fruit simultaneously. There is no notion either of inherent human sin or of women as the embodiment of evil. Youssef, our storekeeper friend, once told me a parable about how Eve fashioned a round loaf of bread and then accidentally let it roll downhill while Adam chased after it. It was, he said, thanks to such female thoughtlessness that men have had to pursue bread ever after. For Yaghnik, as for many Moroccans, however, the differences between men and women turn on the relative strengths of reason and passion, a paradigm that may allow men superiority in a host of legal and social contexts but supplies a rationale for granting increased capacity to women—in law, employment, and the sciences—if their reasoning powers should become more developed through education. His is not the reinterpretation of the early Islamic period when, as the Moroccan scholar Fatima Mernissi would argue, the Prophet's original ideal of gender equality, made possible by the development of self-control through the study and enactment of the revealed word, was subverted after his death by those who sought to maintain their dominance over women as objects of exchange and to "protect" them from the treatment accorded slaves by cloaking them as they moved about in public. Nor does Yaghnik refer to those, like the tenth-century scholar Muhammad ibn Jarir al-Tabari, who argued that if men were to have twice a woman's share in inheritance, they should also have the number of their sins counted as double on the Day of Judgment. To the contrary, for Yaghnik, the girls' school teacher and proud husband of an educated woman, there is nothing, either in the story of creation or in the composition of men and women, to suggest that the pursuit of knowledge may not take precedence over disposition.

To Westerners in particular the whole question of men's attitudes to women in the Muslim world has, when it is not merely prurient or colonialist, been as fascinating as it is subject to easy stereotyping. Whatever else is true, we are confronted with an issue that has to be viewed from a broad cultural perspective. If, for example, it is accurate to characterize Moroccan society as one in which people constantly negotiate their ties with others, then the view men have of women is incomplete without at least taking this factor into consideration. Perhaps, seen in this light, part of the difficulty many Muslim men see in their relations with women is that one cannot negotiate sex. That is, normally relations involve obligations that shift from debt owed to debt repayable in any of a number of convertible forms. But from this perspective, sex is tantamount to chaos in that one

Yaghnik and family, 1967

cannot really bargain with women; men can only dominate them, however benignly, since, from this viewpoint, women's ungoverned disposition to take sexual partners is beyond rational calculation. Women thus contravene the entire scheme of orderly, bargained-for relationships. And since a man cannot be reliably counted on to keep his own passions from interfering with his ability to play the bargaining game, only social chaos can be expected when there is no way to perpetuate reciprocity and hence ensure trust between the sexes.

But, again, this is not Yaghnik's view. Nor is it the way he has organized his life. Fuzia, his wife, is not only educated and, like most Moroccan women, hardly shy about expressing herself, but she too is a person of the middle way. From our earliest conversations, for example, she emphasized that she did not wear a full-face veil but a simple scarf that covered most but not all of her hair. In the 1960s and 1970s it was common to see three generations of women walking down a Moroccan street—one in full covering and face veil, one in a body-hiding djellaba and scarf, and the youngest in an ordinary dress or skirt and blouse. Fuzia, like Yaghnik, thought Sefrou more conservative than Fez in those days, and she often made the drive down to Fez not only to visit friends and relatives but to walk the streets together with her husband and browse in the shops. She was equally clear that women knew their legal rights better than most people assumed, that they did not hesitate to seek redress in court when their situations became intolerable, and that they were more successful in doing so than is commonly imagined—all of which my own study of the courts was to confirm. Neither she nor Yaghnik, then, felt bound to a narrow reading of sacred text or that modern life need alienate them from their devotion to Islam.

Many aspects of human nature are only lightly described in the Quran. Yaghnik emphasized this point when he returned to the Cain and Abel story. The Quran's account of Cain and Abel is quite brief (Sura 5:30–34), stating only that one sacrifice was accepted and the other not. The theme of twins is, of course, common to many Near Eastern creation myths and serves, as in Yaghnik's rendition, as both a formulation of the incest taboo and an explanation of how men are not the product of incest if they engage in sister exchange—itself a not uncommon form of marriage in some times and places in Morocco. It is noteworthy that in at least one Muslim account it is precisely the fact that they did engage in conjugal relations with their sisters that marks the Jews as inferior to Muslims. That came about, some maintain, because the Jews were nearly destroyed when they disobeyed God and had to marry their sisters merely to reproduce themselves, though at the cost of their perpetual pollution.

The Cain and Abel story, with its implications for the incest taboo, is not, however, really about death. It is about the severe punishment that God subsequently prescribed for unlawful killing, since, as the Quran says, "if one man slays another, it shall be as if he had slain mankind altogether" (Sura 5:35). Here, as elsewhere, the Quran constantly harks back to the moral implications of one's acts, to the fate that awaits those who reject God's messengers as God's signs. For Yaghnik and others the Quran is also a charter of explanation for the very organization of human society. What is absent from Yaghnik's account is any connection between the characteristics of individual men and the initial creation of all men. But in some of the Islamic apocrypha there are accounts that link these two concerns. For example, in the material assembled by Abu Layth Samarqandi in the late tenth century, one can find an account of how a man's qualities are a function of that aspect of the Prophet Muhammad that each individual first beheld: "So one beheld his head and became a sultan; another saw his eyebrow and became an artist; another saw his teeth and became charming for men and women. One saw his tongue and became an envoy between sultans; one saw his left arm and became an executioner. One saw the back of his hands and became a miser. Another saw his shadow and became a musician."

Curiously, Yaghnik repeatedly returns to the question of the jnun. Throughout, he portrays their world as parallel to that of humans. For him their world reflects modes of organization similar to those of his own—a place of multiple religious confessions, marketplace chicanery, and unforeseeable accidents. For tribesmen from the countryside the parallel they draw frequently displays features of their own forms of organization. One can, for example, still find accounts, like that recorded by Henriette Willette in the early 1930s, that speak of the jnun as divided into tribes, each with its own chieftain and all subservient to an overarching sultan. One of Willette's informants even said that God was so rushed on the last day of creation that the jnun were not fully completed, hence their odd feet and God's willingness to allow them to remain invisible. The Finnish anthropologist Edward Westermarck, who did extensive research in the tribal area near Sefrou at the turn of the twentieth century, cites many who agree that the jnun are not only invisible or capable of assuming different appearances and moving rapidly across vast distances but that they eat bones and never cast shadows. Yaghnik's reference to those jnun who were converted to goodness by wise humans also recalls the Quran's reference to Harut and Marut, angels who, in King Solomon's time, taught mankind sorcery and sought to tempt men from belief in God. These may be the same rebel angels of the Judeo-Christian Apocrypha, Samhazai and Azazel, who taught men the healing arts and laws and thus benefited mankind by breaking God's monopoly on knowledge. And one can go into the markets of Morocco to this day and find amulets being sold and storytellers relating tales about the ways of turning the jnun to human advantage.

But does Yaghnik really believe in the jnun? This may seem a trivial issue, but in a sense every literate system of faith has a "problem of the jnun," some textually based referent that even the most literal-minded may at times find difficult to swallow. Must a believing Jew accept literally that the burning bush was not consumed, a Christian that Jesus did indeed walk on water, or a Hindu that the universe is actually contained in the mouth of a god? Adherence to the literal and inerrant nature of sacred text had come up previously in our discussions. At one point Yaghnik said, for example, that the punishment of a criminal act must be taken literally: if you fail to punish a man, even by cutting off the hand of a thief, criminals might run amok. However, he added, the burden of such punishment may really fall on the convicted man's family. In the Prophet's day there was a public fund to help such families, and we could do that now, he added. But what if the man repents? I asked. In the Prophet's time, he said, people did not lie, so if a man did repent, you knew he meant it. But immediately Yaghnik cautioned: In these corrupt times it is hard to know if a man is lying, so maybe it is best to leave such decisions to God and be careful how we punish.

Some scholars also point to the practical application of blaming the jnun for acts that might otherwise be regarded as criminal. For example, in some reported cases from the Arab east, a woman has been accused of causing a death. Yet instead of punishing her, a ritual will be undertaken in which the jinn she blames is hanged. Recalling that until early modern times in the West it was quite common to place animals on trial, and even to execute them, in part as a way of shifting blame from a particular person, one could argue that the jnun, whatever their theological posture, offer a sociological opportunity to explain causation without making an attribution that would otherwise require human punishment.

A similar level of textualism and moderation informs the approach of many thinkers Yaghnik admires, particularly as it concerns the literalism associated with belief in the jnun. For example, Muhammad 'Abduh, the great Egyptian "modernizer," sought to reconcile the jnun with contemporary science by suggesting that they are like the microorganisms that cause illness, largely invisible yet obviously potent, while the less renowned Lebanese scholar Hussein al-Jisr (1845–1909), who sought to reconcile Darwin with the Quran, said they were like the air, invisible to men given the way God has created our vision. When it comes to the jnun, a number of Muslim scholars sympathetic to Yaghnik's orientation suggest a parallel universe as hypothesized by mathematicians and physicists. Yaghnik commonly finds some way of amalgamating modern science with a passage in the Quran. The jnun thus become a test not simply of faith in literalism but a way of conceptualization that is constantly reaching for greater incorporation, agglutination, just as Arab poetry, music, and architecture take on accretions as they become ever more extensive. Yaghnik professes to believe in the jnun quite strongly, since to do otherwise would be to deny the truth of the Quran. But his way of "modernizing" them, his orthodoxy in rendering them harmless by uttering the name of God rather than by the use of amulets, his teasing references to the succubus 'Aisha Qandaisha, and his way of connecting her at other times to his understanding of Freud bring these invisible creatures of a netherworld so like our own well within the ambit of his own sense of the familiar.

The fear, or at least the concern, that was felt by people toward the jnun has perhaps been neutralized, domesticated, by Yaghnik in ways not wholly different from those of his orthodox predecessors. But where they kept the jnun close to them for reasons both religious and mundane, Yaghnik's form of domestication may mean that a world through which one could discuss relationships and motivations as if it were one's own, may, at least for this limited purpose, have been lost, perhaps irretrievably, to him and his fellow believers. Reconciling tradition and the contemporary—straddling that middle path—was, in many other ways, to come to the fore as Yaghnik and I continued our conversations over the years.

Then God breathed soul into Adam. And as the soul entered a part of him, he made to seat himself. And God said, "Man is hasty."

—al-Mas'udi (896–956)

Only three things are certain in life: birth, death, and change.

—Arab saying

After an absence of several years I went in search of Yaghnik. I was told that he had bought a small farmhouse on the road leading northeast from Sefrou, and it was there, in the late morning as we sat over coffee that we renewed our conversations. I told Yaghnik that I would like very much to talk with him about what happens after death, but he chose to start by returning to the process of conception.

The child, said Yaghnik, is formed from the fluids of its parents' bodies. A man's fluid comes from the top of his spine and descends from there to his testicles, where it remains until copulation takes place. A woman's seminal fluid comes from the upper part of her chest, running just below the collarbone from armpit to armpit. The fluid passes through her body to her womb, where it mingles with the fluid of the man to form a child. No one knows for sure, but it is possible that if the man's fluid reaches the womb first, the child will be a boy, and vice versa. If they arrive at the same time, he said with a quizzical shrug, perhaps the one with the greatest strength predominates, but this is pure speculation. From the moment the two fluids meet, though, the child begins to be formed, in the following order:

The first thing that goes into the making of the child, male or female, is the seminal fluid. This is followed by the blood, some flesh, then bone, and then more flesh. Yaghnik did not elaborate further, but others I spoke with sometimes added more detail. In Haj's Hamed Britel's account the body is formed in three stages, each lasting forty days (a number that, like the number three, appears frequently in Muslim ritual contexts). The first period is indeed marked by the formation of the seminal fluid; the second by the formation of one's saliva; and the third by soft body parts, so that at this point the fetus has a formless, leechlike appearance. Thus far in their descriptions, both Yaghnik and the Haj conform to the Quranic version (Sura 13:11–15):

> We created man of an extraction of clay,
> then We set him, a drop, in a receptacle secure,
> then We created of the drop a clot
> then We created of the clot a tissue
> then We created of the tissue bones
> then We garmented the bones in flesh;
> thereafter We produced him as another creature.

For the Haj it is at the end of the third stage that an angel enters the body of the pregnant woman and with his fingers forms all the holes in the fetus's body through which the basic life processes will be carried out. The angel also takes the formless mass and molds from it the whole body of the child—arms, legs, torso. Whether it is at forty days, as Yaghnik said, or one hundred and twenty, as the Haj reckons, both agree that once the body is formed God writes in his book the person's name and all the actions the person will perform in life. An angel looking up to heaven copies this fate onto the forehead of the new human being. This fate, says the Haj, is composed of four elements: troublesome acts (*shaqi*) that would lead the person to hell; supportive and felicitous acts (*sa'id*) for which the promised reward is heaven; one's particular fortune in life (*rizeq*), such as one's goods, family, and noteworthy events; and the length of one's days (*ajal*). Indeed, said the Haj, these things were written out for all men even before the world itself was born.

Yaghnik and his fellow Muslims all agree that at the moment of birth two angels settle on one's shoulders. As the Quran says, "Yet there are over you watchers noble, writers who know whatever you do" (Sura 82:10). They record all the deeds of one's life. The angel on your right-hand side, said Yaghnik, is a good angel; the one on the left is not quite so good. The latter always wants to write down the bad things you do, but the good angel rules over him and is often able to get him to postpone writing down something bad. For instance, he said, if you make a nasty remark in haste, the left-hand angel wants to record it immediately, but the right-hand angel will tell him to wait a bit. Then if the person regrets the remark that was made and feels badly about it or apologizes, the right-hand angel will record the whole affair for good. (The Haj even remarked once, with a particularly insouciant smile fraught with purposeful ambiguity, that he is also careful not to blow his cigarette smoke toward one side or the other lest this somewhat suspect habit further offend one or the other of the recording angels.)

Approaching now the question of death, Yaghnik said that when a person dies, the body must be ritually washed. This is necessary not only so that one is ready to be presented before God but because of what happens soon after burial. For as soon as the mourners leave the cemetery, the soul, which has stood apart from the body since the moment of death, now reenters the body, restoring life to the upper half of the individual. If the body has not been washed, however, the soul will refuse to return to it. The corpse then sits up in the grave, and two angels, who would otherwise refuse to approach an unwashed body, now come to question the deceased. This procedure is the same for all people, Yaghnik continued, whether they were Muslims or not. Some people say if the deceased was a good person, the angels will have pleasant faces, and if he was evil they will have hideous faces, but that is not correct, since angels always have ugly faces. The reason for this is a sort of test: if we find the angels repulsive yet still choose their way, our faith will have been proved by a very decisive test. This is particularly true when the angels come to us in the grave, because at the same time that they, in all their ugliness, appear, so does Satan, who, as always, is very beautiful.

The angels then begin to question the person. They ask who is his God, what is his religion, who was God's last prophet, and so on. The good soul will, of course, answer that his God is Allah and Muhammad is his final prophet, and only true faith will let him answer this way in the face of the ugliness of the angels and the beckoning of the beautiful Satan. Because the gates of heaven and hell will remain closed until Judgment Day, the souls of the dead, both good and bad, are then sent to a place called *barzakh*, a liminal zone—the Arabic word itself means "interval," "partition," "barrier," "isthmus"—which is located at some unknown place in God's domains. Those souls who have chosen the way of the angels ascend immediately to a part of barzakh from which they can look at heaven, through whose eight portals lie what will, after Judgment Day, be their eternal reward. However, Yaghnik said, if the dead person chooses the devil, the angels will deliver a blow that sends the person's body into the bowels of the earth, and as his soul then departs for that portion of barzakh looking out toward hell that is reserved for the sinful, he will hear another angel reciting the decree concerning the fate that awaits him.

Not surprisingly, variations of this theme were mentioned to me by others. In the Haj's version, for example, the angel Azrael gathers up the soul of the deceased and looks up to heaven to see the person's fate. If it is a good person, his or her soul is given to a bird, who swallows it, and with the soul lodged in its gullet, flies the soul to heaven to await Judgment Day. The souls of bad people may even be sent directly to hell, though the Haj did not know if they are carried there by a bird. Just as the good will spend their time in barzakh looking out at heaven's delights, so, too, most sinners will contemplate the view of hell and all its horrors. Indeed, he said, just as we in life dream in our sleep or even daydream while awake (a process which, by the way, is God's way of proving to us that we do in fact have a soul, which is quite separate from our body), so, too, the souls in barzakh will daydream about the heaven or hell that will be theirs. Each soul will also see the executor (*'amal*) who will later be responsible for conducting him to the final judgment place. The 'amal of good people, the Haj noted, will be beautiful and will physically carry the individual to judgment; the 'amal of the evil will be ugly and will have to be carried by the man himself. This "dream" will please the good and horrify the sinful every bit as much as their visions of heaven and hell will delight or frighten them. Only one kind of soul will be able to move freely back and forth between barzakh and earth, namely that of the *mujahid*, the man who died in a holy war. He will still be able to help his wife, provided that she reveals to no one that it is her (dead) husband who is aiding her.

Actually, Yaghnik continued, if you went to the graveyard now, you would find all of the graves virtually empty, for the body rapidly decomposes, all except one bone. This wishbone-shaped piece, which comes from the base of our spines where the branching begins to our lower limbs, will not turn into earth. On Judgment Day, when the trumpet is sounded and God proclaims that he shall use his almighty power to raise the dead, the body of each individual will be reconstituted around this bone. Once the body is fully formed, the soul will reenter it from barzakh, and the rejuvenated individual will be carried by his respective executor to the place of final judgment.

Is the time of Judgment Day preordained, I asked, or is it brought on by certain worldly events? Yaghnik said it could be both. The Prophet said that under certain circumstances the time God has set could be hastened by the acts of mankind; others (and here he quoted a saying) hold that "the Last Day will not come until Islam has entered into every home on earth." Indeed, Islam itself could come to an end. There is a hadith that says, "The Messenger of Allah (may peace be upon him) observed: Verily Islam started as something strange and it would again revert (to its old position) of being strange just as it started, and it would recede between the two mosques just as the serpent crawls back into its hole." As for the circumstances that could bring on both earthly catastrophes and even hasten the Day of Judgment, I later found an account that paralleled Yaghnik's, in which the Prophet says:

> When the spoils of war [the state treasury] are not divided lawfully; when Islam is embraced for profit; when alms are given grudgingly; when men obey their wives but disobey their mothers; when people are kind to their friends but ignore their fathers; when voices are raised in the mosques; when the leader of the people hails from its lowest ranks; when a man is honored out of fear of his evil deeds; when wine is consumed and silk is worn; when singing girls and musical instruments abound; when the young generations curse fathers and grandfathers; then they can expect a violent wind, a black sky, or a great shake-up of the earth.

When Judgment Day does come, it will be fearful, said Yaghnik, quoting from the Quran (Sura 82:1–5):

When heaven is split open,
when the stars are scattered,
then a soul shall know its works, the former and the latter,
when the seas swarm over,
when the tombs are overthrown.

At Judgment each confessional group will come forward with its respective prophet, those who have no prophet being set apart. First among those to come forward to the Scales of Justice will be those who are attached to the Prophet Muhammad. Each person will be very fearful and will plead with his respective prophet to intercede on his behalf. Even other prophets—Abraham, Solomon, Jesus, Moses, and so on—will be afraid, and they in turn will come to Muhammad to request his assistance. Each prophet, Muhammad included, will say to God, "These people are with me," but everyone's own record will still have to be told. Each person will read from the book of his life, which will be hung around his or her neck, just exactly as the angels recorded it. Each must read this record aloud so that when Allah delivers the final decree, all the people will know how just He is. The book of a person's life will then be placed on the scales, the good deeds to one side, the bad to the other. This is a particularly fearful moment since, as the Quran says, even a mote of evil may be sufficient to tip the scales and condemn one. But no matter how heavy the weight of a man's sins, even if it be the entire record of his life, if before dying he uttered the profession of faith ("There is only One God Allah and Muhammad is His last Prophet"), the scales will automatically tip in his favor, and he will enter Paradise.

The situation of those who have no prophet and who, as Yaghnik put it, were set to the side on the Day of Judgment, is particularly revealing of mainstream Muslim beliefs. For without having heard from some messenger of God what is expected of them, individuals are in no position to make any moral choice. It is as if they were not fully human. To follow God's dictates is first and foremost a matter of choice, and if one never had the chance to make reason accord with actions, how could one really be held to final judgment? The common answer, expressed as well by Yaghnik, is that Muhammad's message was, in fact, communicated to all the people in the world during the Prophet's lifetime, so no one can claim not to have had the opportunity to follow him. Those people in distant places who seem never to have had contact with seventh-century Arabia did, therefore, hear the message but either ignored it or forgot it. And those, like the ancients, who never had the opportunity to accept or reject God's messenger, stand mute on the Day of Judgment, witness to the fact that if one has never engaged one's intelligence with revelation, one will never have developed the full faculties of a mature human.

Yaghnik had mentioned that the *mujāhid*, the holy warrior, could move between barzakh and earth, but now he referred to him as one of several kinds of people whose bodies do not need to be washed and who do not have to be prayed for when they die because the way in which they died itself assures them of entry into heaven. What would be the purpose, he asked rhetorically, of our seeking God's mercy on such a mujahid when the angels themselves will praise him to Allah? (Interestingly, the Haj went further, saying that a man who works hard for his children is like a man who has died in a holy war, and his soul, too, is certain to go to heaven.) But the mujahid is not the only one who will surely go to heaven. The same is true for those who die by drowning, plague, or a fall from a great height. God likes people to die quietly, peacefully, surrounded by their families, lying properly in bed, said Yaghnik. If someone dies in such a distasteful way, God probably wanted to erase the record of that person's misdeeds and assure his or her admission to heaven. Similarly, God admits without further question those who die while on the pilgrimage to Mecca. Yaghnik offered no overarching theory for this categorization. But as I thought about it later, it seemed to me that the common denominator of those for whom one need not mourn is that they are beyond the principles of ordinary reciprocity. They do not need the request by others for mercy because their accounts, so to speak, have been fixed beyond fear of revision, and hence the interactive relationship with God that mirrors all relationships among men no longer need be called upon to fashion a desired result. It is, in effect, a ritual reversal of reciprocity that confirms, by its very exception, the normal state of things.

There are also those, Yaghnik continued, who are not responsible for their actions and against whom God marks down no evil. Children have no religious obligations: they do not have to fast or pray, and if they should steal or lie or cheat, it does not count against them. Unlike Jewish law, said Yaghnik, which places the misdeeds of a prepubescent child on the record of the father, in Islamic law parents are not responsible for their children's "sins." Crazy people are like children and are also not liable for their actions. Sometimes, too, insanity is God's way of punishing a person for his bad acts. So, too, a person who is unconscious, whether as a result of natural causes or the act of some jinn, is hardly responsible, say, for missing his prayers. And finally a person into whose soul a jinn has entered directly—which can be told by the victim's eyes or mouth being twisted or the person being abnormally strong or weak—can hardly be held responsible when it is the jinn who is controlling that person. Someone who commits suicide, however, will find that on Judgment Day his punishment is to keep killing himself over and over again in the same way in which he first committed this forbidden act.

And what of heaven itself? I asked. Yaghnik warmed to the task. Those who have been admitted to heaven, he said leaning back with a big smile, will find there wonders that are barely imaginable. In heaven each man will have ten wives, live in a gorgeous house furnished with very high cushions (for everyone will be of the same height, exactly thirty elbow-to-fingertips long). Everyone will have a beautiful face (though not all the same), and those who were ill-formed in life will be perfect. In heaven men and women will be equal, and the angels will do all the work. Everyone will have a nice big automobile, but there won't be any smelly exhaust. Fountains will spray perfume rather than water, the breeze in the trees will make the most wonderful music, and no one will ever have to go to the toilet. As in Eden, if you are hungry, delicious fruit will be within easy reach, since all the trees will grow upside down. If you are thirsty, you will be able to drink from one of the four rivers that flow through paradise: the river of water, the river of milk, the river of honey, or the river of wine.

The wine of Paradise is, Yaghnik hastened to add, of a type that does not make a person drunk. It is permissible for a Muslim to drink this wine if he abstained from drinking on earth. If, on the other hand, you did drink on earth but your record was still good enough to get into heaven, you will not be allowed to drink the wine of Paradise. For there will remain certain inequalities in heaven; not all the good things will be permissible to all individuals. After all, did not God tell us that all men are equal except as concerns religion, and is it not on the basis of religion that we will be judged? For example, a very good man will have around him a whole group of scholars with whom he will converse for all eternity. Each person will, then, be repaid according to his merits and in a way that befits him.

And what is hell like? I inquired. All we know, said Yaghnik with a shrug, is that it has seven gates and seven levels, each level being appropriate for the extent of one's sins and the amount of time a person may have to spend there. For example, the higher levels are a sort of prison, a place where those who are not terribly evil remain for a while before going on to heaven. Even hypocrites and those who rejected Muhammad for a time will, if they have ultimately accepted Islam, eventually go to heaven. For those who are irretrievably corrupted, the horrors of the lowest levels of hell are too awful to contemplate. See what the Quran says in the chapter called "The Enveloper." He waited as I turned to the passage (Sura 88:1–7) and read:

> In the Name of God, the Merciful, the Compassionate
> Hast thou received the story of the Enveloper?
> Faces on that day humbled,
> laboring, toilworn,
> roasting at the scorching fire,
> watered at a boiling fountain,
> no food for them but cactus thorn
> unfattening, unappeasing hunger.

There is, then, in Yaghnik's quite orthodox view, no question but that human beings are creatures whose fates have been determined by God. The fate inscribed in the heavens and impressed on our foreheads is not, however, constructed at the expense of our free will: it simply records the choices each person will have made, choices that God has foreseen. It is a statement couched, as it were, in the future imperfect. That is one reason why, after reading in a recent World Values Survey that 65 percent of Moroccans think life is dictated by fate rather than self-control and that the sense of choice is "abruptly declining," I remain skeptical, for such surveys commonly ignore the subtle interrelation of choice and destiny to which Yaghnik and Islam give voice.

Yaghnik was also quick to cite Islamic and European philosophers who took contrary positions on the issue of free will and just as quickly praised those who chose what he called again the middle road of man's freedom and God's own omniscience. The Haj, though fully in agreement with Yaghnik's account, added that God has only set down the main outlines of one's fate, whereas the angels record details that may be pointed out to God by the Prophet as he appeals for mercy to all good men on the Day of Judgment. Recently, Western scholars of the Quran have, however, suggested that some of the terms referring to judgment that are taken literally by contemporary Muslims may have quite different referents. The mention of "virgins" awaiting Islamic martyrs, one linguist has argued, may actually refer to "white raisins," an exotic fruit of rare quality—though perhaps even this is just a metaphor. And while he does not deny the need to read the Quran literally, Yaghnik is, rather like many Muslims of a thousand years ago, far more prepared than contemporary fundamentalists to interpret a number of aspects of the Quran while nevertheless recognizing that some of the terms used in the past are not understood correctly nowadays or that they may need to be understood metaphorically. For him, the written text is at once inviolable yet not necessarily clear in every respect to mortal minds.

Indeed, the whole of Yaghnik's account points up the striking relation in Arab culture between that which is written and that which is transmitted orally. Everything of importance is written down: the Quran, one's fate, the record of one's life. Yet it is vital to appreciate that in each of these contexts, and many worldly ones as well, writing is really a form of redaction, an inscription of that which is essentially oral and which derives its legitimacy from its oral quality. The Quran, of course, derives much of its force from being written down by the illiterate Prophet to whom it was dictated by the angel Gabriel, and its claim of superiority to prior holy texts lies in its not having been changed since it was first transmitted. But the Quran was not given as a written text, like the tablets to Moses, although the Quran itself is God's major sign to man that the Prophet is indeed his chosen envoy. The Quran—the word itself meaning "recitation"—needs to be absorbed by being memorized and repeated; it needs to be chanted and orally shared. It was transmitted in the Arabs' own language, rather than in a manner to which only a few could gain access. Its truths have to be grasped in the interaction that accompanies its oral transmission. And though Westerners commonly imagine that the written is less prone to mistakes, as if scriveners' errors were not a frequent occurrence, anyone who might, for example, get wrong the words sung in a hymn or national anthem and be quickly corrected can appreciate that the oral may be as exact, if not more so, than the merely written.

It is as if the Quran had to be constantly reacquired by being said; it needs to demonstrate its truth value by being uttered; it has to be inscribed in the heart—just as Yaghnik had to learn it by heart—and it has to be communicated face to face in order to bind people together. The same is true of the angels' test of individuals in the grave or that moment when each person reads the record of his or her life before God on Judgment Day. Where Westerners might test a document's veracity by asking if it has been properly drawn or possibly forged—evidence that is thought to exist on the face of the written instrument itself—to Muslims writing is the reduction to script of an oral statement by a particular person, something that has to be tested by asking who this person is, to whom he is attached, and what he has done, not just whether it is inscribed in the correct form. It is thus another instance, like the Haj's rendition of history, in which it is the person who makes the statement believable, not the other way around.

We see this mode of treating the written as if it were oral in numerous domains of everyday Moroccan life. In the Islamic law courts, not only are two official witnesses (*'udul*) always used to validate a document (just as there must always be two angels who record or interrogate men on their acts), but what they record is later assessed like oral statements whose truth depends on the court's acknowledgment of the witnesses as themselves believable persons. (Indeed, in the past, one could be certified prior to any actual cases as a reliable witness if enough people testified to your reputation.) Similarly, if a litigant wants to persuade the court of his claim, he will try to present a document in which at least three and preferably twelve witnesses testify before two notaries and then go before two other notaries and repeat their testimony. The court will then ask of this document how believable these witnesses are, using the fact that they kept their story straight before two sets of inquiring notaries as one index of their credibility. And in certain political circumstances people tend to listen to several reports to see if at least two relaters of diverse backgrounds are saying the same thing, thus adding greatly to the believability of the accounts. The story of Judgment Day thus reflects and guides the way in which the written is evaluated in this world no less than in the next.

Some elements of Yaghnik's eschatology are notable for their tenuous connection to the Quran. The elaboration of barzakh as a sort of interstitial zone may be largely a folk invention. Three times the Quran refers to barzakh: once as the place where the dead reside for a time (Sura 23:100) and twice (Sura 25:53 and 55:19–22) as the place in the sea where fresh and salt water meet, possibly a reference to that part of the Persian Gulf where underground springs form a separate layer, which, like Allah's favors, are never so comingled as to allow choosing only one aspect of His beneficence. Only once does the Quran explicitly refer to "Death's angel" (Sura 32:11), and Yaghnik himself never speaks of a specific angel of death or of the creation of death by God. It is also interesting to note that while Yaghnik sees the dead, at least after their examination by the angels, as truly dead in their graves, he, like many Moroccans (Muslims and Jews alike), claims that saints are actually still alive in their tombs and thus susceptible to human requests for assistance in much the same way they would be involved in reciprocity if ordinarily alive. One cannot bargain across the gap of death, so by this parallel of saints and the living the usual barrier to reciprocity engendered by death is itself undone. Like many urban educated Arabs, Yaghnik does not, however, overstress the role of saints generally. Mothers tend to teach their children about them, and men like Yaghnik are willing to acknowledge the saints' existence. He and Fuzia have visited saintly shrines, but unlike the practice of women who visited Sefrou's patron saint and tied strips of cloth on the fence marking the path to the hill-top as a way of conducing the saint to respond to their requests, in a form of the 'ar, neither Yaghnik nor his wife tends to regard saints as ones who can be bent to one's will. Given their absence from stricter interpretations of the Quran, therefore, Yaghnik does not dwell on the saints or their effect on his own identity. The image of death and judgment, by contrast, reflect more strongly Yaghnik's everyday understanding of the self. For Yaghnik is not alone in expressing a view of the person, notwithstanding God's abil-ity to create things as a series of discrete events, as a unity, the cumulation of all one's traits and ties. To him the self is indivisible, unfractionated, incapable of being assessed only as separable roles or positions. It is the undivided self that exists in this world and that, at the final judgment, God will be called upon to judge.

In a particularly striking phrase the Quran says: "Indeed, we created man in trouble" (Sura 90:5), and nowhere does this come home with greater force than on that Day of Judgment. That each confessional group should be arrayed collectively before God would, of course, give delight to any Durkheimian, especially since, in many accounts, each group betrays its own peculiar social characteristics by who stands where and who says what to whom. All seek, too, in their respective prophet an intermediary, a *wasiṭa*, a go-between, someone who can help them as they stand before the final decision maker. But, characteristically, it is not just someone with a connection that they seek in their prophet: it is someone who, because of his own believability, makes them believable in turn. Just as the Berbers used coswearers in their legal proceedings and Arabs the reliable witness as a guarantor, so, too, at Judgment it is the individual who is made the more credible by the personal record of his chosen intermediary. It will be in the supernatural domain what is so common in the mundane world of patrons and those they protect, an instance (in Clifford Geertz's phrase) of "the dressing of one man in the reputation of the other."

Ultimately, though, in Yaghnik's account, each person stands alone at Judgment. Where Saint Paul could say to the Galatians, "Bear ye one an-other's burdens," the Quran, by contrast, repeatedly asserts, "No soul laden bears the load of another" (Sura 35:18; also 6:164 and 2:116). Not even family can help, "for when the Trumpet is blown, that day there shall be no kinship any more between them" (Sura 23:104). In Islam, it is the in-dividual who bears all moral responsibility, a feature that informs worldly morality in turn.

Indeed, when one sets Yaghnik's account of the end of days alongside descriptions and enactments of a wide range of relationships, it is clear

that for Moroccans, as for most Arabs, the image of the interpersonal contract runs through their worldly and spiritual lives as a constant organizing
theme. God will fulfill his bargains, says the Quran in many passages, if
man fulfills his own. Whether it is through a constraining offering (*'ar*) to
a saint or potential patron, or through the profession of faith at the end
of one's life, Muslims are adamant in asserting that, having once agreed
to the terms of the deal, God must do his part if man does his. The difference between relations with God and those with one's fellowmen is that in
ordinary human interactions one must work very hard to secure and enforce commitments, whereas God, by always keeping his word, never fails
to achieve his purpose even if, as the Quran says, "most men do not know
it" (Sura 12:22).

Finally, there is the image of heaven and hell contained in Yaghnik's
account. His portrayal in this regard is not so far from that of the Quran,
which speaks of heaven as a place of "spouses purified" (Sura 3:13), "wide-
eyed maidens restraining their glances as if they were hidden pearls" (Sura
37:48), "a place of security, gardens and vineyards, maidens with swell-
ing breasts, like of age, and a cup overflowing" (Sura 78:32). And if the
commenters or sermonizers he has read or heard have determined the precise size of people in heaven, or if the image of small children as servants
should bespeak the delight he takes in his own household, or if the capacity to watch, unseen and unaffected, one's parents on a form of television
should convey his own vision of paradise—well, what is heaven for if not
such thoughts? That some Western scholars believe Dante got the idea of
the order of heaven, purgatory, and hell from Islam only underscores the
common bases, yet different variations, that such themes have incorporated in the long contact between Islam and the West.

More interesting, from a strictly theological perspective, is the presence of intoxicating liquors in heaven. In Yaghnik's account, the theme
of heaven as the reverse of the worldly—a place where trees grow upside
down, women do not menstruate, and no one has to go to the toilet—is
further extended by allowing the drinking of liquor. To some commenters,
however, the question of intoxicating liquors in paradise is more richly tex-
tured. Whether or not the Quranic caution about the wines of earth is an
outright prohibition (see Sura 2:216), it has certainly been taken as such
by the orthodox. However, the rationales behind this prohibition vary with
the interpreter. To some medieval scholars, like al-Tabari and al-Razi, the
very word for liquor, *khamr*, which comes from a root meaning "to con-
ceal," suggests that alcohol is undesirable because it veils intellectual powers, turning the most noble aspect of man, his reason, against him, loosing

the hobble cord that acts as a brake on natural dispositions. But in paradise the adverse effects on reason are eliminated: the "rivers of wine, a delight to the drinkers" (Sura 47:16) do not cause men to lose their ability to govern their own acts and thus bring even liquor within the ambit of the permissible. It is one of those ritual reversals that by their inversion confirm the norm yet permit an area of uncertainty and ambiguity through which license may be situationally allowed only for its dangers to be neutralized and society rendered safe.

Other usages have also tested the interpretation of sacred sources. Scholars debating the permissibility of smoking tobacco, particularly in the sixteenth century, had to rationalize their position in ways that did not contravene the Quran or the Prophet's own acts and utterances. Thus some argued that tobacco smoke was like the foul odors the Prophet despised, others that tobacco falls into the same category as disgusting parts of an animal it is forbidden to eat. One clever student even countered his Sufi master's criticism of smoking by claiming that tobacco was the only plant that refused to bow to God after he completed his work of creation, so because of its unbelief it is only appropriate that it be burned!

Anthropologists are fond of describing and analyzing cosmologies, those elaborate images of how, in the eyes of those who believe in them, the world is made orderly, and humankind is granted its proper place. It is an understandable interest. Not only are these normative images often the ones we first convey to outsiders, but they are just the sort of images our theories have told us that all peoples must in fact possess, rational descriptions that make us feel the world is properly organized and comprehensible. Yet at the same time we all know that such stories are, at best, only partly "true"—they guide action only very loosely, coming to the fore more at times of crisis, when some sense of orderliness may render disappointment tolerable, uncertainty bearable, and death defeasible. Yaghnik is no different than many others for telling a coherent tale that may not match the full paradigm through which he actually engages daily life. But as one listens to him trying to make that accounting work in his everyday existence, one must, as he himself does, attend very carefully to the categories he uses and to the process by which his own middle course allows the edges of the ideal to coexist with the demands of the practical and to grant ambivalence and certainty their respective shares in confronting the facts of daily life. It was against this background that, one day in early spring, Yaghnik began to describe the classical Islamic set of moral categories.

All acts, Yaghnik explained, can be arranged along a continuum from the prescribed to the forbidden, the good practices and the bad each being subdivided into three categories. If you start from the best and go to the worst, it works like this: The most desirable acts are *fard*, obligatory—they are prescribed by Allah in the Quran and consist of the Five Pillars of Faith (prayer, the monthlong fast of Ramadan, acknowledgment of God's unity and Muhammad's prophecy, charity, and the pilgrimage to Mecca) as well as such things as the division of property through inheritance prescribed in the Quran. For these acts God will reward you; for failure to perform them He will punish you. Next comes *sunna*, things the Prophet did or told people they should do, acts for which God will reward us, but for which, if we do not perform them, there will be no punishment. So, for example, it is prescribed that you wash certain parts of your body before prayer, while washing other parts, as the Prophet did, is highly desirable but not mandatory. *Mandūb*, which means "recommended," is the next category, and it consists of things the Prophet did sometimes and that it is good for us to follow, as, for example, turning one's back while squatting to urinate, or drinking while being seated rather than standing, or sitting upright rather than leaning while eating.

Then there is a somewhat neutral category, *halāl*, from a root meaning "to untie or dissolve something." These are acts that you are perfectly free to do or not and for which there is no Quranic passage or Prophetic tradition implying clear-cut reward or punishment, though doing these things is really very good: for example, eating all the foods that God has told us it is permissible to eat, or going before notaries to formalize a marriage.

On the bad side there are also three gradations. Least bad is *mubāh*, things Islamic law regards as indifferent or permissible, things you are perfectly free to do but which, Yaghnik made clear, are in his personal opinion rather bad indeed. Here he included such acts as talking during prayers or smoking, which, like the Haj, he said bothers the angels on your shoulders. Worse yet are things categorized as *makrūh*, "reprehensible"—though the word also means "mishap" or "accident." These are things that, if you abstain from doing, God will reward you, but if you choose to do them, you will not be punished. So, for example, it would be makruh if you eat a little bit too soon during the fast of Ramadan or wash yourself above the prescribed line of the ankles in preparation for prayer (thus turning a ritual act into a bath). This is not, Yaghnik stressed, simply the obverse of sunna, however, because makruh acts involve slight infractions of the word of God as well as the words or deeds of the Prophet himself. And finally there are acts that are *harām*, strictly forbidden. Failure to perform an act we have been told by Allah or the Prophet to perform fits this category, or doing anything that we have been expressly enjoined from doing. It can range from murder to eating pork to unjustifiable violence.

As further discussion with Yaghnik and observation of his casual conversation with others revealed, these categories are by no means self-executing. Here, as in so many other respects for Muslims, context matters. To go on the pilgrimage to Mecca, for example, is a required religious duty, but if it would put a severe burden on one's family, it becomes forbidden; to smoke is a matter of some indifference (mubah) to Yaghnik, but if the cost of the habit takes away from feeding one's family, he sees it as haram. Different people use these categories to different ends. Youssef, the storekeeper who found Yaghnik for me, upgraded smoking to makruh, reprehensible—but then, until his fortunes changed, he admitted that he had long refused to sell cigarettes because it brought in some of the riffraff wanting to buy just a couple of cigarettes at a time. Youssef used this same category for looking too much at women—an example, even in the eyes of Yaghnik, that bespoke the grocer's exaggerated sense of propriety. Yet where Yaghnik marked *mubah* acts as allowable but still, in his own words, "very bad indeed," the storekeeper depicted them (using the French term) as *normal*, as things, he said, that have changed with the times and now simply exist as facts of life. Youssef also characterized birth in similar terms: having children is obligatory, while having more children than one can support is *haram*. Others, the Haj included, frequently asserted that only those things that are clearly fard or haram are religiously relevant, and that, for example, birth control is not discussed in the Quran and is at most only connected to certain traditions of the Prophet. Moroccans were well aware that in Tunisia polygamy had been abolished by President Bourguiba on the grounds that multiple wives could never be treated (emotionally) equally, or that a developing nation may be likened to a man who is sick or traveling and is thus free from the obligation to fast during Ramadan until he is sufficiently settled or well. All these instances Yaghnik and others recognized as rationalizations, whether admirable or not, but rationales that could at least be contested through the grid of moral categories that form an important part of orthodox Islamic thought.

Perhaps even more significantly, it is clear that for many Muslims Islam, as Kenneth Cragg put it, allows what the generality do. Certain duties (prayer, fasting) must be performed by each person, while others (leading the prayer) must be accomplished by someone on behalf of everyone if the community is to remain righteous in God's eyes. Not only is the accountability personal, but unless something is clearly required or forbidden, it is regarded as lying within what the Quran calls "the rights of mankind." This is where local custom matters. For custom does not stand apart from Islam: it *is* Islamic in the sense of being within the parameters of men's rights and, if it does not contravene a central tenet of the faith, it will not go beyond what the Quran repeatedly calls "the bounds of God." Thus the powerfully inclusive mentality of Islam allows local variation *as* Islam, not as something in contradistinction to it, a fact that has no doubt contributed to its spread into many parts of the world.

Discussion may, therefore, go forward in terms of the moral grid described by Yaghnik. A sermonizer or politician may try to capture the terms of discussion through his choice of a given category, while an ordinary person may express his conservative approach to women or his progressive approach to interest-bearing loans through the same grid. And perhaps, just as in the West, where the elaboration of a scheme running from the probable through the morally certain affected the development of science, law, and ordinary moral life, the discourse of moral categories may, for some Muslims, support a seemingly nonreligious paradigm by associating it with criteria of moral import. For Yaghnik it is at least a system that suggests an underlying orderliness to life, one that, for a man of the middle way is neither rigidly applied nor uselessly vague just because it partakes of a degree of inherent flexibility. Such conceptual flexibility was particularly vital as Morocco made the transition to national independence in 1956 and settled into new concerns in the succeeding years.

By the mid- to late 1960s, a decade into independence, Yaghnik's world was one in which the first blush of national freedom had passed, the realities of a diminished economy were settling in, and the vicissitudes of party politics and initial reforms had begun to pale in the light of existing circumstance. Often one heard people in Sefrou say that with the Jews and the French gone the economy had declined because the Arabs were reluctant to risk their capital, both monetary and psychological, with one another. Often elections were characterized as just another vehicle through which the game of forging useful personal alliances was played out, rather than being connected to the rectification of abuses of power. Yaghnik, not surprisingly, often cast about for his own course by harking back to elements of the standard Islamic version of history.

When Muhammad took on human form and was placed on earth, Yaghnik said, Satan left the land, Caesar's throne literally toppled, and the great stone in Mecca fell into place. But the Prophet did not try to change everything at once: he shrewdly limited certain practices, like polygamy, so people would not reject him; he did not ban wine drinking outright, but gradually eliminated the land where grapes could be grown. It was like the way we often build houses, Yaghnik said, occasionally adding one room at a time. Throughout the days of the first caliphs people lived that way. But then they began to go astray; they began to ignore the sacred law, the *shari'a*. We cannot go back to those original days, Yaghnik emphasized, but we can get much closer by restoring religious law to its fullest. We should not have laws from other nations, but only the shari'a, ministers should be ulama, and even police commissioners should have a solid knowledge of the sacred law. That would be real democracy, because what is democracy if not truth, and isn't the shari'a simply the truth? The law given to us by God through his Prophet Muhammad is the salvation of society, but the government favors a national law rather than shari'a, and therefore there is very little likelihood that we can recapture the society of those early days. The law should not be treated as rigid, he concluded. It serves us well, though, if we use it as the steadying guide in every domain.

Yaghnik could even find, in the late 1960s, support in the Quran for various instances of foreign affairs, including America's involvement in Vietnam. In the Quran (Sura 18:83–102), he said, we are told that there was once a great king who ruled the world. We call him Dhool Karnain; you call him Alexander the Great. He was opposed by a group of people who lived in the east, in the land where the sun rises, and he was only able to contain them by building a wall in the narrow mountain pass through which they might enter the Western world. On one occasion this wall was in fact breached by Genghis Khan, and he did considerable damage before he and his people were once again contained. If these people, called Gog and Magog, suffer great famine, for example, and once again breach the wall, they could wreak havoc on the civilized world—and I have heard that there is now such a famine in China, and I fear that they may break out of their own lands. That is why I am happy that America intervened in Vietnam to help stop them.

Yaghnik could also employ the categories of his worldview to formulate possible solutions to pressing social concerns. For example, he was, like many, appalled at the cost of bridewealth payments, the sums that, as the defining feature of an Islamic marriage, are presented by a bridegroom and his supporters to the bride or her marital guardian. By the late 1960s it had turned into a form of prestige competition, with only a few villages or settlements, like the nearby one at Bhalil, trying to limit the problem by fixing one symbolic price for all. Yaghnik suggested that the preferable practice is one that some "modern" people were beginning to employ, namely for the bridewealth payment to be very small and for the groom, rather than the bride's family, to supply the household furnishings, which would become the sole property of the wife immediately. This would limit the pressures from the wife's family for the husband to keep buying her things that might ultimately become her property in the event of divorce but that in the meantime puts unnecessary pressure on the newly formed marriage.

Nor was Yaghnik unaware of some of the negative features of focusing too much on religion. When he indicated that an overemphasis on religion was actually bad for the nation, I asked for some examples. The first thing, he said, is that women need more liberty: religion restricts their liberty. Women should be allowed to work in the same places as men; they should just wear a djellaba during working hours. Banks should also be allowed to charge interest, and although we should always have a king, we should also have a parliament whose members have a basic understanding of the shari'a. Once again, as I listened to Yaghnik's list, I heard the man of the middle, the man who (as he himself says) thinks people can be too rigid, too orthodox, and thus miss the practical spirit that he believes is at the core of the shari'a.

As to political development, Yaghnik is not alone in thinking that he is, in some very significant way, actually involved in a democracy. He knows that the media present only rosy views of the economy (when what he sees is the high rate of unemployment of his own family members and students), and he knows only too well what power, corruption, and favoritism have done to the country. But two other elements appeared present in Yaghnik's view, at least through the closing years of the twentieth century. First, he would say, there is a general optimism one encounters among Moroccans, an optimism that to me often seemed hard to explain. Perhaps it was the stress on personalism, the belief (like the player of any lottery) that either I will be the one to win or at least it is worth the chance. Thus one constantly encountered young men who thought they would be the one to marry the foreign woman and get a visa for a job abroad or that they would somehow make the right connection and strike it rich. Moroccans are not, unlike those in many other parts of the Arab world, nostalgic for some imagined past. To the contrary, they are enormously forward-looking and simply do not attend well to the past unless it has some continuing presence.

And secondly, they do imagine that since the power of others depends on their ability to forge bonds of interdependence, there is genuine power in the choice of who one will be dependent upon. This power of weakness, coupled with a deep ambivalence to power and the belief that whoever builds a successful network of allies partakes of a fair share of legitimacy—

and all of it wrapped up in the ultimate limitation of a monarchy that has deep historical and religious roots—yields, for men like Yaghnik, a version of democracy in which power is thought to be limited not by formally structured institutions so much as by the criteria through which one must build and maintain a set of dependents. Given such a view, a government of limited powers possesses far more subtleties of cultural form than can be embraced by elections, partisan attachments, or written constitutions alone.

But even in the latter part of the century, when Yaghnik and others still maintained a high degree of optimism, he was the first to acknowledge that some domains he knew well were deeply troubled. In all the years I have known him, it has been the educational system that most concerns Yaghnik. And few things exercised him more than the prospect of the educational system becoming even less Arabized and more arbitrary in the awarding of degrees. You remember, he asked, how in the mid-1960s the minister of education proposed that certain subjects should be taught entirely in Arabic at the grammar school level and then, particularly for the sciences, partly in French at the next higher level? That much seemed reasonable. But then what happened? In March of 1965 there were terrible riots in Casablanca—which then spread to Fez, Rabat, Marrakech, and other cities—when the minister decreed that students who did not pass on to the higher level could not even go on to technical schools, thus preventing them from ever having a chance at a government job. This, combined with various labor issues raised by the unions, really upset people. I recalled my conversations with Yaghnik and the actions of the king at that moment. Not only did the riots radicalize a number of those who were students at the time and went on to be deeply involved in the country's various political parties, but the king, who suspended Parliament and the constitution for several years, made a speech in which he said to the protestors: "Let me tell you there is no greater danger to the state than the so-called intellectual; it would have been better for you to be illiterate."

To students who were demonstrating about the lack of jobs and more particularly to their parents, such remarks were humiliating. With few possibilities in the private sector, the possibility of a government job—or migration abroad—were the main outlets for those who were educated but unemployed. For most Moroccans in those days the ideal job was a government position—what people (drawing on the French word) called a *mandat*, from the assured income accompanying such a post. Moroccan parents will make extraordinary sacrifices for their children's education, rural people often moving to town in order to make further education for them possible. So parents and students alike were furious when the rules were changed—and not for the first or last time—thereby removing the whole family's opportunity to have one of its members on a steady salary. The government troops, under General Oufkir (the same man who later tried to kill the king in 1972) fired on the protesters during the 1965 events. They said only seven were killed, Yaghnik noted, but everyone knows the count ran into the hundreds. Afterward, the king declared a "state of exception" for five years, during which political and union activities were suspended, followed by yet another change in the constitution giving the monarchy still more power. You cannot simply keep changing the educational system in these ways, Yaghnik concluded, without expecting some reaction.

Yaghnik's account underscored several factors vital to an understanding of the Moroccan style of protest. In many cases the protest may seem to be about one thing but is really about another. Thus so-called bread riots, like the deadly ones that were to occur in Casablanca in 1981 and in a number of cities including Sefrou in the late 1990s, may indeed be triggered by a rise in prices occasioned by a shift in government policy or pressure from international monetary agencies. But they may also be fueled by anger over other matters. When, for example, thousands suddenly showed up for a march protesting Moroccan involvement in the coalition fighting against Saddam Hussein in the First Gulf War, interviews clearly established that the main concern of the protesters was with local economic conditions for which the gathering about Iraq was a partial excuse. Similarly, it is crucial to appreciate that those initiating such protests commonly have a clear sense of whether those who stand by but do not actively participate support their position, a factor that further fuels their willingness to take to the streets. Yaghnik was quite clear that he and all his friends fully sympathized with those who protested in 1965, and on similar occasions, when the changes in educational policy touched deep feelings of economic and political frustration.

At the same time, it is clear that Yaghnik, like so many others, does not feel that the Moroccan regime has been repressive. In the years that came to be called "the years of lead" because of King Hassan's harsh treatment of certain opponents, only those involved in direct actions against the regime, he said, felt the government's sharp edge. Overwhelmingly, I observed, people discussed politics openly and did not feel themselves to be living in a closely watched society where government spies were ever-present. Following his death in 1999 the extent of King Hassan's use of imprisonment became public, and many were surprised not just by the numbers involved but by the fact that it had been done without the populace at large feeling the heavy presence of the central regime. To the contrary, people pointed to the king's more usual practice of closing an offending newspaper and then letting it reopen or demoting an official and then raising him higher (as a clever way of making him more dependent). When, years later, we thought back to these times, Yaghnik understood why, to those in active opposition to the monarchy, these were indeed years of lead, but, perhaps because he saw in the king a man who like himself blended the modern and the traditional, he never thought it had the feel of repression common to so many other countries of the Middle East.

In the face of such concerns it was, then, with some comic relief that I recalled how, in the summer of 1969, I met Yaghnik on the street shortly after Americans first landed on the moon. He congratulated me on the feat. I thanked him, and in the way we both had of poking fun at one another's countries, I asked if he would not, however, have preferred that it be a Muslim who first landed on the moon. Yes, he replied—but that would not really have been possible. Why not? I asked. Well, said Yaghnik, we would have had to send up a man who was a good representative of our people. That is what you did. You are a religious people, so you sent up a religious man—I know because I heard him pray. Our man, too, would have had to be religious. But since the spaceship goes around the earth every few hours before it takes off for the moon and a good Muslim must say his prayers five times from sunrise to sunset, he would have been so busy praying he would not have had time to fly the spaceship. So it is better that it was one of your people who went to the moon!

It should, however, be noted that others, in what may be yet another example of Arab ambivalence to power, saw the arrival on the moon differently. Upon learning of the landing, a Sudanese, no doubt recalling that the moon is often portrayed in folklore as one of the dwelling places of Allah, was heard to say: "Oh, goodness. I hope they don't bring God back with them!" As events unfolded in Morocco and elsewhere, it was hard to believe that the days of either divine punishment or beneficence, unaffected by the acts of men, had commenced.

I do not apply my sword where my lash suffices, nor my lash where my tongue is enough. And even if there be one hair binding me to my fellow men, I do not let it break. When they pull, I loosen, and if they loosen, I pull.

—Muawiya ibn Abi Sofyan (602–80)

The intervening years before I was to meet Yaghnik again were fraught with significant events and trends for Morocco. By the mid-1970s the country was taking in less revenue for its agricultural produce than it paid out for imports, and with the oil shock of the late 1970s Morocco fell into ever-increasing debt. The always uncertain rainfall failed to appear in the early 1980s, and several severe drought years, a fall in the price of phosphates (the country's main source of foreign exchange), and an inexorable rise in the population of some 3 percent annually strained national resources. Two unsuccessful attempts on the king's life in 1971 and 1972 shook everyone. Then in October 1975 the king marched 350,000 unarmed civilians into the Western Sahara in a move aimed at asserting Moroccan sovereignty over the former Spanish territory and further consolidating his own power. The resulting war in the Sahara continued to absorb both money and manpower, and although the king relieved all farmers of paying taxes until the turn of the century, other "contributions" to the war effort continued to drain both resources and optimism. Even as the drought years were later replaced by years of agricultural plenty and Moroccan forces hunkered down behind an earthen wall while procrastinating about possible Saharan elections, small symbols of uncertainty and continuity could be intermittently observed.

In the late 1980s, for example, a new ten-dirham banknote appeared. It was not the musical instrument on the obverse side that caught everyone's attention, even though some people were quick to point out that it had the wrong number of strings for a truly traditional Moroccan lute. What they mainly noticed was the portrait of the king himself. Where earlier bills showed a young man, rather idealized, looking unflinchingly into the middle distance without any hint of a wrinkle, the new portrait was of a man in

King Hassan II, 1960s–1970s

King Hassan II, 1980s

his late fifties who looked at you directly, the hair thinned, the chin weaker, the face slightly puffy, the lines around the eyes and mouth a forger's nightmare. It seemed a remarkably honest, even courageous, portrait, with none of the ageless royalty of an Elizabeth II, the iconic claim to legitimacy of a Juan Carlos, or the advantage granted an American president whose relatively brief tenure may not betray the rigors of high office. The actual and symbolic value of the money itself, however, only tended to become more uncertain. To build the world's third-largest mosque at a cost of $800 million in Casablanca—and thus give that urban center of employment unrest a kind of ritual focus—the king commended "contributions" about which everyone from professors to taxi drivers, their pay often "voluntarily" docked, complained bitterly.

Inflation by the end of the 1980s stood almost three times higher than the official 6 to 7 percent, and unemployment, especially of educated youth, was dangerously high. Riots had broken out on several occasions. In December 1990, troops were called up from the Sahara to shoot at anyone creating disturbances on the streets after rioters in Fez and several other cities had taken out their frustration on some of the symbols of wealth, including a hotel in Fez owned by the king, that marked the increasing gap between rich and poor. Again, protests surrounding the Gulf War in January 1991 were in large part a form of criticism of the king, who also told the nation how much the Saudi and Kuwaiti monarchs loved them when all that Moroccans saw were the extravagant palaces and equally extravagant haughtiness with which these eastern Arabs disported themselves in Morocco. Fundamentalist groups showed surprising organization during that same period, and although the extent of their strength was difficult to gauge, it was clear that they had the capacity to appeal to disaffected university students no less than the urban poor if only the right issues could be found to galvanize support. Professors told me that students in Rabat were divided into "those who pray" and "those who don't pray," and even the former refused to use the mosque built on campus by the government, favoring instead a place they rented and converted for their own use. Now the portrait of the king on newly minted bills showed a man who looks away, and people said it was because he no longer dared to look you in the face. They would show strangers how to fold the new bill so that the Arabic, instead of reading "ten dirhams" would read "he shits on them." Where people always hung pictures of the king in their shops, now in every city I visited it was rare to spot a single picture of the king. When I mentioned this to a very distinguished retired judge, he replied that if I wanted to see the king's picture, I should look for it now in the offices of the large corporations.

Everywhere I went in the late 1980s, people used a word I had rarely heard in the past, and certainly never with such strong overtones. The word *mes'uliya*, usually translated as "responsibility," was no longer used to convey simply an official or role-prescribed act but the failure to treat others with that courtesy and evenhandedness that always made it possible to form alliances wherever beneficial. Now, people said, if you walk unknown into a government office, instead of being asked "What can I do for you, sir?" or even being greeted with a simple *salam u-alaykum*, someone will say gruffly "What do you want?" It was as if the gap had now opened so widely that it was nearly impossible for an ordinary person to bridge it. It was like those houses of the rich, people would say: where in the past a poor relative or dependent never showed discomfort in entering a rich man's house and eating there, the feeling now was that one could not even enter such a place with some sense of deeper equality. Architecture, economics, and everyday civility seemed to strain the very presuppositions of Moroccan society, one of whose key elements had always been that the bases of power were multiple and diffused, thus giving people with different strengths alternative foundations on which to construct a network of supporters. And if that gap becomes too wide, our storekeeper friend told me, if the only way to feel you can be treated fairly is with a bribe, trust will be destroyed and social chaos will take its place.

By the time I returned in the early 1990s, the process had clearly gone much further. The word "responsibility" and the felt sense of injury that accompanied its use were no longer dominant in the vocabulary of morals. It was now a simple given that, more often than not, money alone could speak, and those who did not have enough were not heard. Migrant workers had always been shaken down at the port of entry, but it was now done openly. A government driver told me how he was on the way to the bank one day when a policeman pulled him over. He only had one dirham—worth less than twelve cents—on him, but the cop, so used to getting anything he could, was willing to settle even for that petty bribe. At the post office one might have stood in a slow-moving line to get a needed form only to be told by the teller there were no forms left—until a "gift" suddenly produced the needed document; at a hospital one might have to pay someone just to visit a relative or get an inoculation required for the pilgrimage to Mecca. It was not the purchase of favor, though, that was so degrading but that, like the idea of responsibility, such behavior broke the rules of the entire social game, upset the repertoire of relational possibilities on which alliances are based, and made it no longer imaginable, as the common phrase would have it, to be a poor man in the morning, a vizier of the king in the afternoon, and hanged in the public marketplace the next day.

Popular culture, too, had undergone alteration. In the 1970s television situation comedies were very popular. Audiotapes of particular favorites were readily available in the bazaar. It was a form Moroccans could readily adopt. As people moved into their own marital households instead of remaining with the groom's parents, and as women became increasingly present in the workplace, family comedies could express new tensions and new distributions of power without appearing to threaten the ultimate validation of social conventions. Comedy, George Meredith said long ago, is woman's great friend, since in those situations women can express themselves freely even though at the end, as in all comedies, the genre reveals its conservatism as society reasserts itself in traditional ways. But these shows were largely displaced in the 1980s by imported and domestic soap operas, where the struggle for control in a world portrayed as venal, if not downright corrupt, could strike a more recognizable chord. Yet Moroccans retained in these domains their attachment to the use of language in ways that always test the limits of possible relationships without overstepping the line between seeing what the traffic will bear and giving overt offense.

In such a climate a form of wordplay called *mica* (from the word "Formica") had developed among the young, by which a remark could be made that could bounce off, reflect, resist seriousness—a remark creatively designed to be potentially biting, a bit crazy, and in turn, would elicit a bizarre simile, a joke, an off-the-wall riposte as each participant maneuvered to probe through language play the boundaries of the real. Like the

Arabs' penchant for using jokes as a relatively safe way to challenge the existing order, mica (also called *tmyak* or *'ayn mica,* sometimes translated as a "plastic eye"), as one Moroccan told anthropologist Omar Boum, "is a dangerous practice. [It] betrays the consciousness of the citizen to speak his mind in society."

Even the look of the country was changing. As people sought their own private residences and those working abroad placed their remittances— now accounting for some 40 percent of the country's foreign exchange earnings—in housing built around all of Morocco's cities, the urban land-scape was being transformed. At first, riotous forms of architecture prolif-erated, and different cities tried to mimic the rose-colored look of a Mar-rakech or Essaouira by painting many of the structures a uniform color. In time, King Hassan II insisted that each city should have a distinctly Arab style of architecture and that the main road into each town should reflect this look. Initially, many towns thus took on a Potemkin-like appearance, with arches and plantings that were one street deep, a Hassanized village. Much of the new building was actually illegal, a process that involved con-structing walls at night within an animal enclosure, or building a mosque adjacent to the clandestine structures (commonly named for one of the king's daughters to dissuade their destruction), all built quickly yet some-times in conformity with city codes so the government would not bull-doze them and would eventually grant them water and electricity. The style moved deeper into the new parts of the cities, and as the tide of rural im-migration was slowly replaced by internal growth of the urban population, cities like Fez grew from 300,000 to 700,000 in a single decade, while Casa-blanca grew from 1.7 million in 1975 to 2.7 million in 1990 and a little over 4 million by 2010.

All of these pressures and changes were felt in Sefrou as well. By 1991 it had grown from the 25,000 of a generation earlier to 70,000 and, having been designated a province in its own right, was deeply involved in spruc-ing up an appearance that had become so distant from its earlier charm that at one point the king said he would not visit the town until it was once again rendered beautiful. At first, like other towns, Sefrou experimented with making everything rose colored. Then, playing on one possible origin of the city's name as derived from the word for "yellow," many of the build-ings were repainted in that color, the result being so pale and sulfurous a look that it seemed as if the entire town had contracted jaundice. But by the early 1990s this phase, too, had passed, and in preparation for the ar-rival of its own governor the gardens were refurbished, and the lower por-tions of the trunks of all the trees lining the main entry road were painted white (rather like an old colonial neighborhood), while the pace of new building in all the garden lands around the town continued to cut into the oasis-like appearance for which the city had once been so well known.

On one level the city was doing reasonably well. The health and nutrition of children was improved, and no one was going hungry. Those working abroad faced increasing costs for the numerous villas they were building in Sefrou, but their income helped to create some added construction work in the town. The city council was firmly back in promonarchic hands, as the socialists elected in a protest vote a few years earlier were unable to make significant strides against the entrenched regime. The number of lawyers had gone from zero in the late 1960s to eighteen in 1988 and twenty-four by 1991, a number of them women. Women no longer tied strips of cloth to the fence that led up the footpath to the saintly shrine overlooking the city as a sign of offering for the saint's favors, preferring instead to ride to the top in little taxis. Court officials also told me that the most common clause inserted in marriage contracts was no longer one giving the wife the right not to be moved by her husband to another locale but one that assured her the right to continue working after their marriage.

But when I tried to find Yaghnik in 1988, I learned that he had moved from Sefrou and was living in Fez. I tracked him to a school there, but he was away, and it was not until I returned three years later that I discovered that he was living in an apartment near the railroad station and that he had bought a small café on the same street for his son. I reached him by phone, and we agreed to meet there a few days later.

The café, alas, was not much to look at—little more than a shell with a few tables and chairs out front, the poorest looking of three cafés on that block alone. Not even the name, Café Saadia, "Happiness Café," did much to cheer the heart. In earlier years people would joke about how in other countries people start factories, and in Morocco they start cafés. Or, with so many women employed and so many young men not, people would joke about how all the men do is watch the women work from their perches in the cafés. Even the small boom in private entrepreneurship occasioned by the privatization of many public enterprises had an ironic edge, as people quipped that where once everyone started a café, now everyone starts a bank. The feeling was not eased when Yaghnik's son, now twenty-two years old, greeted me warmly, said that his father would be there in just a moment, and then sat at the far end of the café and stared into the middle distance with just that vague look of ennui and muffled anger that one so often sees on the faces of young Arab men in many other parts of the Middle East, men who do not always have enough to do to capture their energy or confidence enough in what will happen next to bestir great faith in the future.

But when Yaghnik appeared, all was transformed. Ebullient as ever, his hair now gone almost totally white and dressed in a long white gown and cap, he struck me as incredibly elegant and dear. We exchanged the news of passing years, and I learned of his movements since we met last. Yaghnik had stayed in Sefrou until 1984, where for the preceding six years he had been raised to inspector of primary school studies for the region, a job that required travel to numerous towns and villages. He had told me once of a plan for completing his full undergraduate degree through the university in Fez, and after several years and several changes in the university program, he did indeed complete his studies, with a concentration in Islamic law. He also continued his work for the trade union, and with his wife's help, he had developed his small garment business, but he had turned down an offer to become a market inspector in Sefrou even though he still maintained a house there. He had moved back to Fez and taken an ordinary teaching post in order to spend more time with his family and to provide a better education for his younger children.

During his last years in Sefrou, Yaghnik had also taken on the position of prayer leader, or *imam*, in a newly constructed mosque. He was now the imam of an average-sized mosque near his Fez apartment, and partway through our conversation he excused himself for about forty-five minutes while he went off to lead the early evening prayer. When he returned, he told me how being the leader of daily prayers is very important—even more so than delivering the weekly sermon—and he set about inquiring of a Moroccan colleague who was sharing coffee with us and who knew the United States well if there was not a need for a prayer leader among the Muslims of some part of America. It was all done with much humor and self-mockery, but there was also a clear sense of sadness and frustration over then current circumstances.

Look at this café, he said. It cost me over $1,100 just to get the permits and licenses so my son could try to make something for himself. Since even a senior teacher like Yaghnik was at that time earning somewhere between $350 and $450 per month, it was obvious that the sum expended was, for Yaghnik, quite significant. But there simply is no work for boys who don't go on with their education, he continued, and none for many of those who do. If there were work abroad, he said wistfully, I would pack and go tomorrow. The conditions that gave us the riots here in Fez are still present; nothing has changed. As we sat in the waning light, his son isolated on the other side of the café, with that distant unengaged stare, I felt the sadness that lay alongside Yaghnik's natural joy at living. Later, as he walked me to my car, he recited the genealogy of his own automobiles, from a brief flirtation with a Mercedes right back to his little Dauphine, which, patting his ample midsection, he joked would never fit him now. We agreed to meet again that Friday to continue our conversation.

Present at lunch on Friday were several other members of Yaghnik's family. Fuzia, his wife, grayer but ever warm and open, introduced us to her sister and brother-in-law, who had lived and worked in Belgium for the past twenty-seven years and, like so many others working abroad, had made their annual pilgrimage home, their car piled high with European goods, their children unsure which side of the Straits to call home. Yaghnik's younger son, aged fifteen, sat quietly with rapt attention, vaguely remembering the American who used to come visit his father. Now he sat wide eyed at talk of the Gulf War, the Saharan war, the economic war, as if all the hope that had begun to drain from his elder brother were still charged within. A young daughter was still living at home, but Yaghnik's two older daughters had married and moved to other cities; one had recently given birth to a daughter, so Yaghnik and his wife were now grandparents.

The apartment itself was on the top floor of a building just up the street from the Happiness Café. It was a four-flight walk-up that winded his younger guests, but Yaghnik took it swiftly, reminding me that, though heavy, he was still one of those big energetic men who move with a surprising turn of speed, like a rhino or a linebacker or an ordinary sedan hiding its turbocharged engine. The apartment itself was spacious and nicely furnished, in a mix of Moroccan and European styles. A clock on the wall of the living room, identical to one hanging in the apartment I had myself just rented in Fez, repeated the chimes of Big Ben every quarter hour. A cage of parakeets chattered in the background, while a lively ten-year-old mixed collie named Whiskey stared Yaghnik steadily in the eye in the certain knowledge of where his indulgence lay.

During the course of lunch I turned the conversation to the fluorescence of Islamic fundamentalism in Morocco in recent years. I knew that several fundamentalist leaders had significant followings in the country and that the king, ever the master at playing factions against one another, had kept himself in front as the preeminent spiritual and political leader by closing newspapers, imprisoning opponents, outlawing gatherings, and then reopening the papers, granting amnesties, and rebuilding opposition groups to a controllable level. Throughout his reign Hassan would repeat the advice of the Prophet's secretary, founder of the Ummayad dynasty and second caliph, Muawiya ibn Abi-Sufyan (602–80), saying: "Morocco is a country of the golden mean. Moroccans are not a people of excess. Moroccans are sometimes difficult people to lead. My father [Muhammad V]— God bless his soul—always told me: 'Morocco is a lion you must lead with a leash—he should never sense the chain.' So we spend our time adjusting: when he pulls too much, I slacken, and when he slackens, I pull a little."

But the turnout of fundamentalists in various protests, their presence among educated and uneducated alike, and the then current trial of fundamentalist medical students charged with assaulting a policeman during a demonstration had challenged the king's vaunted restraint. In a sense, I thought, Yaghnik might be very sympathetic to the fundamentalist movement, perhaps indeed part of it, given his religiosity and his frustration. His response, and that of the others present, to my inquiries showed, however, that Yaghnik's own middle course remained the guiding metaphor for his thinking.

There are, said Yaghnik, three different kinds of "fundamentalists" (the word he used, 'usuliyin, being derived from the term meaning "root" or "source"). First, there are those who follow the two main leaders of such groups here in Morocco. These people do not want relations with any of the non-Muslim countries. But this is not the era that we live in: we simply have to keep up relations with other nations just to live. To close ourselves off in the name of religion is to be out of step with the times we live in. The second kind of fundamentalist takes a position in the middle: they are sincere believers; they perform all their religious duties and are in the world as it is. For them it is a matter of balance, keeping ties to everyone and keeping faith with the religious law. It is this law that puts a boundary, a shape around things. It keeps people from becoming like the third type, those who only use religion in service of a partisan group, a political end, or the power of the state. These latter people do not really have a knowledgeable attachment to religious law: they don't study the religious texts; they are just puppets for some other purpose.

Many of the students in this country are too young, he added, to be significantly affected by the religious or political issues of the moment. But Yaghnik remained very concerned about their future. His son and daughter listened intently as he noted that the government continues to manipulate the number of students allowed to receive baccalaureate degrees each year—and a few days later the newspaper announced that of the 160,000 candidates in the 1991 cycle, 41 percent had passed, as opposed to 31, 26, 27, and 32 percent in the four preceding years. I thought, too, as he spoke of the increased chances for employment of his female students, that in an ironic way the Moroccan system may actually be working to their particular advantage. For it is a system based largely on unquestioning memorization, a feat that accords well with the image of women not presenting themselves as too challenging in the public domain. As a result, girls generally do better than boys on the exams and get a large number of the available civil service jobs. When coupled with a strict system of seniority in government posts, the result has been a substantial increase not only in the employment of women but, quite strikingly, their rise to significant positions within the bureaucracy. They still reach a "glass ceiling," with men almost always occupying the highest appointive positions. Their rise, however, has not been without moments of institutional uncertainty. For example, it was said that when a woman judge of the court of appeals in Fez was due to become chief judge on the rotational system used by that forum, the male judges sent an inquiry to the king to ask what should be done. The answer came back that they should allow her to take her turn in the seniority system but should not advertise it publicly.

Another factor contributing to women's relative success in the bureaucracy concerns the rules relating to pregnancy. When a woman gives birth to a child, she has a certain number of months to resume her position or lose it. According to all of the young women with whom I spoke around this time, no one could think of a single instance in which the woman had failed to reclaim her job. The usual pattern was to have the maternal grandmother help care for the child. So vital had the position of such wives become to family income that a cartoon in one daily newspaper showed a man marrying a woman who then tells him that she loves him so much that she is going to quit her job and devote herself to him full time, at which point the husband cries out to the departing notaries who just registered their marriage to return and quickly divorce him.

But at the time of my visit in 1991 through to our most recent encounters, dramatic changes had been occurring in Morocco, as in some other Arab countries, in terms of the birth rate. According to Morocco's High Commission for Planning, the fertility rate in the country has been halved, dropping from 7.2 children per woman in 1962 to 4.5 in 1987, 3.3 in 1994, and 2.2 in 2010—barely above the replacement level (and really below that level for urban women, whose rate is 1.8, compared to 2.7 in rural areas). Over two-thirds of women now use contraceptives, the mean age for a mother giving birth to her first child having risen by 2004 to 25.4. Only 9.3 percent of women aged fifteen to nineteen are now married, nearly 30 percent are single at age thirty-five, and the average age of marriage for women is 26.6 years and 31.4 for men, a quarter of all marriages still being to relatives. In 2004, 13 percent of all households consisted of single women, while another 3.6 percent consisted of women living alone with their children. Altogether, by 2013 22 percent of households were headed by a woman. It was noteworthy, too, that by the turn of the twenty-first century the wearing of the headscarf (*ḥijāb*) had increased among younger women but older women were seldom wearing full-face veils. In a sense, the two generations have met in the middle with a headscarf compromise. A significant contributing factor, of course, was increased levels of women's education and employment. Indeed, both Yaghnik and Fuzia were quite pleased by these opportunities for women.

Yaghnik was less sanguine about the jobs available for young men. Many, he said, try hard enough but are discouraged by lack of opportunity. As he spoke, an image came to mind of something I had encountered early and often in my visits to Morocco. Late at night you could see male students sitting on the curb under the streetlamps studying for their exams. Their presence on the streets is, of course, testimony to houses that are too crowded or noisy or hot or ill-lit. But Abe Lincoln, I thought, would have loved it. They sit alone; then, like most Moroccans, unable to stay out of touch for very long, they wander over toward a companion, then wander back, each with a notebook in hand, committing to memory. But Yaghnik knew only too well the problem they would continue to pose for the country's future.

Tickle the bottoms of those in front,
Trouble the noses of those behind,
You win if you sit with the middle kind.

—Arab proverb

There are two kinds of people in the world: the pure and the responsible.

—Archibald MacLeish

Returning to Morocco in 2008, I sensed a country adrift. Most people I spoke with were deeply troubled by the events of 9/11 but even more so by the bombings that occurred in May 2003 in Casablanca (and several less dramatic ones in the spring of 2007). Suicide bombings had been all but unknown in the country, and the fourteen men who took part in the bombings, together with several thousand arrests and numerous jail sentences, scared many Moroccans who felt this simply was not the form of moderation they imagined themselves to represent. Changes had certainly occurred. The new king, Muhammad VI, who took over after the death of his father in 1999, not only had led the movement toward changes in the family law code but appeared to favor programs to assist the poor. He also granted amnesties to many of the political prisoners his father had incarcerated during the so-called years of lead. But if in his lifetime King Hassan II was, in the words of Gary S. Gregg, an "ill-defined figure—benevolent but exacting, a lightning rod for ambivalence—[who] increasingly animates political imaginations and debates about authority and loyalty," that ambivalence had by no means disappeared with the advent of his son's reign. In some respects many people even seemed to have moved away from concerns and identity with nationwide issues and were giving greater emphasis to private life and local needs rather than expecting that their wants would be met at the national level. Whatever else, it was clear that a decade after the turn of the century the political scene was not, despite superficial analogies to other parts of the Middle East, simply reducible to polar contrasts, confidence in the monarchy as a stabilizing institution helping to maintain some sense of balance.

Yaghnik, now fully retired except for a small interest in his djellaba business, continues to represent this middle course, drawing as he always has on some of the most fundamental orientations of his culture. I was particularly intrigued when he told me, though, that he was no longer serving as an imam in his neighborhood mosque. Each Friday, he explained, there is a sermon. The government writes the sermons and expects you to deliver them just as they say. Well, I do not disagree with the general thrust of any of the sermons, but they are not put the way I would do it; I cannot use my own examples, my own ways of saying how the traditions of Islam and modern things can fit together. So I stopped being the imam.

Yaghnik's unwillingness to give up his own style of thinking about Islam is an expression of that individuality that is such a vital component of his personal and cultural orientation in life. It is not unconnected to the Moroccan focus on context, the utilization of different styles of apprehending attachments depending on the larger framework of engagement. Yaghnik has no trouble dressing in trousers in one setting and native garments in another, eating with a fork at one person's house and with his fingers at another, using money as the index of association in one dealing and interpersonal obligation in another. There is for him no disjunction when context legitimizes alternative approaches. Yet it is equally clear that these contexts are not mechanically set out and applied but are negotiable and imprecisely defined. The result is the opposite of role confusion or a sense of uncertainty and inconsistency. It is instead one of freedom to seek advantage and congruence formed by the retention of a repertoire of relational possibilities that can be called upon as required. From the overarching frame of Islam's minimalist requirements and their own cultural stress on the personal and contextual, a number of Moroccans, like Yaghnik, seem to feel that their freedom of action was ebbing away in the face of a country fraught with corruption and a diminished sense of civility.

Many of the concerns for the future of his children and grandchildren that Yaghnik expressed at the beginning of the 1990s have also been borne out in the succeeding years. In 1999 the World Bank reported that those living at the poverty level of a dollar per day in Morocco had risen from 13 percent to 19 percent in less than a decade; it was to rise to fully 25 percent by 2003. At the turn of the twenty-first century 41 percent of adult men in Morocco were still illiterate, while the rate for adult women of 57 percent, which is even greater in rural areas, is higher than that of any other Arab country, including Yemen and Somalia. Children's illiteracy was declining, though: over half of urban girls were literate and nearly three-quarters of the boys. But if women who could find a job in the bureaucracy had a high degree of security—a quarter of all such administrators and managers being women in 1997—those in trades were subject to international price fluctuations and high unemployment. The official statistic for unemployment at the turn of the century was 23 percent, having risen 5 percent in each of the few preceding years, but the real rate was undoubtedly higher. Each year during this period the economy was producing 200,000 new jobs, but 300,000 young people were entering the labor market. Yaghnik felt only too keenly that when over half the population is under the age of thirty but half of them have no job or bank account and the majority live with their parents until they are thirty-five to forty years old, it has become all the more difficult for Moroccans to achieve the one thing that marks them as adult, namely marriage and the start of a family of their own. The problem is compounded by the costs involved in getting married, although the situation is not as bad as in Egypt, where the average cost of a wedding is close to $10,000 (compared to an average annual income of $3,700). At the time of the Egyptian Arab Spring, beginning in January 2011, one could readily understand, therefore, why one young man held up a sign in Tahrir Square in the shape of a pink heart and addressed to President Mubarak reading: "Leave—I want to get married!"

Perhaps there is no better indication of the frustration Yaghnik feels than in the relation of education to employment. As the public educational system continues to deteriorate, with the children of the well-to-do abandoning the public schools to attend a wide array of private institutions, the approach to language continues to remain incoherent, with part of the syllabus in Arabic and part in French, resulting in what Charis Boutieri, in her careful analysis of the actual classroom situation, characterizes as the production of students who are illiterate in both languages. Only a fraction of the 120,000 students earning advanced degrees each year around the turn of the century could find jobs, the overall rate of unemployment for the 400,000 graduates—"the doctors of unemployment"—having risen to at least 30–40 percent. Perhaps the most stunning indication of this crisis concerns the group of blind, unemployed graduate engineers. For more than a decade these young people had been holding a daily protest on the green strip in front of the nation's Parliament in Rabat. On one occasion in the early 1990s, however, I happened to be in a taxi passing the bus station that lies on the far edge of the city when I noticed a group carrying protest signs. When I asked the driver who they were, he said they were those same blind graduates who are usually at the downtown site. When I asked what they were doing way out there, he told me that the government had loaded them on buses and told them they were being taken to the Parliament area but then they brought them here: because they were blind and the government officials wouldn't let anyone near them, he said with obvious disgust, they did not know that they were not in front of the Parliament building! When I returned to Morocco in 2008, a group was still protesting, only this time without being removed from in front of Parliament. "Black marias," like the paddy wagons in the old French films, stood just outside of view along several side streets.

The gap between rich and poor has also been proceeding apace. Essentially, it could be argued, there is no enduring middle class in most parts of the Arab world, since there is no way to pass along one's networks to an offspring or any way to ensure that, even with an education, a job will be available. Any given individual may be in the middle range of incomes in the country, but the persistence of such a position across generations is very difficult to ensure, since networks and their servicing cease when their central figure leaves the scene. Rather, the two groups growing apace in Morocco have been the very wealthy and the very poor. By 1973 Europeans had sold more than 1 million of the 2.5 million acres they owned during the Protectorate, at which point the remainder was nationalized and bought from them. Most of the land owned by Europeans had been sold, usually to the well-off, and when the remainder was nationalized and purchased from them by the government in 1973, most of that land, too, went to royal favorites. So, too, privatized government monopolies also fell into the hands of the favored. These developments were among a number of factors adding to the migration, especially of younger people, to the cities and, for those who were able, abroad, as well as to the effects on both religion and politics.

To Yaghnik these trends are both unwarranted and potentially dangerous. If some of these younger people join others in a form of Islamic renewal, it will not be with his unqualified support. Yaghnik's commitment is to Islamic learning, and he clearly finds such knowledge lacking among many who profess a return to prayer and religious law. He is not unwilling to call himself a "fundamentalist," saying that of course any true Muslim is by definition a fundamentalist, and in this regard he differs from many other strict traditionalists who insist that it is by their lights alone that one can be denominated either a good Muslim or not. Yaghnik does not care for the fundamentalists' telling him whether he is a good Muslim. He does not, therefore, agree with the Adl wa Ihsan (Justice and Spirituality) party and its founder Sheikh Abdesslam Yassine (who died in 2013), which has been formally banned but tolerated by the government. Yassine, like his vocal daughter, had at times been willing to acknowledge the monarchy, while at others he called for the king to step down, questioning both the sovereign's honesty and his alleged subservience to Western mores. As he once said, "our democracy" is not a Western democracy that "begins at pagan Athens and ends in advanced modern societies as a secularist practice, atheistic and immoral."

Rather, Yaghnik finds more attractive the willingness of the moderate, but still very Islamicist, Justice and Development Party (PJD), which has chosen to operate within the system. And though he is pleased that the Adl party turned around and supported the recent changes in the personal status code—changes, he thought, that showed its leaders do harbor somewhat greater interest in the equality of the sexes—Yaghnik still has reservations about the PJD. He is concerned, for example, that following the May 16, 2003, bombings in Casablanca, the party backed the antiterrorism laws that give further powers to the regime, and he is frightened by the PJD's version of Islam, including its opposition to music and cultural festivals. He speculates that this attitude may have accounted for the party having failed to gain as many seats as predicted when, for the first time, it put forward a full slate of candidates in the 2007 parliamentary elections. (In 2012–13, however, the party did join the government, only to find itself relatively isolated when the coalition partners left in protest against the revised constitution's continuing to deprive Parliament of any significant power.) I still support the Istiqlal party, said Yaghnik. It was founded by people from Fez who know what it is to be a Muslim, and who don't think, for example, I should be barred from walking in public with my wife. But I am not surprised that so few people came out to vote in the last elections. Our lives are not made by the politicians the way they were in the years following independence. Indeed, he concluded, the parties, whether Islamic or more secular, have not addressed the big problems of corruption and unemployment, and until they do, we may not go the way of Algeria or others, but my sons and daughters and their children after them will continue to struggle.

Yaghnik might, therefore, seem to occupy that middle ground that is always so hard to maintain in the face of extremes. It is true that fundamentalism spans a variety of social groupings, but in order to translate that orientation into a politically successful movement, such parties would need an issue or a crisis around which to group these diverse interests. At the very least something would have to happen to make moderates like Yaghnik willing to stand on the sidelines while a small group of activists take charge, by which time events will have escaped the choices moderates might otherwise have preferred be made. The violent demise of a king might serve as such an event, but (as attempts on the life of Hassan II in the 1970s and his natural death in 1999 showed) the result would probably be the intensification of individuals' local networks and broad support for a successor in the reigning line. One could also imagine some economic disruption occasioned by the mass return of migrant workers forced out of their jobs in Europe or the reignition of intense resentment occasioned by manipulations of the degree-awarding system within the Moroccan educational system. Already bribery for grades and admissions has become frequent, and as the rich withdraw from the school system and the less rich are finding it a dead end for opportunity, parents like Yaghnik could be radicalized or simply stand by while Muslim fundamentalists take to the streets and press for more sweeping reform. Alternatively, the boom in land speculation and building, which has involved almost anyone with any capital to spare, could suddenly collapse, instantly forging a very large class of similarly affected people.

In any such scenario an issue might be needed that would knit together a common sense of injury, since a common set of specific goals seems insufficient to lead most Moroccans to accept the image proffered by fundamentalists that the ordinary man is not as good a Muslim as they are. Just what narrative would trigger action is impossible to predict, but one does not need a crystal ball to suspect that, as in Tunisia and other countries involved in the Arab Spring, the narrative is likely to incorporate the sense of being sullied by the ever-increasing petty corruption that has come to suffuse every domain of daily life. An index of just how bad the problem has become is contained in the World Justice Project report of 2012–13, where Morocco ranked as number eighty out of ninety-seven countries on a corruption scale, just above India and Uganda, and just a bit worse than Mexico and Moldova.

One area where significant changes have occurred is in the laws of marriage, divorce, and other family matters. Yaghnik favors the changes that have been made over the years in this law (the *Moudawwana*). In 1993 King Hassan II had set up a commission to revise the code, but the changes produced were minor. When, in 2000, the new king indicated his willingness to make more significant alterations, women organized a march of tens of thousands in Rabat in support of the changes. This was met by well-organized Islamist opponents who rallied hundreds of thousands of marchers in Casablanca against any liberalization. For a time the king backed off. But later he convened a wide-ranging advisory group, and in January 2004 Parliament passed a revised code that grants quicker divorces at the wife's behest and changed the rules of alimony, support, property distribution, and marital age. Teams of volunteers have been organized to advise women of their rights, and female legal advisors have even been recruited by the government for this purpose. However, there are concerns that, for all its formal changes, the law may permit an even greater range of judicial discretion than before and that corruption might undermine even these legal improvements.

Yaghnik and his wife, thinking as much about their daughters and grandchildren, see in these legal changes precisely the kind of gradual but significant alteration that makes them continue to believe that Morocco can manage change without producing the chaos of neighboring countries. Fuzia recalls how the wives of Hassan II were not seen in public but his daughters were, in contrast to the next generation, where Muhammad VI's wife is a highly educated and highly visible woman. For her, each step represents the kind of gradual change she and Yaghnik feel is necessary if the country is not to fall into chaos. That confidence may be showing signs of particular strain, though. The popular magazine *Tel Quel* has referred to those like Yaghnik and Fuzia's children as a "Lost Generation," and 42 percent of youth responding to a 2013 survey indicated they would like to emigrate. Though I did not ask him, I have no doubt that Yaghnik is appalled by the fact that since 2011 there have been eighty self-immolations in Morocco, similar to that of Muhammad Bouazizi in Tunisia in December 2010 that set off the Arab Spring. Yet most Moroccans are still willing to support the monarchy and tolerate many problems with the existing system rather than risk the violence that tore Algeria apart for a decade and has affected most Arab countries subsequent to the initial hope of the Arab Spring.

On the political level, Yaghnik told me, people still feel the need to alert authorities through public protests to the danger of restricting access to the great game of seeking advantage wherever one can. This results in a pattern of rebellions rather than revolutions—public demonstrations whose message is not necessarily that one wants to change the rules of the game altogether but that one wants into the game. Moreover, events continue to be largely conceptualized as maneuvers centered on persons rather than crises centered around structural forms. It is not to the restructuring of institutions, then, that attention inevitably turns—for political institutions are themselves seen as largely an extension of the personal power of those who employ them—but to the change of personnel. Pierre Bourdieu has said that, with a degree of freedom to decide their own futures, the Algerians tended to "revolt" differently than people who feel condemned to an eternal present of exploitation: "Revolt is directed above all against persons or situations known to the individual, never against a system that it is the subject to systematically transform. And how could it be otherwise? That which is perceived is not . . . exploitation, but the exploiter; it's not even the boss, but the Spanish foreman."

Moroccans, too, continue to see matters in highly personalistic terms. Yaghnik says that he would, for example, like to see limited terms of office, but at the same time he cannot conceive of structurally limiting the powers of an office, since everything depends on the capabilities and attachments that characterize the personal connections of the officeholder. One repercussion of this political culture is that issues are easily conjoined, such as corruption and school exam changes, thus making it more difficult for groups who speak only in terms of a single issue to mobilize the middle sector of society. Men like Yaghnik, responding in their inclusionary style and with their stress on personalized networks of obligation, have thus far filled in the political middle, like water seeking its own level, squeezing out those groups at the edges from whom change and revolution often stem.

This pattern may not quite accord with the observation by Charles Gallagher that "Morocco is a land of compromise, a role forced upon it by history," since history does not predetermine reactions to events. But it is true that the Moroccan pattern of dispersing power by legitimizing quite varied means of developing obligations, by reshuffling the players as each man's network dies with him, and by attaching these assumptions to their view of Islam does suggest that it is possible that Moroccan society can absorb enormous change without necessarily exhibiting constant disruption. It is a pattern, too, that is deeply writ in the psychodynamics of men like Yaghnik. Moving from context to context focusing on the way ties are formed and (with special emphasis in his case) the moral/religious base against which all situations are themselves contextualized, Yaghnik can maintain a genuine sense of coherence among features that, from the perspective of other cultures, appear contradictory. Katherine Ewing characterizes this pattern by arguing that "as long as an individual is able to maintain contextually appropriate self-representations in interaction with others, he or she may experience a sense of continuity despite the existence of multiple, unintegrated or partially integrated self-representations." It is context, not roles, that is thus capable of being segregated by Yaghnik. One cannot avoid chaos (*fitna*) by reliance on correct role behavior, since incontestably "correct" forms of role behavior are never separable from other aspects of their possessors. Rather, for all their reference to singular features (Fassi, countryman, Jew), personalism continues to trump essentialism, one's baseline identity being readily superseded by information about one's multiple attachments.

This emphasis on the relational may also have been evident when I once spoke with Yaghnik about certain aspects of Islamic sacred art. Yaghnik acknowledges that the arabesque should not be seen as mere repetition but as evidence that choices are made at each juncture. That idea may not be so foreign to Westerners: even for us, as the novelist Ward Just has said, "the answer to chaos is repetition." Much of Western music, for example, is utterly dependent on the internal repetition of themes that nevertheless appear to have been individually chosen. But then, as Stephen Jay Gould noted, "the watchwords of creativity are . . . quirky design, and above all else, redundancy." Perhaps more striking is the recent discovery that Muslim artists understood a highly complex mathematical formula that Western scientists thought they had finally solved only a few years ago. It permits the fabrication of a mosaic of the sort found on a number of mosques, none of whose elements meet at the same exact angle yet all of which are still able to be contained within a singular framework. Perhaps the need for solving such a puzzle motivated these medieval artisans because the cosmos they were representing is indeed envisioned as one in which all men and all momentary relationships are distinctive, no two meeting in exactly the same way, yet constituting a coherent community of belief. If so, the designs are indeed manifestations of reality and prescriptions for constantly creating the way that Muslims envision the world of relationships. For Yaghnik, cleaving to such a multifarious vision means not veering too far to either side lest the fit of the parts undermines the community of believers, the *umma*, itself.

Holding to a middle path is, however, hardly unproblematic. On its face it sounds as though being positioned at the middle must be the easiest of paths. By avoiding extremes one can avoid difficult choices; by dodging pitfalls to either side one can easily prevaricate; by eschewing attachments on either hand one can claim as the high ground an imagined neutrality. In fact, the very opposite is closer to the truth. For the middle path is in fact the most difficult of passages. It demands decisiveness at every step, the capacity to knit together the seemingly irreconcilable without sacrificing principle, the ability to unite individuals and groups who often demand constant attention to their own felt sense of injury. If, following God's ultimate judgment, one must cross to one's fate on the edge of a sword, teetering between beckoning salvation and the circles of hell, so, too, traversing the middle way in life, Yaghnik knows, requires both firmness and faith.

Yaghnik somehow maintains his poise, his sense of wholeness through contextually appropriate images of himself and others, partly because the society he has known has itself been constructed by the collective imaginations of those sharing in just such a view of things. In this Yaghnik is hardly alone. A poll showed that whereas 18 percent of those surveyed in 2001 thought that political and religious life should be separated, that number had risen to 35 percent by 2007. And although Yaghnik would doubtless be among those who wish the religious to inform the political, he would almost certainly agree with those who see, even in this position, that too close an alignment of Islamic fundamentalist politics and support of a moderate monarchy is not in the nation's interest. That is also why, based on our earlier discussions I feel confident that he would disagree with the proposal made in 2013 by Morocco's Supreme Council of Ulama, the body authorized to issue religious opinions (sing. *fatwa*), that apostates should be executed, and that he would instead side with those—including, as it happens, many from the main fundamentalist parties—who rely on the Quran's assertion that "there is no compulsion in religion" in formulating his position.

But it is unclear whether the middle road will remain viable for the succeeding generation. The last time I saw Yaghnik was in the Happiness Café. As he glanced, almost furtively, at his son, I could sense the uncertainty in this ever-optimistic man. Did he see his son as if the boy were pinned in some terrestrial barzakh, and if so was the young man looking at heaven or hell, or simply a world whose rules preclude him from play? Yaghnik has always taken to heart the Quran's assertion that "we appoint you a midmost nation, that you might be a witness to the people, and thus the Messenger might be a witness to you." In the fulfillment of that assignment he has pursued a genuinely intellectual life grounded in the creativity of his religion and his own interpretations of it. Whether standing the middle ground can be passed to the next generation remains, for him and so many of his cohort, the promise and the fear of their remaining days.

Courier of the Horizons:
Hussein ou Muhammad Qadir

ⵜⵓⵍⵓⵎⵣⵓⵜ

Hussein ou Muhammad Qadir

I commend the merchants to you, for they are the couriers of the horizons and God's trusted servants on earth.

—al-Muttaqi, *Kanz al-'Ummal*

Sefrou, July 1966: Something was obviously afoot. The two groups of men who had gathered in the public garden alongside the pasha's office seemed in good humor—they even smiled and joked with one another—but their very presence and separation suggested some kind of dispute. All were countrymen, farmers by appearance, dressed in long djellabas, their soiled turbans tucked and tied in a variety of seemingly carefree ways. I was only just beginning to learn how the turn of a hem or the twist of a headcloth could indicate group attachment, but I already knew enough to realize that they all came from various fractions of the predominantly Berber-speaking Ait Youssi tribe of the Sefrou hinterland. Eager to know what was happening, and eager, too, to acquaint myself with some of the people of the countryside, I approached a man at the edge of one of the groups and asked what was going on.

He had just told me that there was indeed a dispute between the two groups about irrigation rights when a number of the other men from their group began to collect around us. Everyone wanted to explain the situation, and their overall story came out in disconnected bits and pieces, each perhaps anticipating a point he hoped would be made before the pasha or, knowing there might not be sufficient time, using my presence as a welcome chance to air his views. As they spoke, my notice was drawn to one man who stood slightly to the side. As each of them added a point or contradicted another's view, everyone would glance over toward this singular man who, with every passing remark, was gradually being edged forward toward the center. Succinctly and quietly, he would clarify an issue or add an important element. Indeed, the others seemed to be looking to him to do just this, as well as to assert his own views, and in short order he had not only allowed the others to bring out their own arguments but gave their views such coherence that all those gathered watched his responses to my questioning with open approbation.

The dispute itself was not without interest. Each side represented the water owners in one of the two branches of the irrigation system into which the river that passes through Sefrou is divided as it makes its way downstream to their gardens in an area called Beni Mansour. Because the flow of water passes first through the city, the rural administrator had ducked the dispute and insisted that it lay within the jurisdiction of the appointed mayor, in those days still called the pasha, of Sefrou proper. But as interesting as the details of their problem were, I became increasingly intrigued by the man to whom the others deferred, the man who, with such goodwill and obvious humor, with such bright enjoyment of the story and such clear admiration from his colleagues, had made me feel less an intruder than a momentary focus for their own relationships. As the group prepared to go into the pasha's office, I impulsively asked him if he might have time to stop by my apartment later and talk more with me. With a smile suggestive of both shyness and pride, he accepted my invitation.

It was not until late in the afternoon of that hot summer day, sitting on the low cushions in my apartment overlooking the square where we had met, that I began to learn about my guest. When Moroccans meet, they commonly inquire into one another's *asel*, a term that conveys much more than its literal meaning of "origin." "Asel," as we saw in the Haj's usage, implies the sources of one's nurturance, the attachments to others by which one is known, and the ways that people from that region form ties to others and apprehend the bases for a possible attachment between another and oneself. To understand Hussein ou Muhammad Qadir I had to understand what it meant that his asel was that of a Berber from a segment, or fraction, of the Ait Youssi tribe that resided in the Middle Atlas Mountains just south of Sefrou. I also had to understand how, though still a young man, he was building a reputation as a successful entrepreneur and leader.

Hussein was then in his early thirties, a hearty man whose large eyes and bright, ready smile were all the more striking against skin the color of tanned leather. He was dressed in a rough djellaba of the sort he wore in the countryside, but as he settled onto the banquettes and took some of the cold drink I offered him, he was immediately at his ease. He described in detail the irrigation dispute heard by the pasha that morning, and I was all the more struck by his articulate account of the affair. For someone whose first language was Berber, his was the most sophisticated Arabic vocabulary of all the people, Arab or Berber, with whom I had thus far worked, and his grasp of legal and economic details was as astute as that of any pro-

Hussein's village

fessional. When, near the end of the afternoon, I asked if we could work together and told him that if we did so I would insist on paying him for his time, he reached into the large leather purse he carried underneath his djellaba and pulled out several hundred dollars' worth of Moroccan currency. He said that he had just taken out another loan from the bank in town, having paid off an earlier one, and that money was not really an issue. His action was so disingenuous, so much a statement of his being involved as a real player in the game, as to be utterly without pretension. It was simply consistent with his broader account of himself, a view that stressed his relationships with others in a setting of joint ventures and the connections he had forged with the people of his own community and beyond.

Our settlement is located six or seven kilometers out of town, he said, just off the road that cuts through the high plains, over the mountains, and down to the Sahara beyond. Our fraction of the Ait Youssi tribe is known as I'awen (ee-ah-wen), of which there are three sections including our own here near Sefrou and two others at different points farther up in the high country. Our particular settlement, which is called Ait ben 'Assu, has thirty-two "tents" (households) that are home to about 350 people. We're mostly farmers and herders, but a number of us are involved in the sheep trade. We buy and sell animals all over the central part of Morocco, sometimes getting stock from as far away as the pre-Saharan zone and running them down to Casablanca or wherever the prices are good. With my father, and now sometimes just by myself, I have also bought some land downriver from Sefrou, which is how I come to be involved in this irrigation dispute.

In very short compass Hussein had touched on a series of the most vital aspects of his own identity and some of the more arcane issues surrounding the anthropological understanding of tribal organization in Morocco and elsewhere. If, in Morocco, a man's identity is the accumulated associations he has forged with others through the force of his own maneuvering and demonstration of valued traits, then many of the social and personal resources upon which Hussein draws were quickly being laid out for me. Only long and careful study with him—including accompanying him all over the Middle Atlas, and coming to know him and his kinsmen for more than four decades—could begin to clarify for me the social world in which he moved and that he was constantly helping to reconstitute.

The Berbers are, in a sense, the "original" inhabitants of North Africa. Their languages, of which several dialects are spoken in Morocco alone, are more closely related to other Afro-Asiatic languages than to the Arabic of those who brought Islam to the region shortly after the death of the Prophet in the seventh century. People often think of Islam, and Arabic itself, as having spread through conquest alone, as Arab armies fueled by religious fervor poured out of the Arabian Peninsula and gave the inhabitants of conquered territories the choice between death and conversion. But that was not true of Morocco, or indeed most other places. The relatively few Arabs who first arrived from the east could, and at times were, easily overpowered by the Berbers. Though Rome held sway for centuries and the depredations of the Carthaginian-Phoenicians before them were not without impact, the Berbers had never relinquished their own beliefs or customs. But before the arriving Muslims they gave way in religion, though never in language and culture, making their accommodation with surprising speed. There are those Arabs, of course, who still regard the Berbers as only lightly Islamized, but such a view misses an important point. For Islam was, and remains to this day, a religion that regards local practice that does not contravene the few requirements set down in the Quran not as something to be tolerated alongside the formal faith but as itself Islamic. That each converted group can find a place for its own ways *as Islamic* within a universalizing religion was and is a powerful dynamic in the spread of Islam among the cultures of Africa and beyond. For the Berbers of Morocco, once they voluntarily set themselves on the path of Islam, their fights and their alliances, their kingdoms and their political attachments were irrevocably cast in the larger framework of Islamic thought and practice.

To Hussein this Berber identity is enormously important. Like so many others, he first used the word *chleuh,* a general term for Berbers or one of the Berber dialects, with some hesitation, but when he saw that I too used it as a term of description and respect, rather than as the slur some Arabic-speakers imply, his pride and ease were further enhanced. While the distinction is almost entirely linguistic—some 45 percent of the Moroccan population speaks Berber—and most of the people in the Middle Atlas Mountains speak good colloquial Moroccan Arabic as well, Berber identity, as I was to learn, is not without its elements of historical and political revisionism and disagreement. Hussein took great pleasure in helping me to understand not only about Berbers generally but the particular history and structure of his own group of Ait Youssi, especially the subtle, constantly malleable nature of tribes as a form of political organization.

Our own settlement, said Hussein, dates from the period following the death of Caid Omar al-Youssi, in the decade just before the start of the French Protectorate. Everything was chaotic after Omar's death, and the Arab groups living in our area were eager to gain protection from the Berbers who lived nearby. Berbers are great fighters: even the women would

Westermarck's photo of Ait Youssi, 1910

come out to the battle, and if a man ran away, the women would throw some of their red henna on his clothes or face as a mark of his cowardice. As I listened, Hussein's comments recalled something similar I had found in a book published in London in 1609 in which a witness to one such conflict wrote: "For feare of this infamy few forsake the field, but either conquer their enemies, or dye like men, who are presently stripped and buried by these women which follow them." I thought, too, of the time T. E. Lawrence asked an Arab why they fought so hard, and the man replied: "Because the women are watching."

In those days, Hussein continued, we lived a bit farther up in the mountains, some in tents, and some in permanent houses. When Caid Omar died, the Arabs from the Senhadja area just outside of Sefrou came to us. Each of the three Senhadja fractions made a sacrifice ('ar) to the big men of three of our own fractions and received formal protection (mezreg) in return. My great-uncle, Hamou ou Jell, was the one to whom the Ait Genawi fraction of Senhadja made a sacrifice, and Hamou and his brothers then pledged the protection of our whole group to these Arabs. Actually, all of the protection agreements were arranged by a rich man from Senhadja, Muhammad ben Driss, who had made "gifts" to a number of his own people. When they were unable to repay him, he accepted some of their land at cheap prices. Then when Caid Omar died, Muhammad ben Driss needed protection for his own properties and those of his kinsmen. There was no agreement with us about land, but not long afterward the people of my fraction purchased property from ben Driss and some other Senhadjis, and we moved down to their area. We built our settlement in the cluster that still includes the Arabs of Senhadja and the adjacent Arabs who descend from the saint known as Sidi Youssef. One of the other I'awen groups remained at our original site, while the third bought land from their *protégés* and moved a bit closer down the road to Sefrou.

Hussein had begun his account in what I was to learn was a very characteristic manner. His way of placing matters was, in a sense, a combination of personal attachments and their enactment on a particular terrain, the very essence of that idea of *asel*, of the social sources of one's kin plus territorialized nurturance, the same piece of information people commonly seek when trying to identify another. History, for Hussein, is in no small part the history of situated persons, individuals whose connections both embody and reconfigure the relationships that people forge with one another. Indeed, that history would be meaningless without the names of individuals and groups, and some sense of where they are situated in relation to others. Just as I saw with Haj Hamed, as the people and relationships change, the layers of memory that no longer describe continuing relationships recede into a kind of generalized past that, like items in storage, meld into a jumble of past associations whose relational irrelevance erodes their recollection.

By contrast, a relationship that has a continuing impact on present associations will not only stay current, even if it predates later memories that have no ongoing influence, but will be marked with a term that differentiates it from events that no longer have relational effects. That Hussein's settlement is known by various names, including those of his own uncle and a term denominating their engagement in the sheep trade (*Boukherfan*), further highlights the centrality of a peopled place in the identity of each individual's personally fashioned network of attachments. Hussein's approach to his group's history, then, is littered with names he draws upon to show their currency for the present, such that as one uncovers other referents in the literature or the memory of older men, his own process of structured amnesia reveals a good deal about how he employs history to legitimate or explain the present.

Although documentary sources on the history of the Ait Youssi tribe are rather limited, the few that I was able to find do give a fairly clear and characteristic picture of the relations of power that not only confirm the outlines of Hussein's oral history but summarize much of the story of Morocco during the past few centuries. Sources dating back to the twelfth century refer to the Arab tribe of the Beni Hassan, but it was not until the sixteenth century that, owing to pressures from other Saharan-based groups, that tribe began to push into the Middle Atlas Mountains. Behind them came a succession of Berber tribes, principally the Ait Idrassen confederation, who over the years ebbed and flowed along a roughly north–south axis, seldom able to sustain collective action and often engaging in feuds with one another and the dynasts who attempted to assert their taxing power over them. At times they agreed to serve as nominal guardians of caravan routes; at others they expressed even more independence than usual and joined in the overthrow of one monarch or another. By the middle of the seventeenth century, however, under the lash of the great sultan Moulay Ismail, who consolidated the Alaouite dynasty that reigns to the present, the Ait Youssi Berbers were further encouraged to migrate from their center in the high Moulouya region near Algeria to settle in the mountains south of Sefrou. There, various Arabic speakers became embedded among the Berber speakers, sometimes employing their emphasis on saint veneration or claims of descent from the Prophet to influence the practices and beliefs of the local tribes. As one sultan followed another, a pattern had become reasonably well established: the Ait Youssi constituted an essentially Berber accumulation of rather independent localized fractions with Arabic speakers and Jews simultaneously intermixed yet retaining their distinctive language, customs, and forms of association.

Much of this history has, understandably, been turned into a kind of stylized legend by Hussein and his fellow Ait Youssi, as well as by the people of Sefrou. Hussein himself had told me that in the days of the maraboutic "saint" Sidi Youssef ben Hamed Senhadji, for whom the neighboring settlement of Sidi Youssef is named, the inhabitants of the region were indeed an Arab tribe called the Beni Ahsen. When Berbers from the Sahara began to prod the borders of these Arabs' land, he said, the people came to Sidi Youssef and asked him what they should do. "The land wants the Berbers," replied Sidi Youssef. So, Hussein concluded, the Arabs packed up and moved down to the coast, where they live to this day.

This version of events, though highly condensed, nevertheless contains a series of subtle implications. It reasserts the natural conjunction of land and people, an almost "manifest destiny" associated with the Berbers' arrival in the region. It also ratifies their presence through the validation of the local saint, thus adding to the royal mandate they had received as protectors of the caravan routes the spiritual acknowledgment of the Arab patron saint of the immediate area. In its broader form it even underscores the appropriateness with which groups coalesce and fractionate, move and settle in that constant flow of renegotiated ties that lies at the heart of tribal organization, both past and present. And it suggests that the basis for alliance may lie at different levels for different social and political purposes, so that the boundaries of attachment and conflict may vary as the situation and those at their center vary. It is this last feature that is key to an understanding of Hussein's account of Berber tribal organization.

All the people in my settlement, he said, except for those who have married in from the outside, are related to me through my father. Hussein began his familial account in a very organized way, and for a while I thought I was following it. The Arabic word 'adam and our Berber word ighes both mean "bone," he said, and the people related in this line usually live together, help one another, and share a common name. Since our more distant relatives share common descent from a number of "grandfathers," we think of them as people with whom we share a basis for mutual help. In our case the two groups (here Hussein used the term fkheda, which means "thigh") who live farther up the mountains share with us the name of I'awen, and we assist each other in various ways. At a still more inclusive level we all belong to the Ait Youssi "tribe," called a qebila in Arabic, or thaqabilt in Berber.

As I listened to Hussein, all this seemed simple enough; whether through bodily images of bone and thigh or broader metaphors of fraction or tribe, the sense of greater distance and wider inclusion seemed quite straightforward. The problem came only a moment later, when Hussein started to refer to his local descent group, what anthropologists usually call a lineage, by the term he just seemed to be using for the more distantly related group who shared a "grandfather" somewhere back in time (a clan?), and then, just when I thought groups were being sorted in a hierarchy of ever greater extensiveness, he confused me by referring at times to groups at any level of inclusion as "tribes." If a neat array of nested groups, owing duties or holding resources in common, was in some sense being set forth in this kinship system, how could this constant switching of referents make any sense? And if I pushed Hussein to a level of apparent consistency with which he might be uncomfortable, how could I distinguish some highly idealized system from the one within which he operates on a daily basis?

As I worked with Hussein and many others, what initially appeared to be a structure whose "rules" were shot through with exceptions began instead to appear more like a repertoire that had distinct regularities but at whose heart lay precisely that element of malleability that allows both creativity and structure for ordinary individuals as well as highly skilled players like Hussein. The existence of multiple names for different groupings, the opportunity to characterize a more inclusive level of association by the qualities ideally associated with close dependents, and the frequent reconfiguration of associations on an interpersonal basis began to seem less like a nested collection of Russian dolls than a set of tools or an array of possible outcomes that individuals draw upon and negotiate intensely among themselves. Jacques Berque summarized a number of these features when he wrote:

> Each tribe, each group tries to keep its way of life uncommitted. The move-
> ment of tribes and flocks is governed not only by immemorial custom, but
> also by human calculation. The very obstacles it encounters make it more
> deliberate. . . . Hence all the vicissitudes of the story, the constant oscillation
> between deliberation and violence, anarchy and the rule of chiefs, a particu-
> larist and a universalist culture. . . . Between the theory of ancestral unity and
> the real divergence of origins there is a vital contrast. . . . The diversity of
> names, which drives topographers to despair, contrasts with and counter-
> balances the homogeneity of ways of life, and the slight differences which,
> within each group, disrupt and yet confirm these similarities.

Hussein exemplified many of these propositions when he began to describe his actual ties with others. The people of our settlement rely on one
another for a lot of everyday things, he said, but most of the time other
fractions of I'awen or other local groups are just as important. For example,
the maintenance of the irrigation system, which runs through lots of other
groups' land, means we all have to work together. There is also a small
shrine between two of the settlements where people gather for a ritual
meal once a year, though we mostly go to the celebrations at Sidi Lahsen
Lyoussi, the patron saint of the whole Ait Youssi tribe. We even have some
sheep and goats that have been donated for the upkeep of our mosque,
for helping poorer members of the group, or to fund burials. In the old
days the income would sometimes be used to purchase a warrior's horse
and arms if he couldn't afford them himself, or to pay a poor warrior's
bridewealth so he wouldn't feel he could only afford to marry if he moved
outside the group. We have a Quranic school (*msid*) for the little children,
and the men of each "tent" (*khima*)—the households that make up the
settlement (*jema'*)—decide how much each should contribute according
to his ability. Last year (1965), of the thirty-two "tents" in our settlement,
eleven (including me) paid 450 rials each, four paid 300 each, ten paid
200 each, and the remainder paid smaller sums. Early on, a lot of fractions
also had common grain storage places, but that wasn't true for us. Each
"tent" always had its own stores. No matter how hard times get, there is
no borrowing of grain between households: if you need some grain, you

must buy it from someone else. Borrowing is no good because people borrow one thing, then another, then another and often will not pay you back
or will leave you with too little for yourself. For many things, though, you
always need allies beyond your own group.

Before the French arrived, Hussein continued, it was especially necessary to form defense arrangements with other groups. The members of our
own fraction, who lived in the same settlement and were closely related,
would go to more distant relatives, and speaking to them in terms of the
close ties we had to one another remind them of our expectation of help.
It would all be done by one of our "big men," someone who had personal
ties to these people, in the same way that I now keep in touch with some
of these distant people so we can help each other with buying and selling.
Sometimes someone would come to you, as they still do, and say "we are
close kinsmen" (and they use the term for people who have a common
"grandfather") and ask all sorts of "favors" from you. If you want to do
it, you accept their use of that term, but if you aren't that eager for the arrangement, you may tell them, "You are members of the such-and-such"
(and you use the name that implies a more distant grouping), and they
get the idea you aren't so interested in being obliged to them or vice versa.
Nowadays it is about politics and marriage and business arrangements;
earlier on, that sort of thing was often about war or the payment of blood
money.

In the old days, Hussein said, if one man killed another, whether a kinsman or an outsider, there had to be a payment of blood money (called *diya*
in Arabic, or *dith* in Berber). It had to be an intentional killing (*b-niya*): If
a couple of guys were just horsing around and one of them fell and died,
that didn't require payment of blood money. If the deceased was from his
own fraction or one very close, the murderer usually ran away, often to
a group with whom his people had a mutual aid pact (*uṭada*), making a
sacrifice to ensure their protection (*mezreg*). Or he might take sanctuary in
the shrine of Sidi Lahsen Lyoussi. The *jemaʿ*, the heads of household of the
deceased's settlement, would come in force to the *jemaʿ* of the murderer
and demand the *diya* or threaten that someone from the murderer's group
would be killed in retribution. If the killer could afford it, he would pay the
blood money himself. In those days some fractions used a fixed amount,
about 100–120 animals, half of them sheep and the other half goats. Others negotiated the sum based on the murderer's own wealth, not on the
standing of the person who was killed.

Customs did vary even within the Middle Atlas region. Although Hussein did not mention it, a man from the area where the irrigation dispute

that prompted our first meeting told me that among his people, as else-where in Morocco in those days, a woman from the murderer's people could be paid to the fraction of the deceased as a form of the *diya*. It was re-ferred to, he told me, as "giving a soul (*ruḥ*) for that of the murdered man." Such a woman was wedded to a close male relative of the deceased, but without any bridewealth payment (*sdaq*) being made. When the woman gave birth to a son and had finished nursing the child, she had the right to return to her own group. If the husband wanted her to stay, he would have to make a bridewealth payment for her unless it was waived by her father. If the husband died before the wife gave birth to a son, she would become the wife of another close male of that family or, if none existed, be returned home. Something similar applied, he added, when a husband died without violence. The husband's heirs would arrange her remarriage, the bridewealth going to any children of the deceased, while if a woman ran away to be with another man, the husband had to point him out pub-licly, and the man had to pay the husband at least what he had given the girl's father in the first place. If all this did not happen, violence and the *diya* might kick in.

If a blood money payment was agreed upon, Hussein continued, but the murderer couldn't afford to pay it himself, he had to rely on his kins-men to raise the money. The big men of the *jema'* would decide how much each member of the fraction had to contribute to the *diya*, again each ac-cording to his wealth, not how closely related he was to the murderer. Only the person who was most affected by the killing—or his heirs in the proportions set by the law of inheritance—received the payment; blood money wasn't shared with other members of the dead man's kin group. If the *diya* wasn't paid, the family of the murdered man would wait their chance and kill a man from the close kin of the murderer, if not the mur-derer himself. Sometimes a man would stay away for years, even his whole life, never returning if the *diya* had not been accepted or a settlement made.

All this happened in our own "family" in the days after Caid Omar died. My mother's brother, from the Ait Chou, was killed by a man from the Ait Bouteyeb, both of them fractions of I'awen. The killer packed up his tent and gathered his family and immediately ran away. He took his family— that is to say, they were eager to go—because the score could have been evened by killing any of the males of the murderer's kin group. I've heard that the dead man's family refused a cash settlement and that sometime later the brother of the dead man surprised and killed a member of the murderer's own family. Others say that big men of the tribe agreed among themselves to a settlement (*sulḥ*), and a *diya* was paid. Maybe both parts are true. The important thing is that members of a lineage (*ighes*) had to support each other in such instances; more distant relatives, even friends or allies, might be asked to contribute, but that depended on your own ties to them.

Several pieces of the puzzle were now beginning to fall into place. Clearly, from the description of Hussein and many others, and with the support of numerous documentary sources and comparative studies of tribes elsewhere in Morocco and beyond, it became apparent that the interaction of territory and kinship, as influenced by the actions of singular figures, was crucial to the way people and groups took shape. But the range of possibilities—the recognizable and acceptable forms of permissible relationship—was deeply influential in these maneuvers. This appeared increasingly true as I traced the types of alliances people could make with one another in Ait Youssi social history.

From Hussein's accounts it became possible to see that in pre-Protectorate times there was, broadly speaking, a fluctuating emphasis on multiple bases of intratribal affiliation and the imposition of sufficiently centralized political control, so that the wide array of available alliances could lie dormant until other events or other personalities might precipitate their utilization. So, for example, genealogical proximity might form a foundation for regularized expectations of assistance in minor disputes or the payment of blood money, while territorial ties might either supplement or trump kinship if someone could capture the terms of the relationships or events in such a way as to give them priority. "Your neighbor who is close is more important than your kinsman who is far away," says a proverb common to both Arabs and Berbers. It was, therefore, far from uncommon for outsiders—whether through intermarriage, flight from one's group of origin, or genealogical manipulation—to become incorporated within a tribal fraction of the Ait Youssi. Rates as high as 70 percent have been reported for the inclusion of strangers in High Atlas tribes, and doubtless very high figures would apply at different times and regions in Hussein's territory as well.

In a system of such open texture, where each must guard his own well-being and bear some responsibility for those nearby, the concept of a neighbor thus goes well beyond physical proximity. Numerous arrangements, hedged with supernatural ritual, reflect this emphasis. For example, mutual labor agreements, based on either kinship or locality, continued to be important in the days when Hussein and I first met. Indeed, Hussein had actually performed labor at the area where the irrigation dispute occurred to firm up his ties to those people. Unlike those who trace descent to a saint or seek legitimization in a dynastic line, ordinary Moroccans give genealogy rather little emphasis, its terms being more like available templates that the clever builder of a network of ties can draw upon in forming and legitimating his set of dependencies. Similarly, there were formal agreements that were made for mutual protection or precipitated only in the event of warfare involving larger confederations of localized groups. Several of these are still referred to by men like Hussein and could have considerable currency as circumstances demand.

One form of alliance is known as an *uṭada*, Hussein explained. It was formed between two or more "fractions" (though here he used the term *qebila*, which can imply a clan that specifies precise descent to a specific ancestor or a tribe claiming generalized descent from some eponymous predecessor); such pacts were never just between individuals. The original formation of an *uṭada* pact is hedged round with an extremely strong form of the 'ar, he said, which like its other manifestations—for example, a sacrifice intended to obtain the protection or intercession of a saint—will bring about God's punishment if violated. Again, such agreements were always instigated by a big man on behalf of an entire group. Representatives of the groups would meet and exchange turbans or cloaks, which, like a sacrifice, is also called an 'ar and carries enormous supernatural power. In fact, Hussein added, long ago, when some of these pacts were formed, the men of each group would suck on the breasts of the old women of the other group as part of the 'ar ritual. For some groups—though not us—the *uṭada* was so strong a form of alliance that you were not supposed to marry within the pact or even to trade with one another so as to avoid possible conflicts. Oaths would be taken on one's commitment as an *uṭada*-mate, and if a dispute occurred within one of the contracting fractions, a big man from the other group would render judgment on it.

The agreements could have various purposes. Sefrou has been our main market for a very long time, Hussein said, and we have always needed to be able to go there on Thursdays to buy and sell. Sometimes the agreement made between various tribes or fractions was to ensure the peace of the market, as, for example, when various groups would agree that none of their people would fight while in the weekly market. If men who had disputes met there, they would just walk away from each other or risk very heavy fines, even death, at the hands of their own fraction-mates. Or the agreement might concern free and unimpeded access to a given road or might be established to secure a general peace in their home regions. Most important, Hussein emphasized, these alliances committed both groups to mutual defense. Again, these pacts were mainly initiated or revitalized when there was chaos in the countryside, and their defensive purposes might, in peacetime, be replaced by other forms of mutual aid. When I asked Hussein for an example, he mentioned several.

Not long ago, he said, there was an election for a minor political office. A man from over in the Ait Khalifa area was running for the post. He came to our I'awen group and got us to promise support based on our being *uṭada*-mates. Later, when he realized that he had no chance of winning and wanted to pull out in time to get his deposit back, he made a deal with another man to hand his votes over to this second guy. But when he came to us and asked us to turn over our support to this new man, we felt no obligation to do so because the new guy wasn't from a group with whom we had an *uṭada* pact. Only some of our people gave him their votes; most of us voted for someone else. When I asked Hussein if he would feel obliged to give an *uṭada*-mate a loan, for example, he said: If he is known to be an honest man, you would definitely lend him the money because otherwise God will punish you—maybe not right away, but eventually. But if you think he isn't really reliable, you would just tell him you are a bit short at the moment and can't help out. Often, he added, if someone moves to town, he will seek out an *uṭada*-mate and ask his help in getting settled, and usually some form of assistance is forthcoming. Intermarriage had also been common to strengthen these pacts, and people still have a tendency to seek marriage partners from an allied group, just as they may now use this attachment as a basis for establishing a commercial relationship.

War chiefs also were crucial in this pre-Protectorate period. The leader of a settlement/lineage like Hussein's (the man himself being referred to as an *ahemil*, or "bearer") was often allowed, on the strength of the abilities and connections that brought him this recognition, to commit everyone to a mutual defense agreement. At a higher level, a war chief (at this level called an *amghar*) would be picked on an ad hoc basis to lead a whole range of groups in battle, as for example against the invading French in the early years of the Protectorate. Such a special-purpose confederation might also serve to guarantee safe passage for caravans or to broaden the range of protection that a particular *ahemil* wished to give to a Jewish trader. Alliances of this sort depended entirely on the big men who brought them into existence, and after one of them died, it would only hold together if there was some equally forceful person who could effectuate their continuation.

All of these forms of alliance, I could see, were—and, to the extent that they have a role or analogues at present, are—characterized by their personalistic and situational nature. As several scholars put it fifty years ago: "The effects of a [pact of alliance] are strictly personal and do not extend to the family of the linked individual. Consequently, upon the death of one of them, the pact ends, and the other party is freed from any obligations." I also remembered coming across a statement, while preparing for fieldwork, by T. E. Lawrence: "Arabs," he said, "believe in persons, not in institutions." Like so many of Lawrence's assertions, this one is both true and untrue. Of course there are institutions—the mortmain property system, the judges and scholars of the law, the monarchy itself—but for Hussein and others the idea of persons as utterly separable from their various roles is contrary to the way they orient themselves in the world. When I once referred to American judges who say they are ruling contrary to their personal beliefs, Hussein, like so many others, began a series of Socratic questions: Who is this man? Where is he from? Who is he connected to? The thrust was clearly to show that if I did a proper search for information about the judge, I would not find any contradiction in his statement, since a man is not an accumulation of separable roles but an indissoluble composite of all his traits and ties. The self, in this view, is not fractionable. Hussein's way of putting it is to say that a man always has his senses alert to everything around him and that it is the whole man who attaches himself as needed to better himself and those dependent on him. People may occupy positions, then, but it is as whole persons, not sets of roles, by which they are known.

Moreover, Hussein made it clear on many occasions that not only does the person make the position but the ambivalence that attends any individual's qualities and powers carries over into every realm of social and religious life. So, for example, a descendant of a saint, like those living nearby at Sidi Youssef to whom Hussein's predecessors had given protection, may be called upon to act as an intermediary in a dispute and will bring the supernatural attachment he claims to bear on the legitimacy of their intervention. But *who* the particular man is, whom he is attached to, and how he has acted on other occasions will be far more decisive than spiritual descent alone. Indeed it will be these worldly effective features that demonstrate that the spiritual power said to have been passed to him (when, for example, his predecessor ritually spat upon him) actually took. It is, in a sense, a system in which you are only as good as your last performance, since the power of a saint or a king who claims descent from the Prophet himself can dissipate as surely as it must be corralled.

Indeed, no one is beyond the ambivalence shown to all forms of power. This quality is revealed, for example, in the attitude toward enemies, who are rarely pushed to destruction, since they may become allies at a later time. As John Waterbury has put it, Moroccans have "an acute sense of the temporary nature of victory." So, too, when I saw the descendant of a Saharan saint come through a rural market one day carrying the flag of his brotherhood and imperiously demanding contributions from every man he approached, it was not surprising to see that, after reluctantly shelling out a few coins, each man in turn mumbled something negative as the "saint" departed. People also only half-jokingly refer to the pure white birds that follow a man plowing a field eating the insects he has dug up as *marabouts* (saints or their descendants) because, they say, the farmer does all the hard work and the "saints" take the benefits without even getting themselves dirty. The same ambivalence is expressed about powerful political figures and even one's domineering relatives.

In earlier times, in various parts of North Africa, ritual reversals underscored this ambivalence to power. In some marriage rituals, for example, the bridegroom would first be dressed as a woman and then gradually transformed into a man; in the ritual appointment of a student as sultan for a day, the young man could command a favor from the real sultan. Other examples abound: in times of drought men may have been obliged to wear women's clothes, judges may have been stoned and beaten, women (sometimes quite naked) might form opposing teams in a game, and the coffins of saints could be turned upside down and the flag covering their tombs taken outside and destroyed. This aspect of the tribal structure, in which power is leveled lest it become too consolidated, or in which the powerful may be temporarily humbled in order to bring divine benefits to the people, is a recurring theme through many North African tribal systems. The model may even have been the Prophet's act of turning his garment in asking God to change an existing circumstance. Inversion and ambivalence may be separate or conjoined elements of seeking alteration and underscoring the need for limitation, each having the effect of reinforcing the constraints placed on existing power.

One can, then, speak of tribes in organizational terms. But one can also entertain the idea of a set of features commonly associated with tribal organization that may be referred to as a "tribal ethos." For just as one need not be a Protestant to exhibit aspects of the Protestant work ethic, so, too, one may or may not be a member of an actual tribe yet manifest some of the features associated with that set of political forms. Indeed, the ethos associated with tribes may even suffuse the broader society to whose formation they have been integral. Tribes, in this sense, often place structural limits on power, using various leveling devices—gossip, jokes, proverbs, rituals, structured rotations—toward this end. In addition, this ethos holds that no one can claim to be morally superior to any other ab initio, that reciprocity is inherent in all relationships, and that roles commonly crosscut relationships to bind society together. Regarding all power and all persons ambivalently does not render action beyond accomplishment, but it does limit power being fixed in particular social units or automatically passed from one generation to the next. Thus many of Hussein's own actions that would seem internally contradictory can only be understood against that very ambivalence to power that is integral to his, and many other Moroccans', idea of freedom.

While this ambivalence to power characterizes both Arabs and Berbers, other features are more distinctive to Berber custom and structures. During the months following our first meeting in the mid-1960s I had begun to work in the local court, and I asked Hussein about the role that Berber law once played in the organization of his fraction and the larger Ait Youssi tribe. Usually, said Hussein, everyone knows who has done what—it's a small place—and you just take care of things among yourselves. Now, with gendarmes and police and people moving around a lot, big things go to the government, and Berber custom isn't involved. But all through the French period, especially when the French tried to split the Berbers from the Arabs by trying to put us under Berber law and the Arabs under Islamic law, and until Berber law was eliminated altogether at the time of independence in 1956, Berber law mattered a lot. It is gone now, replaced by state law, he said without regret: "What is past is past and what is missing is known only to God," we say. But when Berber law was active, if, in trying to decide among the parties to a dispute, you didn't know what actually happened, you would have to use a group of people swearing an oath. It worked like this:

If someone made an accusation against another, the accuser would pick one man from the lineage of the accused, who in turn would pick four others from that fraction to take an oath alongside the man first chosen. It didn't matter who the four were: the key was the lead oath taker, called a *noqran*. You would always pick a man who was respected, who had lots of ties to other people, who wouldn't risk taking a false oath because he feared God and didn't want people to distrust him. If five oath takers couldn't be found, the guilt of the accused was presumed, and he had to return, say, the stolen item or pay the equivalent of its value and maybe a small fine. People who thought he was guilty would rather help him pay the money than take a false oath. But if the coswearers were willing to take the oath, they would go on a Friday to the mosque or a saint's shrine, take the oath—the *noqran* being the first to swear—and the accuser would have to be satisfied that the accused was indeed not guilty. Formerly, said Hussein, the coswearers could be from any I'awen group, because it was really one lineage (*fekheda*). But once we split up physically, the oath takers had to come from your own localized fraction.

Hussein's account was wonderfully reminiscent of those forms of fact finding that occurred in numerous cultures in the past, including medieval Britain and Europe. One feature that makes the Berber custom so distinctive, however, is that it was not just a form of group swearing but one in which the accuser chose the lead oath taker from the accused's own associates. It demonstrates how important it is for a person to balance his local (usually kin-based) ties with alliances made beyond, and how a man's "word" (*klam*)—his assertions and hence his worldly consequent ties to others—are put into play in such an event. It was almost as if such trustworthiness, rather than the guilt or innocence of the accused, were the central concern of the process. As we saw in the use of reliable witnesses described by the Haj in the Islamic law courts, it is not the oath that makes the person believable but the other way around.

And yet, Berber law has all but died out. In the former Spanish zone of Morocco it had been assiduously eliminated in the 1920s under the lash of the devout, if ultimately unsuccessful, rebel Abdel Krim, while in the rest of Morocco it was given minor deference by the central government for a short while after independence. But perhaps it was because Berber law was so much aimed at containing internal conflict that, when it was able to, the independent Moroccan state saw this role as indispensable to its own functioning, and Berber law lost its purchase. I had assumed, therefore, that Hussein was correct when he said that coswearing had already ceased to exist in the postindependence period. But I was later to encounter Berbers from other fractions farther up in the mountains who told a different story. They said that as late as the early 1970s an accused might go to the government-appointed sheikh, and if he and others felt that it would not be good to bring the police into the matter, they could agree to use coswearers. Whether this rather surreptitious practice has continued in some few areas I cannot say with certainty. But that the forms were remembered and admired may mean that some elements of Berber law—a highly developed system that often involved written codes and specialized lineages of experts—may not be wholly forgotten in the Middle Atlas region. On the other hand, the fact that the Berbers have relinquished a system of law that operated for centuries in favor of a national law may be yet another example, along with malleable group identification, of specific forms receding for a time while the more generalized tribal ethos remains dormant or displaced.

Hussein had, by his account of the structure of the Ait Youssi tribe and its constituent segments, also raised some very fundamental issues about tribal organization that have exercised anthropologists for decades. Tribes are extraordinarily fascinating forms of political organization. For all their diversity, they display some common approaches to various questions of political organization: How is power conceptualized in such systems, and how does it relate to the concept of the person that appears evident in a number of domains of the social and cultural life of those sharing in a common identity? How shall mechanisms be constructed so that people are bound in various ways across a multiplicity of relationships, thus holding the tribe together when necessary but not so restricting the ways power can be acquired that it can fall under the permanent control of the few? And how, in the case of North Africa, shall a religion at once universalizing and highly localized fit with this distribution of power? The answers offered by social scientists have been quite varied, and North Africa has, as a result of the interests of some who have studied it, become a major site for testing alternative theories.

Morocco became an intellectual battleground in this regard for Western scholars when Ernest Gellner, who was bringing his work in Morocco to fruition about the same time I first met Hussein, formulated his assessment of these tribes' organization. A British philosopher of Czech background, Gellner had found in Morocco the opportunity to test one of the fundamental questions that had long exercised central European political philosophers, namely: How is anarchy possible? He had found in the writings of the British anthropologist E. E. Evans-Pritchard, who had studied the Nuer of the Sudan, and in the work of a French sociologist of Morocco, Robert Montagne, the framework he sought to test in his own research in the High Atlas Mountains.

Evans-Pritchard had argued that tribes like those of the Nuer of southern Sudan were, at least ideally, organized by a principle of segmentary opposition: less inclusive kin groupings, which might fight among themselves, were allied at ever higher points on the genealogical charter, such that at the highest level an entire tribe could be mobilized for common purposes. The balanced opposition of less inclusive kin groups maintained order without any overarching authority through such diverse mechanisms as the rules of feuding, the constraints of intermarriage, the use of religious and nonsaintly mediators, and the implications of violating interlocking affiliations. Such mechanisms for limiting violence could, it was argued, thereby perform the work that might otherwise be accomplished by a centralized government. For Gellner this was an appealing paradigm:

it fit both his intellectual affinity for singular principles informing diverse forms of real political life—he was soon to write a book declaring himself a proponent of monism and a strong opponent of pluralism in philosophy—and it seemed a real-world solution to the question of anarchy's possibilities. When, in his book *Saints of the Atlas*, he was to give his full analysis, one could see how he thought that the saintly lineages present in Morocco could be inserted between fractions, thus balancing hostilities that commonly occurred at various levels of segmentary consolidation and fractionation.

Accounts like the one Hussein had been offering, however, gave me some pause, as it concerned this argument for segmentarity. If that model really described common practice, why were the terms Hussein and others applied to these units so varied in their actual referents, sometimes relating to one level of inclusiveness and sometimes to quite another? Why, when I began to ask about specific historical and contemporary alliances, did it so often turn out that it was not a case, to borrow the classic formulation, of "me and my brother against my cousin and both of us against an outsider," but of "me and a distant relative (or even an unrelated neighbor) against my close kinsmen (or even my brother)"? Gellner's own account included very few specific case studies of alliance, and he frequently spoke of "kinks" in the system, instances where segmentary alignment was hardly automatic. Evans-Pritchard himself had referred to segmentarity as an "idiom," thus suggesting that it was far from being a self-executing mechanism. Indeed, as I began to see evidence in a host of domains of the constant negotiability of relationships—negotiations that were themselves highly regularized but not restricted to genealogical proximity alone—the segmentary model began to slip through my fingers.

Of course it could be true that such a model existed in the past, that Hussein was living at a time, following French conquest and the bureaucratization attendant on national independence, when the old tribal ways no longer applied. But that did not fit his account any more than it fit those found in the older literature or more contemporary arrangements I was to witness. The sources and the descriptions of elders from many parts of the country clearly showed the centrality of individual persons in the fabrication of networks of interdependence, and everything—from the sliding-scale referents to the manipulations of claimed attachments in disputes both past and present—suggested that this was not a matter of historic change alone. Indeed, other anthropologists had been arguing, for example, that segmentarity might work predominantly as an adaptation to the expansion of groups into new territories, a useful tactic because kin-based groupings could maintain their own separateness yet call on more distant kin to assist them as they moved into the territory of alien peoples. Morton Fried had even argued that tribes do not come into existence unless confronted by a state: until such moments the main political unit is the band of localized kin. At the same time, research in the Sudan and elsewhere was beginning to suggest that even Evans-Pritchard may have seen the Nuer at a particular expansionist moment in their history, that the theories of British anthropologists of the mid-twentieth century were affected by the fear that the discipline might fall back into the errors of an earlier social evolutionism and that it was this fear that precluded them from developing theories of change that focused on the histories of the people they were studying. When the segmentary model also seemed to some of the political scientists studying Morocco at this time, most notably John Waterbury, to suggest analogues to the way the king played political groupings off against one another, the idea of segmentarity took root in the discussions among Moroccanists and students of Middle Eastern societies more broadly.

But the account of Hussein and many others suggests a rather different view not only of Moroccan tribes but, as one studies the matter comparatively, of tribes as a family of political forms more generally. Far from being sharply delineated and structurally exact, tribes have qualities that make them a great deal more flexible in shape and disposition. Indeed, they are quite malleable, fashioning themselves to fit the context of the moment. The typical colonialist approach—"take me to your leader"—may, in many cases, precipitate someone who appears as the group's headman, but that is only because leaders may be cast up for special purposes or because they are really only spokesmen and not the central nodal points in a set political structure.

Similarly, as groups move across the landscape or encounter changing political climates, localized kin groups and their larger coalitions will commonly shape themselves to fit the new context. Thus Hussein also described situations in which people who were "always" Ait Youssi but who were at a given moment involved in a land dispute that brought them into closer alliance with an adjacent tribe would simply claim to be of that latter tribe all along and, owing to the care taken in forming their ties, they were then able to make the claim stick. At the individual level, as Robert Murphy found to be true among the Tuareg of Niger, "kin terms may be adapted to conduct rather than conduct to terms." In other instances, as Hussein pointed out, a whole kin group may redefine itself as the need to cast up a leader, to take on a given political shape, or to achieve a tactical advantage called for reconfiguration. Analogies are always dangerous, but I came to think of tribes as being less like crystals than like amoebas for their quality of shape-shifting. Amoebas are not without defining capabilities, though, any more than are tribes. It is just that it is an error to focus on their momentary form rather than on the qualities that allow for a particular range of reshaping without loss of overall integrity.

There may, of course, be a highly adaptive aspect to this form of organization, an aspect that does not, however, have to lead us back to a simplistic evolutionary view. Here another analogy comes to mind, that of a wallpaper pattern design. If the tip of a triangle is cut off, whatever else may be true of it, the figure is no longer a triangle. But if a pattern is replicated innumerable times, and then a portion, even the vast majority of the design, is lost (by disease, conquest, migration, or the like) the fundamental design remains and may be rebuilt. Whether in Morocco or elsewhere, this malleability and capacity for potential replication may thus be quite fundamental to an understanding of tribes as a class of political forms. Small wonder, then, that the seeming repetition of the arabesque should serve as the model for a world in which reconstitution from decimation was all too frequently necessary.

From our earliest conversations, then, Hussein's descriptions were consonant with some of the general features to which scholars of tribal organization have pointed and some of the wider features of Moroccan political culture that may contain a tribal element. Pierre Clastres, in his *Society against the State*, for example, argued that societies that do not have state structures actually strive to negate power: they have, he says, a "premonition that power's transcendence conceals a mortal risk for the group, that the principle of an authority which is external and the creator of its own legality is a challenge to the culture itself." Although a number of Clastres's characterizations do not fit the Moroccan case (and most are put in rather romanticized terms), it is true that, as Hussein's own account clearly reveals, a leader may indeed be cast up for a purpose, and people may place themselves under his direction for a time. As soon as the crisis passes, though, and sometimes before, the competition for alliances is renewed, and power is rendered vulnerable to whoever can grasp aspects of it next. In this sense, Hussein's tribe is less like those that are exceptionally small and more like that amoeboid form that is capable of varying its shape depending on the larger polity with which it may have to contend.

Various political commenters have also seen "tribal" elements in the structure of current political cultures of the Middle East. A number of them, however, use the concept with little explanation and less precision. Thomas L. Friedman, in his Pulitzer Prize–winning book *From Beirut to Jerusalem*, concludes that the internal political maneuverings of disparate factions in Lebanon, at least at the time he was reporting on them, are explainable in terms of tribalism. But he offers neither an analysis of tribal political forms nor an extended discussion of the meaning of this statement in the Lebanese context. David Pryce-Jones remains at the level of stereotypes when, in *The Closed Circle: An Interpretation of the Arabs*, he says that "tribal societies are a closed order" and that the Arabs have trapped themselves in this closed system where "no institutions evolved for common consent for common purposes," a system, he claims, in which lying and corruption are integral to the quest for power. And the American military operating in Iraq, and later Afghanistan, referred to the tribes as "Indian country" and, regarding them as contrary to nations, ignored them until their approach to US forces—not the so-called surge—began to alter the military equation. Such assertions and policies, then, do little to further our understanding either of tribes generally or of the meaning of power in Moroccan political culture in particular. But each does highlight elements that, when pulled together, offer better insights into the larger context of Hussein's account.

If tribes are, in no small part, organized to preserve and replicate themselves by eschewing too much power in too few hands for too long, then the particular variant of tribalism found in Morocco may be reinforced by other aspects of the culture. As each person builds up alliances within and beyond his own kinsmen, he must constantly hedge himself against changing circumstances. Moreover, one must establish to the conviction of others that one is indeed a reliable ally. Such credibility, however, cannot be for a single event alone. Since anything done for another may be called up as a debt in some other form later on, it is essential not only to distribute one's associations but to have, or leave open the possibility for, ties that involve more than a single event. Many cultural features reinforce this pattern. In much of the past, fights, even warfare, were of limited extent and duration, as in most tribal cultures, since complete destruction of one moment's opponent might be the destruction of the next moment's ally. Brett and Fentress note that often a Berber leader even had to have the recognition of his enemy in order to have legitimacy in his own group: if he were to be relied upon to bring others around to agreements he made or keep his own people in line, then even opponents had to demonstrate that they approved of him. This placed limitations on his actions against outsiders who, after all, might turn out to be allies in the next encounter. Similarly, one might belong to multiple opposed groups at the same time without any sense of contradiction, each being an acceptable base for alliance formation. By crosscutting groups and time, therefore, individuals and whole settlements could hedge against the vicissitudes they perceived in their personal and collective lives.

The formation of bonds of indebtedness, of course, carries a variety of risks. One may miscalculate another's reliability, not be able to conduce the desired reciprocation, or (in the Moroccan case) be unable to pass an obligation on to a successor. There is, then, a tincture of fear associated with such a system. To the old saw that if you owe the bank a small sum, they have you in their power, but if you owe them a lot, you have them in your power must be added several other factors: the debtor may try to force you to accept less than what is owed, you may lack the knowledge to calculate an alternative form of recompense or may have to oblige yourself to another to get the needed information, you may look foolish or unwise for having linked yourself to a particular other, and so on. The character in a British novel may speak for many Moroccans as well when he says of the relative strength of the parties to a debt: "It will depend on many things. On timing, or whether you need each other, or other opportunities, on who has more powerful friends. It is a question of hidden balances. Men trade for greed. But debt is about fear, and fear is stronger than greed. The true power, the weapon that defeats all others, is debt. Fools search for gold. The wise man studies debt. That is the key to all business."

The emphasis on trade as an expression of greed and fear may overstate the case—certainly from Hussein's perspective. But one incident was especially revealing. Hussein, like several others under similar circumstances, once came to me after I began studying the local courts and asked me to draw up an agreement between himself and another man for a particular loan. Though he eventually decided he had better do it with the court notaries, Hussein had first explained to me that he did not want to have to pay the notaries the "extra fee" they always seemed to expect and did not want others to know of his loan to this man, an individual who he was quick to note had a poor reputation and from whom he could not necessarily expect repayment. The man had powerful connections, though, and Hussein saw the loan as the price of either tapping into those ties or avoiding actions that the other might engage in to Hussein's detriment. In short, debt in this instance was an entanglement that summed up all the advantages and warnings that accompany a life of trade, the life of a man acting "freely" in a world of running debt. Like his attachment to his kin and settlement, these debt relations always incorporate ambiguities that nevertheless serve to retain a man's ability to maneuver in the ever-changing game of relationship.

Embeddedness in groups is thus countered by the strains of constantly forming personal networks. This became particularly clear when, in the spring of 1967, several members of Hussein's family, knowing of our work together, came to me privately and urged me to convince Hussein not to move out of his father's house. From the way they spoke, it sounded as if Hussein was preparing to move to the far side of the moon. Married and already a father, he had, like many men, initially brought his wife to live in his father's house. But at some point it was clear that Hussein had to make a break with his father in order to ingratiate and build networks in his own name, to be a separate member of the settlement's *jema'*. As it turned out, Hussein was only moving next door, but that made all the difference in the world for his being able to forge alliances in his own name.

Interpersonal entanglements are always multiple and crucial to one's identity. For example, the defining feature of a marriage is the agreement to a marital contract and, as its most central element, the conveyance of a bridewealth payment that seals the arrangement. While colonial-era observers sometimes characterized this payment as proof of the "sale" of the bride, the transfer of procreative rights in her, or proof that marriage is really the alliance of two groups rather than two persons, it may be more useful to see marriage in Morocco (and the Arab world at large) as the major transition to adulthood for a man (and in a different way, of course, for a woman). Islam has very few rites of passage: no baptism or sacraments, no advancement by cohort to established responsibilities or ritual quest for a spiritual consort or patron, and even circumcision occurs at such a young age as hardly to constitute a change of social position. Instead, what makes one a man is establishing a set of interconnecting obligations. And raising the bridewealth, from kinsmen and others, is the main way to prove one has such connections. It is, however, a two-edged proposition, for it demonstrates, on the one hand, connectedness and worldly consequence and, on the other, that one is now deeply embedded in a web of obligations that places constraints on one's actions. Young men have often come to me to complain about this predicament, especially when their marriages were unhappy and they could neither afford to offend those upon whom they depended for the bridewealth payment—a portion of which may, by agreement, still be owing upon divorce to the woman or her marital guardian—and the difficulties of raising a new payment, with all its attendant obligations, in the event of remarriage. Yet it is the bridewealth that more than anything else symbolizes that one has moved to the stage of manhood, notwithstanding the potential discomfort of the ensuing bonds.

Hussein himself did not seem to feel the adverse tug of kinship too intensely. True, he had balked when his future brother-in-law tried to shake

Hussein's wife, Hada

him down for a larger sum of money than the token often given the bride's brother as a form of ritual release or compensation. And he had moved out of his father's house. But his own success gave Hussein a measure of leeway in choosing his obligations, and the very acquisition of this freedom was itself a not insignificant factor in the motivation for his financial pursuits.

By the time I got to know him in the mid-1960s, Hussein had already been married, divorced, and remarried. With his first wife he had three children; a son and daughter died as infants, while the remaining daughter went to live with her mother. Although Hussein had an agreement with his former wife for the daughter's support, the wife's family had recently made her sue Hussein for additional support. Hussein won in court, but when the family sent an intermediary who made a sacrifice at his door, Hussein gave them a full year's added support but made it clear that he had no further financial attachment to either mother or daughter as a result of the way her family had acted. With his next wife, Hada, he had another son. But the boy was born with a malformed brain, and from the medicine bottle Hussein once showed me, it appeared that he suffered seizures as well. As with all his children, Hussein was intensely affectionate. He cuddled the little boy and wiped his mouth as he cradled him on his lap, but it was clear that the boy would never be fully functional. With both wives there had been a ritual period of in-law avoidance, which usually lasts about a month, followed by a ritual sacrifice. Hussein explained that this was to reduce tensions at the outset of a marriage. One reason, though, for marrying a close relative, he said, is precisely because the existing relationship may ease the tensions that accompany bridewealth negotiations and financial considerations attendant on the marriage. In his own life, however, Hussein has never married someone who is closely related by kinship.

The use of magic in such relationships is also common, and Hussein is a great believer in the efficacy of such magic. There are many ways to use magic, he told me on various occasions. Stones can be arranged the way disputing people are located physically, and the man who understands magic can arrange them to favor one party or another. Or there is a man over here in Senhadja, Hussein pointed out, who is learned in the Quran and can write magical phrases on a piece of paper. If you want your wife to return to you, you take that paper and tie it to a tree, and when the wind shakes it, she will come back. Or if you want to make a man impotent, you bury the paper where he will walk over it. A jealous woman who doesn't want another woman to have a child will have the phrase inscribed on the blade of a knife and bury it where the woman walks, and until it is removed, she will not conceive. People also have the phrase put in a pouch and worn as an amulet to make an opponent fail in war or in business: Caid Omar had such a powerful amulet that made him invulnerable to bullets, and it was only after he lost it in battle that he was killed. A mother may use magic to make a child divorce his wife, but a man would never use magic against his mother. A man may choose to "sell" his property to a favored son to keep it away from daughters and their husbands. I know sons who have used magic to make their fathers do this, Hussein said, even though it is terribly shameful, since the Quran sets out the rules of inheritance, and people should not try to go around them.

I used magic myself once about fourteen years ago, Hussein added with a smile. I was crazy about a particular girl and wanted her to be equally attracted to me. So I went to a Jew in Sefrou—their magic is about the most powerful there is—and paid him a lot to write out magic papers, and I buried one along her path and set another in a tree. She then told her mother she really liked me. But her father had already arranged a marriage for her. Even though I didn't get her, he concluded, the magic worked because she did want me.

Hussein's belief in such magical practices is revealing. Not only does he see certain figures who are normally regarded as relatively powerless and "unmanly" (scholars, women, and Jews) as possessing such powers, but through the relationships where it is employed or thought effective one can see the places of greatest social strain and desire. Hussein, too, refers at times to family ties as cloying: "Close kin are like scorpions," he once told me (reciting a proverb that plays on the similar sound of "kin" and "scorpions" in Arabic), because they hold you close, but over your head, unseen, grabbing you from behind, comes the stinger. Perhaps that is why, like so many others of his generation, Hussein could seek a kind of emotional relief, and not just a less enmeshing social tie, in his relationships with various Jews.

Hussein often waxed ecstatic about his relations with the Jews of the region. Even the Jewish women, he said, learned Berber, and you could always trust the Jews in their dealings. But once independence arrived, he said, most of the Jews moved out of the countryside, while others felt that the Arabs and Berbers had grown closer together during the struggles at the end of the Protectorate and that without French law and protégé status they would get squeezed out in their dealings with us. Jews and Muslims have the same nature (*nafs*). Yes, the Traditions of the Prophet (*ḥadith*) say that they have neither this world nor the next because they don't recognize the Prophet, and yes, I have heard teachers say that they will go to hell, at least until they recognize the legitimacy of the Prophet Muhammad. But I am not sure this is true. It is a sin for someone to talk about things he knows nothing about. And you could always tell a Jew something without worrying that he would tell others.

Thus for Hussein, as for so many of his generation, the emotional proximity to a Jew was, perhaps, in proportion to his commercial tie with him, and as the Jew was not part of the same group dynamic as his fellow Muslims, that emotional bond was not subject to constant, interchangeable claims of assistance. As the resident stranger the Jew stood outside of the rules applicable to the crosscutting demands of any relation with a fellow tribesman, kinsman, or in-law and hence was both an exception to and a confirmation of the rules of maneuver within the world of one's other contacts.

For Moroccans like Hussein, then, it is not that groups, as opposed to

Jewish barber bleeding Berber client

individuals, are primary or subordinate but that the range of permissible gambits is vast. Like an elaborate game the board is limited and violation of basic rules leads to fear of the repercussions of social discord. But the moves remain creative, virtually infinite, and to those who take pleasure or are simply caught up in the game it embodies the natural way of things. Much can happen to make the social forms that may have developed when tribes were autonomous or semiautonomous units take on quite a different appearances as modern bureaucratic states engulf them. However, the ethos, values, and orientations of tribal forms may retain considerable force, as they clearly do for Hussein, provided we see tribes from the outset not as solitary groups that retain a crystalline structure but as highly flexible, shape-shifting entities that have long adapted to changing circumstances. Aspects of these qualities were added to Hussein's account as, over the course of many months and years, I began to learn about how he had been building up his own economic and social position and how his view of the national political structure fit with his personal and collective sense of identity.

An intelligent enemy is better than an ignorant friend.
Trust him—but pray from behind him.

—Arab sayings

I visited Hussein several times in the 1980s and early 1990s. Each time I would drive out to his village, over the tough, rock-strewn track. As I rounded the bend and descended to the settlement, I would see all sorts of domesticated animals collected in and along the shallow stream that runs through the area. It was a scene of extraordinary beauty, a pastoral setting that, in the midday sun, explained why, when I asked him once why he did not move into the city, Hussein simply answered by motioning around him. I remember, too, one visit when we climbed to the flat roof of his house. In the cool evening he draped one of his heavy Berber burnouses over my shoulders. Then, pointing in the direction of the setting sun, he asked if it was true that the earth was round. Yes, I answered. You mean, he said, pointing westward, that if I go all the way in that direction I will come back from the east? Yes, I said. He gave me a look of genuine wonder, but I also think it was *me*, more than any scientific evidence I might have adduced, that he chose to believe.

Another time I asked Hussein if I might take his picture. Just a moment, he said, and reaching into the purse he carried under his djellaba, he withdrew a large-denomination banknote and holding it folded in the hand by his side asked if I had the bill in the picture. I thought it odd at first, but then interpreted it somewhat along the lines of our wanting to be in good clothes or with our hair properly combed in a picture. It was as if he were saying, "I am not a Berber bumpkin who is just in from the sheep trade, but a man of some substance." It is an image Hussein must constantly project in his associations, one he sought to make visible in the picture through the symbol and the reality of his financial success.

Typically, upon my arrival at the cluster of houses, the children of the settlement raced alongside my car, jockeying to see who would be first

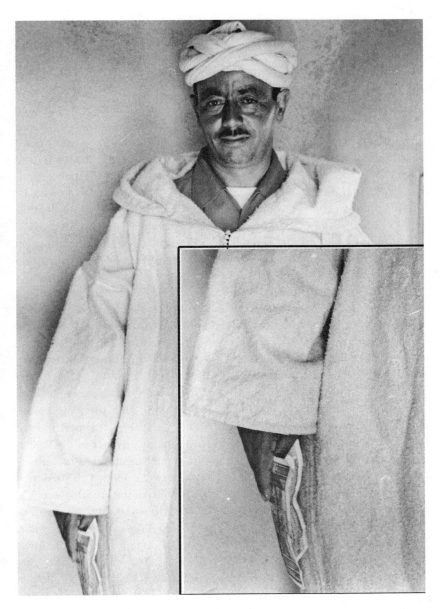

Hussein holding currency

to climb in after I stopped. Then one of them would dash into Hussein's house to announce the visitor. A moment later Hussein would appear, smiling broadly, and once we settled into his guest room and exchanged our most recent news, he would begin to share with me his latest thinking about the country and his own Berber people.

In an age of renewed ethnic strife the role of the Berbers of Morocco constitutes a fascinating test case. Hussein is immensely proud of his Berber identity: he speaks the language constantly at home, teases himself and others about the words used by Arabs to taunt Berber speakers, and loves, in turn, to tweak the Arabs for their inability to make certain sounds used in Berber. Once, while discussing politics during a walk in town, he commented on the more pragmatic, less arrogant stance of the Berbers by pointing to a group of Berbers seated in the shade near a group of Arabs standing rigidly in the sun. He then repeated a well-known comment about Arab hauteur and Berber practicality by saying: "Where you see an Arab standing up, you will see a Berber already sitting down." Attitudes toward the Berbers, particularly on the part of the colonizing French and in very recent times, have, however, not remained static. Indeed, such attitudes become a good index of the larger political context of their moment.

Early on, many of the French were quite enamored of the Berbers of the country's south. They saw in them a kind of warrior nobility that they felt contrasted with the abject demeanor of the decadent, pietistic, and untrustworthy urban Arabs. Berbers of the Middle Atlas, however, were commonly portrayed in a very negative light until, after the main battles of 1913–14, they were defeated and became the object of some cosseted imaginary. Some of the ethnographers who came in advance of the French troops were perceptive enough to note the greater similarities than differences between Arabs and Berbers, a perspective that tended to be downplayed once domination became the principle aim of the French. As part of their general colonial practice the French sought to skim off the cream of these rural notables and, with hollow promises of *liberté, fraternité, egalité,* to train some of them in French-run schools to become the handmaidens of their empire. Eager to avoid the mistakes, as he saw them, of the Algerian example, Resident-General Lyautey sought to keep Arab and Berber, French and Muslim more separated than elsewhere in French North Africa.

However, as colonial experience progressed, what began as a romance of the Berber became involvement in their protracted resistance—admirable militarily, perhaps, but certainly not administratively. To some extent the French replaced the Moroccan state in its relations with the tribes, and the ever-malleable tribes adapted for the moment accordingly. The notion, current in much of the academic and administrative literature, that tribal regions were either *bled el-makhzen* (government-dominated lands) or *bled es-siba* (dissident lands), even when it referred mainly to the payment of taxes, belied a great range of contacts and accommodations. The extremes of romanticization and bureaucratic incorporation may have been modulated at those moments when the French did not want tribal cooperation to appear as simple collaboration. At other moments, however, there was a tense joinder of interests as each kept the other close enough to know him, to restrain some actions, and to keep all options open.

At the same time, however, rumors kept appearing that the French were seeking to convert Moroccans, especially the Berbers, to Christianity. Lyautey was concerned to restrict the teaching of Islam in the curriculum of the schools set up for the "sons of notables," and small-scale missionary groups, mainly British and American rather than French, did operate in the country. Protests took various forms, none more amusing, perhaps, than the time, as C. R. Pennell describes it, when, after the Bishop of Rabat urged that efforts should be made to convert the Muslims, "one group even retaliated by getting the Bishop's secretary drunk and announcing he had converted to Islam."

Though such rumors were not unimportant, it was a much more direct act that helped fuel nationalist sentiment among the Berbers. Throughout the interwar years French policy drifted. As Jacque Berque put it, "If a policy consists of systematizing in a collective practice the significance extracted from a historic whole, there was no French policy in North Africa between the two world wars." So, when the ill-conceived Berber Dahir (edict) of 1930 sought to place Arabs and Berbers under separate legal regimes, the die was cast. What early ethnographers had stressed—that the Berbers were not all that separated from the Arabs in religion and social interaction—was now reinforced by common political resistance. Indeed, the 1930 Dahir truly infuriated the Berbers. Hussein put the matter very bluntly: Our customary law *is* Islamic law, he said, thus underscoring a point neither administrators nor Orientalists have ever fully grasped about Islamic law in all periods and places. The result was greater alliance between the two for purposes of achieving independence than might otherwise have been the case.

Yet concern that the Arab-Berber distinction might decrease the post-Protectorate push toward national unity was by no means eradicated. For years the independent Moroccan government, afraid of invigorating such a distinction, forbade the use of Berber dialects in the schools and banned their use in some state-controlled media. At other moments the government seemed to be more accommodating. In 1978 King Hassan II (whose mother, only incidentally, was a Berber) had Parliament approve a national institute of Berber studies, but it was never actually set up. Following the rise of greater Berber awareness in Algeria and the institution of a panna-tional Berber cultural gathering, the Moroccan government, in the mid-1990s, added to the long-standing radio broadcasts in Berber five-minute televised news summaries in each of the three Berber dialects. At that time, though, as one outside report said, the broadcasts "are—according to Ber-ber activists—horrible translations of the Arabic original." Still later, fol-lowing his accession to the throne after his father's death in 1999, King Mu-hammad VI announced the creation of a new Berber institute and allowed teaching of the language in six private schools. But within months the gov-ernment also banned the meeting of a Berber activist association, contin-ued a ban (first instituted by the French in 1933 and renewed in 1997) on the use of Berber names for civil identity registration, and required parents to choose their children's personal names from a government-approved list of Arab and Muslim terms, a practice that is, however, sometimes ig-nored locally. In yet another turn, following the events of the 2010–11 Arab Spring and demonstrations in Morocco known as the February 20 Move-ment, a new constitution was promulgated that recognized Berber as "an official language of the State, being common patrimony of all Moroccans without exception."

To Hussein all of this has long seemed both ridiculous and insulting. He accepts the undocumented estimate that nearly half the Moroccan population—perhaps as many as fifteen million people—identify them-selves as Berber, and while he has supported the *Mouvement Populaire* (the so-called Berber Party) at moments in its political history, his approach, like that of most people in the Ait Youssi territory, is pragmatic rather than ideological. In one election, he said, the Berber candidate arrived in a beat-up old car, and the Arab from the other party arrived by helicopter. So, Hussein asked, leaning close and wagging his head with sardonic effect, which one would you vote for? If at times the ethnic card is played, then, it is neither with an exclusive ethnic agenda in hand nor with any expecta-tion of enduring attachment. Indeed, for Hussein, Berber identity is an-other among the array of personal attributes that are not exclusive but one among a concatenation of features that constitute a person. The trick, then, is to maneuver within and among these attributes to greatest personal ef-fect. And the result, in a collective sense, is an intriguing political phenom-enon: perhaps half the people of a country who have never felt an over-powering need to identify themselves separately accept instead the broader cultural norm that Berberness, like other features, is part of being Muslim (just as Berber custom has been seen as deeply Islamic) and part of the repertoire one draws upon in forging ties with others. Hence the rise and fall of minor government policies toward Berbers are, Hussein believes, petty annoyances that only people who don't understand how things really work get exercised over.

Hussein's identity and connections as a Berber are, in many respects, outweighed in importance by his involvement and his great success as an entrepreneur. Since our first meeting by the pasha's office, I had wanted to understand, by following the career of someone like Hussein, how such a person actually becomes a "big man." From our earliest encounters Hussein seemed exceptionally clear in describing how commerce and the construction of social networks worked in his world and, by implication, how he became a master of both. From the outset Hussein was also remarkably open with me about his finances, and he showed me, beginning in the mid-sixties, the details of his costs and assets. Like many people with a natural talent—but unlike many who cannot describe their own gift—Hussein began by indicating how easy it is to get rich.

At the time we first met, Hussein already owned, in addition to properties at his home village site, some forty hectares of unirrigated and seven hectares of variously irrigated land at the Beni Mansour area where, he reminded me, his group had certain social ties. All of the land had been titled with the land registry office, which uses the Torrens system of registration, in which the state maintains a registry of titles that cannot later be legally challenged if properly certified. Under this system all those who profess to have an interest in the land being registered must bring forth their claims within a specified period of time or lose them. Thereafter, any lien must be registered at the titling office so that when land is resold a unified record of liens exists, and purchasers do not have to search numerous records, endure a long period of written and verbal notice, or risk later claims affecting their title. The system had been introduced by the French colonists in Tunisia and Algeria in the latter part of the nineteenth century and was also used by the French (as Moroccan historian Abdellah Laroui has said) "to legalize dubious titles." Reading through the land records in the registry office, I could see how this worked. Titles went back to a point where, unable to produce further documentation, sometimes because owners fled in the face of military action or at the expiration of a nominal lease, the land came into the hands of the French. Thus, to take just a few examples: 30,000 hectares of land was seized during military operations in the Chaouia (where Haj Hamed had gone to fight) in the period 1907–

12, while in the central Moroccan region around Beni Mellal in just two years in the 1920s over 62,000 hectares of private land (*melk*) was seized. Other legal changes whittled away at the indigenous land base. A tribal assembly, for example, could agree to allow collective land to be alienated, while other lands were seized by eminent domain or obtained with (often inadequate) compensation.

Hussein was well aware of the abuses to which the land registry system, along with other forms of colonial appropriation, had been subjected. Though he could not cite the specific numbers, he was not surprised to learn that by 1932 the French had confiscated over 2 million acres (837,000 hectares) of native lands in Morocco. He knew more particularly that the French had annexed large portions of the forests and pasturages in his own local area. In fact, as Hassan Benhalima notes in his study of Sefrou and its region, 75,000 hectares of forest land was taken in 1930, 5,000 hectares of the best farmland between 1925–30, and another 8,000 hectares from the area just north of Sefrou in 1949. He further notes: "At Louata [El Ouata, just to the north of Sefrou] for example, irrigated land 'bought' for 400 francs [about 15 cents] and dry land for 300 francs [about 10 cents] per hectare was distributed after 1930 to 26 Europeans farmers, 4 Jews and 8 Muslims, who immediately registered it with the Land Registration office." Reading many of the land records myself, I repeatedly came across titles in which the basis for the European ownership of the land was either obscure or based on confiscatory pricing. Hussein, ever the sardonic realist, shared a laugh over the story about the Berber who, upon being asked by a foreigner how the Moroccans lost their land to the French, replied by asking if the man did not know the story of the monkey and the mouse:

> There was once a mouse who had a piece of cheese. He was very proud of the cheese and decided to show it to his friend the monkey.
>
> "What a lovely piece of cheese that is," said the monkey. "In fact, it looks just perfect for my favorite trick."
>
> "What trick?" asked the mouse.
>
> "Why, the one in which I balance a piece of cheese on the tip of my tail."
>
> "Balance a piece of cheese on the tip of your tail!" cried the mouse. "That's impossible. I don't believe it. I just bet you can't do it!"
>
> "Here," said the monkey, "I'll show you." He took the cheese out of the mouse's hand and placed it ever so delicately on the tip of his tail. The cheese hovered for an instant and then toppled to one side.
>
> "You see," said the mouse, "you can't do it."
>
> "Nonsense," said the monkey. "It's just that the cheese is a bit too heavy

on one side. But that's easily fixed." And with that the monkey took a small bite from one side of the cheese and set about balancing it on his tail once again.

This time the piece of cheese was barely set in place when it teetered and fell to the other side.

"We'll just have to even that up again," said the monkey. And as the mouse watched, the monkey, with a great show of technical expertise and craftsmanship, nibbled away another small piece from the other side of the cheese.

Each time the monkey placed the dwindling piece of cheese on his tail. Each time it toppled to one side or the other. And each time, with careful explanations of the intricacies involved, the monkey tried to meet the mouse's challenge by nibbling away just enough from one side of the cheese or the other to insure that the outcome would be properly balanced.

Finally, however, the monkey had bitten away all of the cheese. With an expression of great chagrin he said to the mouse: "Well, I suppose you win the bet." He quickly turned and walked away, leaving the poor little mouse to wonder how it was that he won his bet but lost his beautiful piece of cheese.

And that, concluded the Berber, is how the Moroccans lost their land to the French.

If Hussein saw the bitter humor in this story, he also realized early on that, whatever the historic abuses of the registry system and other laws introduced by the French, under the alternative system of traditional Islamic law, where a sale is validated by notaries or claims supported by witnesses, any property may be the subject of endless litigation. As a means of social disentanglement, no less than financial certitude, Hussein vastly preferred, therefore, to secure his independence through this land registry innovation. Indeed, said Hussein, I used to sit in on court sessions dealing with property and contract cases in order to learn exactly how the law handled such claims—and how people got trapped in dealings with relatives and neighbors who are trying to get you to do things for them. Modeling himself explicitly after other big men (as well as the French farmers with whom they, in turn, were familiar), Hussein decided he would secure all of his land with registered titles.

The registration process, of course, requires more time and expense than some are willing to expend. A published announcement must be made at the commencement of the registration process, as well as an oral announcement at the market nearest to the property. Claimants must register their objections within a period of several months. In the late 1960s the prospective registrant had to pay a fee of 8 percent of the sale price of the property plus a small amount for secretarial work. The cost of a traditional property transfer arranged through the notaries was in theory somewhat higher: an 8 percent government tax on the sale price plus a fee of 3 percent (declining to 1 percent on a sliding valuation scale) paid directly to the notaries. When one deals with the notaries, however, there may be other problems and expenses, quite aside from later claims. Put bluntly, the notaries have always been a source of some corruption. For a sum of money paid under the table, said Hussein, they will often register a lower sale price; for more they will put clauses in the contract of sale that may preserve to the seller a later claim against the buyer. There is even a saying about notaries, he added with a smile: If you give them a certain sum of money, they will write a document as long as your arm; if you give them twice as much, they will write one twice that length; and for a still larger sum they would even be willing to write on both sides of the scroll (which, of course, is never done)! So eager was Hussein to avoid the notaries that, as noted earlier, he initially came to me to have a document written about a loan he felt compelled to make to a particularly shady character who was nevertheless well connected. Thus, to avoid later entanglements and the shenanigans of some of the court personnel, Hussein quickly took to the land registry system introduced by the French.

In the early years following independence Hussein was well aware of the larger context within which he was working. Figures show that in 1956 almost all rural farmers worked less than two hectares, while half a million rural men, lacking any land of their own, worked as sharecroppers, often on the farms of Frenchmen or rich Moroccans, whose holdings averaged some 170 hectares. Nationwide programs to modernize native holdings through mechanization were counterproductive in that the costs passed on to small-scale farmers only increased their indebtedness. However, Hussein saw that there were also certain advantages to such programs and quickly took to renting tractors, often in combination with others, to till the lands he owned that were large enough to benefit from such an operation.

Hussein used his titled property, in turn, as collateral for loans from the local bank. In 1966, when he was still quite early in his career, Hussein was paying 4.25 to 4.5 percent interest on loans of $2,000, though on one $500 loan for one year he had paid interest of $50, or 10 percent. The bank would only lend with titled collateral, but once you have paid off a loan of your own, he noted, the bank will let you cosign for others, thus allowing a man like Hussein not only to avoid certain entanglements that might accompany loans from a kinsman but to become a patron to others. Although Hussein has had very close ties to Jews throughout his career, he never needed the small loans (often in those days of no more than ten dollars) made by a few of the remaining Jews at rates up to 5 percent *per month*.

In the late 1960s dry land in the Beni Mansour area was selling for $250–$300 per hectare, while the lower-quality land near Hussein's own village went for about $140 per hectare. (Still better dry land, in the areas near Sefrou taken by the French, cost as much as $500–$800 per hectare, though one European farmer eager to leave after his crop failed from lack of rain was selling his land for only $210 per hectare.) Irrigated land, by contrast, cost $500 per hectare in Beni Mansour but $2,000 per hectare near Hussein's village. The latter figure was so high because it included the cost of the water itself, which can be bought and sold separately from the land, while people in the Beni Mansour area actually prefer dry land and the grain crops they can grow on it. (For example, in 1966 water was scarce, and an allotment of water lasting about five hours—from the 'asr prayer until the 'asha prayer—and used once a week for the whole year was selling for $700.) Prices also vary with the ability of the soil to hold moisture. Hussein particularly likes the land at Beni Mansour because it is "cold" (i.e., it holds rainfall well) and because if you plow it with a tractor to the greater depth than is possible with draft animals, you can ensure more moist soil for your crop. Although Hussein never engaged in the practice, a number of other farmers raised capital by selling their crops "green." A buyer would pay a skilled farmer half of what they agreed the crop should bring at harvest time. Farmers would only sell a limited part of their crop this way, about 20 percent. It was primarily Jews who were engaged in buying crops green, and with their departure the practice has largely disappeared.

Traditionally, Moroccans have also used a variety of sharecropping arrangements for those who work on their lands. The _khammes_, or "fifths" system, employed on dry land divides the crop into five parts, with one share each going to the owner, the renter, the worker, the supplier of the seed, and the supplier of the plow animal. Various combinations are thus possible. Someone who, for example, rents a plot and supplies all the seed, work, and draft animals may contract for 80 percent of the crop. There are no minimal guarantees, and each person takes his chances against crop failure. Similar arrangements apply on irrigated lands, though here the worker receives one-fourth of the crop, the owner supplying everything else. People sometimes refer to the sharecropper facetiously as a sultan because, Hussein said, he is not the owner of the land, contributes no seed or money, the work of plowing is done for him by dumb beasts, and even at harvest time he brings in his family and neighbors who do the hard labor for nothing!

Other partnership forms also exist. A shepherd who keeps another's animals for eight years gets to keep one-quarter of the entire herd. Or, if the arrangement is a yearly one, he keeps one-quarter of that year's lambs. If the shepherd contributes half to the purchase of the sheep or goats, he gets half of the wool, milk, and butter produced. Those who care for olive trees on irrigated land usually receive cash equal to one-fifth of the value of the harvest. Islamic law and custom are famous for the variety and inventiveness of their forms of partnership and risk distribution: in Lebanon, Fuad Khuri reports, the bus driver even gets to keep an animal born under way. Hussein has been quick to adopt and develop several forms of employment and partnerships in his own business practice. In each case he has also amalgamated some arrangements learned from European farmers.

In particular, Hussein adopted a system for his lands at Beni Mansour that came to be referred to as the *resemi* system, from a word meaning "entitled." Each of the four workers operating on this system with Hussein in the late sixties received the standard government rate for farm workers of $1.20 per day for each of the five to six days per week they actually worked during the seven-month agricultural season. (By comparison, a European farmer employing more than fifty resemi workers nearby was paying eighty cents per day plus fifty kilos of grain per year for a family of six, two of whom were full-time workers.) Hussein also supplied accommodations for each worker's family, houses that cost him $500 apiece to construct. During the off-season (October to early March) the men continued to live in Hussein's houses while tending any flocks of their own but without receiving any pay or food from Hussein.

To place these figures in some context, it should be noted that in 1966 a laborer living in Sefrou and supporting a small family would, according to the court experts I consulted, need for his monthly expenses about $31 for food (which was enough to include one kilo of meat per week), $24 for the rent of a single room, and $12 for his children's school expenses. A lower-level civil servant or craftsman with a good trade would have spent about $80 for food and rent. By comparison, monthly earnings for a small shopkeeper were around $60, for a low-level uniformed government aide (*mokhazni*) $70, for a white-collar government clerk $200, and for a well-off butcher anywhere from $400 to $800. An unemployed man working on the roads under a government welfare program received $5 for twelve days plus a sack of flour, or $10 and no grain. Those who fought in the French army during World War II or in Vietnam received veterans' benefits ranging anywhere from $100 to $300 per quarter depending on their rank (and more if wounded).

For a worker, then, who earned $1,000 for the season, risked no investment, got paid even if the crop failed, had a roof over his head, and may have earned other monies in town during the off-season, Hussein's version of the resemi system offered a good income and clear advantages over many sharecropping or homesteading arrangements. For Hussein it meant definite costs and a stable supply of labor, as well as that form of patronage through which others would come to see him as a reliable and important benefactor. Through additional small gifts to his workers—for example, a meal a day to each of his dozen sharecroppers, even though it exceeded any customary practice—Hussein further secured his workers' obligation. Over the years, these "salaried" workers have not become an indentured and landless peasantry: they see their earnings as well above those of low-level civil servants and, in an economic and ecological environment where fluctuation is rampant, they prefer to find a man like Hussein on whom they believe they can depend.

With his land and labor costs more or less settled, Hussein was able to turn his attention to other markets and opportunities. Hussein's holdings by the late sixties already included one contiguous plot of twenty hectares of dry, but not rocky, land of good soil planted in hard wheat (*gmeh*), for which the following cultivation expenses were incurred on a per-hectare basis in 1966: $40 rental of tractor and driver from the government co-operative for initial clearing (a cost that would decline to $6 after the first year); $7.50 per hectare for 250 kilos of good phosphate fertilizer; $18 per hectare for 132 kilos of seed (not counting the value of the excess seed Hussein usually sells after the first purchase); $8.40 if he hired workers receiving $1.20 per day to harvest all twenty hectares in a day (or $10 to rent a mechanical harvester for two days); $2.10 for threshing by seven men using ten mules at $1.20 per worker per day (Hussein's actual cost being lower, since he owned six mules himself and borrowed the others); plus a tax on the crop of $40, a figure Hussein regarded as quite low. Thus, while it is difficult to compute his costs per hectare exactly—since his "salaried" workers also work on his other plots, because grain buyers give farmers "gifts" to get their business, and because though he pays no social security, Hussein has always paid the costs of anyone injured while working for him, etc.—a cost of roughly $115–$120 per hectare, or $2,200–$2,400 for all twenty hectares, appears to be a good approximation.

A very good crop in those years would, in turn, yield about 4,000 kilos per hectare, though farmers with poorer-quality land in this area and not using fertilizer to full advantage could expect only 3,000 kilos in a good year. At a sale price of $11 per 100 kilos, Hussein's twenty-hectare crop of 80,000 kilos sold for a total of $8,800, or about four times his investment. By rotating crops (grain or barley every other year, with chick peas or beans grown in between) Hussein has been able to ensure that the land never needs to lie fallow, thus, in theory, continuing his profits on a regular basis.

To mention costs and profits so neatly would, however, be to convey a far simpler picture than is accurate. For the climatic variation across even adjacent regions and certainly across just a few years is extraordinary. Rain may literally fall on one hillside but not the next one over, and land that looks like a desert one year looks like a garden the next. As Clifford Geertz quipped, in his comparison of the cultural ecology of monsoon Indonesia to littoral Morocco, in the former all you need to know to predict the weather is which way the wind is blowing, while in the latter you would need to penetrate the mind of God. Even sultans knew, as the saying goes, that a monarch may not survive three years of drought. Throughout Moroccan history such moments have been fraught with political distress. The Haj, for example, recalled how much the drought years of the late nineteenth century and the period around World War II had affected political events. Small wonder, then, that King Hassan II once told a French journalist: "Faced with a choice between an intelligence report and the weather bulletin, I will put the intelligence report to one side."

With rainfall so variable, prices obviously fluctuate just as greatly. To take just the two years from this early period in Hussein's career, 1965 and 1966—the former an average good year for rainfall, the latter a year characterized by a severe lack of rainfall—compare these sale prices for commodities in Hussein's region: onions 1–2¢ versus 6¢ (and as high as 10¢ in Casablanca); tomatoes 4¢ versus 7¢; green peppers 7¢ versus 10¢; beans 6–7¢ versus 8¢; corn 5¢ versus 6½¢, potatoes 8¢ versus 11¢ (though two other types of potatoes remained constant at 7–8¢ because they are raised on irrigated land). A factor affecting price, of course, is the strategy that farmers use in the face of uncertainty. Moroccan farmers typically vary crops within and across their fields and constantly hedge their bets against the vicissitudes of weather, labor, market price, and political circumstance. Indeed, as Hussein continually asserts and demonstrates, it is necessary to hedge in all of one's interactions, from placing one family member in one political party and another in the opposition to the formation of personal alliances based on a wide variety of obligational bonds. Hussein plays on this pattern in numerous ways.

Agriculturally, as we have seen, Hussein early on began to mix dry and irrigated landholdings. But he has also mixed the purchase of parcels in his own village area with those at Beni Mansour. The latter area is populated by a different and unrelated fraction of the Ait Youssi tribe and is under a different administrator, so Hussein has thereby distributed his social ties and his political contacts and vulnerabilities. Already in 1966 he owned (partly with his father) some thirteen hundred olive trees, eleven hundred of which were planted more than six years earlier and had thus already reached maturity. He made $130 from each of the seventy trees he harvested that year. He had also placed other assets in different regions: seven cows were kept near Beni Mansour, but another four were kept farther up in the Middle Atlas Mountains at Guigou. His own flocks of a hundred sheep and a similar number of goats were also kept up in the mountains, where he had a seven-year contract for division of the profits with a man who watched over the herds. Indeed, it was only after many months of working with him that I learned accidentally about these additional assets. Hussein explained: If I keep the herds near our own village, everyone will think I am such a rich man that they will always be asking me to do things for them—pay for the Quranic school teacher, help them with their bride-wealth payments, and so on—so I find it best to keep some things with people I trade with and know but who aren't related or nearby. That way everyone doesn't know everything about my affairs.

There is yet another factor of risk distribution, one that connects Hussein and the other members of his settlement to areas beyond their own, namely the pattern of transhumance. In the case of Hussein's own settlement, the Ait Ben ʿAssu, locally maintained herds of sheep and goats were kept near their village during the summer and mild winters. In more difficult winters animals were taken to any uncultivated land in the Beni Mansour region, further underscoring his attachment to the people of that area. According to Hussein, it was a tradition that any Ait Youssi could bring his herds to such places in the winter. Others, however, told me that in pre-Protectorate times groups commonly had to make an ʿar sacrifice to be allowed into these lowland regions, but the French ended that practice by declaring uncultivated lands open to any fraction of the tribe. Hussein acknowledges that conflicts were not unknown but notes that grazing land at Beni Mansour is plentiful, and no special areas need to be set aside for each household or lineage. Indeed, throughout Ait Youssi territory, pastures are used on a first-come, first-served basis and pasturage is nowadays seldom the source of conflict it once was. Nevertheless, this may be one example in which such "traditions" are, in fact, recent inventions. Whatever its actual "truth," the mutual acceptance of this version of history as a practice of long standing forges yet another tie between Hussein's group and those at Beni Mansour.

Hussein's success has, of course, come about through lengthy endeavors, including partnerships with his father and floating bank loans. But that does not mean Hussein would be averse to getting rich quick, particularly if it involved a hunt for buried treasure. The problem, however, is that one may have to contend with the antics of the jnun. For Hussein, like Yaghnik and the Haj, not only believes in the existence of the jnun—those creatures of the netherworld noted by the Quran who may cause grief or be summoned for help—but believes that, even though such buried treasures do indeed exist, it is also true, as the saying goes, that "over every treasure sits a jinn." On one occasion, Hussein said, we heard that there was such a treasure buried near our settlement. So with a couple of others we put Quranic phrases around our necks to protect us from the jinn that would be guarding the treasure, and went out to find it. We sprinkled barley around just as you would if you were sowing a crop, and where the grain seemed to collect indicated where the treasure was to be found. But when we started digging, one of the men suddenly dropped his shovel with a shriek and said that he had been struck hard on the forearm, no doubt by a jinn. We decided to stop until we could get a Quranic teacher to write out some phrases that would protect us. Meanwhile we are keeping it all a secret and getting back to our farming and trading.

Indeed, treasure hunts aside, listening to Hussein talk about how to succeed one is easily left with the impression that it all sounds so simple, like the Oxford groundskeeper who nonchalantly told an American who asked the secret to the college's elegant lawn that all you had to do was plant the seed and take perfect care of it for three hundred years. To Hussein his achievements seem so transparent that one wonders why the entire nation is not filled with successful farmers and herdsmen. Of course, luck plays a significant role. Not only is rainfall unpredictable, but the machinations of rapacious officials, uncertain neighbors, and tendentious kinsmen—to say nothing of crop disease, animal infection, and world market prices—are among the myriad factors with which any entrepreneur must contend. Nevertheless, several factors come through with great clarity as I have tracked Hussein's career from these early days: the intense focus in all of his ventures on the persons at their center, the need to build social support for any undertaking, and the wisdom of carefully hedging one's bets.

From that first day outside the pasha's office through to our most recent encounters, I have seen how much Hussein's "presence"—his command of language, his calculation of others' needs, his capacity to see several moves ahead—have made him someone others choose as their patron. In a world in which, at least throughout most of his life, multiple bases have existed for building alliances, Hussein has been a master at accumulating attachments to construct a broad and diverse base of dependencies. By placing his assets, both material and human, in domains that are not equally and simultaneously vulnerable to the same adverse effects, he endeavors to secure himself in a world of uncertainty; by making his own word the centerpiece of his reliability he convinces others to choose him, rather than someone else, as the man to depend on. Like a high-wire artist or a successful investor, he has his recognizably legitimate stratagems, and like them he is so adept at the performance that one sometimes forgets just how hard it is to pull it off with seemingly effortless aplomb. Hussein also understands perfectly well that the same techniques of hedging, forging disparate alliances, and relying on persons rather than impersonal forces informs politics no less than the marketplace, but he clearly believes that the latter is both more worthy of one's efforts and more admirable than the former.

For as long as I have known him, Hussein's attitude toward organized politics has been one of sardonic humor and overt skepticism. In the 1960s, when the first blush of national independence had not quite faded, he showed pride in the clever tactics used by Berber freedom fighters against the French colonists. But even then he expressed boyish playfulness rather than personal animosity or ideological fervor, and his admiration for the French farmers' techniques and his pride in knowing several of those who remained in the area belied any sense of estrangement from their common enterprise. Nominally allied through the main urban Arab-dominated Istiqlal party initially led by Allal al-Fassi and more directly with the Berber Party founded by Mahjoubi Aherdane, Hussein regarded those who were too ardently attached to any party as naively limiting their ability to engage in flexible relationships and deluded in imagining the constancy of their fellow party members. We have a saying, he once told me: "Every shout drives the cattle," and there are plenty of people, he concluded, who are foolish enough to be driven in just this way by any politician with a loud voice. Like most Moroccans he has always been skeptical of the machinations of the king's ministers rather than blaming the king directly for any missteps. He would often make teasing remarks, too, of the obsequious personnel surrounding government officials and would no doubt have had a good laugh at what Ruth Knafo Setton has written about a story her father used to tell: "Every time I see Hassan II's unsmiling but oddly benign face, I remember Dad telling me how he went skating once on a mountain lake in Ifrane. Mohammed V, the father of Hassan, the future king, was there skating with his two bodyguards. Whenever he slipped, the body-guards had to fall too."

At the same time, Hussein has always remained a strong supporter of the monarchy, or perhaps more accurately, of a strong monarch. In Hassan II he saw a clever calculator of advantage, a man who could play the shortsighted against one another and, as Hassan himself used to say, guide the Moroccan lion sometimes by easing on the leash he held and at other times by reining it in hard. While Hussein rejoices in the differences of custom and style he encounters in the marketplace, he would, I feel sure, readily acknowledge the truth of Abdellah Hammoudi's insightful statement that "the authoritarian government must have diversity in order to appear as the mediator." And while he admired the king's boldness, his go-slow approach to change, his clever fluctuation of force and forgiveness, and the similar qualities of some of the local tribal political leaders, Hussein continually rejected any efforts made by his own allies to put him forward politically. Indeed, like many Moroccans, the more ardent partisans and intellectuals perhaps excepted, Hussein does not appear in all instances to see his fate as tied to that of his nation's. Faced by challenges from the outside, as in the Algerian border disputes and to a more limited extent the whole Western Sahara venture, he rallies to Morocco's claims. But his identity is not so deeply attached to the country as to override his choices at every turn. To the contrary, as promises of national development have flickered over the years, Hussein has maintained a strong attachment to the local, whether it be in his modes of forging associations, his vision of safety and well-being, or in his forward-looking memory. These tendencies were only to become more marked as the years went by.

A known mistake is better than an unknown truth.
Before you enter, be sure to check out the exit.

—Moroccan sayings

In anthropology, as in psychoanalysis, it is important to know when to stop. (A friend undergoing psychiatric training called once to say that, after earlier sessions had taken him back through the stages of his development, during his most recent session he remembered being born. I suggested that perhaps it was time to stop because if he continued, he might drown.) At the time of my initial fieldwork in the 1960s the decision about when to break off from a period of fieldwork was mainly dependent on the need to complete my degree. Later, the mundane pressures of expiring grants and the need for employment were more decisive. But when, as I prepared for a trip back many years after that first encounter, I recalled how, in the summer of 1969, with degree and the offer of a postdoc in hand, and then on various other visits, I was able to watch as Hussein developed his finances and his standing within the community.

At the time of one such revisit I had arrived the same day there was to be a redistribution ceremony at the local stadium of lands seized from colonists and now being handed out to a few local farmers, an event the Haj was eager for me to see. We made our way up into the stands and watched as the pasha's brother, then serving as minister of information, handed out titles to several rather ragged-looking countrymen. When one man, obviously illiterate, held the document upside down, the minister actually upbraided him for not knowing how to read; when another gave his name not in the usual patronymic form but as son of a woman's name, the minister shamelessly teased the man for not knowing who his father was. But it was after the minister and his entourage departed that, looking down at a line of rural men gathered before the assembled crowd playing native tambourines and singing that I noticed Hussein among them, clearly having the time of his life playing along and, as he later said, watching the minister, like most politicians, make a fool of himself. Indeed, when we got a chance to sit down together, Hussein could not help but rush to bring me up to date.

If there is much to be said for stopping fieldwork, there is just as much to be said for return visits to the field, however brief, not least because people are so flattered you have returned that they pour forth their news while the anthropologist, fresh from realizing how much remains to be understood from the last go-round, rushes to ask all the things he hoped would not be brought up in the dissertation defense. Although I could only visit him briefly on some of these occasions, it was immediately clear that Hussein was prospering, but not without some cost to his moral sensibilities.

My brother and I bought a truck, Hussein told me that day in 1969, a Berliet, that can carry sheep in two levels and cost $6,400. If we aren't using it for sheep, we take vegetables all the way from the Middle Atlas to Casablanca. Wherever we go, we look around for something to sell at a profit in the next place. Buying and selling, said Hussein, is our "salary," our *mandat*.

This term had become the watchword of the day. For what everyone said they wanted in these years, especially for their children, was a steady government income, a *mandat*. Education was seen as the key, and no effort was too great, for urban and rural alike, to secure it. People will do anything to send their kids through school, Hussein said. Many of them rent a place in town and have their wife or a family member move there to take care of the student. Hussein's comments recalled a Moroccan saying: "Without the sons of the poor, scholarship would die." That proposition has long been applicable to students from the countryside who would attend Quran studies at a mosque, though it applies to broader education as well. But the government does not always play fair, Hussein continued. Each year they set the number of those who will be allowed to pass the baccalaureate exam, and in March (1969), when they changed the proportion at the last moment, some people took to the streets of Sefrou and many other towns in protest. Recalling what Yaghnik had told me about the same events, I asked how widespread the protest was. People may not participate in a protest, Hussein commented, but the fact that it is widely believed they support it means that they are saying to others, "Go ahead and take the lead," which any good leader knows makes a big difference in whether the protest will go forward at all. Such marches in which those who stand by effectively license the protest in the first place, or in which the ostensible point of the protest (e.g., some recent government policy change) masks the true point of disagreement with government actions were to become a pattern Hussein would often note over the coming years in Morocco. Time was short for me during some of those visits, but I looked forward to keeping in touch about these and other issues through regular return trips.

But it was nearly a decade, not until the summer of 1978, before I was to see Hussein again. Not finding him at home in the settlement, I returned with several village men to the café in Sefrou, where they said he might be found. Sure enough, the Berliet truck was parked nearby, and the boys told me to just go upstairs and surprise Hussein. Looking up as I entered, I saw Hussein leaning back against the rail, his yellow turban tilted at a rakish angle, his stubbly beard a few days old. Just then he turned, saw me, and broke into a huge smile while calling aloud, "Ah, Larry!" I rushed up the narrow staircase and around the men at the table to embrace him. The others seemed to know who I was, and we all began relating the news of the passing years. Occasionally, Hussein would break into Berber to tell the others something about me and then turn to me and apparently say, "Isn't that so?" as if it was only expectable that I would understand the Berber he spoke.

Clearly Hussein was prospering: on the way down from the village one of the men even joked that Hussein could afford to buy a Rolls Royce, and Hussein himself acknowledged that he had been doing very well in the sheep trade and had, in addition, substantially increased his landholdings at Beni Mansour. He had dissolved his partnership in the truck as a result of some disagreement with his partners, but, as he said, you never should break with someone entirely, so he purchased a twenty-five-hectare plot from a departing Jew and formed a partnership with his former trucking associates to work it. The mid-1970s, I knew, had, at one level, been a boom time for some in Morocco: annual growth hit 7.3 percent as foreign borrowing fueled national debt. When I asked about his sheep herds, he said that he no longer keeps large numbers at various locations. It is too hard to get shepherds, he said, now that many of the young boys are attending school. Kids, he said, want TVs and cars and radios now and show rather little interest in rural life, even though the diploma you get in life is worth far more than the one you get from school. Hussein told me that he had, in typically Moroccan fashion, also added to his house, building rooms around the formerly open roof area and furnishing them with handsome banquettes and pillows where he could entertain guests. He was also in the process of building a new house, which, like many in the village at that time, would be situated separately in one of the gardens rather than clustered among those in the main part of the settlement.

Politics was a natural subject of discussion, too, when we returned to the settlement and were joined for a meal by a number of the other men. Settling back in the somewhat grander new guest room, Hussein picked up the thread of our earlier conversations. The recent parliamentary election had been a contentious affair, and Hussein's humor and disgust were once again on display. It was a nasty business, he said, with some of the supporters of various Arab candidates making bad remarks to us and our kids. This fellow here, he said, pointing to the man next to him, was beaten up by one man's supporters, and this one here, he said, playfully grabbing another young man, is our little socialist: the local caid rounded him and some others up, left them without food or water for two days, and kept them so long at the caid's office that now we call *him* "caid." When I asked whom he supported, he said: Aherdane, from the Berber Party, came and said the Socialist leader was a liar, would promise anything, and is really against the king. Besides, Aherdane had airplanes fly over the crowd after the speech he gave here. Aherdane had airplanes and cars and money and everything, and the Socialist didn't even have a donkey. So whom would you vote for? It is all just silly politics anyway. I don't want anything to do with parties anymore; buying and selling is much more interesting.

The attitude of Hussein and his companions was equally skeptical when we turned to the most important political developments of the intervening years. Twice, in 1971 and again a year later, attempts had been made on the life of the king, once at his birthday party, when he apparently talked young cadets out of shooting him, and again when he fooled attacking aircraft into believing that their fire had already killed him. Reasons for these attempts varied, from rampant corruption to the oddity, recalled by many from a few years before, of the king placing a huge portrait of himself near the new mosque, located close to the palace in Rabat, a portrait not of him as Commander of the Faithful riding to prayers with his black guard carrying an umbrella over his head but of him dressed in his golfing togs, putter in hand. These attempts on the king's life were wrong and stupid, Hussein said, and yes, the cadets came from the nearby training facility in the Middle Atlas and, yes, the perpetrator of the second attempt, General Oufkir, was a Berber. But this was not a Berber plot, and the people who did this should be severely punished. Hussein nodded his affirmation, too, when I mentioned the remark of another man who said, when I asked what would happen if the king was assassinated, that there would be a king in every police station. The king is clever, Hussein said, clever for the people: he gets us foreign aid when the crops are bad, and he plays politicians off like a master. The parties have done us no good. Remember that agricultural election when you were here last, when a rural guy upset the richest man in Sefrou, but the big shots from Rabat still wouldn't let him take office? I told you then that it was someone else's turn to get rich. That's still how it works.

I recalled how much Hussein and others emphasized the need for strong leaders, men they thought were lacking at the local level nowadays. Caids today, said Hussein, are not men of "force." In the past they worked hard. You would go into their office and you would see one aide in one kind of uniform, others in another kind, and all of them with a hat or something to show you their position. Now they all wear trousers and suits, and you can't tell who is who. Before, they would always be out in the countryside. You could see them coming from miles away, and when their cars pulled up, an aide would jump out, open the door, salute, and the caid would quickly complete his business; then the process would be reversed, and he was off again in a cloud of dust. Now what do the caids use their aides for? They send them to the market—like women—to buy tomatoes and peppers! For a caid then it was forbidden, shameful to just sit idly in a café—he was always working, powerful. Now they practically live in the fancy cafés of Rabat and Fez. The caids today, he concluded in one of his very rare moments of using a French phrase, c'est fini.

I then asked about the other key occurrence of the intervening years, the Green March in 1975, when the king declared that the Saharan zones the Spanish relinquished were Moroccan territory, and he marched over 300,000 unarmed men into the area. It is crazy to send men in unarmed, said Hussein. Did they go by choice? I asked. Actually, he answered, the ones I know about who went were forced to do so by the local sheikh, who threatened to put them in jail if they refused. There were a few people from here who went expecting to get free land, but they are being foolish. They will get nothing. Even the land that is being distributed around here by the government, which they say is freehold land, cannot be passed by normal inheritance rules and can be lost if you move away from it for a time. How can you call it private land when you aren't free to deal with it? What Hussein did not mention was that the Saharan venture was absorbing twice as much national expenditure as all the other programs of the government and that by the late seventies, while few voiced direct opposition to the Saharan takeover, strikes and protests by teachers and unionists had been fueled by the distorting effect of the venture.

Throughout his remarks Hussein was voicing a widely shared set of themes: that political parties exist not for their ideas but as bases of association that may be useful (such that fathers not infrequently place one son in one party and another with the opposition); that getting allies to show up for something is the surest indicator of success; and that the legitimacy of the king, like those who imitate his legitimacy at lower levels, must at all times be shown to be operative, whether it is in the claim to spiritual potency derived through a line of predecessor saints, by virtue of Prophetic descent, or through claims of notable lineage. Politics, for Hussein, is, then, not the more to be admired for being a displacement of war but the more to be scorned as a lesser form of doing business.

If Hussein's finances were flourishing, however, some elements of his personal life were not. Both Hussein's father and his uncle had died; "They went to Allah" was his culturally standard response, and then, in a wonderfully apt metaphor of his whole ethos, he added, "They are traveling." Hussein's brain-impaired son was also doing very poorly. After various medical opinions were explored, it was clear that the boy's ailment was incurable. Fellow villagers urged me not even to ask about the boy because Hussein and his wife felt ashamed of his ailment. Hada had, however, given birth to a daughter two years before and to another son two years before that, a lively little boy who would stand naked on the running board of Hussein's truck and shake my hand with great self-assurance. The elder of Hussein's daughters had married the son of Hada's brother. Recently, this husband had struck Hussein's young son. I never really liked the man, Hussein told me, and his remark reminded me that years before, Hussein mentioned that this man's father had sought a ritual "bribe" (_rshwa_) from him, well beyond the customary token amount, when Hussein married his sister. "Corn yields seed for corn, and grain for grain," Hussein added: To know what a boy will be like, just look at those who gave birth to the seed. Our custom is that if you want to end a marriage, the father can just return the bridewealth payment and have the divorce registered, and that is exactly what I plan to do. Later, he said quite casually, I will find a better husband for my daughter.

Hussein has a rather jovial view of marriage generally. We Berbers often change wives in the spring, he joked, and we can have lots of them. How many wives can you have in America? When I answered that we only have one at a time, he laughed and, mimicking a man going to bed, said it was better to be able to rest your head one night on this one and one night on the other. But isn't it really tiring having more than one wife? I teased. See that old man over there dozing? Hussein said. It may be a bit much for him but not for a strong man. Yet as well-to-do as he had become, I noted that Hussein still had but one wife. It was the oldest son he was to lose.

One morning in late July a boy from the village came to find me. He told me that Hussein's son had died early that day while Hussein was marketing up in the mountains. We drove out to the settlement and paid our condolences to Hada, who looked drained, surrounded as she had been all morning by crying women. She asked if we could drive over to Azrou and tell Hussein the news. With one of their kinsmen we drove to the hilltop overlooking the market. Down below we spotted Hussein, and when his kinsman approached and told him the news, we could see Hussein, dressed in a dark brown djellaba and a beige turban tied in the Saharan style, brace himself, gather a few colleagues, and prepare to return home. When he came up to the car, we expressed our sympathy. He smiled wanly and simply said it was God's will, and we all piled into the car for the quiet ride back. At the settlement, as we quickly prepared to leave, Hussein's expression turned from contemplative to somber, as he reflected perhaps not just on the death of his son but on the boy's whole tragically short life.

Movement is a blessing.

—Arab saying

June 1988: When I mentioned to a young Moroccan the sometimes strange feeling of returning to the field after a number of years, he said that I should think of it as rereading a favorite book. The analogy is apt, for even if a book may seem to be complete within its own parameters, the passage of time and the very open nature of the text may lead to different impressions than those acquired at first reading. As always upon arriving in Morocco, I asked about the rainfall, but this time with special concern, since a number of years in the 1980s brought serious droughts. Many people said the drought years were not such a bad thing, though, because they led to the digging of wells that frequently provided rich new sources of water. On the king's land near Fez, they noted, water was quickly discovered, thus reinforcing the view of the king's spiritual potency. Additional irrigation schemes, based on those the French had planned for what they imagined would be an endless Protectorate, helped to ameliorate the situation, at least for the wealthy, while foreign aid shipments secured the monarchy from further pressure.

In Moroccan parlance particular years are sometimes singled out for a defining event: 1945 was long known as the year of the ration coupon ('am l-bun) and 1975 as the year of the Green March ('am mesira). Similarly, 1988 was soon to be known as the year of the mosque ('am mesjid) because of the $800 million mosque the king decided to build in Casablanca, always a hotbed of opposition and itself lacking the historic religious sites of a Fez or Marrakech. But these names usually reflect a time when social ties have been jumbled and are subject to being rearranged, and the fact that the king's call for voluntary contributions to build the mosque was followed by unofficial wage deductions and coerced donations that upset relationships of interdependence did not sit well with anyone. (A joke at the time concerned two worshippers at the new mosque who could not get in because of overcrowding. One says, "We should complain." Horrified, the other says, "No, he will just build another one!")

Rain had been plentiful in the period just before I arrived, however, and Morocco was having one of the best agricultural years since independence. During the preceding drought years the king had suspended all taxes on farmers until 2000, but such taxes were, in fact, very slight in any event. Throughout the country one was seeing the effects of a new government approach: privatization. Bus lines, some utilities, and many cooperatives were being sold off to investors, and where people had emphasized the desirability of government jobs for their children, now they spoke more in terms of the private sector. Remittances from abroad had risen to 40 percent of GDP. The gap between rich and poor was becoming even more visible as new quarters in every city contained huge villas, and the old city and squatter settlements grew rapidly from within. The country was politically rather quiet. As always, the king was playing one faction against another, never loosening the grip of his own power while appearing to foreign nations to be the very model of a moderate Muslim monarch.

Once again I drove out the Boulemane road to find Hussein. At what I thought was the turnoff, I picked up a young man who came from the settlement. Interestingly, he did not recognize the name Ait ben 'Assu as that of the group of houses, the name Boukherfane having become more common. It was an example of how a man who no longer has an impact on people's lives may have his attachment to his base settlement be replaced by a name that refers to the endeavors—in this case of sheep-dealing entrepreneurs—of those who come after. Along the way, the young man filled me in on some of the changes in Hussein's life.

Shortly after I had last seen him, Hussein divorced his wife Hada. I do not know the reason why, the young man said. Hussein did seem to want more children, and that may have been a factor. He told me that their son, now fourteen, lived during the school year in the house Hada owns in Sefrou and goes back to the settlement during the summer. Hussein could certainly have afforded to take a second wife, but I knew from earlier conversations that, for all his joking, he did not care for polygamy, even though he thought that the law had no business telling a man how many wives he should be able to have. If a woman and her family don't mind that she is the second or tenth wife, Hussein had said, it should be up to them. People should be free to make whatever contractual arrangements they want. Though Hussein himself was not a polygamist, he had, around 1981, following his divorce from Hada, taken a new wife, a Berber woman from high up in the Middle Atlas. They now had three small children, two boys and a girl, the young man continued. He described Hussein as sixtyish, reasonably healthy, dressed in a djellaba, a turban, and a big purse—a description I took as emphasizing that Hussein still looks very much the Berber when many other men were wearing Western clothes. When we arrived in the settlement, Hussein's wife came out to greet us. Young, pretty, and very lively, she told us that Hussein would not be back for some time. So it was not until the next day that we met in the café on the main street of Sefrou.

The past decade had left its mark on Hussein. His greeting was as warm as ever, but the boyish smile now revealed that he had lost many of his teeth. He also carried a cane, his right knee and ankle obviously giving him a lot of pain. He had put on weight and looked ruddy and rather puffy. Yet in the sweetness of his smile and in his own shy and utterly unselfconscious way, he continued to be amazed by our friendship. I joined him while he shopped for dinner, and then we headed out to the village, arriving a bit before sunset.

Hussein was living in the same house, rather than the new one he had been building, but the rest of the roof area had now been enclosed to form a room some forty feet by twenty feet, its walls tiled, the banquettes covered in rich brocades, a large photo of Hussein as a young man hanging opposite the entrance, and all the trappings of a big man's entertainment room—large tea kettles, trays, carpets, etc.—on full display. As we sat and talked in the glow of the propane lantern, others came and went—a worker discussing some business, a couple of young cousins seeking quick advice—until dinner was served near midnight.

Hussein, I learned, was continuing to buy and sell sheep, but he now owned several houses in Sefrou and still more land at Beni Mansour. The drought has not much affected us, he said. Much of my land is irrigated, new wells seem to hit water at less than ten meters, and in areas along the coast where the drought was especially bad, I was able to purchase sheep at a good price and find plenty of pasturage for them back here in our hills. I was asked by the Berber Party to get involved in politics, but those people who do so are just foolish. They fight over nothing when buying and selling is more interesting and profitable. I do have two lawyers working on a lawsuit that has been going on now for three years. I had a contract to buy a piece of farmland for 10 million francs, but when the owner got an offer from someone else for 12 million, he refused to complete our deal. The court ruled for me—they even fined the man when he wouldn't follow their order—so now we are waiting for the appeal.

On our way out to the village Hussein told me that Mr. Tobaly, the only remaining Jew in Sefrou, had asked us to stop by. This turned out not to be Jacob Tobaly, who had been my landlord back in the 1960s, but Mimoun, who still owned a gas station at the edge of the old city and had long been involved in financial dealings with people from the countryside. What was striking was how he and Hussein embraced, joked, teased one another about various deals, and clearly felt a closeness that had always been part of that special relation of the Jews to the tribesmen of the region. We miss the Jews, Hussein said later, because they made money go around, almost like gambling (*kif swirti*), whereas the Arabs just sit on their money and don't circulate it. I was struck, too, at how many others expressed regret at the Jews' departure, often telling me that they could say things to them that they could not say to fellow Muslims, that it was a kind of psychological intimacy they could find nowhere else in their lives.

It was at this point that Hussein used the word I had been hearing since my return from many other people, including Yaghnik, *mes'uliya*. The root verb means "to answer," but in this form it refers to "one who must answer," who must be answerable, and hence it refers to the broader idea of "responsibility." In the past, said Hussein, everything was about kinship (*ḥabab*), then it was about "friendship" (*saḥab*), and now it is about money (*flus*). Earlier on, if you wanted to deal in the world, you had to rely on kinfolk, or people you could treat as kin, but as people moved around, you had to establish your own ties of "friendship" as I have in Beni Mansour. Nowadays even that is not enough. Now you have to have money to enter "the game," and if you don't have it, no one treats you respectfully or feels the need to give as well as take. You go to a shop or an office in the past, and someone would say, "How are you?" and would even offer you a glass of tea; now they say, "What do you want?" in an abrupt and impolite way. There is no civility now.

Hussein's optimism, in the face of colonial intervention, corrupt officialdom, mendacious associates, and the constraints of capricious weather and shifting alliances never ceased, though, to amaze me. Staying mobile, in every sense of the word, seems to be key to Hussein and his compatriots' approach to such uncertainty. Thus, through the 1980s, as before and since, Moroccans sought work wherever in the country or in the world they could find it. Over the years, I have encountered people from the Sefrou region in France, Colorado, the Low Countries, and California. It would be easy to attribute this mobility to some romantic vision of tribal nomadism or the determinative push of economic necessity, but that would miss the terms through which Hussein and others render this flow meaningful. He repeated a saying I heard often from others when discussing this subject: "Every absence increases prestige" (*kull l-ghiba katzid l-hiba*). It means that a man has to understand how other people act and think, he explained, so that if you are going to have a relationship with another, you need to know the customs by which he operates. Isn't that what you are doing here? Won't people in America listen to you when you speak, because you have traveled and learned our customs?

Once, I showed Hussein a copy of A. J. Arberry's translation of the Quran I kept with me, and he asked what passages those little stickers marked. I shamelessly translated back into the only Arabic I speak not the word of God but the colloquial of a Moroccan Everyman the passage that says: "Had I wished it I could have made you all one nation." Hussein smiled broadly and said that it is exactly those differences God put there so we would have to make the effort to understand each other's ways. If, I remembered Houari Touati having written, "Muslim men of letters of the Middle Ages were mad for travel" because, as they sought the purest forms of Arabic, the truest relation of what the Prophet said or did, the least contaminated rendition of religious knowledge—all of which accrued to their own authority as spokesmen for right conduct and right thought—Hussein traveled to know the range and kind of human difference, thus enabling him to guide others in the best ways to negotiate such a multifaceted world. Like his other favorite Quranic passage—"Seek knowledge even unto China"— Hussein clearly equates useful information with moving through a peopled world.

For Hussein movement is both natural and necessary, not only to learn how to connect to others but because movement defines the space and content of the world a man occupies. Yet movement is not the same as being unattached. Hussein often used the Arabic word *rbet*, which like the Berber *thqef* means "bound" or "attached," to refer to an association with a smart teacher or leader, as well as to bonds of kinship and residence— but always with that ambiguous sense of being simultaneously linked and fettered. Only movement, whether across terrain or through networks of relationship, can define a man. I even wondered at times if Hussein might not be a bit of a natural Wittgensteinian, or if the philosopher may have unknowingly been a bit of a Moroccan, for seeming to say with the Austrian philosopher, that "the axis is not fixed in the sense that it holds fast, but the movement around it determines its immobility." Whether it is in the older marital custom of dressing a man as a woman, tying his hands, and then ritually releasing him into a state of manhood, or in answering the simple inquiry "How are you?" (literally, "What is your news?") by answering, "I am in the world" (*ana f-dunia*), movement for Hussein is made free by forging connections wherever they may be had. On more than one occasion he also reminded me that in their language the term for Berbers means "free men" and that the ideograph in the Berber system of writing for "free" is an abstract representation of a man. Nowadays, though, Hussein mused, people move around so frequently you can't tell much about them: even people of good "origins" are unpredictable. As with the departure of the Jews his tone was one of sadness, of a world that does not conform to the sense of interdependency and civility that is so vital to his sense of propriety and order.

For Hussein, as for many others, the absence of "responsibility" was also related to the significant increase in everyday corruption, a point that came home quite vividly when, in the course of a gathering in his guest room after the Friday prayers, Hussein turned from the assembled men and posed a question to me: Is there corruption in America? Yes, I answered. Give us an example, he said. So, as the room quieted, I gave an example of a kickback arrangement. Ah, no, said Hussein, as the others shook their heads in unison, that is just buying and selling. So I mentioned the Watergate scandal. No, no, Hussein replied to common assent, that is just politics. So I gave an example of nepotism. No, no, no, all voices cried out, that is just family solidarity. So, as I struggled to think of an example that would maintain the honor of my country for being every bit as corrupt as anyone else's, Hussein turned to the others and said, with genuine admiration, You see why America is so strong: they have no corruption!

When I asked the men at Hussein's, as I have so many in the Arab world over the years, what passes for corruption in their view, I received the same answer: corruption is the failure to share with those with whom you have formed ties of dependence whatever largesse comes your way. Theirs is a world in which the defining feature of a man is that he has formed a web of indebtedness, a network of obligations that prove his capacity to maneuver in a world of relentless uncertainty. Failure to service such attachments is thus regarded as not only stupid but corrupt. The dictionary defines corruption as "morally debased." But context matters, and it is not enough to see things, as Hussein and others in his world do, as "eating the beneficence" yourself. Set in a bureaucratic order where delay and prevarication are rife, where underlings fear blame and every official holds his or her position at the whim of someone higher up, corruption ironically becomes a mode of efficiency: with the right timing and amount of "grease" (to use their own idiom) desired ends can be quickly accomplished. And because Moroccans are constantly negotiating the definition of the situation anyway—asking, for example, are we members of the same "fraction" or just the more distant "tribe," did your words or acts constitute a validation of an obligation, or were they just another turn in the bargaining process?—it is often the terms of the situation that have to be negotiated, with the payment constituting its confirmation. Corruption can even contribute to transparency in an odd way because, in the constant quest for information, one has to show connections, indeed even secrets, in order for one's maneuvering capacity to attract others to you. From a somewhat functionalist view, therefore, one could point to some "useful" aspects of corruption, even as Hussein and his colleagues define it.

This approach to "corruption" came out in remarks I was hearing from people of quite different backgrounds. A professor of geography drew me a diagram of a series of people, each of whom arranged his contacts in his own way. The only French word he used in the conversation was *ambivalence*, a word he used to describe Morocco generally. There is, he said pointing to his diagram, a "contradiction" as each person sets about organizing his own arrangements; people want laws, but they also want the freedom to make their own arrangements, even when that means getting "favors" the laws might restrict. Another man, returning for the summer from employment abroad, told me that he would prefer freedom with corruption to rigid laws that tie a man up. And a lawyer remarked that laws are like different shoes: you need one sort for running and another for hiking across rocky terrain, and favoritism is integral to the choice of the proper footgear needed for a given purpose. For all its undoubted evils, then, corruption can yield a certain efficiency and enable the search for knowledge even as it circles back to reinforce the need for more information and more contacts in the first place.

Yet the pain of dealing in a world of petty corruption is palpable for Hussein. The police will stop our truck for no reason at all, he said, and will accept even a small amount as a bribe just so they get something. A bill inserted in a pack of cigarettes, a "present" carried for the purpose—we have to do it for the smallest of things. We Moroccans (I recalled another man saying) are the "technicians of bribery" for all the ways we can think to do it. The extent and impact of having to pay for what should be part of an official's duty-bound acts cannot now be underestimated. Indeed, matters were only to get worse over the years. In its July 2013 report Transparency International stated that half of all Moroccans have paid a bribe at some time, usually to police, but also to people in the judicial system, to hospital and medical personnel, to teachers, and to bureaucrats. When Hussein and others speak about such matters, the words they use carry the implication of being made dirty, of prostituting one's values (*fasad*), of not being able to engage others in a relation of trust through reciprocal expectations. Their sense of corruption is one of deep-seated loathing made all the more offensive by what they recognize as their own necessary complicity.

But there is also humor and insight connected with the florescence of corrupt practices. Talking with the men in his guest room on another occasion, Hussein brought me up short by saying: You know, corruption is our form of democracy. While the others smiled, waiting for yet another clever turn to Hussein's words, I expressed complete bafflement. Well, you see, he said (gathering his heavy winter cloak around him and smiling broadly), if some big man says do such and such, but I can pay someone below him not to do it, is that not a check on the big man's power? And isn't democracy all about keeping big men from having too much power over you? As the assembled men nodded and chuckled at Hussein's words, I was once again reminded of his much-admired ability to use language as a form of what Muslim scholars call "lawful magic" (*sihr halal*).

Hussein was also mindful of the delicate ways in which another's power can and should be limited. He spoke, in effect, of the power of weakness when he was careful to note that a man can often choose upon which of various more powerful men to be dependent. He was quick to joke about the powerful generally, using stories and proverbs to cut them down to size. He told the tale of a fussy Arab type who derided the countryman's use of the colloquial. Can you write Arabic? asked the countryman. Of course, huffed the self-important Arab. Well write this, said the rural man, and he made a sound like one spitting. Hussein knew the two-edged nature of such remarks. We have a saying, he once told me: "When a Moroccan succeeds, people applaud—and when he doesn't succeed, people applaud." So, he seemed to be saying, not only are there pressures not to convert one form of success into a form of power over others, but where everything depends on the praise of others, success and failure may, in fact, yield similar results.

Hussein's approach to power, then, often seemed to be one of indirection. Indeed, he himself emphasized this point. You do not want to have to say "no" to someone with actual or potential power, he would say, so you do not take what they say as a directive but as a suggestion. You also don't look at what it gets you to do something for him in the short-term: you concentrate on what sense it makes for you looking way down the line. And you don't just pay attention to the bad things, even the stupid things, a person with some power says. "You ignore many things from a liar," we say, because if you fail to realize that, as much as a man may lie, there are still some truths in what he says, you will lose sight of those parts you shouldn't have ignored. In his typical admixture of tolerance, pragmatism, and eclecticism, I was later to think how much Hussein might have agreed with what Rifa'a al-Tahtawi, an Egyptian sent to Paris in the early nineteenth century wrote:

> Don't reject an idea if it is suitable,
> Or Truth even if it comes from error.
> Pearls are precious to acquire,
> But it is not the diver who decides their worth.

What I also understood Hussein to be saying was that it is the whole process that matters. Later I came across something that André Aciman, the writer of Egyptian background, said: "Process is a tricky word: it embraces neither the present nor the future tense, but something grammarians might call the imperfect conditional. In other words, neither here nor there." Perhaps that is why foreigners often think Arabic a strange language for having no infinitives and for letting context sort things out when, as we saw one scholar suggest, every word in Arabic seems to mean something and its opposite. Process is all in Hussein's world—whether in the style of assessing another in court, in politics, or in marital negotiations, or in the way truth is established in the marketplace. It is a world in which words and relations are kept relatively open ended, and hence a world in which the command of language to pin something down to a momentary context makes all the difference.

It is also a style of language use that can be easily misunderstood by outsiders. Westerners often characterize Middle Easterners as prone to exaggerated rhetoric, as if the worst excesses of a Nasser or Qaddafi were the norm. By contrast, Hussein provided no end of examples showing that a person of worldly consequence must (in the idiom of his culture) "have word." For example, once, as we sat in his guest room with the other men, the discussion turned to the annual cleaning of the settlement's main irrigation canal. A well-to-do man speaking Arabic said that he would be hiring someone to perform his share of the work. From the corner came the voice of a poor man. I do not remember his exact words, but I vividly recall how he spoke quite elegantly of the cleaning as a communal act, not something whose meaning could be converted through money or palmed off on others. He cited other examples, the words of his predecessors, the need for men to work together, and what I took to be a Berber proverb or two. By the time he was done, he had so captured the terms of the situation as to render the wealthier man's resources totally irrelevant to the situation. Competition to capture the terms of discussion can, as someone once noted of Moroccans, render conversation a blood sport. And the reason why poets are so admired (and in the Quran so reviled) is that they may define a circumstance in ways that undercut the words of the learned and the powerful. Countrymen even engage in song duels in which two groups settle differences by appealing to the opinion of the surrounding crowd through the teasing by each of their lead poets. I also came across the statement a Syrian intellectual once made to the reporter Neil Mac-Farquhar concerning a person's command of language: "In our mentality the man who speaks well is more respectable than the man who works well." However, I think Hussein and his colleagues would put it somewhat differently. For them language is a resource, along with many others, that can be turned into advantageous relationships, and in that sense to speak well *is* to work well. It is a quality that kept appearing as our years of work together stretched out.

The only fence against the world is a thorough knowledge of it.

—John Locke

In the variety of knowledge lies safety.

—Muslim character in Joseph Conrad's *Outcast of the Islands*

I returned to Morocco in January of 1999. Rain had finally begun to fall the month before, ending yet another drought and a period when temperatures broke more than a half century of records. But if the relief was palpable, so was the sense of entropy. The beautifully patterned sidewalks dating from Protectorate times had never seemed right for Morocco: they crack quickly, and as the rigid pattern chips and the whole effect crumbles, the attempt to impose some Cartesian design on a far more dynamic underlay seems utterly misplaced. Tempting analogies abound. Driving up to Sefrou I was again struck by the characteristic etiquette of the road. The style is one of pressing to advantage any opening while still recognizing that, if others have some cognizable "right" they actually and effectively assert, they will be acknowledged. There is little of the free-floating road rage that accompanies the denial of one's status or rights in other countries—little of the Mediterranean refusal to back off a claim no matter what, the German pecking order of vehicle brands on the autobahn, the Egyptian quest for an account that needs to be settled. Pedestrians and animals wander into one's way, and the flow seems more like that of opportunistic waves than determinable tides, not a river in the sea but a stream of whorls and eddies. Traffic is synoptic, casuistic, a shared story whose every encounter builds from predecessor and context to a coherence that is one of process rather than prescription. Like so many other features of what has been called the Arab frame tradition, where music or buildings or poems or relationships are not closed by a preexisting design but reach out in numerous directions to take on new additions, to be alive is to be in the game and to sense how the process *is* the form. A young attorney standing alongside such a road once told me he thought of law in the same way. A right does not exist unless asserted, and the broad outlines of the highway provide identifiable shape to what is within, he said; it is not a free-for-all but a process of swerving and braking, probing and deferring that matches the law to the ways of the society it serves.

Entering Sefrou I was surprised at how built up the city had become. Streets had been widened in front of the city's old walls, villas had been constructed on prime garden land, the French hotel at the outskirts had lost the hedge through which those making their way to the bar used to pass now that the bar itself was gone. The public garden was well maintained, and from the rim of the hills overlooking the city, or at the waterfall that marks the urban perimeter, one could recall Collette's description of Sefrou as an "earthly paradise . . . a pool of fertility, lush, shimmering with laughter and water." Anthropologists, Lévi-Strauss once quipped, are radicals at home and conservatives abroad. Whether as the perpetrators or the victims of functionalism—a theory that emphasizes the contribution of each element to the continued working of a whole society but that, as a result, has always had trouble accounting for change—we anthropologists often have to make a real effort when we study others to note the alterations such theories may obscure. And, wary of appearing judgmental, we often avoid discussions of discontinuities unless we can imagine ourselves allied with the politically correct side in the equation of power. Morocco in particular may not seem to lend itself to a focus on discontinuity. Instead it seems to embrace the continuous—one king for decades, one dynasty for centuries, one religion for millennia. It sometimes becomes an exercise in pressing the limits of predilection and profession, then, to attend to change when neither the subject nor the theories are altogether hospitable to it.

Throughout the 1990s, change often seemed to come from features that had already appeared clearly on the horizon. But at a certain point even quantitative increase can seem like qualitative shift. The statistics for that period and the early part of the twenty-first century help tell the story. Even as the birth rate had dropped between 1980 and the end of the century from 5.9 to 3.4 as the average age of marriage increased for men to twenty-nine and for women to their midtwenties and the number of women using contraceptives had risen from roughly 17 percent to nearly half, the "population momentum"—internal increase coupled with those now entering their childbearing years—boosted the national population from twenty-five million in 1990 to over thirty-one million at the end of the decade and as many as thirty-four million by 2009. (It was less than thirteen million when I began work in Morocco in the mid-1960s.) Life expectancy from birth increased from 56 years for men and over 59 for women in 1985 to 69 and 74 respectively, by 2008, even though infant mortality had dropped in the same period from 93 to 38 per 1,000 live births, the proportion of those under the age of 15 had declined from nearly half of the population to less than 30 percent. Already in 1982 a quarter of the 39,000 people living in the city of Sefrou had migrated from the countryside—the city's proportion not being very different from those of other Moroccan cities—

and the local unemployment rate, though less than the national average, probably hovered around 20 percent. If so many people were now in the cities, what, I wondered must be happening out in places like Hussein's settlement?

As I left Sefrou and drove into the mountains to the south, the feeling was one of depopulation. Climatic fluctuations had contributed to the exodus. When average rainfall in Fez, for example, varied by a factor of four within the space of a couple of years, and when national grain production cycled from 2.5 to 10 to 4 million tons within the compass of five years, what may once have been common occurrences now had uncommon effects on migration, urban growth, and the diminution of the agricultural sector to less than a quarter of all workers. Literacy rates were up by double digits in the 1980s, reaching almost half of the population by the end of the century, and by 2000 a quarter of all women were in the workforce. But according to the UN's Human Development Index, which combines a number of socioeconomic factors, in 1998 Morocco ranked 124th out of 174 countries (and in 2007, 130th out of 182), about the same level as Myanmar and Gabon. With 8.1 percent of the nation's population having emigrated abroad (three-quarters of them to Europe), remittances in 2007 ranked Morocco one of the highest such recipient countries in the world. Poverty at the lowest levels was so persistent as to rank the country alongside Haiti in international ratings.

But if the nationwide rate of those living below the poverty line had risen from 13 percent at the start of the decade to 20 percent by the midnineties, its rise to 25 percent by 2003 only indicated that much of rural poverty had simply been transferred and rendered more visible by movement to urban areas. The World Bank estimated that, in 2010, 44 percent of Moroccans still lived in rural areas and that the growth rate for those areas was virtually flat, while urban population was growing at a rate of 1.6 percent. It may seem astonishing, too, that, at the start of the 1990s, 22.5 percent of urban households and 16 percent of those in rural areas were headed by a woman. But here, as elsewhere, continuities kick in, for recent historical work suggests that in many parts of the Middle East female-headed households have long been underestimated.

In Sefrou itself the press of increased population was palpable. Geographers have described the population movement in Morocco as being like a cascade: first there is partial movement of rural people into a nearby market town, then they pour over more permanently into the nation's smaller cities, and then surge irreversibly into the major urban centers. And certainly cities like Sefrou had become a waypoint for some, an endpoint for many, in this long, slow drainage from the countryside. One contributing factor was that the 1980s had also marked the start of a program of privatizing not only government industry holdings but some land as well. I was reminded that more than 1 million acres of the 2.5 million owned by French farmers in 1973 had been sold to wealthy Moroccans and that much of the remainder went to military or royal favorites. The gap between rich and poor became increasingly visible, especially with the construction of huge villas built by the well-to-do, which were quite unlike the older medina dwellings that hid their status behind obscure walls and stolid doors. Many of the villas were referred to as being "Gulf" or even "California" style, the latter term perhaps being related to the many ways in which Moroccans had tried to develop their agricultural economy along the lines of that state. At moments the growing disparity of wealth intensified local tensions: nationwide strikes and riots in December 1990 and in Tangiers in middecade were ostensibly about food prices, but the anguish ran to a wide range of concerns; in 1992 in the village of Bhalil, just down the road toward Fez from Sefrou, young men publicly protested the way in which a local politician used the *'ar* sacrifice to conduce support, insisting instead that they should be able to select their own leaders without ritual constraint.

Politically, Morocco seemed to cycle through changes that changed little. In 1993 a coalition government offered, at least to the partisan classes, some hope of fundamental change, and after the constitution (through the sixth referendum on that foundational document since 1962) was altered in 1996 to allow direct election of the lower house of Parliament, it seemed the king was willing to permit greater popular involvement. Indeed, two years earlier the king had granted amnesty to 424 prisoners, thus suggesting that a line had finally been drawn after the attempts on his life of the early 1970s. And when, in 1998, the socialist leader Abderahmane Youssefi was appointed prime minister in an opposition-led government—what the king was pleased to call a government of *alternance*, a term that suggested that everyone could play at taking turns—the politically committed were all the more encouraged that democratization from within was possible. *Alternance* seemed an especially appropriate term, since in Arabic the word for "state" or "nation" (*daula*) comes from a root meaning "to rotate." So it seems appropriate that in short order the Youssefi government showed itself stalled and inept, and the king's usual game of pitting parties against one another, yielding no real power and rendering opposition figures complicit in the status quo, demonstrated that real change was not at hand. Unsurprisingly, in the face of the Arab Spring of 2011 a new king again

King Hassan II, 1990s

reformed the constitution, this time allowing the leading party represented in Parliament to supply the prime minister. But without any real powers, that minor alteration effected little real difference in its turn.

The returning anthropologist also grasps at other continuities, familiar artifacts against which to try to measure alteration. When I arrived at the beginning of 1999, my attention was again drawn to the portrayal of King Hassan II on the currency. Miraculously he had become young again, but his face was once more turned away and looking without expression into the distance, perhaps, as Yaghnik and others had remarked, because he is too ashamed to look us in the eye. On the side of each denomination was a blank circle, but if you held the bill up to the light, the king's face, now looking straight at you, suddenly appears, as if he had been watching you all along, yet without that sadder, older, full-face view of an earlier iteration. On the reverse of the 100-dirham note a white dove hovers over those engaged in the Green March to the Sahara, the king's brooding presence, revealed only when raised to the light, overseeing it all.

Once again, as the century came to an end, the unpredictable hand of nature also showed itself. Severe droughts in 1999 and 2000, compounded by labor demands, simultaneously weakened the national economy and strengthened the central government. On the one hand, the government seemed the ultimate source of security against such natural disasters, negotiating foreign aid and dispensing its favors strategically, while on the other, several political parties (and soon several fundamentalist groups) showed up ahead of the government to offer help and set the stage for later garnering protest votes.

I met Hussein at the same café on the main street of Sefrou where the Haj and I so often started the day. When I mentioned a number of these statistics to him, Hussein's reaction was characteristic. To him the most significant factor was the government program of privatization, a program he regarded as desirable but flawed by the fact that it was used to favor the rich and well connected. Land that had belonged to French farmers who had left, he explained, gets handed out to a few farmers in such small pieces that they can't make much of a living from it, while the rich get the best and the largest of the farms. Do you remember, that time a couple of years ago when you were watching from the bleachers as they handed out land titles in a ceremony at the stadium here in Sefrou, how the minster himself made fun of one man because he was called by his mother's family name, when we all knew that was because his father wasn't known, or how he teased the man who held the title upside down because he was illiterate? Do you think he would ever have treated a wealthy landowner that way?

Hussein also did not believe in some local version of the trickle-down theory of economics or that the presence of the opposition parties in the government was anything more than a form of co-optation. He could not cite statistics showing that, in fact, half of all state revenues go to pay the salaries of bureaucrats, but he continued to have mild contempt for those who limited themselves by such dependence. While privatization seemed to encourage rampant capitalism, Hussein noted that almost all the benefits went to a small number of well-connected people, reports I read suggesting that thirty-six families actually control two-thirds of the privatized economy. But, said Hussein, the transfer of many government-held enterprises to a few rich people also made these entrepreneurs more dependent on the government. They think they can rely on the central government, he said, these urban businessmen, but they will have to play the way the big men in the government want them to and will not have even the same independence they had before. They will be like animals on a leash. That is what it will be like for these people who get everything from the government, he concluded: they will think they are free, but they are tied with ropes they cannot see.

Many people from the Sefrou region—including men from Hussein's own group—had long been working abroad, but the pace of attempts to find such jobs, he said, had continued to rise. The statistics were to show still greater increases in the following years. By 2003 there were roughly 2.5 million Moroccans working abroad sending back $3.6 billion per year, the fourth-highest amount of all developing nations. (By 2005 the amount had risen to $4.6 billion, accounting for over 9 percent of the country's

GDP.) Most sought work in Europe. But whereas an earlier generation of foreign workers had sent money back to build homes to which they expected to retire, now many were staying in Europe because Morocco offers no retirement or social welfare benefits. Their children are often caught between worlds. They are teased in Morocco for their ignorance of things Moroccan and subject to various forms of discrimination in Europe, leading them to speak of themselves as being "homesick everywhere." Hussein regards these youngsters as something of a lost generation: When they come back to Morocco to visit, he noted, they can't speak good colloquial Arabic and don't seem to know what to do. For the younger generation generally, he concluded, buying and selling is neither attractive nor always possible.

But something else had happened over the years, something that may have occurred quite gradually or that may have punctuated the flow of perception in moments of national stress. It concerns the nature of memory. Anthropologists and historians are, of course, quite used to people reinventing their views of the past to fit current rationales or creating instant "traditions," and certainly Hussein was as susceptible to these processes as others. He could tweak a tribal genealogy to fit a pressing claim, he could describe a relationship gone sour as never having really engaged him, he could vary the terms suggestive of closeness as his ties to a given kinsman improved. But I sensed that more was at issue than the reinterpretation of the past. As with the Haj and others, what seemed to be changing were the very terms by which events were now being explained.

For example, in the first decades of our work Hussein almost always traced the cause of an event to some individual who made it happen. Whether it was the decision of his tribal predecessors to form a given alliance or the course of a national policy, it was always some *one*, not some *thing*, that could be pointed to as the cause. But when, years later, I was to review with Hussein the same events he had described to me years earlier, two things stood out: that without failing to place great emphasis on individuals, he was also now describing those events (and much more current ones) in terms of how some *thing* could be the effective cause. He would speak of how the world price of a commodity affected the whole market, how the attraction of urban life influenced residence and kinship, how court proceedings had come to include circumstantial evidence and not just the determination of a person's reliability based on knowledge of his web of worldly consequent relationships. In years gone by he used the word that now means "probable" to mean "authoritative," a shift that, while paralleling the Western history of that term's alteration, was clearly an independent development. Just as the Haj had initially described his reasons for not using fertilizer in his garden as being because of *who* said it was not helpful and then, years later, spoke in terms of how things affect things, so, too, Hussein's emphasis showed a subtle shift from the highly personalistic to the more physical explanation of causation and thus seemed consonant with his sense of diminished interaction with knowable others.

To some Moroccans such a shift in causal explanations to one that might appears to accord with the style of European thought seems an appropriate subject for irony. A teacher had told anthropologist Charis Boutieri that "French is Cartesian, it's a cause and effect language. Arabic is a juxtaposition, for example when you ask someone to answer your questions, he will not do it but will make a long speech about how competent he is to do it." Humor aside, for Hussein the issue is one of information rather than logic, and as the sources of social attachment have become less clearly defined, the style in which that information becomes available to him, and with it the ability to predict causal connections, has also become more problematic.

Similarly, what counts as a relationship with continuing effects—the very marker of time itself—appears to have undergone subtle alteration. Like so many others, Hussein feels the uncertainties of predicting and influencing others' affiliations as the countryside becomes comparatively depopulated and the marketplace less personalized. Deborah Kapchan, in her study of the Moroccan bazaar, says that people are nostalgic for an earlier time when, as they say, people "had *niya*," when they operated with intentions that were both transparent and susceptible to forming a basis of trust. That a time should be marked as one of genuine intentions (*kan niya niya*) does not, however, simply equate with the usual notion of nostalgia. For neither Hussein nor Moroccans generally express the sort of nostalgia one encounters in, say, Egypt, where the vision of an earlier, rather pristine time from which society has fallen away is a dominant theme in song and story no less than common discourse. To the contrary, what Hussein and others rue is the lack of clarity on which to base relationships that must at some point incorporate a leap of trust, and it is uncertainty of where to find that base, rather than some image of a golden age to which one would seek to return, that is central. It is an expression of a world grown somewhat indistinct, not a loss of confidence in being able to nonetheless find one's way within it.

In July 1999 King Hassan II died, ending a reign of some thirty-eight years. The transition to his thirty-six-year-old son, Muhammad VI, was smooth. The change afforded many people an opportunity to pause and rethink the past. Already in the early 1990s Hussein, for instance, did not

agree with the incipient revisionist view that Hassan was merciless and repressive. He regards the years of Hassan's reign as ones in which people
spoke openly about politics, and only those who actually lifted their hand
against the monarch were imprisoned. That Muhammad VI released nearly
eight thousand prisoners, reduced the sentences of thirty-eight thousand
others, and established a reconciliation process that revealed details of his
father's regime (though without allowing any direct criticism of Hassan II)
seemed consistent to many with the amnesties that Hassan and his predecessors had long employed. The advent of his son's reign was also trum-
peted as the beginning of great concern for the poor, many of whom lined
up at post offices around the country and sent messages—with a return
receipt requested, in the hope of establishing a personal form of obligation
with the king! For the entire forty-day mourning period, however, Berber-
language news and music was taken off the air and replaced by Arabic programs. When we spoke again during a return visit, Hussein saw the new
king's emphasis on the poor as likely to be more show than substance, but
he admires the young king's entrepreneurial skills and increasing economic
power as a balance to corrupt politicians.

The events of 9/11 were seen by not only Hussein but many Moroccans
with whom I spoke as having gotten the attention of the Americans on
Middle Eastern concerns but in a manner and at a price that would not
receive approbation if repeated. And the bombings in Casablanca in May
2003 that killed over forty people, followed by numerous arrests, sixteen
condemnations to death, and more than fifty persons being given long
prison sentences only reinforced the belief that the fundamentalist parties
would, from the perspective of men like Hussein, act no differently than
other politicians were they to extend their gains from recent elections. The
so-called bread riot that occurred in Sefrou in September 2007 was, like
other such events in Morocco, more about the actions of local officials
than national economics, he said, and was seen as consistent with the
30 percent turnout in that year's elections, in which 20 percent of the bal-
lots were turned in blank, often with insulting comments written in. Similarly, the later iteration of palace-controlled political musical chairs, called
"transhumance," could hardly seem to be a shift toward limited monar-
chical rule. "Authoritarian pluralism" and "liberalized autocracy" may not
have been phrases Hussein shared with the country's intellectuals, but
the majority of Moroccans led daily lives in which national-level affairs
were not their central concern in any event. (A poll showed, for example,
that 95 percent of young people did not identify with any party.) Partisan politics continued to supply Hussein with resources for high humor.

The long-term claims on the Sahara remained popular, and after having to apologize for not including the disputed Western Sahara on its map of restaurants in Morocco, McDonald's began marketing a McSahara Burger, to the amusement of those who saw it all as an example of the absurdities of politics.

By the end of the first decade of the twenty-first century, the approval rating of King Muhammad VI was over 90 percent. But when a poll asserting this appeared, the publications were seized and destroyed because the monarchy was deemed above polling and debate in any form. And though Hussein and his colleagues are unwavering supporters of the monarchy and of a strong hand against those who would challenge the stability it affords, little had changed in the attitude toward ministers and politicians, who are rarely regarded as having the people's interests at heart. It was Hussein, for example, who, apropos of the tendency to blame ministers rather than monarchs, reminded me that there was a man in Sefrou who had only one eye whom everyone called "the king" because, they said, he could see only half of what was going on around him. In the words of a popular Moroccan song, "The king is a doctor and his subjects are wounded, but there is not a single government official who will tell him of their plight." But then, as Joseph Braude has noted, "Such fables, wisely believed by the population, can hold a system together for a very long time."

For many Moroccans a certain degree of what one scholar calls "depoliticization" appears to have occurred over the years, a process that nevertheless does not seem to have delegitimized the monarchy. When asked, however, neither Hussein nor any of his fellow villagers ever expresses his views in terms of some kind of conspiracy theory. Indeed, Westerners who attribute such conspiracy-mindedness to Middle Easterners usually fail to hear the way events are being explained. For it remains vital to Hussein's and others' view of society that they still see persons as the primary causal agents of events, not that there are constant, hidden cabals. And though they are more prone now to discuss how things can make things happen in a world in which people move around so much that predicting or conducing behavior based on group attachment has become more problematic, their focus on persons rather than impersonal forces continues to be a crucial factor for an outsider trying to understand their lives.

The honest, truthful Muslim merchant will stand with the martyrs on the Day of Judgment.

—al-Muttaqi, *Kanz al-'ummal*

It's what makes the world go 'round, differences.

—Charles Todd, *Legacy of the Dead*

I once mentioned to Hussein, as I had to several shopkeepers, that in many instances Islam was brought to new lands not by soldiers or missionaries but by merchants. More recently I mentioned that traders may have played a similar role when the Berbers along the old Roman frontiers accepted Islam, a time when, as scholars have described it, "Islam was no longer called upon to identify the conquerors in relation to the conquered, so much as the merchants in relation to their clients." Hussein expressed delight at these notions, but not surprise. Our Quranic schoolteacher keeps reminding us that the Prophet stressed the need to keep to your contractual commitments, he remarked. We even say, "It is by the grace of God that contentiousness is put between the buyer and the seller." Why? Because differences make you pay attention to *who* that other person is and how you should be dealing with him. Hussein also has implied that the market itself works best when there is diversity and difference at its core. And though he has always respected my scholarly work, I feel sure that, on the Moroccan equivalent of the theory that the seed falls close to the source, it was my father's career as a small businessman and my grandfather's as a peddler that has made Hussein believe I might share the marketer's appreciation of diversity.

There is, then, a morality to this man of business, but not one of pretense and professed superiority, of exclusiveness and vaunted religiosity. Hussein, like many others, views the marketplace as being in and of the world, not as an exception to it, a world that embraces cleverness and even craftiness as much as it does candor and trust, and all without inherent hypocrisy, posturing, or contradiction. As in every other domain of Moroccan life, there is a felt sense of ambiguity in market dealings. As Deborah Kapchan has said of those involved in Moroccan market life, "There is no transaction without some sincerity, but no profit in sincerity alone." In the market, as indeed in the ethos of tribal relations, a certain leveling takes place, and like those wily thieves who, as Fadwa Malti-Douglas explains, appear in classical Arabic crime narratives, cleverness better informs the momentary loser about the ways of the world—indeed renders him in many respects interchangeable with the thief, someone who nevertheless should not be so severely punished as to fail to be a potential ally on another occasion. Being clever is not, then, an example of moral blurring but of the need to consider relations of identity across transient differences and to take steps to keep avenues open that unbridled conflict could otherwise render unavailable.

It is not surprising, then, that Hussein constantly emphasizes that an adversary at one moment may be an ally at another, an ethos that calls for gauging, and often limiting, one's willingness to take differences to an irreversible point. Whether it is in his references to earlier forms of tribal warfare or contemporary instances of political contest, Hussein advocates a middle course, which he regards in no way as a sign of weakness but as its exact opposite. His words recall those of North Africa scholar Jacques Berque, who once wrote: "The recourse to negotiation, to a bargaining that weighed adversaries up, and to cynical reversals of position was . . . not just a taint of military weakness or a sign of duplicity. It contained a long tradition that prefers manoeuvre to war. It does not, therefore, compel the admiring scorn that such behavior, observed in subtle partners, inspired in Bismarck. It is the characteristic of intelligence braving coarseness, of energy palliating lack of means."

Nor is the market merely a zone of financial transactions. Indeed, without in any way romanticizing it, the market is also for Hussein the premier place for the enactment of Islam. For the market *is* in a zone of religion in one crucial sense: the Quran, along with the stories of the practices and sayings of the Prophet, make clear that this world is a stage, a platform, a zone limited by the "rights of God" as well as the place within which the "rights of man" to contract and abide by their contracts, to explore difference yet claim no moral superiority based on difference, challenges humankind to fashion bonds in such a way as to render the world a proper "community of believers." It is not the occasional seller's bluster that "it is by the beard of the Prophet that I know these goods to be what I say they are" that renders this a space tinged by the religious, for such utterances may be regarded as no more to be assessed for their truth value when unsubstantiated by a recognized mode of validation than is a price mentioned in the process of a negotiation. Rather it is the practice of fabricating a world of bargained-for attachments that renders the market a mundane instance of the supernatural model, a human version of that indispensable aspect of being a Muslim—living in a community configured by negotiated difference. Religiosity, then, lies not in ritual or prayer alone but in the enactment of that God-given reasoning power that renders men able to create their own relations and in doing so to achieve conformity to the divine will.

Thus, to Hussein, as to many others I have encountered, the marketplace and Islam meet on a terrain of realism, whether about human nature and relationships or the likely course of human affairs. Hussein especially loves it when people refer to those Quranic passages where contracts are commended, where one is encouraged to travel and learn the ways of others with whom one buys and sells, and where bargaining is understood to be of the essence of mankind. After all, he has heard Quranic teachers say, did not the Prophet Muhammad himself bargain with God over the number of daily prayers required of believers, reducing the number from fifty to five? It has been people like Hussein, too, who demonstrate that any utterance may be like a price in the marketplace and thus not subject to being assessed as true or false until some relationship is undertaken with reference to it. But once truth does attach, lying becomes especially serious because of the premonitory fear of social chaos that may be produced by a lack of interdependencies constantly serviced by individuals who must deal with one another face to face.

Similarly, for Hussein and his companions "tribe" and "Berber" are concepts of great situational importance. In the West "tribal" is often used as a derogatory term: it implies narrowness, intolerance, backwardness, and self-defeating exclusivity. But tribal attachments commonly incorporate a much more open-textured structure than Westerners imagine. Far from simply embracing the proposition that one should "do unto others what has been done to you," actual tribes play up each other's particularity and rarely seek its eradication. Hussein revels in this variety, which for him accords with the nature of reality and his moral obligation to pursue knowledge and safety in that variety. Although I have never mentioned it to him, I strongly suspect he would agree with Robert Lowie, who stressed the existence of crosscutting associations (what anthropologists have called "sodalities") that he said "reveal a tribe's capacity to sample alternate social forms, without necessarily adopting them as the central components of its social machine. Each tribal population appears almost to toy with patterns that are fundamental to its neighbors." The "tribe" (along with Hussein's overall identity as a Berber)—however bounded, however conceptually malleable—forms part of a conceptual repertoire that does not stand in contradiction to the state, to the universalizing claims of Islam, or to the modern world. It is, for Hussein, a resource, a terrain of verbal and physical acts that reveals the intent of men, a point of attachment in a world of constant inconstancy. There may, of course, be a price to such attachments. David Hart has said: "Tribesmen make poor nationalists and palpably poorer fundamentalists. Their reactions to Islam are secular and lay reactions, ones of instinctive defense of their faith. It is a defense based more on cultural inculcation and respect than on intellect or understand-ing, a defense which invokes the notion of *jihad*, the effort and self-striving which may result in holy war should Islam be perceived as threatened, al-though it is also a defense which is by no means necessarily beclouded by fanaticism. The reactions in question are, in short, those of the fighter."

But this is true only to a limited extent. Hussein is strongly attached to Moroccan national identity, as are his fellow Berbers, which may be one reason why Morocco has never descended into warring enclaves based on ethnicity or level of education. There was a time when, as one of the char-acters in a well-known Moroccan folktale could say: "I am a man of the saddle and the sword, and you are one of transactions and trust." But such dichotomies do not resonate for Hussein. In fact, he sees transactions as the best means to *avoid* the sword, and his emphasis on solidarity with fellow Berbers, as well as at the more inclusive levels of Moroccans and Muslims, is part of his initial, if not always persistent, response to a situa-tion of conflict. If I see an Arab mistreating a Berber in the marketplace, I come to the Berber's side, he has said me. But no one, he continues, should claim to be better than someone else just because he is a Berber, a *cherif*, a Muslim, or a Jew. When the angels on our shoulders record our deeds ("just like bank accounts"), he concludes, they will be more interested in what you did than in what rituals you performed, and any man who places himself above others, who thinks he is better than others just because he is a descendant of the Prophet or is a haj or a rich Arab increases the sins that the angels will record. That emphasis on process over structure, like the vi-sion of sovereignty as one of relationships more than of boundaries, may thereby render Hussein's ability to sustain both national identity and local attachment part of a shared conceptual orientation that in other countries cannot be so easily sustained.

The years surrounding the turn of the twenty-first century saw Hussein resting to some extent on his achievements. He made his pilgrimage to Mecca, an act that for him, as for so many Muslims, was not one that can be reduced to piety or fear or the status accorded back home. For what it really demonstrates to a man like Hussein is that worldly consequence includes the spiritual, underscores that the proper sphere of humanity in-cludes attachment to the sublime, and incorporates being in a world made for man to traverse and comprehend. He continues, too, to express oppo-sition to any violent change in Morocco's political structure and thus re-minded me of a famous passage in Tocqueville, where that trenchant ob-server of American democracy says: "I know of nothing more opposed to revolutionary mores than commercial mores. Commerce is naturally the

enemy of all violent passions. It likes even tempers, is pleased by compromise, very carefully flees anger. It is patient, supple, insinuating, and it has
recourse to extreme means only when the most absolute necessity obliges
it. Commerce renders men independent of one another; it gives them a
high idea of their individual worth; it brings them to want to handle their
own affairs and then to succeed at them; it therefore disposes them to freedom but moves them away from revolutions." Combine this proposition
with what Charles C. Torrey wrote at the end of the nineteenth century
about Islam, and one can see how a more localized version of such propositions takes shape:

> The mutual relations between God and man are of a strictly commercial na-
> ture. Allah is the ideal merchant. He includes all the universe in his reckon-
> ing. All is counted, everything measured. The book and the balances are his
> institutions, and he has made himself the pattern of honest dealing. Life is a
> business, for gain or loss. He who does a good or an evil work ("earns" good
> or evil), receives his pay for it, even in this life. Some debts are forgiven, for
> Allah is not a hard creditor. . . . At the resurrection, Allah holds a final reck-
> oning with all men. Their actions are read from the account-book, weighed
> in the balances; each is paid his exact due, no one is defrauded.

Such features may contribute not only to Hussein's skepticism about the
sorts of actions taken elsewhere at the time of the Arab Spring but his continued embeddedness in his own local group and his fellow Moroccan
merchants.

I had often thought that as Hussein's stature increased, people in the
settlement would refer to their place, as they often have done in the past,
by the name of its current "big man," and thus that the cluster of houses
might now be known as Ait Hussein. But much has changed. The young
depart; the city of Sefrou and even more distant towns seem ever closer.
Many rural enclaves have become less dependent than they once were on
the ability of a leading figure to intercede or mediate to the outside on
their behalf. And so the settlement has remained Boukherfan, the name
suggestive of its members' engagement in the sheep trade rather than their
reliance, once so prevalent, on the intermediation of a big man. That subtle shift of terminology may signal one of the ways in which association
through enterprise may be displacing identity through a figure at the center
of an entire community's web of affiliations.

But if the time has passed or been set in momentary abeyance when
attachment to a big man was indispensable or tribes served as the preemi-

nent political units, the ethos that lingers, interwoven as it has long been with the agglutinative embrace of mainstream Islam, forecloses any simple reduction of society or faith to party or ritual or boundary. If Hussein does not need the fundamentalists to tell him how to be a proper Muslim, it is also too facile to call his approach to Islam unintellectual. For to him the market, the pasture, and the guest room are no less places of religious enactment than the mosque or the shrine. "A merchant is the beloved of God," said the Prophet. And since, for Hussein, it is only through action that faith, like any other intellectual concept, is made real, it will always be in the spaces where a man is free to move that Hussein will demonstrate his unwavering attachment to his people and his vision of the way the world is really composed. Until the last it is through his motion in this world that he will demonstrate the ever-present motion of his mind.

A Nation among Nations:
Shimon Benizri

Shimon Benizri

Lo yisa goy el goy echad.
No nation is a nation alone.

—Hebrew song

Sefrou, Morocco, June 5, 1967

The radio had gone silent. For several days I had been switching back and forth among Moroccan and European broadcasts, following the growing tensions between Israel and the surrounding Arab states. But when the Moroccan national broadcast was abruptly interrupted, I knew events must have taken a turn for the worse. A few moments later the station resumed— but now with martial music and exhortations from the government, politicians, and doctors of Islamic law. In the absence of solid news I tried to convince myself that perhaps it did not really signal the start of hostilities. That hope, however, was short lived. As I raced back and forth across the dial, I soon heard the Moroccan station announce that what was later to be known as the Six-Day War had indeed commenced.

Initial reports on the Moroccan stations were contradictory. One said that Tel Aviv had been bombed; another played classical music interspersed with announcements that could only suggest Israeli advances. The radio also indicated that Moroccan troops would be sent to combat Israel, and it was said that America was assisting the Jewish state. My own situation, however, was not deeply affected. A few days later the chief judge of the district in whose court I had all but completed a study—a man whom I would later get to know well and for whom I have the deepest respect and affection—said that it was too much trouble for the clerks to be getting records out for me and that I should not return to the court for the time being. Even Haj Hamed suggested we keep our heads down and not do too much traveling for the moment. During my seventeen months of fieldwork I had not once encountered any difficulties, and though I had not focused my research on the significant Jewish community still residing in Sefrou, the tenor of communal relations had never been a cause for concern. Nor did I feel any anxiety as a result of my own living circumstances.

At the time the war began, I was residing just outside the old city walls in one of four apartments that shared a small courtyard above the shop of Malka, a Jewish furniture maker. One of the apartments was occupied by a young Muslim couple—she an Arab from the city, he a Berber from the nearby Middle Atlas Mountains. The other two apartments were occupied by Jewish families. To one side lived a couple, the Poneys, she a thin fidgety woman always nervously tweaking a headscarf of the type married women of the Jewish community commonly wore, her husband a sickly-looking man invariably dressed in a gray djellaba and black beret, the latter having once been the sign of a French protégé or, for others, something of a protest against the pre-Protectorate garb expected of Jews.

But it was the other family I came to know best. For just across the tiled common space lived Shimon and Zohara Benizri and seven of their eight children—he a quiet man in his late fifties, a warm smile permanently affixed on his boyish face, she a short, bustling, ever-optimistic woman efficiently managing a household of rambunctious children. In those first few moments my thoughts turned to all of the city's Jews and to what this war might mean to their continued willingness, unlike most of their coreligionists in Sefrou and Morocco as a whole, to remain in the country. But it was not until I went out to talk with others that I could begin to see, in this moment of potential crisis, just how entangled were their lives with those of their Muslim neighbors.

The Benizri and Poney families, 1967

A group of Muslims gathered around the post office spoke animatedly about how the Jews were now going to get their comeuppance while others used phrases—"May Allah bring good things," "It is all in Allah's hands"— that by their very indirection often signal that matters are not always as obvious or predictable as they seem. Elsewhere I saw Jews and Muslims speaking quietly to one another. I talked with a number of the Jews, who seemed mostly confused and helpless rather than threatened, but who nevertheless went about their business normally. Later, one of the Benizri children told me that Muslim kids had gathered around their school and were throwing stones until the police were called and dispersed them. I even learned that one Jewish man had gone to donate blood for the Moroccan troops who were to head for the front. But the Muslims who later told me the story laughed and said that while it was a nice gesture, they would, of course, have to throw out his blood, because everyone knows that Jewish blood doesn't work on Muslims. The most striking moment, however, came that first evening when a visitor arrived at the Benizri residence.

The visitor—who also brought his wife and teenage boy with him—was the son of a man named Caid Said, who had formerly given his protection to Shimon, and before him to Shimon's father, when they lived and traded in the mountains. He was an elegant man, dressed in a flowing djellaba and carefully wrapped turban, his sun-ripened face framed by a blazingly white beard. He was also a wealthy man who had twice gone on the pilgrimage to Mecca and who was the undisputed leader of his tribal fraction located in that part of the Middle Atlas Mountains where Mrs. Benizri had grown up. As soon as the war broke out, he had begun the long trip to the city with his young wife for the express purpose of assuring the Benizris that no matter what happened in the Middle East, they had no reason to fear for their personal safety or that of their property. He spoke calmly and reassuringly of the fact that they were all Moroccans and that the government would protect them. He offered his personal help, specifically suggesting that during the next few weeks they jointly rent a house in the old Jewish quarter where the Benizris could live upstairs and he and his family downstairs, between them and the outside world, a partnership arrangement that was actually not uncommon at many times and places in Morocco.

Shimon graciously refused the offer, saying they felt quite safe where they were (especially with their American neighbor so close by). The visitor then suggested that they at least allow him to leave his own son to sleep outside the staircase leading up to our apartments as a sign that any attack on this family would be an attack on him as well. Again, Shimon and Zohara demurred, pointing out that the house could easily be locked and that it was only children who were causing any disturbances. Upon learning of the children's stone-throwing, Caid Said's son reminded Shimon that the Berbers could offer better protection than the government should the Benizris at any time change their mind and decide it would be best to leave the city for a while. They parted late that night with the Berber assuring the family that he and some of his boys would be keeping a watchful eye on Shimon's stall in the marketplace in any case.

Throughout the six days that the war lasted, life in the city remained virtually unchanged on the surface. Those people who felt most strongly about the war expressed the greatest opposition to Israel's continued existence, and those who were most certain of a quick Arab victory came mainly from the segment of educated urban Arabs. The poorer people of the city and the Berbers of the countryside talked about making a peaceful settlement and the difficulty of keeping straight who was who in the war. (Does Iraq have a common border with Israel? Where exactly is Syria?) And they stressed that the whole business should certainly not affect the Jews of their own city.

Beneath the surface, however, among Muslims and Jews alike, the dominant feeling at this point was one of uncertainty. As one Jewish man told

Shimon in his shop

me, "Everything would be all right if people today respected the old ways and continued to treat us as individuals. But nowadays there are so many unemployed people in town who could be turned against us at any moment." A Muslim shopkeeper spoke in similar terms: "You have to understand the custom in this country," he said. "People do whatever some big man tells them to do. *What* they are told to do doesn't matter nearly as much as the fact that someone takes hold of things and tells people how they should act. If the government does nothing and someone tells people to kill the Jews, that is what they may do. If the government tells us to be good to the Jews, we will follow their directions." An attempt to provide some such authoritative direction was not long in coming.

On June 12 the newspaper of Istiqlal, the main conservative political party in Morocco at that time, called for a boycott of "all those who have close and distant ties with 'Israel' and her sinister allies." They also published a list of companies that, they said, dealt with Israel and should be boycotted. The more conservative Arabs of the city now had their direction: they said they would have no business dealings with Jews, since all Muslims must unite in the face of the outside enemy. Jews remained off the streets, some even afraid to try buying food. Unarmed soldiers—including one stationed, symbolically, at the gate of the old Jewish quarter in the center of the city, a place where no Jews any longer resided—joined the local police in casually patrolling the city as the government began to clarify its own position. On June 14, the Moroccan representative to the United Nations spoke at length of the favorable treatment Jews had always received in Morocco, particularly when the late king, Muhammad V, resisted the anti-Jewish legislation of the Vichy regime during the Second World War. A similar statement from the Royal Cabinet released two days later further emphasized that none of the citizenship rights of Moroccan Jews would be altered in any way by the current situation. Meanwhile, on June 15 the government seized the Istiqlal party newspapers; when the papers reappeared two days later, the call for a boycott was only slightly toned down, although no specific nations or companies were mentioned by name.

The Jews of the city, meanwhile, played for time. With the boycott in partial effect and some of the Muslims actually intimidated into not patronizing Jewish-owned shops, individual Jews reasoned that they could close their businesses on Wednesday and Thursday (June 14–15) for the Jewish holiday of Shevuoth, open briefly on Friday (the Muslim "Sabbath"), stay at home over the weekend, and go back to work on Monday—the day before the Muslim holiday celebrating the Prophet's birthday. The Jews felt that in the interim many even normally unemployed Muslims would become busy harvesting the area's first grain crop in two years. Moreover, unless the fighting in the Middle East resumed and the local Muslims were forced to remain united against an enemy whose presence they could be made to feel personally, internal Muslim differences would reassert themselves, and the Jews would once again be able to work within the context of their personal and social relationships with the Muslims.

Realizing, however, their complete political impotence, the Jews feared that in the days following the war they might find themselves used as pawns in the struggle among the various Moroccan political factions.

For the most part this fear proved groundless. Intent on preserving public order and not allowing the politicians to seize the initiative, King Hassan II took a strong stand in favor of protecting all Moroccan citizens—Jews and Muslims alike—from violent action. As the United Nations debated on into deadlock, Istiqlal continued to call for a boycott of Jews and the nationalization of some Western-owned firms. Dubbing the boycott an act against the order of the state, the government struck back on July 5, charging that "the boycott is not an Islamic principle. . . . Those who incite people to participate in it commit an act that is criminal in thought, in law, and in spirit." Then on July 8, in a most remarkable televised speech, the king himself argued that it was not surprising that the world should regard the Arabs as the aggressors in the recent war, since it was they who called for a general mobilization a week before the fighting began and it was they who closed the Gulf of Aqaba. He said that one should never enter into a war until one's own country is at least the economic equal of the opponent, and he stressed the point that internal chaos is far worse than an undesirable international political situation. The king's verbal determination was expressed in action a few days later when the head of the largest labor union in the country was imprisoned for charging that the Moroccan government itself had fallen into the hands of pro-Zionist forces. The papers of the Istiqlal party, threatened with another seizure, turned to a direct attack on those whom they regarded the king as coddling, and they initiated a series of articles on the Protocols of the Elders of Zion, the notorious forgery about the Jewish world conspiracy of which the Nazis had made such effective use. Yet even here it was clear that the Moroccans, like President Nasser of Egypt, had to borrow their anti-Jewish text from another cultural tradition simply because the Arabs lacked a well-developed anti-Semitic literature of their own.

Significantly, however, within the city itself the impact of this struggle for power and influence on the national level was minimal. The king's strong stand concerning any sort of illegal action against the Jews was not without its effect, but the local situation had already begun to ease well before Hassan's position was fully clarified. Most Jews reopened their shops right after the holiday of the Prophet's birthday, and Muslims and Jews joked and conversed in near normal fashion. With the passage of time and the continued bickering among the various political factions, the people of the city reasserted their suspicions about all national party leaders and their abiding faith in personal judgments based on face-to-face relations. Those Jews who practiced trades or sold goods without competition from Muslims were fully patronized. Some urban Arabs and fewer Berbers, perhaps hedging against any later claim that they had supported Israel's friends, avoided Jewish shops that were in direct competition with Muslims while still remaining cordial in their relationships with individual Jewish businessmen. Rural people practiced this avoidance even less on market days, when there were enough of them in town so they could not easily be intimidated by some of their more partisan urban brethren.

Witnessing the events surrounding the war, I often found myself intensely curious about the relations between the Muslims and Jews but not especially surprised. Much of what happened—from the extraordinary visit of the son of the Benizris' Berber protector to the king's speech—fit with what I had come to understand about Moroccan communal history. That it was by no means an unambiguous history was made all the more apparent when, sometime later, I began to place Shimon's own life story within the broader context of Moroccan social history.

> There was, until there was, in times so fair,
> When basil and lilies grew here and there,
> And God was to be found everywhere.
>
> —Traditional story opening

I was born in 1910, Shimon began, up in the Middle Atlas Mountains, at a place called Almis d-Marmousha. My father and all those before him came from Midelt, a high-plains area about a hundred kilometers south of Sefrou, between the mountains, where numerous small villages dot the plateau that runs along the Moulouya River. My father had spent seven years living in Tlemcen, in the northwest of Algeria, but he finally returned to Morocco, first to Midelt, though eventually he settled in Almis. Like Jews elsewhere in the mountains of Morocco he traded through the Berber territories. He first bought cotton cloth in Fez and got someone from there to accompany him safely back to Sefrou. Then, under the protection of two local big men—Caid Said ou M'hammad from Guigou (the one whose son came to our house just after the war began in the Middle East) and another man from the Ait Seghoushen fraction of the Ait Youssi tribe—he traded the cloth for wool and sheep throughout the central Middle Atlas. He then returned with those goods to Sefrou, where they were sold to a buyer who forwarded them to Fez. In my experience no one ever violated the protection those big men afforded, not the protection they gave me or my father or any of the other Jews who lived and traded in the mountains. In those days in Midelt, where I mainly spent my early years, there were about 20 Jewish families, maybe a total of 120 individuals in that whole general area. We lived mixed in with the Muslims, each with his protector, not like in Sefrou and the other cities where there were separate Jewish quarters.

In 1933 my father died, so I and my mother and several of my siblings came down to Sefrou. In the mountains I had a small store where I sold all the usual things: cooking oil, cotton cloth, grain, sugar. In a country store you have to sell everything. But in Sefrou I was able to open a shop selling only cloth, many of my clients being the rural people I already knew who came to town on the market days. Six years later, after I had already been married once and divorced, I wed Zohara, who was from a place called Seghina, near El Mers, also up in the Middle Atlas. We were introduced by people I knew in El Mers from the days my father traded there under the protection of Caid Said. All the Jews living in that area, including Zohara and me, spoke Berber, unlike the Jews in Sefrou, who rarely did. Later on, the people in El Mers asked me to return and settle there, so I moved back up into the countryside and stayed there from 1939 until 1957. After Morocco gained independence from France in 1956, many Jews decided to emigrate: indeed, several members of my own immediate family—my mother, two of my brothers, and two of my sisters—were among those who moved to Israel. But I decided to stay in Morocco. I brought the family back to Sefrou, where the children could attend school and where I once again opened a cloth stall in the main market area.

Shimon's account immediately touched on a number of themes common to the situation of Moroccan Jews, particularly those who had ties to the country's rural hinterland. No one knows for sure when Jews first arrived in Morocco. There are those who would trace Jewish presence in Morocco back to Phoenician times, while others offer evidence that Jews who left after the destruction of the Second Temple in 70 C.E. made their way across the whole of North Africa, possibly converting some of the Berber tribes along the way. In the process, it seems likely that many of these Jews settled in the mountainous regions, where the protection of a local big man was vital. What is clear is that a distinction can be drawn between those Jews who were already resident in North Africa and those who arrived following the expulsions from Europe, the descendants of each group possessing distinctive linguistic, culinary, and liturgical characteristics. However, according to a number of Jews with whom I discussed family history, few of the Jews in Sefrou originally came from Spain or other European countries; they mainly (as they would say) "came from Palestine a long time ago."

For centuries Jews had been scattered all along the caravan trade route (the so-called Royal Road, *triq as-sultan*) that stretched from Fez to Sefrou and then across the Middle Atlas Mountains all the way down to the pre-Saharan zone, where it linked up with trade across the desert to Timbouctou. The Moulouya Plateau, where Shimon's father settled, was an important way station along various trade routes, while settlements like Almis and El Mers, where Shimon resided, were collecting points for the trade in hides and wool that flowed into the caravan route and the markets of central and northern Morocco. Since many of the caravan organizers and most of the local groups in the mountains were Berbers, the resident Jews learned the local language, taught their children some liturgical Hebrew, and managed to maintain a number of their distinctive customs.

Families like Shimon's that settled, at whatever date, in the hinterland of Morocco were, however, deeply influenced by their incorporation within the tribal territories. To many Westerners the nature and degree of Muslim-Jewish interaction, whether in the mountains or the towns, cannot easily fit with the experience Jews had living in Europe. Indeed, the tone in which Shimon and many of the Muslims spoke about one another initially took me by surprise.

Shimon and his wife were especially enthusiastic when speaking of their life among the Berbers. Certainly before the consolidation of French control, protection from a local big man, particularly for those like Shimon and his father who had to move among different tribes and fractions, was indispensable. As a Moroccan Jew from the High Atlas Mountains phrased it to anthropologist Moshe Shokeid, "We traveled through different governments." And while it is tempting to regard Shimon's account and those of other Jews as occasionally romanticized, the evidence is clear that any violation of a patron's protection was a very serious matter indeed. Instances of theft and to a much lesser extent murder are the mainstay of such stories. Clifford and Hildred Geertz, for example, collected the story of a Jewish man whose animals were stolen by rivals of his Middle Atlas protector. The latter called up his allies and subdued the offenders. He had the offending tribesmen drive their sheep into a narrow gorge, lined his own men on one ridge and those of the defeated group on the other, and then sent the Jew into the valley between the arrayed forces to pick out for himself the number of the offenders' sheep necessary to restore the patron's honor.

The image of the Jew taking his time to carefully choose the best animals while the two Berber fractions stood watch from above is, however, not unique to Morocco. S. D. Goitein relates similar stories of Jews in Yemen, called "protected comrades," on whose behalf the tribesmen would go to war if one of their protégées was attacked. Indeed, if a member of another group murdered a protected Jew, it was said that were such an act to go unavenged, the murdered Jew would ride on the back of the murderer on the Day of Judgment. For while Muslims can forgive one another, only God himself can avenge an unprotected Jew. David Hart summarized the situation of most rural Jews in Morocco in the following terms: "The keynote of Jewish behavior was that of safety in humility; conversely, for a powerful man to have 'his own' Jew was considered a sign of prestige. Because the Jews stood entirely outside the political system, and because their occupational services were much in demand, many informants said that to kill or even to molest a Jew was an infinitely worse offense than to kill a fellow tribesman."

Such protection was, of course, far from unambiguous. On the one hand, the Jews who could find reliable protectors might be able to organize their personal and communal lives in relative safety. On the other hand, the Jews were required to remain weak and dependent. It was commonly accepted that Jews did not or should not possess the capacity for self-defense. Hence a significant part of the claimed reliability of a Muslim seeking to build a network of allies was, like his control of women (to whom the Jews were frequently compared), both an indicator and an artifact of his success. Symbolically, the Jews' inferior status might be demonstrated in a host of ways. In the countryside the men were distinguished by their cloaks and squared hats, the women by their scarves; in urban areas the men were not permitted to pass through a Muslim graveyard, were commonly required to wear distinctive clothing and hairstyles, and had to ride (like a woman) sideways on a pack animal. Whenever they passed the door of a mosque or the house of a notable cherif, the Jew had to remove his hat and shoes and carry them in his hand. As always in Morocco, personal connections could modify circumstance such that, according to Haj Hamed and others, in Sefrou rich Jews only had to remove their shoes; they could keep their hats on. (Curiously, in the High Atlas Mountains Jews sometimes wore white cloaks instead of the black characteristic of Jews elsewhere, white often being associated with descendants of the Prophet and thus like these distinctive figures perhaps emphasizing that the Jews were marked as protected and off limits, or at least as yet another category of people possessing ambiguous powers.) Moreover, when a Jew died, the corpse could be removed from the city only through Bab Sitti

Messaouda, the "back door" of Sefrou, and the procession would then go to the graveyard via a circuitous road under the supervision, in troubled times, of an armed Muslim guard. Following an early Muslim tradition, Jews were also forbidden to ride so noble an animal as a horse but might, however, take solace in the assurance that so regal a creature as a lion would never lower itself to eat a mere Jew.

Physical arrangements differed in rural versus urban areas. In the countryside, as Shimon was quick to point out, Muslims and Jews did not live in separate areas. Beginning in the nineteenth century, by comparison, sultans required Jews, mainly in the coastal cities, to live in a distinct quarter (*mellah*), in part to dominate their finances and in part as a symbol of the ruler's legitimacy as a protector. Travelers from abroad frequently commented on these Jewish quarters and their residents. On August 20, 1883, Charles de Foucauld, on reconnaissance as a French army officer before his entry to the priesthood and accompanied by a Moroccan rabbi, entrepreneur, and guide from the south named Mordechai Aby Serrour, arrived in Sefrou disguised as a Polish rabbi. He described Sefrou as the most beautiful Moroccan city he had seen: "I enter the gardens, immense and marvelous gardens, such as I have never seen in Morocco; dense trees whose leaves [and] thick foliage spilled over the land an impenetrable shade and a delicious freshness, where all the branches are charged with fruits, and the perpetually green landscape rustles and murmurs with innumerable watercourses." Foucauld went on to describe the town's Jewish community as one of the two happiest in the country. It is also a measure of the size and importance of the Sefrou community that he put the number of Jewish families at that time at some three thousand souls (out of a total population of six thousand), the same number as in Fez, where the total population was about seventy thousand. His stay, however, was rather brief.

It was during my initial fieldwork that a Jewish businessman named Jacob Tobaly told me the story: In those days my maternal grandfather was the richest Jew in Sefrou, he said, and whenever visiting Jewish dignitaries passed through, they stayed at his house—No. 1 Mellah, just inside the main gate and to the left. Foucauld had been staying at my grandfather's house for about a week. But when it got to be the Sabbath, my grandfather saw Foucauld cleaning his fingernails, something he knew no rabbi would ever do on that day. So he told Foucauld he knew he was an imposter and made him leave the next day. (A published account differs slightly. There, it is said that while staying at the house of David Laelyel, also spelled Aoulil, the latter's wife saw Foucauld sketching on the Sabbath. The chief rabbi, Shalom Azoulay, was informed and after quizzing Aby Serrour, agreed, as

Jewish quarter (mellah), 1967

did others along their way, to keep secret for ten years the nature of Foucauld's mission.)

Other travelers offered equally glowing descriptions of the Jewish community of Sefrou in the late nineteenth century. Robert Kerr, for example, wrote: "The Jews of Sefrou are very industrious, many of them being engaged in gardening, while others carry on a good trade with the surrounding tribes, bartering, as they have comparatively little money. The Jewesses of Sifroo are famed for their smallness and exceptional beauty." So close was the Muslims' association with the Jewish population that to this day people from elsewhere remark on the Sefrouis' frequent use of words and pronunciations as being typical of the Jewish speech style. Sefrou was singularly distinctive, too, because the Jewish quarter was situated right in the middle of the town rather than, as in other Moroccan cities, at its walled edge. With only one access gate at the end of a small bridge over the river (until a rear entryway was created after the Protectorate began) and with the backs of the houses, often rising four stories, forming something of a defensive barrier, the quarter could be shut off from the rest of the city and cushioned to some extent from outsiders by its own walls and the surrounding neighborhoods.

The ties with Muslim neighbors, in both the city and countryside, were close and complex. Shimon pointed out, for example, that Muslims and Jews even engaged in some of each other's rituals. This is particularly true in the veneration of those figures, commonly referred to in the Western literature as "saints," who are believed capable of channeling their spiritual powers to benefit those associated with them. Throughout Morocco Muslims and Jews to this day share a number of such saints. In Sefrou a cave—variously called Kaf el-Yahudi, Kaf Daoud, Kaf el-Moumen, "the cave of Rav Shimon," the cave of the seven sleeping saints, and the resting place of Rabbi Isaac Mul el-Mila—is located on a hillside above the Jewish and Muslim graveyards. Women in particular still visit the site for the saint's powers affecting their capacity to bear a child. Once a year there was also a special celebration attended by members of both faiths. In Morocco as a whole, scholars have counted at least 134 saints venerated by both faiths, of which 88 all agree are Jewish, 33 are claimed by both groups, and 13 even the Jews agree are Muslims. Instances are also recorded of financial disputes between Muslims and Jews being taken to the grave of a Jewish saint where oaths would be sworn and even of cases where two Muslims would lay hands on a Jewish saint's tomb and settle their claim with a decisory oath. Indeed, in much the same way the living descendants of Muslim saints may intercede to mediate disputes, those regarded in their lifetime as Jewish saints could also be called upon to show the way to a peaceful resolution of an argument. Stories of such saints abound.

Tales are especially told of the miraculous powers of the saints to protect the Jewish community, whether by transforming themselves into some other substance or merchandise that Jews did not want it known they were trading or by magically saving the community by turning evil men into dwarves. Other tales refer to a rabbi who uses a long-forgotten prayer to tame a wild animal or describe how, for example, the Sefrou rabbi Hayyim Yosef David Azoulay saved the town's Jews from marauding tribesmen by making himself invisible. On other occasions, however, saints are rumored to have been the focus for intercommunal aggression: it is said that in a few instances Jewish holy men were actually murdered and then buried in Muslim graveyards so the Muslims' dead relatives might benefit from the saintly figure's presence among them. In more recent years, with government encouragement, Jews from abroad have returned in large numbers to visit the shrines. On several occasions artifacts and remains of Jewish saints have even been moved to Israel, where they have become the focus of massive pilgrimages by the Jews of Moroccan descent.

When there was drought or other troubles in the country, Shimon pointed out, it was also the practice to have the Jews, as well as the Muslims, make special prayers. The particular form of these rituals and the ways of describing them reveal some of the ambiguities in the communal relationship, as a number of early travelers' accounts indicated. Louis Sauveur de Chenier, in his book published in 1788, says:

> The Moors . . . think importunity will oblige God to grant their requests. In the time of heavy rains the children all day run about the streets, and bawl for fair weather; and, in the time of drought, for rain, making a hideous noise. . . . Should God not listen to the children, they are joined by the Saints and Talbes [*tolba*, scholars], who proceed altogether into the fields and call for rain. If this still prove ineffectual, they go barefoot in a body, and meanly cloathed, to pray at the tombs of their Saints for rain. . . . Should all these efforts fail, they at last drive the Jews out of the town, and forbid them to return without rain—"For," say they, "though God will not grant rain to our prayers, he will to those of the Jews, to rid himself of their importunity, and the stinking odour of their breath and feet."

One Muslim I met did indeed refer, jokingly, to the smell of the Jews being the cause for God's sending down the rains. But most people, pointing to both historical and modern examples of the practice, agreed that the Jews were not forced to participate in these prayers but were enjoined to do so. This was confirmed by many other Jews with whom I spoke, including Jacob Tobaly, who said the prayer at the saint's cave was led by the chief rabbi and that when the prayer was finished, "the Muslims would greet the returning Jews with a great show of appreciation, clapping and dancing all around." Shimon agreed with what Haj Hamed had told me, when the latter explained why Jews and Muslims alike would go barefoot out of the city and turn their djellabas around when they sought divine aid: "We and the Jews pray to the same God," said the Haj. "We are like a single river from which different irrigation canals branch. Sometimes we each follow our own paths, but before God we are all just one stream. This is the way it is when we come before this one God to ask for rain or when we come before his saints." Such accounts are, therefore, closer to that of Xavier Durrieu, who, writing in the 1850s, notwithstanding a number of anti-Semitic comments characteristic of some French explorers of North Africa in the late nineteenth to early twentieth century, noted that

> when war or pestilence desolates the country, when a great public calamity is dreaded, the Sultan orders that, to appease or turn away the anger of Heaven, prayers should be put up in all the mosques. Despised and detested as the Jews are, they then become the objects of the most eager solicitation, and the most lively attachment on the part of the Pachas and Cadis [Islamic law judges]; and they are no longer commanded, but entreated to be good enough to pray God in their synagogues to show himself merciful to every human being living under the dominion of the Sultan. Covered with ashes—their clothes torn, their persons attenuated by fasting and maceration—Israelites and Musulmans traverse the country and the streets of the towns in procession. . . . But when the public panic is once dissipated, the Jews take good care to keep themselves concealed for some weeks; for the arrogant Musulmans, ashamed of having associated the degraded children of Moses in their grief and terror, should they meet them in the first moment of humiliation and anger, would make them expiate severely the crime of having dared to implore for the privileged family of the prophet, the mercy of a God who rejected them.

Stories of such mutual prayers are known from many other sources. The last rabbi of Sefrou, Rabbi David Ovadia (born in 1913), reports a noteworthy story concerning one of his predecessors of the nineteenth century, Rabbi Raphael Moshe Elbaz (1823–97), indicating the extent to which religious coexistence was enjoyed. Ovadia writes: "[At times of famine] it was the custom of the great head of the Muslims to ask him [Rabbi Elbaz] to pray ardently . . . because they considered him like an angel. And sometimes, when the imam climbed up into the minaret at dawn to welcome the day with hymns, the rabbi would also respond to him [*oneh liqrato*] from the window of his house with songs and supplications [*baqashot*] in Arabic. The imam remained quiet, listening to him." More recently, in the winter of 2013–14, when drought once again threatened Morocco, King Muhammad VI requested that the Jews offer up special prayers for rain.

Although rain prayers were offered separately by each confessional community, other occasions involved the direct participation of Muslims in Jewish rituals. During the final days of Passover a celebration called Mimouna was held that incorporates various ideas of seasonal renewal. It was a time, Shimon said, when Jewish peddlers who had left their families in the city—often for many months at a time—returned to visit them, while others celebrated the festival in their small rural enclaves. The festivities included young people wearing fancy clothing, some men dressing in the turbans and cloaks normally worn only by Muslims, and most residents moving outside of the mellah to hold picnics and rain prayers in the nearby fields. Muslims not only brought dairy products and wheat at the outset of Passover and accepted the foods that the Jews dispensed with in preparation for the holiday but on the last day brought them supplies of bread and sugar to replenish the foods they discarded in making their homes kosher for Passover. Most significant was the gift of yeast brought by Muslim friends, which a Jewish memoirist, writing of the event in 1950 in his High Atlas home of Demnate, described as part of the blessedness (*baraka*) so central to Moroccan spiritual discourse: "The piece of yeast, huge, sat in flour, as if on a throne, symbol of plenty and luck—symbol of mimouna. It was put on a tray loaded with all sorts of goodies, bowls of fresh butter, of honey, dates, walnuts and almonds. People sang, congratulated each other and danced before lifting this baraka, which was accompanied by flowers, green branches, green beans in stems, and mint."

Three days after the completion of the holiday the Jews in turn would bring gifts to the homes of their Muslim friends. Both communities viewed this as part of the ritual of renewal that benefited all, and it served in many cases to reconfirm the interlocking economic ties of the individuals who engaged in its attendant exchange. Moroccan-born Haim Zafrani, of the University of Paris, could therefore conclude:

> Muslims very often appeared as partners in the celebration of the [Mimuna] rites. . . . They could make a considerable contribution to the preparations for the festival and its procedures and sometimes stood at the center of a ritual in which they were the protagonist, even the archetype and model. . . . The Mimuna remains an affirmation of the deep links which attached the Jewish minority to the Muslim majority. It was evidence of the existence of an area of convergence that must be taken into consideration where the two groups found each other and met. . . . It constituted one of the elements in a remarkable symbiosis and a mainly peaceful co-existence that lasted for nearly two millennia on the hospitable soil of the Maghreb.

Mimouna was not the only such ritual of this sort. Others were practiced particularly, but not exclusively, in Berber communities. In the southwest of the country a masquerade would take place a month after the Muslim holiday celebrating Abraham's sacrifice, during which Muslim men dressed up as Jews—even as Jewish women—and engaged in sexually explicit satires of government and religious figures, prostitutes, and other marginal groups. They sang songs about wonder-working Jews and employed the occasional Hebraized word in greetings to one another. Masks and costumes, often quite outrageous, mocked the wearers no less than others. Similar rituals could be found in other parts of the High Atlas Mountains in which Muslim and Jewish roles are reversed as one enters a new moment in the religious and agricultural calendar.

Mimouna and similar events thus perform a vision of self and other, of communal association and confessional antipathy, of interpersonal relationships and structured roles. Ritual reversals are common in many cultures, of course, and in cases like the rain prayers that follow the practice of going into the fields and reversing one's garments, as it is said the Prophet himself did on such occasions, the ambivalence toward Jews is palpable. Indeed, to some Muslims this is yet another instance in which there is some trepidation in one's approach to certain Jews who, they believe, command special powers. That was why Hussein went to a Jewish mystic to seek love magic, why others have reputedly stolen a Jewish saint to bury in their own graveyard, and why, in Sefrou as elsewhere, the Muslims continue to maintain and venerate many Jewish shrines. The reverse, of course, can also be true: as recently as the 1970s Norman Stillman records an instance of a young Jewish girl going to a Muslim female seer to ascertain whether her intended would indeed be a good spouse.

The interaction with shared saints and fortunetellers and the ritual of Mimouna, as Abdellah Hammoudi points out for the latter event, also serves to enact a genuine sense of belonging, as much for the minority Jews as for their Muslim neighbors. It demonstrates that inequality can be bypassed, that gifts do more than indebt, and that indeed a gift, whether of yeast or of participation, demonstrates that a challenge to moderation has been met. That sense of moderation, so central to the Moroccan concept of personal and collective identity, was neatly caught in a recent comment to Charis Boutieri by a schoolteacher who said: "We have always been exposed to multiple elements—the Berbers, the Jews, the Andalusians, the Arabs: That was our contract for being Moroccan."

Such exposure did, however, vary by location and circumstance. In the countryside, Shimon and Zohara insisted, Muslims and Jews mixed freely. However, when Shimon first moved back to Sefrou in the early 1930s, most urban Jews still lived in the mellah, although some of the more wealthy ones were being invited by Muslims to live in other quarters where it was felt they would make better neighbors than the poor people who were beginning to move into the city. Mellahs like that of Sefrou had been developed at different times and with different physical arrangements in the course of Moroccan history. The mellah of Fez, for example, dates from 1438 and may have been so named because it was on the site of an old salt mine, rather than because Jews were sometimes called upon to salt the heads of criminals. Most other mellahs date from the nineteenth century, when they were developed, in part, as a sign of royal protection. Crammed into restricted space the residents of the mellahs suffered all the ills attendant on such arrangements, including various problems of public health, privacy, security, and limited education. George Orwell, whose general opinion of Jews was always mixed, was recovering from illness in Marrakech in 1938–39 when he famously if one-sidedly described the situation of the Jews in that city:

When you go through the Jewish quarters you gather some idea of what the medieval ghettoes were probably like. Under their Moorish rulers the Jews were only allowed to own land in certain restricted areas, and after centuries of this kind of treatment they have ceased to bother about overcrowding. Many of the streets are a good deal less than six feet wide, the houses are completely windowless, and sore-eyed children cluster everywhere in unbelievable numbers, like clouds of flies. Down the centre of the street there is generally running a little river of urine. In the bazaar huge families of Jews, all dressed in the long black robe and little black skull-cap, are working in dark fly-infested booths that look like caves. A carpenter sits cross-legged at a prehistoric lathe, turning chair-legs at lightning speed. He works the lathe with a bow in his right hand and guides the chisel with his left foot, and thanks to a lifetime of sitting in this position his left leg is warped out of shape. At his side his grandson, aged six, is already starting on the simpler parts of the job.

Crowding was indeed common. Each house in the mellah of Marrakech at the turn of the twentieth century reportedly contained ten families, or about sixty people. Throughout its history the mellah of Sefrou was one of the most densely populated in the country and would qualify as one of the most densely populated living quarters anywhere in the world. For example, in 1948 the density of Sefrou's mellah was 415,815 people per square kilometer (twice that of Casablanca's mellah), a figure that is considerably higher than the Warsaw Ghetto in 1940 at 129,412, ten times that of the single most densely populated city in the world at present (Manila at 43,079), and well above the current figures for Manhattan at 27,227, Mum-

Mellah residents, 1913

bai at 22,937, and Gaza City at 9,982. Even in the 1970s the influx of rural people into the former mellah has only resulted in a density of 183,330 per square kilometer. So dense was the mellah that when the sultan Moulay Hassan I passed through the area in the 1890s, he reputedly said that he would construct a second mellah to relieve the unsanitary conditions of Sefrou's Jewish quarter, a plan that was not pursued after the sultan died during that campaign. In those days epidemics frequently decimated the quarter. Aubin notes, "In the summer of 1899 small-pox carried off 2500 children at Marrakech, and in 1901 a typhus epidemic at Fez was the cause of 3000 deaths within four months." To this day, as one walks through its remaining alleyways, its storied residences overreaching the narrow streets and blocking the sunlight, where women cluster at the water fountains and children play in the tiny spaces available, it is not difficult to replace in the mind's eye the poor rural people who now populate the quarter with the Jews who were once cloistered there.

The demographic density of Jewish quarters like that of Sefrou was matched only by the convolutions of its internal organization. Muslims have long pointed to the Pact of 'Umar, a peace accord reputedly offered by a seventh-century caliph to non-Muslims, that permitted the Jews, as People of the Book, to practice their religion and to organize their internal governance relatively free of Muslim control, provided they paid a protective tax. The formal structure of communal organization developed by the

Jewish community in Sefrou, portions of which may have been borrowed from the Spanish immigrants and thus differed little from that of other cities, was very elaborate. It basically consisted of a central group of elders and wealthy figures, called in Hebrew the *va'ad* or *ma'amad* but often referred to by the later French term *comité*, who oversaw the application of a rich array of communal ordinances (in Hebrew, *takanot*) that covered everything from charity and sumptuary laws to the rules for settling disputes with Muslims and fines for infractions of the accepted standards of behavior. Violations of the ordinances could result in relatively minor penalties—having to fund a communal meal or the payment of sums then distributed to the poor—all the way up to excommunication. Weekly collections of food and money overseen by the central agency were regularly distributed to those in need. Fearing their loss to the community, Jewish officials were particularly careful not to allow individuals to fall into total poverty, whether by overspending on marriages or nearly bankrupting themselves on elaborate circumcision ceremonies. Jessica Marglin cites documents from Meknes in the first half of the nineteenth century in which the use of middlemen was forbidden because, in particularly hard times, they were driving many into poverty, thereby threatening the well-being of the community as a whole. Edward Westermarck, who conducted extensive research in the Middle Atlas area at the turn of the twentieth century, thus noted that apropos of the expenditure on ceremonial occasions: "An old Moorish proverb says that the Christians spend their money on lawsuits, the Jews on religious festivals, and the Moors on weddings."

Indeed, numerous documents, dating back to the seventeenth century, attest to just how tightly Jewish officials exercised control, even over minute details of sumptuary life, in their communities. Haim Zafrani quotes regulations from that early period specifying in minute detail, on pain of anathema and excommunication, that at a family festivity one "is permitted to make only one single meal, which must exclude chicken, pigeon, and poultry of any sort." A committee ruling from 1804 is even more detailed: it set fines for not going directly to morning prayers, for women's "wild behavior" in the streets during weddings, and for involvement in the quarrels of others and cautioned against the excessive visibility of women (which would make them think bad thoughts) and "sitting in rows in the streets," especially on the Sabbath. Similarly, in 1904 a regulation signed by Rabbi Azoulay severely limited the entertainment of guests or serving of food on the occasion of a circumcision, at the conclusion of a marriage agreement, or at a naming ceremony or funeral. A 1923 rule further limited giving guests at such rituals more than tea and a single egg, while a proposal emanating from the Rabat rabbinate in 1948 and ratified by the Jewish officials in Sefrou blamed women's competition with one another in such celebrations for detracting from monies required for their children's education and other familial needs.

The committee of any Jewish community was, therefore, rightly described by Roger LeTourneau as "the management council of the mellah firm," inasmuch as these prominent men (four in number until some younger members forced an increase to six around 1940) directed most of the internal organization and external contacts of the community as a whole. In addition to the centralized regulation of many communal activities, each individual in the community belonged to one of several sections into which the entire Jewish population was divided for purposes of various charitable and social duties. Beyond this there were multiple groups to which individuals could belong, from burial societies to study groups to philanthropic associations and defense networks. Interestingly, by no later than the nineteenth century most synagogues throughout Morocco were privately constructed and operated. Rich or powerful men would establish a place of worship and, according to documents from the early nineteenth century, the rabbi would usually be paid not from member fees to the synagogue but by the patron himself. (The decision of a court in 1945 appointed by the government, however, may have been revising history when it agreed with the Sefrou committee, who argued that the revenue from privately established synagogues should, "on democratic principles" and because such a practice was "once customary," be shared with the public, except for sums needed to sustain the rabbis, so long as the latter "please" the public.)

Moreover, as Shlomo Deshen points out, Jewish inheritance law also shifted in the nineteenth century from a regime in which some family property was held jointly by the widow and surviving sons to the new system in which a man's wealth was divided only among his sons, to the detriment of the widow. As Deshen notes, "Again, the social implication of the new practice was to enhance the position of the individual. . . . In the nineteenth century the role of the family, as a corporate property-holding group, declined."

Another index of the role of increasing individuality was the elaboration in this period of the system of protégés. Those Jews, predominantly the wealthy and well-connected who had obtained protégé status from a foreign consul, might escape formal taxes and the depredations of local caids, but they were, compared to the Jewish population as a whole, few in number: reports from the Alliance Israélite Universelle (AIU) put the

270/ A Nation among Nations

total number of protégés in all of Morocco at 463 in 1860, of whom 103 were Jews. However, C. R. Pennell suggests that the total of seven to eight hundred protégés in Morocco (one-quarter of whom, or 3 percent of the country's total Jewish population, were Jews) reported by Pierre Flamand for the late 1870s was probably less than a third of the real figure, since a number of consuls made informal arrangements that were not officially counted. Whatever the correct numbers, the protégé system is yet another example of how, by freeing up individual economic activity, personal patronage, which is so central to Muslim organizational forms, became an increasingly important part of Moroccan Jewish social structure as well.

That individuals might belong to a wide range of associations—some of which were formed on the basis of patrifiliation and others that crosscut ties of kinship and marital alliance—may have had the dual effect of knitting together the community in a dense array of intersecting attachments at the same time that it undercut communal pressures for total conformity. The organization of the Jewish community was, in its use of multiple formal institutions and what Clifford Geertz called its "plutocratic paternalism," significantly different from that of their Muslim neighbors, who, despite such important organizations as religious brotherhoods and the charitable endowments (habus, waqf), tended to emphasize personal networks over more impersonal institutions. In many other respects, however, they were quite similar. One way in which the social organization of the two communities appears quite close was in the emphasis on patron-client relations.

Within the Jewish community, patron-client relationships were crucial, particularly when formed with those individuals who, being wealthy and well connected, served as intermediaries within the community, especially in dealings with the Muslims. The hierarchy of the community typically involved small peddlers, like Shimon's father, near the bottom (sometimes referred to as "riding Jews," since they could be away from their home base for weeks or months at a time); craftsmen of varying degrees and urban shopkeepers (also called "sitting Jews") a bit farther up the socioeconomic ladder; scholars, rabbis, and knowledgeable elders still higher up; and at the top those wholesalers, major importer-exporters (sing. *tajjar*), and high government counselors who were closely attached to the caids, pashas, foreign consuls, government ministers, and the sultan himself. Indeed, just as in the case of those famous Jews of Moorish Spain who rose to be key advisors to Muslim rulers—men like Hasdai ibn Shaprut, vizier to the tenth-century caliph Abd al-Rahman III, or Samuel Ha-Nagid, vizier to the Berber king of Grenada Habbus al-Muzaffar, in the eleventh century—a number of Moroccan Jews have, from time to time, brought their skills and connections to the service of the monarch. Even now André Azoulay, a longtime advisor to King Hassan II, continues as a valued consultant to his son, King Muhammad VI.

In most urban Moroccan Jewish communities up to Protectorate times, the Muslim government, usually with the consent of the Jewish authorities, also chose a communal leader (*nagīd* in Hebrew, in Arabic *sheikh el-yahūd*) to oversee various aspects of internal security and to act as representative to the Muslim officials. Sefrou, however, may have experienced a somewhat unusual history in this regard. According to the documents described by Shalom Bar-Asher, in 1712 the nagid of Sefrou, Judah ben Harosh, demanded that the community reimburse him for expenses incurred after he was imprisoned for the misuse of royal funds. Apparently the community balked and, following further missteps by Judah's brother Isaac, an ordinance was passed in 1723 abolishing the post of nagid altogether. Instead, the duties of the nagid were assigned by lottery to two men out of a group of twelve for a limited term. Three years later, however, Judah had himself recognized as nagid by the local caid. The leaders of the Jewish community reacted by refusing to pay any of his expenses and issued a number of legal rulings against him. Judah, in turn, simply tore up the 1723 decree abolishing the office. But in 1727, with the concurrence of the rabbinical law court of Meknes, the leaders in Sefrou passed an ordinance that limited their earlier position by simply barring all members of the Harosh family from ever serving as nagid and condemned any of them who might seek, directly or indirectly, to occupy that role to automatic excommunication. The rule stood until 1780, when another member of the family, Machluf ben Harosh, a reputedly honest and capable man, was willing to serve as nagid. Rabbi Shaul Abitbol ruled that even though earlier ordinances are binding on later generations, the system of rotation was producing corruption and disorganization, and thus for the good of the community the earlier edict could be viewed as applying only to Judah and not to any later member of the family.

This early conflict is revealing in several significant respects. Clearly the community was eager to retain its own internal organization and not to have a Muslim official place someone in the position of nagid without their consent. Structurally, the appointment process was not unlike the choice of an Islamic qadi, for while the government could fill the position of Islamic judge on its own, it was broadly understood that the notables of the region could successfully disapprove of the designated individual. However, on at least one occasion in the early twentieth century the sultan, finding the members of a family who had long supplied the nagid to be irritatingly stubborn, insisted that someone from a different family be chosen to represent the Jews. Moreover, there has always been a certain tension between the individual Jew's contacts with Muslims outside of the community and the concerns of the collectivity as a whole, a conflict that risked greater attachment by an individual to the former than the latter. One communal regulation in Sefrou signaled this tension by condemning visits by the father of a groom and his male relatives to the home of the bride on festive occasions because when they "go and submit themselves to others," they are giving greater emphasis to personal patronage ties than to the bonds of kinship. Thus, the early fight over the appointment as nagid of Judah Harosh shows not only that internal strife was not unknown in the Jewish community but, more to the point, that such disagreements required some flexibility if the well-being of the community as a whole was not to be threatened. Since the period in question was one of frequent drought, inflation, and chaos following the death in 1727 of the powerful sultan Moulay Ismail, the willingness of Rabbi Abitbol to employ the concept of communal good—which is very similar to the Islamic idea of modifying a rule as a matter of the public interest (*istislaḥ* and *istiḥsan*)— demonstrates the highly practical approach taken in both Jewish and Islamic law in Morocco.

Judah's initial misstep may have been occasioned by the fact that Jewish community officials were also responsible for, and hence capable of, misappropriating the collection of taxes payable to the Moroccan government. Several types of formal taxes were imposed specifically on the Jews. The most distinctive was the traditional "protection" tax, or *jizya*, sanctioned by Islamic law and payable yearly by all adult males. The amount was set by the community leaders based on their assessment of the individual's worth, though the most wealthy were at times protected from the depredations of acquisitive Muslim officials by being taxed at the rate of the next level down. Since the wealthy might also serve as intermediaries for the community and be called upon for special contributions in times of difficulty, practicality, to say nothing of professed attachment to rabbinic texts and local ordinances, also played a role in the assessment of annual taxes on the well-to-do. In some instances local Muslim officials simply left it to the Jews to raise the appropriate sums peacefully. In others, the process was less benign. Thus, in 1815 in Mogador (Essaouira) the Jews were locked in the mellah without food or water while sorting out the payment from each class of resident. The four groups into which the rabbis divided the population of six thousand comprised four merchants in the first group (who paid over half the entire sum), the petty traders in the second group, crafts-men in the third, and the mass of poor laborers in the fourth. In the words of James Riley, an American who witnessed the event:

The Jews soon appeared by classes [before the local caid]; as they ap-proached, they put off their slippers, took their money in both their hands, and holding them alongside each other, as high as the breast, came slowly forward to the talb, or Mohammedan scrivener, appointed to receive it. He took it from them, hitting each one a smart blow from his fist on his bare forehead, by way of receipt of his money, at which the Jews said, *Nahma Sidi* (thank you, my lord), and retired to give place to his companion.

Thus they proceeded through the three first classes without much dif-ficulty, when the fourth [i.e., the poorest] class was forced up with big sticks. This class was very numerous, as well as miserable. They approached very unwillingly, and were asked one by one if they were ready to pay their *gazier* [*jizya* tax]. When one said yes, he approached as the others had done, paid his money, took a similar receipt, and then went about his business. He that said, no, he could not, or was not ready, was seized instantly by the Moors, who throwing him flat on his face to the ground, gave him about fifty blows with a thick stick upon his back and posteriors, and conducted him away, I was told into a dungeon. . . . At the end of three days more, I was informed that those who were confined to the dungeon were brought forth, but I did not see them. The friends of some of these poor creatures had made up the money, and they were dismissed; whilst the others, after receiving more stripes, were remanded and put in irons. Before the next three days had ex-pired, many of them changed their religion, were received by the Moors as brothers, and were taken to the mosque, and highly feasted, but were [in ac-cordance with Islamic law] held responsible for the last tax notwithstanding.

Other taxes, like those mentioned by Haj Hamed, were also invoked, including the "informal" payments expected by caids and royal officials, to say nothing of flat-out bribes. The burden of these taxes could be oner-ous, depending on the times and the acquisitiveness of those to whom they were due. And while the occasional looting of the Jewish quarter was hardly part of the ordinary system of taxation, it could be so tied up with the financial burden Jews sometimes had to endure that, as the British envoy Sir John H. Drummond-Hay noted in his *Western Barbary: Its Wild Tribes and Savage Animals*, published in 1844: "It is a proverbial retort given to this day by the Jews to any Moor who asks money of them—'were you not present at the pillage of the Jewry?'"

Indeed, from an analytic point of view, moments of attacks on the Jews are, for Jews and Muslims alike, a fascinating test of the nature of memory itself. The Muslims, I have suggested, seldom dwell on any event whose impact on the present is regarded as irrelevant, while, as Ruth Setton says for many Moroccan Jews, "We suffer from a sort of cultural amnesia. We forget what happened to us yesterday, the coming and going of the French, the dynasties of Sultans. A great blur of darkness buries us." Perhaps there were too many incidents; perhaps they could not all be memorialized. Maybe it is too much to expect the descendants of those who lived in Spain to remember the slaughter of a hundred thousand of their coreligionists throughout the country, especially in Castile, when Jews were blamed for the Black Death in 1391. Maybe it is understandable that few can cite how, on May 14, 1465, almost all the Jews in the mellah of Fez were killed when rebels used the excuse of a Jew being appointed as vizier to overthrow the Merinid dynasty, or that in the same area famine killed some twenty thousand Jews thirty years later, following the Jews expulsion from the Iberian Peninsula. Perhaps some have read how the sultan Moulay Rachid in 1670 burned a Jewish counselor in order to strike fear among the Jews and then tore down synagogues and imposed enormous taxes on the community. And maybe some have heard how, in the overall chaos following the end of the sultan Muhammad III's thirty-three-year reign in 1790, there was a massacre of Jews in Tetouan, while at Fez the Jews were driven out of the city, leading their rabbinical judge, Yehudah b. Obed Ibn Attar (1725–1812), to write: "And our faces became like the under side of a pot because the sun looked upon us; and we lived in tents like the sons of Kedar and Arabia and we were left without knowledge and understanding without worship, prayer, and Torah, because our minds had become disoriented with sorrow and grief."

Incidents closer in time may, however, have formed their own sediment of memory, some more readily recalled than others. The tragic story of Sol Hashuel, beheaded in Fez in 1835 after she recanted her conversion to Islam, has entered the realm of story and myth, while some of those from the north have not forgotten that when war broke out between Spain and Morocco in 1859, over four hundred Jews were killed. Others from the Marrakech region may not be surprised to learn of the deaths of 307 Jews in a variety of incidents in the years 1864–80.

Not all such incidents ended in official complicity or avoidance, however. When I first arrived in Morocco, older Jewish men, along with Haj Hamed, could recall that after the attacks on various Jewish communities following the death of the sultan Moulay al-Hassan in 1894, the new sultan was convinced to do more to protect the Jews. In November of 1896 an order was sent to Sefrou's Caid Omar al-Youssi, as to caids all over the country, ordering him to guard the Jews' persons and property. Some even knew that this was not the first time sultans were called upon to issue such directives. Famously, in 1863 Sir Moses Montefiore, the internationally known British baronet and philanthropist, already eighty years old, ill, and traveling fifteen miles a day on a camel over rugged territory, had come to Fez in response to the execution of a fourteen-year-old Jewish boy falsely accused of murdering a Muslim. In the course of just eight days he got a number of Jewish prisoners released and obtained from the sultan an order that read in part:

All Jews residing within our dominions . . . shall be treated by our governors, administrators, and all other subjects, in manner conformable with the evenly balanced scales of justice, and that in the administration of the courts of law they shall occupy a position of perfect equality with all other people, so that not even a fractional portion of the smallest imaginable particle of injustice shall reach any one of them. . . . Nor shall any tradesman among them, or artisan, be compelled to work against his will. The work of every one of them shall be duly recompensed, for injustice here is injustice in Heaven, and we cannot countenance it in any matter affecting either the Jews' rights or the rights of others, our own dignity being itself opposed to such a course. All persons in our regard have an equal claim to justice, and, if any person should wrong or injure one of the Jews, we will, with the help of God, punish him.

In another instance from this period an AIU teacher wrote:

In Sefrou, a little town near Fez, a poor cobbler received, on the orders of a caid's son, seven hundred blows of a stick, for not having made some slippers as perfectly as those shown him as models. As for another Jew, the caid forced him to work without paying him anything. Others who took themselves to markets or nearby settlements were financially exploited by functionaries and employees of every level. The complaints of the Jews got to the sultan; he issued an imperial order (*dahir*) to assure the security of the Jews of Sefrou; he ordered the caid's son to pay an indemnity of 250 francs to the cobbler who was so cruelly beaten.

Several of the Jews in Sefrou whom I interviewed in the 1960s could also point in detail to the events in Fez in 1911 when disorganized tribesmen attacked the city and a number of the Jews were robbed and killed. A Jewish teacher wrote in a letter dated June 4 of that year: "At Sefrou as well the Jews lived for several weeks in profound agony. . . . Our co-religionists are forced to supply [the Berbers] munitions, arms and money. This poor community is ruined." Jews were not, however, necessarily disarmed, and they did at times defend themselves. Robert Assaraf, relying in part on the materials brought to Israel from the Sefrou community by their chief rabbi, David Ovadia, supplies the details:

On a Thursday, the market day, after having been informed by some of their Muslim friends of an impending attack, the Jews, under the leadership of their nagid, Mordekhay Seba, took hostage several tribesmen who were in town. Mordekhay then distributed guns from their hiding places and had stones and boiling oil carried to the rooftops and parapets. He tried to negotiate with the tribesmen threatening the mellah from his position on the walls by offering certain financial guarantees. Several Muslim guards were also offered money to assist in the Jews' defense, but with little certainty that they would not then join their fellow tribesmen seeking to attack the quarter. That night the marauders used pickaxes to create a hole in the wall. The defenders wanted to repulse them, but Mordekhay told them to wait. Then when the first intruder was able to get himself through the hole, Mordekhay gave the order to shoot him, along with those of his fellow tribesmen who sought to recover the man's body. The Berbers panicked, and the Jews were able to seal the hole. Mordekhay then drew on his diplomatic skills to free the hostages, who were lowered from the high walls by rope. Rabbi Ovadia picks up the narrative at this point:

On Sunday, the Muslims [*Arabes*] made it known that they wanted to make peace with the Jews. But the Jews were always afraid to leave the mellah to parley. With his usual daring, Mordekhay offered himself up, accompanied by Aharon Azoulay. The negotiation went on so long the families of the two men began to fear for their lives. They returned as night fell. They then informed the community about the results of their negotiations. The Muslims had insisted above all that the mellah's weapons be turned over to them, but the men had refused, denying they possessed any. Ultimately, it was decided that the community would pay a ransom of 20,000 francs, in monthly installments, and in return the big men of the tribes agreed to themselves mount guard around the mellah every Thursday, the market day. Moreover, the community was required to provision the rebels every day before they departed for Fez with flour, sugar and tea.

In a speech that year to visiting representatives of the AIU, Shalom Azoulay praised God for sending the French "to save the Jews from being destroyed by Ait Youssi" who could not be kept at bay notwithstanding the bribe of 20,000 francs, while a legal ruling by 'Aba Elbaz held that even widows and orphans, who would normally have been exempt, must contribute to the taxes the "Philistine" rebels opposed to the sultan were extracting from the community. The treatment by the tribesmen of Sefrou as "their village" was, therefore, a mixed situation for the townspeople. Particularly at times of weak central control, the presence of rural people in the market could be disturbing to Muslims and Jews alike. Writing a few years earlier from Fez, Eugène Aubin had observed:

If the Berbers were good customers they were occasionally rather awkward ones. Sometimes they arrived in a band with the fixed idea of pillaging some shops. In a moment the *souks* were in a panic, merchants shut their shops, and made haste to quit the bazaar, leaving the tradesman who was attacked to settle matters with his assailants by himself. The news of the incident would soon reach the Mellah, whose entrances were, as a precautionary measure, guarded by a detachment of *asker* [soldiers]. Without the slightest motive a panic would break out in the Mellah, and might last for several hours. Women wept and wrung their hands, men ran madly in every direction, of-

Jewish quarter of Fez after 1912 riot

fering the melancholy spectacle of a population to whom fear has become a habit.

Such fears were not without foundation. A number of Jews clearly recollect the events in Fez in the spring of 1912 when the sultan's troops mutinied and dozens of Jews were killed as the soldiers and others rampaged through the city. In an attempt to reduce the flow of ammunition to rebels outside the city, officials sought to disarm both the Europeans and the Jews living in Fez. The former refused, but the Jews agreed to turn in their arms for fear of greater reprisals by both French and Moroccan officers. When the troops mutinied in mid-April, they not only attacked the Europeans but rampaged through the streets of the mellah, killing forty-five, injuring another twenty-seven, and pillaging all of the shops and homes. Writing to the minister plenipotentiary of France a few days later, Amram El-Maleh described how "no home has been spared. There is not one where there were not dead or wounded." He reported that thirty-five hundred Jews were given refuge by the sultan inside the palace grounds, "and even there," according to a news account published at the end of the month, "they are confronted with extreme misery . . . mainly from starvation." Dr. Félix Weisgerber described visiting the sultan and the mellah during these events, when the whole population of the mellah, some ten thousand souls, was gathered for safety in and around the palace. Of his visit to the mellah he wrote: "The main street of the *mellah* is nothing more than

Jews given sanctuary at Sultan's menagerie, Fez, 1912

a heap of ruins, of eviscerated furnishings, of smashed household items among which lie bodies of men, women, children hideously swollen and mutilated surrounded by bands of rats. Along the collapsed walls, several dogs, too sated to move, content themselves by showing us their fangs. A scroll of the Law, torn and soiled, trails in a dark pool of coagulated blood that gives off a terrifying odor."

In fact, during the worst moments the sultan gave shelter to many of the Jews by opening the empty cages of his menagerie where, as Ruth Setton's father bitterly recalled, his mother and the other Jews were only able to survive by being for a time a part of the monarch's zoo. In the words of the Paris correspondent for the *Daily Telegraph*, "Scores of women and children have found no other refuge but in the Sultan's menagerie. Here a lion dozes or a bear plays antics in a cage, and in the next cage, instead of wild beasts, there are women and children camping and cooking odds and ends of food in strange pots over primitive fires." However, it should be noted that, in addition to the sultan's protection, the Muslims of Fez, particularly the merchants, also cared for the Jews and took up a collection to aid them.

When these and similar events are recalled, all of the ambiguities associated with Muslim-Jewish relations come rushing back in. Informants note that Muslims, too, were attacked when sultans died and regimes were up for grabs and that it was not one's neighbors who engaged in such attacks, but outsiders. Raids were aimed much more at theft than at murder, and the Jews, who were at times armed, resisted these attacks, occasionally alongside Muslim allies and mercenaries. Moreover, as people also stress, since any moment that is likely to give rise to such attacks is also a test of a big man's claims as protector and guarantor, the situations become all the more complex and ambiguous. In many respects the late nineteenth century did, of course, mark the end point of a style of governance and the range of factors that came into play as Muslims and Jews had, in ways that were always ambiguous and even contradictory, adapted to one another. Matters did not cease to be any less ambivalent and tangled when, following the establishment of the Protectorate soon after the events in Fez, the Jews had to accommodate themselves to the effects of an imperial power directly occupying the country.

Sefrou—April 2, 1916
M. Nigrine, head of the Jewish school in Sefrou, describes in a letter to his superiors how some of the young Jewish men have begun to replace the black hat previously required of Jews with a new red one and how a policeman had arrested and briefly jailed one of the Jews for violating the established dress

code. He relates his conversation with the French chef du bureau, *in which the lieutenant says: "But listen, M. Nigrine. You know that Morocco is an independent country (I smile in spite of myself, he smiles, we understand one another)."*

The initial years of the French Protectorate had only an indirect effect on Shimon. Until his early twenties he was still living up in the mountains, an area whose more remote parts were not to be fully "pacified" by the French until 1931. As we sat one day in the late 1960s around the table in his kitchen, Shimon drew me back to those early days. When I was about twelve years old—it would have been around 1922—the road from Fez and Sefrou into the mountains was still "cut" by rebels, he began. My father and his brother had come down to Sefrou during that time, so Caid Said ou M'Hammad sent them a letter asking them to gather up some trade goods and bring them out to the countryside. The caid promised to send men to Sefrou to accompany them out of the city under his protection. The brothers took the letter to a translator who read them Caid Said's message and prepared their response, indicating they would accept the caid's offer. Although this was an area that Caid Said dominated, Shimon explained, there were others competing for control. Somehow the letter the translator prepared got intercepted and fell into the hands of a Muslim official in Sefrou who was an ally of another caid named Mouloud who was trying to wrest control away from Said. The translator came to the Muslim official and said: These men are under my personal protection (*mezreg*). Do me a favor (here Shimon used the European word *fabor*, since there is really no word in Arabic for a deed done with no expectation of reciprocity): Send me and my brother to jail for three months in place of the Benizris. The official thought and thought. Then he said: The Jews don't have to go to jail, and neither do you and your brother. But the Jews must leave the city. So my father and his brother left Sefrou and moved to the small settlement of Azzaba, just to the east, where, through other friends, they were able to sneak enough goods out of Sefrou to supply Said.

Indeed, said Shimon, it was also in 1922, after years of resistance, that the French began to send airplanes into the area and bomb the Muslims' settlements. At this point several of the big men of Almis came to my father. They said to him: You lived in Tlemcen, in Algeria, and you know the French. What is their custom, how do we make peace with them? My father told them to gather ten of the most important men and go to meet the advancing French. They also brought a bull with them. My father also told them to carry a piece of white cloth with them. Then the ten men with the bull walked down the road to meet the French. With my father acting as the go-between they showed the white cloth to the French officer who came up. They told him they didn't want to fight anymore, that they didn't want to be bombed, and that many of the young men who still wanted to fight had run away from the Almis area. The Frenchmen accepted their surrender: they did not sacrifice the bull. Afterward, Shimon concluded, the French kept sending planes over on reconnaissance, but they didn't drop any more bombs. It was not until 1924–26, a few years later, that most of the tribes in that part of the central Middle Atlas Mountains were finally "pacified."

The first years of the French Protectorate did, however, inevitably lead to changes for those Jews who, like Shimon, lived and traded in the Middle Atlas. The French concentrated their efforts in the region on the lowland areas their farmers gradually infiltrated. "Useful Morocco," as they called it, could be tilled and irrigated, and if the flocks of the mountain tribes brought down for winter pasturage could be restricted, these areas could be more readily developed for *colon* farmers, and the tribesmen could be drawn into working for them. In the late nineteenth century, for example, some 120,000 sheep were driven into the region around Fez; by 1931 that number had been restricted to just 37,000. Caids continued to press locals for taxes (because the colonial power allowed them legally to retain 6 percent of whatever they could extract), while lands held collectively by tribes, most of which originated as royal grants in exchange for ostensible protection of roads and maintenance of peace, were, along with water rights, effectively appropriated and turned over to French farmers by 1919.

Many of the rural farmers whose cultivation of unirrigated cereal crops was further subject to the vicissitudes of the weather began to work on the newly developed French farms; Pennell notes that by the mid-1930s the average-sized *colon* farm employed about fourteen Muslim families. The results of these measures backed up into the mountainous region where Shimon and other Jews lived. Caids adapted their actions to suit the new overseers, transhumance patterns were dependent on French concerns rather than tribal agreements or conflicts, and trade was increasingly affected by the control of domestic and foreign markets that linked Morocco to a wider economic system. The development of roads and the security of the French regime also meant that traders in the countryside were not as fully dependent on individual Berber protectors as they had been previously. Moreover, as the colonial presence really took hold, said Shimon, even the relatively isolated communities of Jews that had remained unchanged became increasingly affected by what was happening in nearby cities like Sefrou.

Sefrou in the early years of the Protectorate was still a small city of about six thousand people, half of whom were Jewish. The residents, of course, had had various contacts with the French since well before the onset of the Protectorate. In addition to a few of the local Jews becoming protégés of the French, a Jewish man named Schlomo Debdoubi, who was a purchasing agent and adviser on dealings with foreign consuls for Caid Omar in the late nineteenth century, sent his son Shimon to Tangiers, where he became the first Sefroui to learn the French language. In the spring of 1967 Haj Hamed invited me to meet this man, by then quite old. We sat at a small table outside a café on the main street of the new part of Sefrou, the Haj as always in his djellaba, Turkish trousers, yellow slippers, beige cap, and cigarette, and Debdoubi in a rather elegant and distinctly Jewish cloak and embroidered hat. The Haj was especially eager to introduce us because, he said, Debdoubi was a really fine man: quiet, gentle, and honest. At the Haj's urging Debdoubi and I spoke briefly in French. I did not learn until years later that he was the one who acted as the interpreter for the French when troops entered Sefrou in 1911 and thus failed to ask him about that incident. But a week after our first encounter, when I came across Debdoubi and the Haj sitting outside our friend the storekeeper's store, we did have a longer conversation.

Debdoubi, whose ancestors came from Spain and settled in the town of Debdou before moving to Sefrou, said there were only 620 Jews left in the town and only two of the seven synagogues still operated. Two *hazzans*, who have the authority to perform marriages and oversee ritual slaughtering but who cannot make legal judgments, came up from Fez as needed. After the Haj left, Debdoubi mentioned that the grand rabbi, David Ovadia, and most of his own family had gone to Israel but that his relatives there found it difficult to get work. When I asked why they emigrated, he said wistfully, because "they wanted to have their own land." How strange, I thought: Was I hearing, in Arabic, that ancient lament about the land, now embodied in a phrase from the Israeli national anthem: "So long as the eye looks eastward, gazing toward Zion, our hope is not lost—that hope of two millennia, to be a free people in our land, the land of Zion and Jerusalem"? Or was the emotion I sensed, as I was later to learn from Haj Hamed, far more complex?

For it was the Haj who subsequently told me that Debdoubi's own daughter had, within the previous decade, married a Muslim man and converted to Islam. The father tried to block the marriage and conversion, said the Haj. He even carried his appeal to the king himself, but the daughter told the king that she acted of her own free will, and the king said there was nothing he could do about the matter. Fear of conversion has deep roots in the history and psyche of the Jews of Morocco. The names of various Muslim families are frequently cited as indicative of their Jewish origins; I even had a travel agent in Fez named Haj El-Kohen. An eighteenth-century Jewish court document from Meknes speaks for the anguish such conversions pose to the community: "For in these times conversions are common and people do not refrain from intermarrying with partners who have converted relatives." Once again, as Shlomo Deshen points out, social and commercial ties with Muslim partners and neighbors could threaten Jewish communal ties, even leading (as also occurred in Meknes) to one of the parties revealing confidential information about the finances of various Jews to outsiders with whom they had formed patron-client, much less marital, relationships. Thus, close friendships with individual Muslims were not without their perceived risks to the Jewish community at large, including the loss of members through conversion to Islam.

In the early years of the Protectorate, when the Haj and Debdoubi were entering manhood and Shimon was still a boy, Sefrou, like other urban

Municipal council of Sefrou, Pasha Lamuri, Jewish and French members, ca. 1920s

centers, also began to take on the Protectorate's administrative apparatus, including French oversight of the courts, the restructuring of the municipal government, and the promulgation of municipal health and planning regulations. However, the greatest impact for the Jews, short of the *Pax Gallica* itself, came through the establishment of schools by foreign organizations. In 1911 the AIU, the most prominent of these organizations, sought to establish a school in Sefrou similar to those it had founded beginning in the 1860s in other parts of Morocco and the Middle East. In its 1860 Declaration the AIU made clear its mission and its view of the people it sought to help: "What was, what is, the aim of the Alliance? . . . In the first place, to cast a ray of the Occident into communities degenerated by centuries of oppression and ignorance; next, to help them find work more secure and less disparaged than peddling by providing the children with the rudiments of an elementary and rational instruction; finally, by opening spirits to Western ideas, to destroy certain outdated prejudices and superstitions which were paralyzing the life and development of the communities."

Many of the local Jews, however, resisted the introduction of AIU schools. In a letter dated August 19, 1911, AIU teacher Samuel Malka wrote that the Jews of Sefrou claimed "that French lessons are illicit under the Mosaic Law, and would lead to the conversion of young Jews to Christianity." The Jews who resisted probably understood full well that the AIU mission was more than the mere teaching of the French language. It was a moral project as well, one in which the "civilizing" effect of learning the language was intended to carry in its train a wide array of Western values. Indeed, the AIU saw the Moroccan Jews' own language as the key obstacle to be overcome in their broader mission. In a letter written by one of the AIU teachers from Casablanca in October 1898, the image of the backward Moroccan Jews and the difficulties of bringing enlightenment through language is clearly expressed:

> We must not lose sight of the fact that there is nothing more difficult than the study of French for the children who speak popular Arabic; the very spirit of their maternal dialect is so distant from the European spirit! The sounds, the expressions, and the ideas of the two languages clash when they come into contact. If the idiom spoken here [among the Jews] were closer to Arabic our task would be much easier! But it is a jargon, a jumble of expressions, from Arabic, Chaldean, Spanish, even Berber, composed without logic, mixed together in a small number of molds so narrowly formed that it is impossible to pour a new idea into them. There is not room for thought to function, only a very limited stock of clichés, applied more or less aptly to the diverse

circumstances of life. There is no base to work from: ideas, words, and constructions must be created whole. . . . Here we keep strictly to French from the beginning. It is imperative that their jargon be completely discarded, that translation be forbidden, and that the French form be imposed in its direct relation to the object, the gesture, or the action to be expressed.

As its declaration implies, the AIU was also opposed to the Jewish practice of saint veneration and pilgrimages, practices they regarded as depraved and contrary to Talmudic rationalism. Oren Kosansky cites several communications from AIU teachers in the Moroccan town of Ouazzane in this regard, one of whom, writing in 1910, says: "Our institutions should be a place to uproot these beliefs [in saints and miraculous cures], but students are absent from school on [pilgrimage days]." Twenty years later another teacher could still write: "It is a commonplace to recall the rapid movement that carries the Moroccan Jewish masses towards modern progress and civilization. . . . The notable fact is this forward march, this will to turn away from the past, to forget forever times of disgrace and oppression, to let go of ancient customs, of all the ridiculous superstitions. . . . In this general commotion, the cult of saints . . . is maintaining itself and even growing to a significance unknown in the past."

Commenters in the colonial period were equally critical of celebrations centered on a given saint. Pierre Flamand wrote: "It is difficult to render an account of the kind of frenzy that one sees at the time of the major pilgrimages, with their bacchic disorder and heavy drinking." Indeed, *mahia*, that potent fig liquor the Jews of North Africa brewed in rooftop stills, was described by a French traveler as "an unctuous *eau-de-vie*, [that] has no parallel in animating a conversation." Even fire walking did, and still does, take place at these rituals. Letters and reports from AIU teachers in the period around 1911 also commented adversely on the practice of marrying girls as young as six or seven to boys aged fourteen to sixteen, though this may have been a way of trying to ensure that the children would not subsequently be lost to the community through intermarriage.

Eventually, the Jews of Sefrou did agree in 1910 to the establishment of an AIU school, which initially could only handle 65 of the 150 who sought entry. The chaotic events of 1911–12 led to the frequent suspension of classes, but correspondence from the period 1915–16 suggests that at least by that date the school had begun operating regularly. Still, parents often objected to the subjects studied. The director of the Sefrou school in 1916, M. Nigrine, wrote that, given their parents' attachment to biblical literalism, it was especially difficult to teach the children scientific concepts without getting into trouble with them. Ironically, even though the AIU was not part of the French government but was in many respects in step with the Protectorate's *mission civilisatrice*, the AIU and the Protectorate government parted company in that the French largely promoted the preservation of Muslim and Jewish shrines, seeing in them a kind of authentic Moroccan syncretism that was preferable to Jewish assimilation and the conservative Islam of the urban Arab elite. This approach has sometimes led commenters to the mistaken belief that the French were also responsible for ending annual celebrations (sing. *moussem*) among the Muslims for fear that such gatherings might serve as focal points for resistance. For example, contrary to some local beliefs, the annual festival at the shrine of Sidi Ali Bouseghine, the "patron saint" of Sefrou, was not in fact ended by the French but by the offspring of the saint, who thought the celebrations were getting too disruptive and were exacerbating feuding among the different lines of the saint's descendants. Despite the modernizing work of the AIU and the Protectorate authorities, the shrine at Kaf al-Yahudi and other small Jewish shrines in Sefrou retained their importance for members of both faiths.

Notwithstanding some initial opposition, the fact that so many students sought the proffered AIU education is consistent with the eagerness with which many of Sefrou's Jews welcomed the greater freedom French rule offered. In short order a number of girls (and a bit later many boys) learned French and took French *prénoms* in addition to the Hebrew names they retained for ritual and documentary purposes, names like Nicole and André becoming all the fashion. As in other parts of the Muslim world, the Jews also began to avail themselves of activities previously not regarded by the Muslims as consistent with their status. Disputes over proper Jewish men's wear, like the dispute over hats in Sefrou, were common in many other places in the Muslim world. As late as the 1930s in Yemen, for example, a crisis occurred when a Jewish rabbi began to ride a bicycle, it having to be determined whether such a conveyance was like the horse that Jews should not ride or some permissible category of transport. In Sefrou, as well, in the early 1930s a Jewish café at the main gate to Fez just opposite a Muslim cemetery was the subject of considerable dispute, heightened by the presence of liquor and singing, all of which eventually led to the refusal of authorities to renew the café owner's lease. As elsewhere in the country, matters were also exacerbated by the anti-Jewish sentiment of some French officials and civilians.

Shimon was still living in the countryside during these years, but Haj Hamed, who came up with some frequency from Safi, remembered the

Jews and rural clients in market

situation very well. Throughout the 1920s, he said, there was a French-man, whose name he pronounced as Captain Matir, who oversaw both the troops and civil affairs in Sefrou during the time when the pasha Lamuri was both the pasha of Sefrou and the caid of the Ait Youssi tribal area. According to the Haj, Matir promulgated a number of laws specifically aimed against the Jews. When the French took over—and for some time prior for those who were French protégées—the Jews stopped wearing their traditional (and Muslim-imposed) dress and began to wear better-quality garments, more varied in color, and more stylish. Matir ordered them to return to wearing black slippers, black caps (sing. *chechia*), and black djel-labas made of only the poorest cloth. More importantly, he forbade the Jews from peddling in the countryside, forming commercial partnerships with Muslims, or lending with interest. He also stopped the Jews from pur-chasing green crops, that is, lending money against a portion of the har-vest. Whether his motives were anti-Jewish or his way of trying to further Resident-General Lyautey's vision of how best to maintain order and sepa-rate the Jews from the Muslims, Matir's directives put a severe crimp in the economy of the Jews. (Lyautey, it may be noted, regarded the Jews of Morocco as so used to being submissive that, playing on the Arab term for a given tribe, he referred to them as the "Beni Oui-oui.")

Pasha Lamuri, too, seemed cast in the mold of the older caids when it came to dealing with Jews or anyone else. Jacob Tobaly, for example, told me a story that, he said, showed how much Lamuri wanted to be seen as a protector. The pasha was approached once by a Jewish peddler who said he had been robbed near Sidi Boumediane. Lamuri, who had his guards round up the most likely culprit, was one of those men, Tobaly said, who can see through to the tiniest lie: he would simply look at a man very closely and, usually without asking a question, determine if the man was guilty. He told the suspect to pay up or be cut in two. And even after the accused man paid, he was publicly flogged and thrown in jail for a year. The comments by the Haj and Mr. Tobaly are supported by a contemporaneous letter from Rabbi Simon Haim Ovadia, who states: "An overlord, Mohamed Lamori Seraradi, governs the town of Sefrou. This potentate is particularly cruel to the Jews and the Muslims, putting whoever he wants in prison, inflicting fines and beating Jews, which is contrary to the law even though the French now have control over the cities, which is of no use anyway because the French governor doesn't see anyone and this official [Lamori] comes and goes, lying to the governor who believes him."

That Rabbi Ovadia mentions Lamuri's rough treatment of *both* Jews and Muslims is especially noteworthy and quite consistent with the accounts offered by others. It is true, Jacob Tobaly concluded, that Lamuri expanded and improved the mellah, but his harsh methods and his own cupidity began to work against the French view of how things should be conducted. Like Captain Matir, he eventually lost local support, and pressure was brought by many parties to have both of them removed. However, even after Matir was transferred to Fez, the Haj said, his successor, who apparently shared his views of the country's Jews, did not initially change a number of Matir's policies.

The issue of buying crops green came up, too, in my conversations with Jacob Tobaly. Himself a grain merchant approaching fifty when I knew him in the late 1960s, he said that those who did engage in this practice would commonly pay the farmer about half of what the crop should sell for. If the previous year's crop was good, the farmers might sell no more than 10 percent of the expected harvest, but if the previous year was poor and the farmers' stores had run out, they might sell as much as 30–40 percent of their future crop this way. If the crop failed, the money paid the farmer was considered a loan that had to be paid back the following year. Alternatively, some Jews loaned money directly. Rates were very high: several percent per month. The number of Jews engaged in such lending was, however, always rather limited. Nevertheless, there were a few Jewish lenders who, when a farmer could not repay his loan or had overextended himself in the sale of green crops, would pay the court notary to "forget" the loan arrangement, make the farmer an additional loan, and when he was unable to repay the cumulative amount, purchase his land cheaply.

A wide variety of partnership forms also existed between Muslims and Jews, contracts being drawn in such a way that the Muslim prohibition on charging interest was circumvented by diverse methods of profit sharing and legal fictions. Mohamed Kenbib notes that in a number of instances throughout Morocco Muslims who could not obtain the advantages of being a protégé of a foreign government in the late nineteenth century would enter into specious contracts with Jews and, as "sleeping partners," benefit from the seizure or sale of lands from farmers who could not repay the debts to their Jewish "partners." Though such practices alienated both local Muslims and foreign consuls, it does indicate the willingness of Muslims and Jews to form partnerships with one another. Similar practices continued into the Protectorate era, notwithstanding the end of the protégé system. It may have been because of the occasional abuses, coupled with the French view of Jews as rapacious lenders and widespread French anti-Semitism that led Captain Matir and other colonial officers to seek limitations on the economic activities of some of the Jewish merchants. In many other instances Muslim-Jewish partnerships were fully sanctioned by law and involved a wide range of economic and interpersonal ties.

The overwhelming majority of urban Jews, of course, made their living not from lending money or engaging in large-scale ventures but as small shopkeepers and craftsmen. A number of scholars, commenting on the economic position of Jews in various Middle Eastern countries and periods, have suggested that the range of occupations that Jews could practice was quite limited. But more recent historical work shows this was not the case; indeed this may be one of those instances in which what was thought must be true in the Muslim world was based on expectations from the experience of Jews living in Christian Europe. As historian Mark Cohen notes: "The Jews of Islam, in contrast, participated in a 'commercial revolution' that began with the Arab conquests in the seventh century and had plenty of room for all participants. The Jews pursued a diversified mix of economic endeavors that largely integrated them into the Arab marketplace. The Islamic economy for the most part did not impose confessional boundaries restricting members of the minority religions to certain economic activities."

Daniel Schroeter's detailed studies of Essaouira (formerly Mogador), which could be applied as well to many areas, support this proposition: "On a business level Jews interacted with Muslims in the wide open spaces of the urban market. . . . In the urban markets, ethnic barriers were broken down. . . . The requirements of business overrode religious differences." Similarly, Clifford Geertz, who did an extraordinarily detailed study of the Sefrou marketplace, concluded: "Jews mixed with Muslims under uniform ground rules, which, to an extent difficult to credit for those whose ideas about Jews in traditional trade are based on the role they played in pre-modern Europe, were indifferent to religious status."

Sefrou was thus not unusual among Moroccan examples regarding the occupational range and integration of the Jews. Massignon's list of occupations practiced by Muslims and Jews in Sefrou in 1924 (table 1) is instructive in this regard .

Note that all of the tinsmiths and porters, for example, were Jews. This, older Muslims told me, was because the tinsmiths were also plumbers and had to enter a Muslim's house where they would see the women and the belongings of the homeowner. But whereas the Muslims were not eager for fellow Muslims to see such things in their homes, the Jews could be expected to remain discreet and, since they were not potential marital partners or political allies, their knowledge of one's household situation was not going to bear on subsequent relationships. Jewish porters, who reportedly numbered three hundred earlier in the century, were perhaps especially numerous because they worked a good deal with Berbers.

By the time of the 1960 census Jews were still practicing a very wide range of occupations, though with less representation in the crafts than earlier. What such lists do not show, however, is the frequency with which Jews and Muslims entered into a variety of partnerships. Detailed study of the land records in Fez reveals that quite a few houses and gardens that were titled under the system the French introduced were jointly owned by members of both groups. This was hardly a recent or localized development. Moroccan records contain documents that memorialize such agreements going back centuries; other sources, such as the famous Geniza documents that were discovered in Egypt, reveal a similar pattern dating back to the early Middle Ages. As recently as my initial field studies in Sefrou, I gathered lists of such partnerships, ranging from the names of Muslims who acted as intermediaries for Jews who loaned money or bought crops green to Hussein's list of the few remaining Jews engaged in partnerships with his fellow tribesmen, all of whom either accepted some of the profit instead of charging interest or by then charged the same low rates as the bank. Jacob Tobaly also insisted that mutual investing replaced loans sometime in the midcolonial era.

When an agreement between a Muslim and a Jew was contested, matters commonly went to the Muslim court. More striking, however, was the

Table 1. Massignon's List of Occupations Practiced by Muslims and Jews in Sefrou in 1924

Occupation	Number Muslims	Jews
Saddlers	10	0
Jewelers	6[a]	6
Rope makers	16	0
Wheelwrights	4	0
Lime burners	16	0
Soap makers	0	3
Tinsmiths	0	6
Blacksmiths	21	0
Masons	16	0
Horseshoers	16	0
Carpenters & barrel makers	5	3
Wool carders	0	5
Olive oil millers	24	0
Cobblers	44	24
Sawyers	15	0
Tailors	12	0
Weavers	70	0
Bath operators	3	0
Barbers	12	4
Donut makers	2	2
Butchers	26	16
Bakers	30	0
Café operators	8	0
Charcoal makers	5	5
Nail makers & dealers	2	4
Auctioneers	8	9
Upholsterers	6	40
Greengrocers (beqqala)	8	12
Spice, herb sellers ('attara)	43	51
Inn and corral (funduq) operators	8	0
Dried fruit sellers	15	0
Roofers	2	0
Wool merchants	12	6
Vegetable dealers	25	0
Grain measurers	4	0
Flour millers	12	12[b]
Musicians	8	3
Candy makers	3	0
Porters	0	25
Cook shop operators	12	0
Teamsters (intercity)	0	25[c]
Straw and palmetto sellers	7	0
Hide dealers	0	5

[a] Coppersmiths
[b] 50 workers
[c] Having 100 mules

fact that Jews not infrequently went into the Muslim courts to have their own disputes with a fellow Jew settled. Such practices were often discouraged by Jewish officials: a document from 1804 has the committee setting a fine for going to a non-Jewish court; another from 1856 inveighs against a Jew who, in a dispute with another Jew, brought to the synagogue a Muslim advocate who apparently argued the matter according to Islamic law; and in 1862 a wife who agreed to no support as a condition of her divorce was bound to that stipulation by the Jewish court, at which point she went to the Muslim court, which granted her alimony. There are even examples of two Muslims coming to a respected Jewish figure like a *hazzan* to have their matter arbitrated. Particularly in the countryside, Jews might avail themselves of several different legal systems, Islamic, Berber, and Jewish. An important Muslim entrepreneur of a community in the deep south of Morocco, discussing partnerships with the Jews, thus told Omar Boum, as was true elsewhere in the country: "We needed Jews for our economic survival; they depended on us for their personal security. We had to coexist to endure the desert. We had to agree on a fenceless space and a legal framework that organized our relationship. The market and the *shariʿa* made this interdependence not only possible but also sustainable."

Once again, partnerships and legal pluralism were not limited to the modern period or Morocco; records show this to have been common throughout the Ottoman Empire and other regions as well, though the rare instances of Muslims actually coming to Jewish authorities appear to be unique to Morocco. Jessica Marglin's study of the courts of Meknes in the nineteenth century shows instances of Jewish merchants obtaining legal documents simultaneously from a Jewish and a Muslim court as well as Jews representing Muslims as their spokesmen in legal proceedings. Jews also absorbed some of the customary practices of Islamic law, as, for example, in disguising interest as return on the initial investment. Far from seeking to limit the jurisdiction of the Jewish courts, most of the Moroccan monarchs and local big men once again demonstrated their protector status by reinforcing local Jewish autonomy in the governance of their own affairs. What is striking, however, is that each appears to have sampled and been directly involved at times in the others' localized institutions.

During the 1920s, when Shimon was still growing up in the mountains, the effects of developments taking place in Morocco's urban centers had a less direct impact on his life than when, during the period 1933–39, he moved for the first time to Sefrou. The Jews had been eager to get out of mellahs all over Morocco for some time. By 1934 all resistance to the French had ended in the south, and large numbers of French had moved into the country. Within Sefrou proper the Jewish population had risen steadily from 3,444 in 1926 (in addition to 4,894 Muslims and 140 foreigners) to 4,346 in 1936 (compared to 7,288 Muslims and 246 Europeans) and 5,757 in 1947 (still half the city's total population) before declining to 4,360 in 1951–52 and 3,041 in 1960 (less than 20 percent of the Muslim population) before dropping precipitously through the next decade to just 222 in 1971 (out of a total population of more than 28,000). In the 1930s, however, the Jewish community, both urban and rural, was still very vibrant. But the impact of outside events on the Jews of Morocco was only going to increase as the decade drew to a close.

Shimon admits that he was largely unaware of the major transformations occurring in Europe when, in 1939, he accepted the offer of reestablishing a store back in the Middle Atlas Mountains. Indeed, he candidly acknowledges that the war years were relatively quiet for him. He tended his store, and he and Zohara raised their family. Except for the shortages of numerous goods associated with the war, the situation of his own small community seemed little different from any other time when the weather, tribal politics, or the activities of the central government kept the Jews reliant on their local relationships. Elsewhere, the effects of the war on Moroccan Jews were not so easily ignored.

In October 1940, after the fall of France that spring, the Vichy regime applied its "Law of the Jews" to France's North African possessions. The law placed a quota of 2 percent on the number of Jewish doctors and lawyers who could practice their professions, and a limit of 10 percent on the number of Jews enrolled in secondary education. Jews were also barred from government posts, military positions, educational appointments, and jobs in communication. The Moroccan sultan Muhammad V, in conformity with Islamic law, which holds that religion is not a matter of race, succeeded in having the law modified so that converts to Islam would not be regarded as Jewish. He also succeeded in getting the law modified so Jews could continue to participate in their own educational institutions. Then in June 1941 Vichy extended the list of occupations, mainly commercial, in which Jews could not participate. While restrictions were far harsher in Algeria, where the French citizenship of Jews was revoked, and in Tunisia, which was occupied by German forces after the American invasion of North Africa, Morocco was the only country where the Jews were required to move back into the mellahs. Rations, always limited in these years, were also set at a lower level for Jews than other groups. Some Jews hid their property with Muslim friends, fearing that the listing of assets required by the Vichy governors would be the first step in their confiscation. In many instances this trust in their Muslim counterparts proved well-placed; in other instances, however, the Jews were deceived by their partners. Importantly, though, expressions of support for the Jews came from the sultan himself.

For while Muhammad V, who had no independent powers of his own under the Protectorate, did sign the Vichy laws, he also took significant steps to ameliorate the situation of Morocco's Jews. He had not only gotten Vichy to acknowledge that religion was not based on race, but he made clear his desire to protect the Jews. He arranged for a group of rabbis and Jewish leaders to be sneaked into the palace, hidden in a wagon, and assured them that he would tolerate no distinction among his subjects. Then, on the occasion of the Festival of the Throne he invited the Jewish leaders to join in the celebration, and he again publicly stated in front of the assembled Vichy officials that he regarded the Jews as being under his protection. He also reiterated to the Jewish invitees his commitment to their equal treatment. Indeed, a telegram discovered in the early 1980s that was sent to Vichy headquarters describes the sultan's actions at this event:

> On that occasion, it was the custom for the Sultan to hold a guest banquet which was attended by French officials and distinguished individuals from Moroccan circles. For the first time, the Sultan invited representatives of the Jewish community to the banquet and placed them most obviously in the best seats, right next to the French officials. The Sultan had wanted personally to introduce the Jewish individuals present. When the French officials expressed surprise at the presence of the Jews at the meeting, the Sultan told them: "I in no way approve of the new anti-Semitic laws and I refuse to be associated with any measure of which I disapprove. I wish to inform you that, as in the past, the Jews remain under my protection and I refuse to allow any distinction to be made among my subjects." This sensational declaration gave rise to lively comment within French and indigenous communities.

When the Vichy officials required a census that appeared to be preparatory to the confiscation of Jewish property, a delegation of Jewish notables made a traditional 'ar sacrifice of four bulls to the sultan, who then met with them and indicated that his signing the Vichy law that had been presented to him was only intended to affect assets that might leave the country. He then said in the presence of others, and confirmed his statement in a second meeting with the delegates: "Rest assured, I will sign nothing else concerning Moroccan Jews. I consider you to be Moroccans in the same capacity as Muslims and your property, like theirs, will not be touched.

Should you hear bad reports concerning the Jews, come and let me know." Then, on July 13 a delegation of Jews invited by the pasha of Fez attended the reception held by the sultan in Rabat celebrating the circumcision of the monarch's sons. In a document reproduced by Haim Zafrani the sultan is described as asking the Jews to a private meeting following the reception where he said to them: "My palace is open at all times for you to come and find me when you hear something unpleasant about yourselves." The document goes on to say of the sultan that afterward "He was so good as to ask personally that his steward serve them tea and traditional cakes."

But the sultan was powerless to control events: he could not even employ the air of overseeing a slow-moving bureaucracy to much effect, since real power remained firmly in the hands of the French, assisted in part by the sultan's anti-Semitic centenarian vizier Muhammad El Mokri. In addition, the Jews were confronted with a number of anti-Semitic French officers at every level. Governor-General Charles Noguès and a number of other French officers serving in North Africa, like the overall head of the Vichy government (and former leader of French forces in Morocco) General Philippe Pétain, held racist beliefs long before they received Nazi instructions. These officials also had support from an elite group of Legionnaires and right-wing colonists who, according to Haim Zafrani, had sworn an oath "to combat democracy, Gaullist dissidence and Jewish leprosy" and had planned an attack on the Jews of Casablanca for November 15, 1942, which was only frustrated by the landing of American forces on November 8 and their entry into Casablanca three days later. During 1941–42 the French authorities in Morocco also raised no objection when the Germans began to establish detention camps in each of the North African countries.

Robert Satloff, who has investigated the existence of these camps, reminds his readers that in the 1942 film *Casablanca* there is mention of these facilities when a Gestapo officer tries to convince Ingrid Bergman, portraying the wife of a Czech partisan, that her husband should surrender to the Germans; otherwise, he insinuates, "It is possible that the French authorities will find a reason to put him in the concentration camp here." Indeed, such camps—one of which was actually situated at Casablanca— held about seven thousand people, two thousand of them Jews, the vast majority of whom were from other countries and were either caught in Morocco or sent there from Europe. The camps in Algeria and Tunisia were especially known for the brutality of the French Foreign Legionnaires and the local guards who ran them: men were beaten, starved, made to lie for days in shallow graves, and subjected to extremes of heat and cold. Aside from the facility located near Casablanca, most of the thirty camps in Morocco were along the Algerian border, in barren areas well away from the public eye.

Although little remarked upon by Westerners, the camps were not altogether unknown to people in Morocco. One was even located in Missour, not far from El Mers, where Shimon was living during the war years. A listing of its inmates shows that, like the hero in *Casablanca*, some of those incarcerated there were indeed partisans from Czechoslovakia. In his thorough listing of the camps Oliel notes that the inmates of the Missour camp, mostly politically active (particularly Communist) foreign prisoners (but, as elsewhere, also some Moroccan Muslim and Jewish leftists), were treated as badly as those in the Algerian camps at Djelfa and Djenien-bou-Rezq, which were noteworthy for "the severity of the conditions inflicted on their internees." But as best I could tell, Shimon was never aware of the camp's existence. Even after the American troops landed in 1942, Roosevelt did not move to have the camps closed immediately, as he and Eisenhower were intent on keeping the local French forces, which had initially resisted the invasion, from doing anything that might interfere with the allies' push toward Italy.

A good deal of mythology and controversy has grown up about the role played by the sultan Muhammad V in "protecting" the Jews during those early years of the war. Some claim that when Vichy threatened to require the Jews in Morocco to wear a large Star of David, the sultan told the French to bring enough copies so he and his family could don them as well. Many Jewish leaders in Morocco argue strongly that his statements, public and private, went a long way toward preventing the sort of actions that occurred in Algeria and Tunisia. Others are equally adamant in insisting that while the sultan's gestures were not without symbolic meaning, neither fanciful stories about wearing a Star of David nor any of the monarch's statements made any difference to the Jews' situation.

In recent years a number of influential members of the remnant Jewish community of Morocco and some supporters in Israel, including President Shimon Peres, have proposed the sultan's inclusion among the Righteous Gentiles honored at the holocaust memorial Yad Vashem. Although a number of European and Turkish Muslims are so honored, there are none from the Arab world, even though, as Satloff and others have documented, there were indeed Arabs in France and North Africa who would be worthy of consideration. Since the criterion for inclusion is that one must have risked one's own life to save Jews and clear evidence to that effect appears lacking in the case of Muhammad V, no formal application has been made. Two things, though, do bear noting. First, what Muhammad V did may be seen as yet another instance in which some portion of any Moroccan monarch's legitimacy resides in his claim to be a protector of his people, for which the Jews are the traditional test case. And second, Muhammad V was not about to let fissures in his citizenry open up that would undermine his overarching goal, namely, to retain sufficient national unity to achieve Moroccan independence once the war was over. Shimon and Zohara, like most Moroccan Jews who lived through that period, strongly believe that, whatever his motivations, the sultan did do what he could to protect the Jews, and they, along with most of their coreligionists, have continued to honor his memory even after leaving Morocco.

If Shimon, nestled in the countryside and still the very image of the compliant Jewish storekeeper and protégé of his Berber big man, lived a relatively peaceful existence, the country as a whole was subjected to the ancient ills of drought, famine, and disease during the latter years of the war. The loss of flocks, which ranged up to 70 percent in some parts of the country in 1943, was not quite as severe where Shimon lived in the Middle Atlas region of El Mers. But in the cities it was a different matter. Food, particularly bread, was in short supply, and under the Vichy rules the Jews were the last to receive any provisions.

Throughout the war the French in and around Sefrou were divided between Vichy supporters and Gaullists, neither being particularly sympathetic to the situation of the Jews. In the summer and autumn of 1944 incidents broke out in several cities. In Sefrou, on July 30, following a minor altercation between a Jew and a soldier who had wounded the former's brother, four hundred soldiers (*goumiers*) fueled by the statements of pro-Vichy administrators attacked Jews celebrating the holiday that marks the destruction of the Temple in Jerusalem, wounding dozens of Jews and violating the synagogue and Talmudic school. The police, instead of restraining the attackers, arrested two hundred Jews, imposed on them a four-day curfew, and barred them from public places outside the mellah. As Rabbi Ovadia noted, "The Jews of Morocco, not having had to suffer from the Nazis, our enemies, under cover of the French administration, had thus found it propitious to effect the evil designs they had always fomented against us." After similar attacks occurred two months later in Meknes, the sultan called in representatives of the Jewish community in an attempt to reassure them of his protection.

But the famine of 1945—what Moroccans still call the year of the ration coupon (*'am l-bun*)—put additional pressure on many relationships. For Shimon the food shortages only intensified dependence on his protectors and theirs on his connections to Jewish suppliers in Sefrou and Fez to make outside goods available to his rural clients. Agitation for independence was further fueled in these years by the demands of the developing nationalist parties and unions, leading to violence in Casablanca and Fez, deportations of some leaders, and further polarization of the French population. As markets for traditional Moroccan products and services dried up, many of the Jews began to drift to the larger cities, seeking both economic opportunities for themselves and better education for their children.

Starting with the invasion by American forces in November 1942 and continuing to the end of the Vichy presence—and more particularly after the war itself ended and the French could focus attention on North Africa again—the city of Sefrou, like many others, began to expand outside of its ancient walls. Beginning around 1940, but with greater significance right after the war, gardens in adjacent areas became the site for new apartments and housing clusters, and many of the Jews who could afford to do so moved into these neighborhoods. The French had discouraged the migration of rural people into the cities, but a trickle that was later to become a deluge was beginning all over the country. Perhaps in an attempt to reestablish the "traditional" order after the war, some officials, both Moroccan and French, sought to keep Jews in their prewar roles. In 1946, for example, when Rabbi Ovadia became the chief rabbi of Sefrou, he took off the garb previously worn by such persons, only for pressure to be brought to bear on him by government officials to once again don the appropriate costume.

But the forces of change, some legislated within the Jewish communities and others that were external to Morocco, were becoming irresistible. Inheritance laws were once again subject to alteration, as the rabbis had to respond to the condition of women who were experiencing greater education and mobility. Assets now had to be divided equally between a wife and up to four children; in 1952 the rabbis, in a wrenching decision that contravened biblical law, even declared that a woman could not be required to marry her deceased husband's brother. Couples could now meet with chaperones present before their marital agreement was drawn up by their parents. The Jewish population of Morocco in the postwar period is variously estimated at 250,000–280,000, roughly one-quarter of all the Jews living in the Middle East, including Turkey at that time.

Along with the arrival of American troops and the development of an incipient nationalist movement, the most dramatic event for the Jews, of course, was the founding in 1948 of the State of Israel. In Morocco, the repercussions were varied. On the one hand, the creation of Israel appeared to many the fulfillment of a millenarian promise. On the other, the immediate outbreak of war in the Middle East put the Jews in the position of being at least emotionally allied with those fighting the Arab armies. Several incidents occurred in which Moroccan Jews were attacked. Near Oujda a mob killed thirty-nine Jews and wounded a number of others in an incident that scholars like Haim Zafrani suggest may have been fomented from abroad. In Sefrou, the committee announced that Jews leaving town for more than forty-eight hours had to register with them, and if they failed to do so, the persons' families should report the absence to local officials. For the most part, though, locals still drew a distinction between Jews and Zionists.

Following the cessation of hostilities in the Middle East, Israel stepped up its efforts to gather the Jews of all the Arab lands into the new nation. Agents who were sent to Morocco reportedly told Jews, especially those in the most isolated rural regions, that Morocco would be the next Germany, and it was imperative that they leave while they could. Undoubtedly there were those who saw the advent of the Jewish state not only as the fulfillment of biblical promise but as an opportunity to reject altogether the lives they had led under Muslim cultural and political domination. In this respect they may have shared the sentiment of the twelfth-century Jewish poet Judah Halevi, who famously wrote from Spain:

> My heart is in the East—
> and I am at the edge of the West.
> How can I possibly taste what I eat?
> How could it please me?
> How can I keep my promise
> or ever fulfill my vow,
> when Zion is held by Edom
> and I am bound by Arabia's chains?

But even though the combination of millennial allure and newfound uncertainties led some eighteen thousand Jews to emigrate to Israel at this time, there was even greater movement by Jews of the interior to the large cities of the coast, mainly Casablanca. Thus, notwithstanding events in the east, the attachment of Moroccan Jews to their homeland remained strong.

As attentive as all Moroccans were to the creation of Israel, the increase in nationalist sentiment was the primary concern to most Muslim Moroccans at this moment. To this day many people believe that President Roosevelt promised the sultan Muhammad V at the time of the Casablanca meeting with Churchill that the United States would return Morocco's fa-

Sefrou before 1950 flood

vor of having been the first country to recognize American independence by urging the French to bring the Protectorate to an end following the war. In the latter part of the 1930s, but with greater impetus in the immediate postwar period, a few of the more highly educated Jews in the larger cities joined with Muslims in organizing political groups and trade unions pressing for independence. Like their Muslim counterparts, most were politically well to the left and perfectly aware that the sultan himself had expressed nationalistic leanings on a number of occasions.

However, 1950 marked a quite different occasion in Sefrou's history. On September 25 (at the time of the Jewish holiday of Succoth), following four hours in which four and a quarter inches of rain fell, a major flood occurred. Apparently, debris got clogged at a point just above the heart of the city, and when it burst, the river suddenly rose by some twenty feet. The mellah, being right alongside the river at the city center, was the primary site affected. This was not the first time the mellah was flooded: in May 1916 a flash flood left ten Jewish families homeless, and twenty-seven years before that another flood caused considerable damage. But the 1950 deluge was far more severe: 21 Jews and 26 Muslims died before the waters receded; 286 Jewish families were left homeless. Afterward, the channel of the river was dug out some fifty feet, but to this day if one walks alongside the river's bank and looks up at a fading line drawn twenty feet up on an adjacent building, one can see the limit the floodwaters reached. So serious was the damage and so close was he to the pasha of Sefrou, Si Bekkai ben

Sefrou after 1950 flood

Jewish laundresses at river

Embarek Lahbil, that the sultan Muhammad V paid a visit to the stricken city and offered assistance in its reconstruction. Jewish women, who had long come down to the river to wash their clothes—an image so associated with the city generally as to be memorialized in numerous paintings and postage stamps—returned in time to their routine, but for those who lived through it, the flood remains one of the most vivid memories of their entire lives.

In this same period on the political front, the French and their Moroccan allies were becoming sufficiently dissatisfied with the sultan's support of the nationalists that, in August 1953, they succeeded in dethroning him, sending his entire family into exile, and replacing him with the puppet sultan Ben Arafa. The Moroccan population at large was incensed: people who emphasized his descent through the line of the Prophet even claimed to see the exiled sultan's face in the moon, and Si Bekkai, as pasha of Sefrou, came out with a clear statement of support for the deposed sultan, though fearing his removal would create more problems than it solved, the French authorities left Bekkai in place. The Army of Liberation—a term used in the Sefrou area for a broad range of groups rather than a single organized entity—began its own campaign of hit-and-run attacks. Several French-owned farms in the Sefrou area were burned, and Jews were cautioned not to support the colonial power. Jews were harassed in many parts of the country, including Sefrou, where outsiders demanded free goods from Jewish merchants, who then chose this unsettled period as the time to emigrate. However, Muhammad Zade, in his *Résistance et Armée de Libération au Maroc*, indicates that less than 2 percent of the 4,061 acts carried out nationwide by the Army of Liberation in the period 1953–56 were against Jews.

Although Sefrou remained comparatively quiet, throughout the early 1950s violent incidents increased across the country, some carried out by colonists who felt the government was leaning toward accommodation with those seeking independence, others by Moroccans seeking to convince the French that the price of retaining dominance was too high. Finally, on November 16, 1955, the French, their loss in Vietnam and their ongoing battle in Algeria weighing heavily on them, reached an agreement with the exiled sultan for independence, and Muhammad V was returned to enormous national celebration. Si Bekkai, no longer pasha of Sefrou, was assigned the task of forming a cabinet, in which he served as prime minister, while the caid of the Ait Youssi of the Sefrou region was installed as interior minister. Along with four of his fellow religionists in the Parliament, a Jew was appointed as the first head of the postal and telegraph ministry.

Once again, the Jews of Morocco were faced with wrenching decisions. In one sense, as Norman Stillman argues, the Jews' closeness to the French may have been their undoing; it disrupted their earlier interpersonal relations with Muslims and allied them too closely with French culture and aspirations. On the other hand, their situation had become increasingly untenable because of a variety of factors, from the changes in their socioeconomic role to the international political climate, rather than as the simple result of identification with the colonial power. The Jews of Morocco had never been made French citizens, as their coreligionists in Algeria had been, and had not collectively taken up positions favoring the continuation of the Protectorate. They had shown solidarity with the sultan and had not massively abandoned the country with the founding of Israel. Moreover, the nationalist leaders knew that the talents of the Jews and the image of the state as protector would be no less desirable after independence than it had ever been. One leading Moroccan political activist told a British reporter in 1947 that there were only three Muslim doctors, six lawyers, and six agricultural engineers in the whole country, while in 1956, according to a study by Noureddine Sraïeb, "the European population's children all attended school. The Jewish Moroccan population was at 80% while Muslims at only 13%. . . . In 1955, Morocco counted only 19 Muslim doctors and 117 Jewish doctors, 6 Muslim and 11 Jewish pharmacists, about fifteen engineers for each of these denominations and 165 high ranking executives [mainly Muslim] in the government." Thus many of the nationalists knew that Jewish involvement in an independent nation would be desirable, if for no other reason (as the head of the Istiqlal party Allal al-Fassi argued) because other Arabs did not want the largest group of Jews in the Middle East further populating Israel. Worries over precisely how a Muslim government would handle the economy and political party wrangling, was, in the early blush of national independence, balanced for Moroccan Jewry against confidence in a monarch who had protected them from Vichy, the American presence at a major military base, and the government's relatively benign approach to Israel. Nevertheless, as for so many other Moroccan Jews, it was a time of major transition for Shimon and his family.

Within a year after Morocco gained its independence, Shimon and his immediate family moved to Sefrou. At the same time, Shimon's mother and several of his siblings emigrated to Israel. When asked what prompted these decisions—and especially why he chose to remain in Morocco—Shimon was rather diffident. He responded simply: My father had been dead for many years, and my mother and siblings, one of whom was a rabbi, were all very religious and wanted to go to Israel. As for himself, he said, what would he do there? He could not just open a little cloth shop, he did not want to separate from his Berber customers, and he was getting on in years. But I did move to Sefrou, he added, mostly for the children's sake. There was no future for them in the countryside, and schooling in Sefrou was necessary for whatever future they were to have.

In fact there were by that time several Jewish schools in Sefrou. One, called Em-Habanim, was started by wealthy Moroccan Jewish women who wanted a modern alternative to the AIU school. In 1954 there were close to 610 enrolled in the school, another 611 at the AIU school, 50 more at a Lubavatcher school for girls, and 40 at the Bet David Yeshiva. One of Shimon's daughters, Collette, eventually became a teacher at Em-Habanim. All of the Benizri children went mainly by their francophonic names, spoke good French and no modern standard Arabic (*fusha*) or the Berber their parents spoke so fluently. The contrast of the younger generation's Western clothing to that of their elders, inevitably quite sharp, was caught in this period by one writer in the following somewhat sardonic terms:

> As they leave the mellah the Jews of both generations are arrayed before you. Here is the older generation. It has a long beard, a drab jellaba, the old-fashioned skullcap of the oppressed. Nevertheless, in its way of maintaining itself there is a fierce humility. It is the regal misery of the sages.
> Here is the new generation. It has taken on the ostensible appearance of

the children of its century, adorning itself as if by an unbreakable law in the style of Marlon Brando. . . . Wanting to be at the cutting edge of progress, it winds up at the juncture of every form of affectation.

The generational difference was especially striking in the Benizri family, given the long duration of the parents' lives in the tribal countryside and the children's thoroughgoing orientation to a world beyond their current experience. By the time I got to know the family in 1967, one daughter was living in Casablanca awaiting her divorce, while the younger ones were chafing at life in small-town Morocco. The community was now entirely out of the old mellah, most having moved to the neighborhood just outside the walls where we lived, Shimon said, others up to the new town the French had constructed, primarily on a street called the Rue du Serpent because of its winding shape. A few Jews, like Shimon and Zohara's brother, still kept their stalls in the medina hard by the main mosque, where merchants rented them from the pious foundation (ḥabus). Celebrations on religious holidays still brought people close, and Shimon's contacts with his rural clientele who came each week to market remained undisturbed. Yet each new event carried with it added justification for anxiety. When, on February 26, 1961, Muhammad V died suddenly during a minor operation, the Jews felt that their protector was gone and that his son Hassan II was untested in this regard. Clearly the community was aging, and whether it was to be by moving to Casablanca or Rabat or to a home abroad, there was little doubt, particularly after the Six-Day War, that almost all of the Jews would soon leave. For the Benizri family that time came the very next year.

---

lo vashuv od l-veysoh, velo yakirenu od mekomo.
And the places that knew them shall know them no more.

—Job 7:10

What good are roots if you can't take them with you?

—Gertrude Stein

Petah Tikva, Tel Aviv, Israel—July 1977
Of all the images I retain of Shimon Benizri, few remain so fixed in my mind's eye as the moment when Shimon stepped out of his apartment in Israel to greet me. It was not just the warmth of his embrace or the joy at seeing him safely settled with the family in Israel. It was the hat. In Mo-

rocco I cannot recall a time when Shimon was not dressed in a dark djel-laba, white shirt, native-style open-backed slippers, and a French beret. The other garments that Friday evening were unaltered—the same Shimon I had always known—but the beret was gone, replaced now by a Western man's hat. Hats had always carried great symbolic import for the Jews of Morocco, from the black *chechia* (with its overtones of religious identity and Muslim imposition) to the beret (with its implications of being a European protégé) to this new hat (with its association with the Orthodox of Israel). Somehow, I thought, this must be Shimon's concession to his new environs, his way of melding into a new set of contradictions. Inside the apartment, though, it felt like we were all back in Morocco. It was only a bit later, with several of the children joining Shimon and Zohara around the table, that I was able to ask about their passage to the Holy Land. It was Collette who began:

It was all arranged through a Jewish organization in Morocco, she said, and the trip did not cost us anything. There were ten of us in our family—my parents, the children, everyone. We went first to Fez and then by car to Casablanca. My father had sold everything from his business and ex-changed the money on the black market, at a loss of 30 percent, for French francs. We were able to take many of our personal belongings, though. In Casa, in the dead of night, we were then taken to the airplane. I think all the people on board were immigrating to Israel, but my brother Haim thinks some of them may have been tourists. No one checked any of the things we brought with us or looked to see if we were taking money out. They didn't even look at our papers—it had all been arranged. The flight went to Marseilles, where we were put up for several weeks while awaiting the plane that would take us to Israel. In France my mother bought a re-frigerator and others items of the sort we had to leave behind in Morocco, things that were sent to Israel by boat. After a few weeks we boarded a plane around midnight. On board the El Al flight were immigrants from all over North Africa and maybe Yemen. Some were dressed in torn garments and had no baggage at all. We arrived in Israel at 5:00 A.M., just as the sun rose. It was an incredible feeling!

We were given two apartments—this one that my parents occupy and one other—here in Petah Tikva, just northeast of Tel Aviv. Each apartment has two bedrooms, a bath, a living room, and a kitchen. We were also given $100, and the apartment was, and still is, rent free. We brought a number of things from Morocco you can see here—the large clock, the dining room rug, the covers in the dining room, the ritual objects.

After a few weeks my father was put to work in an iron factory. It was hard work, especially for a man of fifty-eight. He worked there until 1975, when at sixty-five he retired. The other children also worked: Haim picked oranges. I too worked. I had taken a basic certificate during three years of study in Morocco, but my father said there wasn't enough money to continue my studies. So I taught Hebrew to the children in the school in Sefrou. What I taught was biblical Hebrew, and I couldn't speak modern Israeli Hebrew when I arrived here. Without a skill and not knowing the language, all I could get was manual labor. It was very hard. I had many jobs. Like Haim, I picked oranges. Oh, how I hurt after a day of picking oranges! I worked at that for only a few months, and then I had to stop.

Six years ago I got married. My husband is also from Morocco. His father still lives in Casablanca and works for the agency that got us to Israel. It is still difficult. Everything here is very expensive.

I asked the boys how they were doing. Haim said that he felt it was much better here in Israel than staying in Morocco. There, he said, a Jew couldn't walk around at night. Maybe it was easier for those who already came from a big city in Morocco, but for us coming from a small place like Sefrou it was hard getting used to a big city here. Elie, the husband of another daughter Miriam, himself of Iraqi origins, joined in. We boys have to go to the army, but Collette and the girls are all categorized as religious, so they are exempt. That is fine with me because even though I disagree with the people who are very religious about the way they control marriage and divorce and matters of that sort, I am willing to pay the price of their rigidity because they are what is distinctive about us as Jews. We are all pro-Likud, Begin's party, the boys said; at least they tell the truth and stick to it. I would even like to see representation in Parliament of the Black Panthers, the Moroccan activist group, said Haim. They are the ones who stick up for us Moroccans. There is a lot of tension between us Sephardim and the European Jews, the Ashkenazim. They think they are better than us because they have an education. If you don't speak Yiddish, you can't get anything here, he concluded. But Collette said she thought they were crazy to favor Likud. It means more war—absolutely, she said.

Later, when I spoke alone with Shimon's wife, Zohara, she told me, in hushed tones, her version of their departure from Morocco. A few months after you left Sefrou (in September 1967) things had gotten much worse, she said. Children kept throwing stones at the Jewish school. One of my daughters came home one day with blood running down her face from a cut on the head when some Muslim kid threw a stone at her. People in Sefrou wouldn't buy anything from Shimon, just a little. The Muslim couple who lived in the same courtyard with us—the Berber man and his

Arab wife who fought a lot, you remember—they wouldn't talk to us, they avoided us. The wife turned very nasty and one day told me we should get the hell out of the place. I became afraid to go out of the house or to leave the children alone, and now with the hostility of our neighbors, the people with whom we shared the small courtyard, we couldn't even trust them. We told people we were just moving to Casablanca. We sold our things. The Muslims knew we were really leaving for Israel: we had something to sell— they gave us a few pennies for it. We said okay because we wanted to go. Everything was done through the Jewish organization.

When the time came, we left Sefrou with whatever we could carry. It was night. We boarded a taxi and went straight through to Casa. Everyone was afraid. We didn't know if there would be trouble. We didn't have much money—we changed a bit for francs, but we had very little. In Casa we went straight to the airplane. There were Jews from all over Morocco. There were ten in our family, including my brother, who also had a stall where he sold cloth alongside the river in Sefrou, and his family.

We flew to Marseilles. There they gave us a place to stay—they fed us, they housed us, they gave us clothes, everything. After some fifteen days we flew to Israel with people from all over the place—Jews from Tunis and Morocco and everywhere. We arrived in Israel, and they took us to this apartment. We walked up the stairs, here to the top, and this is where we have been ever since.

It was hard. We didn't know Hebrew. There was no water or electricity at first—not like it is now—there was nothing. The children worked—oh, such hard work! Poor Collette: in Sefrou she taught children; here she picked oranges. And Shimon. You know what he did? He worked in a factory. Polishing metal. He never did that sort of work. It was so hard for him, poor thing. And he got paid very little; everything was so expensive.

The children had all sorts of difficulties. One of the boys cried a lot. Look at the children now, she said, look how quickly they age. Elie was here last night. His face is so drawn; he has to get up so early in the morning, go all the way from Natanya to Haifa, work, come home, do his army service. If there is only one breadwinner in the family, they can hardly make ends meet. The children here become old too soon.

Shimon himself, ever the quiet man, was quiet through most of the discussions. He acknowledged that work in the factory had been very difficult. The metal shop had 160 employees, he said, some of whom were from Arab countries, so I was able to talk to them. Watching the boys go off to the army was even harder. Shimon was unable to read either Hebrew or Arabic; I was never sure if he could even read the Hebrew prayers. He acknowledged that he understands Hebrew well enough but cannot speak it much. I watched later as he looked through the pictures in the newspaper, always the wide-eyed gaze of benign curiosity mingled with the mien of one who cannot grasp the accompanying words but knows the power they possess, eager to rely on the goodness of others while knowing that, as a Moroccan journalist once said of the oblique speech of those who traffic in power, "every word that we don't understand is dangerous—dangerous, dear sir." Surrounded, though, by his family and feeling that they were comparatively safe was comforting. But, he said, it will take until my grand-children's generation for us to feel truly comfortable here. In the meantime it will be even harder for the children born in Morocco than for me.

In many respects the story of Shimon and his family is typical of those whose lives spanned Morocco and Israel in this particular period. It has been said, with considerable accuracy, that, from the period of 1948 on-ward, the Jews of Morocco left the country from the bottom up: it was those who were poor and mostly rural who departed first, and only later, often having first moved to the big cities of the country, did the middle class begin to depart in numbers. Several Zionist organizations began to operate in Morocco after 1948, often in competition with one another. The kibbutz-based groups preferred to recruit poor rural Jews, mainly from the High Atlas Mountains and areas in the south, who they thought may have been farmers and would be more easily adaptable to agricultural com-munities in Israel. Transit camps were established in Morocco and in the countries through which they would pass on their way to Israel. The num-ber of émigrés rose dramatically: in 1954, 8,171 left the country and the next year, 24,994.

When Morocco achieved independence in 1956, the legal and politi-cal climate changed significantly. From 1956 to 1963, under pressure from some Arab countries and the nation's main political party, Istiqlal, the gov-ernment prohibited emigration to Israel. Zionist offices and transit camps in Morocco were closed. In the spring of 1956, with several thousand Jews stranded in the camps, pressure was brought to bear on the king by presidents Eisenhower and Pierre Mendès-France that resulted in a total of 12,600 Jews being allowed to leave the country on the pretext that they were not really going to Israel. That fall the government stopped issuing passports to Jews. In 1959, following parliamentary elections that brought a number of leftists into the government, the Jewish minister of post and telegraph was removed and communication links to Israel cut. The Jews felt they were trapped. Bribes to officials to leave the country were followed by the arrest and mistreatment of a number of Jews.

As a result of these circumstances the Israeli secret service, Mossad, initiated its own plans for extricating the Jews. In 1961 it arranged for a man named David Littman, who posed as a Christian and actually thought he was working for a Jewish agency rather than the secret service, organized Operation Mural, which evacuated 530 children by pretending to take them for a holiday in Switzerland, an act for which he received special honors from the State of Israel in 2008. Unlike his son and successor, who chose greater proximity to Western countries, Muhammad V tried to position himself alongside the unaligned nations, inviting Egypt's Nasser to attend a conference that discussed Arab-Israeli and Third World concerns in January 1961, an event that caused Moroccan Jewry some concern. Following the death of Muhammad V, a month later the Jews' sense of trust in a protective monarchy was more deeply undermined. It was in this environment that Mossad also distributed thousands of pamphlets claiming that "any certainty of finding a place in an independent Morocco has disappeared." In that same year tragedy struck: a ship, the *Pisces*, overloaded with Jews seeking to slip out of the country, went down with the loss of over forty lives. The outcry from American and foreign Jewish groups following the loss resulted in the Moroccan government agreeing, in exchange for payments ranging up to $250 apiece, to allow some eighty to one hundred thousand Jews to leave the country. While King Hassan II thus appeared to be somewhat accommodating, a letter written to the AIU magazine in the winter of 1962 summarized the view of many: "In short, it seems that fear of a bad future has more influence than present proofs of equality."

In one other way the pattern of emigration was also changing. Ultimately, 90 percent of the Moroccan Jewish emigrants went to Israel, so that by the time the Benizris arrived, one out of every six Jews in Israel was from Morocco. (According to one Israeli source a total of 224,883 Jews left Morocco during 1952–72.) But by the 1960s a number of the migrants were going to France, while others went to Canada, where, as one writer put it, there is "less danger of assimilation than in France." Indeed, Muslims used to refer to Canada as *bled el-yahudi*, the land of the Jews, because many of the Moroccan Jews would get landed immigrant status there, travel to Israel, and then present Canadian papers when they wished to visit family or do business back in Morocco. Another wave of migrants departed after the Six-Day War in 1967, leaving only sixty thousand Jews in the country. The two failed attempts on the king's life in the early 1970s shook the remnant community, though when the news reached Sefrou that the king had survived the 1971 attack at his palace in Skhirat, the few remaining Jews went out on the streets and celebrated. By then, however, the total Jewish population of Morocco was down to thirty-five thousand, the vast majority of whom were clustered in Casablanca and Rabat. The diaspora abroad continued: in 1981 there were 80,000 Moroccan Jews in France, 18,000 in Montreal, and about 10,000 in Los Angeles. The country-side and the smaller cities were all but drained of their Jewish populations. Sefrou was no exception: in 1972 there were only 47 families, comprising 199 individual Jews, left in the town, while only a couple of dozen remained by 1980.

At the national level all the ambiguities of Moroccan approaches to the Jews were on full display through these years, even though comparatively few members of the community remained. Prime Minister Yitzhak Rabin visited Morocco in 1976. The next year General Moshe Dayan came to Morocco—where he toured the markets of Marrakech disguised in a mustache, wig, and sunglasses—and used the occasion to forge contacts through King Hassan that eventually led to Egyptian president Anwar Sadat's visit to Jerusalem later that year. Morocco even had a Jewish *chef du cabinet* in the Ministry of Defense in those years, and following the insertion of Moroccans into the Saharan territory abandoned by the Spanish in 1975, the new government newspaper, *Le Matin du Sahara et du Maghreb*, carried each day's date in the European, the Muslim, and the Hebrew calendars on its front page. It was an open secret, too, that agents of the Israeli secret service met frequently with and participated in the training of Moroccans and assisted in the building of a barrier in the Sahara aimed at keeping out the Algerian-backed and anti-Israel forces of the Polisario. Even King Hassan admitted that he could easily contact the Israelis without having to go through any of the usual diplomatic channels.

In a sense Moroccan policy could go several ways. The king could continue, as he did, to express the protective role of the monarchy, thus drawing on the image of the Jews as protected people (*dhimmi*) but shorn of the special taxation or terminology of that traditional Islamic status. He could employ what might be called the *tajjar* model, in which an elite from the Jewish community would serve in important national and transnational roles—a kind of global intermediary for certain financial and diplomatic ties—while simultaneously leaving internal Jewish community affairs to be overseen by this elite. Or he could stress the position of Jews as citizens of the nation who would be regarded as no different from any other citizens. Each approach had its contradictions: being a "protected" people suggested an attitude of inequality; using an elite smacked of indirect communal rule at home and an image of Jewish internationalism abroad. And neither the political parties nor the younger generation could fully separate

Jewish from Zionist, thus failing to include Jews in the postindependence image of the state despite the efforts many had made to assist in the quest for separation from France and Spain. As a former member of the Army of Liberation in the south, noting how the Jews of his region supplied food, clothing, and trucks ("which they themselves drove to the battlefield"), told Aomar Boum: "Jews left for many reasons, economic, political, personal, and religious. But many left because we failed as nationalists to incorporate them even though we claim to the contrary." In the end, elements of each model seemed to remain in play, with all of the contradictions each incorporated left unresolved. For those Jews who stayed in Morocco, such contradictions only reinforced their felt need to keep one foot in the country and one abroad; for those who emigrated to Israel, France, and other countries, many of the same contradictions followed them into their new lives.

If the Moroccan government's style of handling relationships with the Jews was not fundamentally altered in these years, the situation of the Moroccan Jews who had left for Israel had already been undergoing certain changes when the Benizris arrived there in the late 1960s. Earlier on, most new migrants were taken to transit camps of tents or mud huts, where they might be stuck for several years. Jews from North Africa clearly received far less favorable treatment than their "white" coreligionists from Europe and later Russia, most of the Arab Jews eventually being shifted to agricultural settlements and development towns. These settlements were commonly in barren zones and were often near the border with hostile Arabs. One can see in such films as *Routes of Exile* and *Turn Left at the End of the World* the dismay, and often resistance, with which the Moroccan immigrants confronted their new environment.

The situation of Shimon and his family represented the later alternative, namely the provision of an apartment in a suburb of a large city and a job doing manual labor. Petah Tikva, to which the Benizris were assigned, began in 1878 as the first agricultural settlement of the Zionist movement. It was there that David Ben-Gurion initially settled following his escape from Poland in 1906. In his memoir, the future prime minister of Israel rhapsodized about the place: "The howling of jackals in the vineyards; the braying of donkeys in the stables; the croaking of frogs in the ponds; the scent of blossoming acacia; the murmur of the distant sea . . . everything intoxicated me." Perhaps by comparison to the massacres in Odessa and elsewhere, when Jews were blamed for fomenting the failed revolution of 1905, Petah Tikva did indeed look good to Ben Gurion. Sixty years later, however, it was mainly high-rise apartment blocks with orchards and factories beckoning men like Shimon who had been small shopkeepers or craftsmen whose skills (like making pack saddles) simply could not translate to their new situation.

But if many of their occupations had to be left behind, the Benizris, like other North African Jews, did bring a good deal of their cultural baggage with them: theirs was, as the Tunisian Jewish writer Albert Memmi has said, a "portable homeland." True, the European Jews saw them as "black," untutored, and uncouth, and they discriminated against them accordingly. Shimon's eldest son, for example, noted that he had parachuted twice into Sinai and Golan during the 1973 war yet complained that in the late 1970s there still was not a single soldier of North African origins admitted into the highly prestigious ranks of the country's fighter pilots. It is also true that many of the North African Jews began to admire the Hassidim who shared their ritual devotion, something they felt the secularizing Jews from Europe and America were rapidly losing. Others regret the loss of a distinctive tradition of Sephardic scholarship. Dr. Eliyahu Eliachar of the World Sephardic Federation and former president of Jerusalem's Sephardic Council, addressing a younger generation of Oriental Jews, has said:

> Our present decadence began a hundred and twenty years ago when the Alliance Israélite Universelle . . . began to erect elementary schools—lycées—all over the world. They were established with the best of intentions, to help raise the standard of living in poor Sephardic communities. Under the guise of eliminating centuries of Oriental superstition and backwardness, however, the Alliance did irreparable damage to our Sephardic traditions and customs. Throughout the Middle East and North Africa, lycées began to supersede and replace the yeshivas. . . . These yeshivas were the backbone of our Sephardic identity. Many of our brighter young men, who formerly would have gone on to rabbinical studies, contented themselves with elementary schooling in these lycées and then went on to white-collar positions to earn money for their families. This, in essence, is what befell your father's and mother's generation in Jerusalem.

Notwithstanding such concerns the Jews of Arab lands have maintained a distinct identity of their own. There are now some one million Jews of Moroccan origin in Israel—about 15 percent of the total population—who brought their traditions with them. In particular, they transferred with relative ease their celebration of Moroccan saints. Since a number of these revered figures had themselves been buried in Israel and the remains of some others were being moved there, the cult of the saints was not just sustained but vastly revitalized in Israel. Thus, at yearly celebrations, called *hilula*, at shrines of figures like Yisrael Abuhatzira (1889–1984, also known as Baba Sali, the miracle working "Praying Father" who was born in Tafilelt, Morocco, and is buried in Netivot, Israel), literally a hundred thousand or more Jews from North Africa may now arrive for prayers, feasting, and reasserting their common cultural identity. So numerous are the Moroccan Jews in Israel that Mimouna has become a national holiday. In many respects the reinvigoration of the saints is associated with the Moroccan émigrés' efforts to assert a collective identity in the face of the discrimination many experienced in their new home. Politically, as the Benizri boys indicated, many of the Moroccan Jews felt that only those political parties identified with religion, like Shas, or others on the right, like Likud, could respect their needs. Many also favored the proposition, eventually supported by the Israeli Knesset, that having lost most of their possessions when they left the Arab lands, either Arab Jews should be compensated by those countries for their losses or there should be a clear recognition that an exchange of populations and lands had taken place.

Through it all, and for each generation in somewhat different ways, one eye was still cast back to Morocco, to the memories of a life that was never easy but never without its benefits, and to a certain wonder that there was a time when they truly felt themselves at home as Arab Jews. Appreciating why that should have been so, why for people like Shimon the memories should remain so vivid, is vital to comprehending who they—and their Muslim compatriots—understand themselves to be.

I wish I could forget. But memories are branded into me. I feel as if I'm recreating a world that's dying before my eyes. We've been in this country for seven centuries, and no one remembers anything! When I look back into our past as Moroccan Jews, it's dark, like the mellah.

—Ruth Knafo Setton, *The Road to Fez*

From the film *Tinghir-Jerusalem: Echoes from the Mellah*, 2012, in which a Muslim in a small Moroccan town speaks in Berber to a Jewish former resident of the town now living in Israel, the Berber man says: "You must come to Tinghir—check your roots. This is your country here. All those years you never forgot Berber. We live in peace here—do you live in peace?" The Jewish man replies: "I always think about the village and its people. I never forgot Tinghir. [*naming individuals while drying his eyes*] I had Muslim friends. We were real good friends."

Rabat, Morocco—July 1991

Mustapha takes me to a café owned by a Jew who has converted to Islam. Everyone knows the conversion was phony, that he did it to marry a Muslim woman. The people come for the food, mostly Jewish delicacies. On each table is a bottle of Rabbi Jacob wine, labeled "Kosher for Passover" in Hebrew. But it is not the food that is the main attraction. It is the singing. For late in the evening the owner begins to sing old Jewish songs. And all those present—all of whom are Muslims—join in; they know the lyrics by heart and sing with relish. The songs are mostly laments for lost loves, tragic affairs of the heart. At the back of the café sit a couple of heavyset men in tight-fitting suits. My friend says they are government guys, there perhaps to ensure that the songs are not too political or merely to show the protective presence of the regime; no one pays them any attention. When I sneak a look at them later, I notice that they too are tapping their feet in time to the music.

Los Angeles, California—July 2007

In the evening, following a conference honoring the late Clifford Geertz's work in Morocco, a concert is held at the university auditorium. The huge hall is filled with Moroccans, many of them having dressed themselves and their children in traditional festive clothes. A famous Muslim singer has been brought from Morocco for the occasion. He is joined onstage by a Moroccan Jewish cantor, now living in Los Angeles. Together they begin singing old Jewish songs. Suddenly from behind I hear many of the members of the audience joining in. I turn and see that many are also filling the aisles, swaying, holding children in their arms, their eyes moist. The Muslim singer is enchanted. He and the cantor move closer to the front of the stage. Every time they seem to be bringing the evening to a close, the audience urges them on. No one wants it to end.

How, in looking at the experience of Shimon and his fellow Jews, are we to make sense of their life among the Muslims of Morocco? How can we account for this strange admixture of antipathy and succor, condescension and care? Why, given such a history, should so many of the Jews and Muslims of a certain age so clearly miss one another?

The answer commonly offered by Shimon and other Jews is that it was bad people, poor and displaced people, people who lacked wise leadership or knowledge who engaged in acts against them, not the sensible, educated, or honorable city dwellers and tribesmen. Yet this may not suffice as explanation. It is true that some of the early puritanical movements—great Berber dynasties like the Almohads and the Almoravids who dominated Morocco and Spain in the eleventh through thirteenth centuries—did regard non-Muslims as anathema and that some contemporary Islamists follow in their footsteps. But even in those instances simple analogies to European anti-Semitism do not apply, for the Moroccan experience was neither one of widespread attempts to purge the Jews nor even one of reviling them in literature or song. Bernard Lewis has said: "On the whole, in contrast to Christian anti-Semitism, the Muslim attitude toward non-Muslims is one not of hate or fear or envy but simply of contempt." However, even that assertion speaks to only one end of the continuum. Rather, all the ambiguities attendant on Muslim social and political structure appear to have been extended, if not integral, to the place that Jews occupied in the larger context of Muslim life. Indeed, the Jews were for the Muslims a limiting case, a test instance of much of what the Muslims needed in order to understand themselves.

Thus, to the question whether Jews were subjected to oppressive treatment or were treated with consideration and respect, the answer is—undoubtedly—both. The historical record is certainly filled with instances of attacks on Jewish communities, both by tribesmen from the countryside and from within the urban communities. Yet two factors are important to keep in mind. First, on most occasions when there were attacks on the Jews, there were attacks on Muslims as well. The death of a sultan or other axial event was a moment when protection by the center was especially problematic, and it was common for depredations to occur as much against fellow Muslims as Jews. And second, such moments also afforded those who sought to assert their leadership the opportunity to do so precisely by protecting the Jewish community. Thus the Jew served as an indicator of many factors for the Muslims: they were the vehicles through whom one showed dominance yet reliability as a protector; they were subjected to some forms of social ostracism yet were alluring for their constancy, their magical powers and the attraction of their women; they were segregated for centuries in their mellahs, yet they were intimate strangers who could be allowed to see what fellow Muslims were discouraged from observing.

For such a system of relationship to flourish, however, it is not enough for there to be men and women of goodwill, nor is it sufficient for there to be idiosyncratic moments of intimacy and fellow feeling. There must also be a structure, a vessel through which the relationships can be given shape and limit. Just as one cannot share a sentiment with another—or perhaps even recognize it within oneself—without a set of linguistic or other symbols that can hold its meaning and design, so, too, the style, the feel, the arc of Muslim-Jewish relations had to have a set of cultural norms and organizational forms capable of making it recognizable to all. How the Moroccans structured these features into their society and culture, how they created and maintained mechanisms through which this accommodation—a term that may be preferable to "toleration"—has been made possible are central to the organization of each community and to their interactions with one another. Three features may be of particular importance in understanding these structural elements: the nature of reciprocity and the role of the Jew as an internal stranger; the qualities associated with the particular Moroccan variant of a tribal ethos; and the role of ritual in the expression and enabling of Muslim-Jewish relationships.

Central to an understanding of Muslim-Jewish relations in Morocco is the role of reciprocity in the dominant Muslim culture. For Muslims it is essential to build up a network of persons with whom one is entwined through a variety of obligations. Whether it is in the actual formation of a financial debt or in the "favors" granted that may be called up in another way and at another time, the system of reciprocity is so deeply writ into the culture that there really is no term for an act done with no expectation of potential return. Hospitality in one setting may yield an attempt to get another to help in a marital alliance; access to desired goods in the marketplace may be called up when one is seeking political support. If a Muslim man is, therefore, identified by his web of obligations, the Jew occupies a particular place within that construct. For whereas the fellow Muslim might be asked to reciprocate in any convertible form, the Jew lies outside this pool of reciprocity, as one does not commonly imagine him as a marriage mate or as a political ally. It is thus possible to have a more distinctly economic tie with a Jew that will not have all the implications of later and not fully predictable claims of another kind. Such a limited tie also means that there can be a certain intimacy, like the stranger on the train to whom one can tell things one might never tell a close friend.

Protecting one's network is also crucial. Just as a Muslim man must protect his womenfolk, so, too, he must service his bonds of social indebtedness with great care, particularly in an environment of political, climatic, and relational uncertainty. Therefore any attack on the Jews was an attack not only on them but on their partners, protectors, or psychological intimates. Since an attack was often followed with some gesture of protection, it was also an opportunity for those vying for power, particularly in the vacuum created by chaotic events, to step in and offer themselves as protectors. The Jews, recognizing that attacks rarely if ever involved any racial hatred, did not so much forget these incidents as understand that they were, in the logic of the local, not simply about them, especially as they were not the only ones assaulted at such moments. Anyone who was sufficiently weak could be the vehicle through whom one contested dependencies or overlordship.

Given this pattern, it is not surprising that one still hears Muslims expressing their sadness at the departure of the Jews, indeed expressing a true sense of having lost a vital aspect of their own social identity. One of Morocco's most famous novelists, Tahar Ben Jelloun, gives us a character, Moha, who, in speaking to his Jewish friend Moshe, expresses this loss in the following way:

> You know, Moshe, for every Jew who leaves this country a bit of me goes away too. One day I am going to find myself without any body, with just a shadow. They are all leaving. But what are they afraid of? What misfortune! It seems moreover that the Jews of Europe and America, you know, the richest ones, mislead our children. They are not happy out there, I assure you! They arrive with suitcases full of illusions and afterwards realize it is difficult to live without their roots. They wither away from nostalgia and melancholy. None of them speaks a word of Hebrew. They know only Arabic or Berber. I know they are not happy there. No one leaves his country so easily. The land remains inside of you.

Other comments make sense against this background. Muslims in Sefrou, for example, have said to me that ever since the Jews departed, the urban section of the city's river—which is still called the Oued El Yahudi, the Jewish River—has not had enough water in it. Others speak about the way Jews kept their money circulating—like a game of chance, some say—whereas Muslims just sit on their capital. One Muslim merchant told me: "The Jews pulled people out so that together they would get rich. Now with the Jews gone the Muslims are like stingy old men. Without the Jews the market does not work." Daniel Schroeter notes a similar circumstance in one of the coastal cities when he writes: "The Muslims today look back nostalgically to the days when the ambulant Jewish peddler circulated in the countryside. In the town of Essaouira, the economic eclipse of the town is attributed to the departure of the Jews. In recent [2004] Moroccan parliamentary elections, a Jewish businessman from Meknes was popularly elected as deputy for Essaouira by the town's almost entirely Muslim population. It appears to reflect the belief that Jewish business acumen might still have the chance to restore the prosperity of Essaouira."

A second aspect of Muslims' social organization that bears on their relationship with the resident Jews might be called the tribal ethos. Just as one need not be a Protestant to display aspects of the Protestant work ethic, so too one need not be an actual member of a Moroccan tribe to exhibit features of a tribal ethos. Just as Protestantism is a vital backdrop to many aspects of American culture, so too the contribution of tribal existence in Moroccan social history suffuses and informs features at a broadly cultural level. These may include a strong belief that too much power should not remain for too long in too few hands, an approach that is given form through a set of leveling mechanisms—from pressures to share one's largesse to gossip, tension-relieving joking, and double-edged language play—all of which structure the redistribution of power and support the deep-seated ambivalence to power that pervades political, religious, and gender domains. It is important in this regard to note that the concept of ambivalence, a term that in English comes from the Latin meaning to be equally vitalized by two things, in Ian Leslie's phrasing, "is not the same as indifference, with which it is often confused. Someone in an ambivalent state of mind is experiencing an *excess* of opinion, not an absence of it. An ambivalent person may feel very strongly about the subject at hand without reaching anything like a coherent point of view on it."

This potential incoherence may, however, be structured within a cultural scheme so as to ameliorate its most debilitating effects. In Morocco, we can see elements of this structuring in a number of ways. In the accounts of the Haj and Hussein, for example, we can see that power is always suspect and that while the sources of legitimacy may be shared, so too are the mechanisms by which it is constantly undercut, whether in the demand that reciprocal obligations be proven to the breaking point or in the hedging of attachments to a patron through contacts with his rival. We can see it in the potential fault lines along which joking takes place or in the need to have one's own leadership acknowledged by one's enemies. We can see it where Moroccans have managed monarchy without allowing hierarchy to run through all other sectors of society. That even saints are subject to such double-mindedness leaves open the option of contesting anyone's claims of authority and power. The Jews have their place in this structural pattern, too, insofar as concerns about their knowledge of the marketplace and magic may, just as with women, raise questions about where power really lies and who may be able to employ it at any given moment.

As we saw in Hussein's discussion of Berber organization, the anthropologist Robert Lowie once spoke about the ways in which tribes sample one another's social and cultural forms, and that process surely applies as well in the Moroccan context. This is as true across seemingly impermeable religious boundaries as among seemingly fixed tribal borders. Moreover, it is common in societies that display this aspect of the tribal ethos for people not to be bound by category. An example may help in this regard: One day in the marketplace I saw a powerful man, stripped to the waist, hawking a patent medicine. "This medicine will cure everything that is wrong with you," he cried. "*Even a Jew* will be cured by it!" This was not a slight against the Jews but an example of what Bernard Lewis has called the *trajetio ad absurdum* mode of Arab expression, in which one shows by the example that does not usually apply that individuals are not, in fact, bound by the way they are commonly categorized. Thus, contrary to her usual propensity, *even* a woman may be a knowledgeable person and *even* a Jew could be cured despite "normal" differences in their dispositions. It is also why Haj Hamed can sincerely believe that Shimon Debdoubi, through his studious development of his rational faculties, is a man of great maturity and knowledge, even if the Haj thinks most Jews tend to be more wily than wise.

Rituals, too, are one of the premier vehicles through which the structure of relationships may be expressed and maintained. Whether it is in drawing people together in the enactment of their shared orientations or in learning how to feel what society takes for granted, rituals can display and enforce a vision of people's places in the order of things. Moreover, the reversal that may take place through certain rituals can have special potency because it allows an interstitial moment of license before reasserting and underscoring the acceptable social norms, a period of experimentation with new possibilities that is nevertheless especially fraught with danger, since there is always the risk that things—people—will *not* get back where they must for society to be able to operate and replicate itself. Thus on the occasion of the Prophet's birthday soldiers from the Haouz region were reported by Aubin a century ago to put on a carnavalesque "series of scenes, a sort of review, in which a certain number of types figure in the midst of a flood of obscenities—disgusting Jews, howling *derqawa* [religious brotherhood members], Kadis [judges] of Fez, fortune-tellers, popular Sheikhs, little boys trained for the lascivious dance." Degradation is also commonly an indispensable aspect of ritual reversals if one is to be temporarily torn from an existing structure before being reintegrated and renewed. Edward Westermarck, working at the turn of the twentieth century among the tribes of the Sefrou region, offers a particularly striking example in this regard. A Muslim who wants to conjure up a Jewish genie for his own benefit, Westermarck writes, does all kinds of disgusting things. He eats his own excrement, and dirties his clothes with them; drinks his own urine if thirsty, and sprinkles his clothes with it . . . makes an ablution with his urine, and prays with his face in the wrong direction, that is, not towards Mecca. He writes on the paper the name of the jinn . . . burns the paper together with some coriander seed and in burning it recites the name of the jinn and some passages from the Koran and the word Allah and other holy words exchanged for *sitan* [the Devil], and continues this recitation until the jinn comes.

An equally stunning instance of reversal is supplied in a letter dated April 22, 1912, when, following the attack on the Jews of Fez in the wake of the mutiny of Moroccan troops, the writer reports on the women revealing their nakedness: "During the revolt the Moorish women of the lower classes assembled on the house tops, exposing their breasts and inciting the revolters [*sic*] to kill the Christians."

The ritual reversals that inform Muslim-Jewish relations in Morocco are, therefore, excellent indicators both of the participants' cosmological orientations and of the ways in which they sample one another's lives before reverting to their own. Thus the moments when each burlesques the other holds both the allure of possessing the other's forbidding powers and the possibility that society can only be predictable and replicated if each manages to get back to where he started. In the Moroccan case it underscores both dependence and freedom. For the Muslim such rituals reinforce their role as protectors; for the Jew such rituals demonstrate the power of the weak, the ability of the seemingly subordinate to choose his protector, and through his use of connections and the powers of his saints or leaders to have a dramatic effect on how dependable a man will be regarded by his fellow Muslims. Jews, therefore, are compared to women by Muslims in that both are indicators of one's reliability as a person who has succeeded in constructing a network of indebtedness. And like women, Jews are to be approached with some degree of caution, for they may wind up as the holders of one's good opinion of oneself. Women and Jews may, therefore, seem powerless, even obsequious, but the appearance may be deceptive. Shimon's humility is not Shylock's wiliness or even his demand for justice but a forceful claim to acceptable domains of difference and to that intimacy of the self-effacing stranger that makes one so vital to the other's self-image. Small wonder, then, that this same feature—the approval of the seeming opposite—should be played out in other ways in Moroccan social structure, as when it is one's enemies who must essentially approve a man as the head of his own group, or when the formalities of the acknowledgment of a monarch, which may seem to be extraneous to his actual grasp of power, is vital to denying equal claims to a rival.

Ritual reversals, then, are only one among many ways in which the dominant Muslim culture structures the license necessary for constantly challenging power and creating new bonds of indebtedness without permitting existing networks to become ossified or easily transmitted from one generation to the next. When even a saint or a king must constantly prove that his powers are indeed effective, new gambits and new players appear without changing the basic cultural rules of the game. The sense of ambivalence pervades all domains, then, and often gives rise, in play or poetry, folktale or humor to forms that support its essential vitality. The sense, too, that things are often best understood through their obverse may be encountered in the many Arabic terms that contain a meaning and its opposite, in taking on the role of the other at certain ritual moments, and in the Arabic proverb that says, "The thing, having reached its end, turns into its contrary." It is a mode of grasping reality perhaps most stunningly caught by the ninth-century Arab poet al-Buhturi, in his *Hamasa*, when he wrote:

> You are lost if the riddle approaches.
> If it turns its back you guess it.
> You see that you see no matter right
> Unless you methodically reverse it.
> To the lamp of noon night fetches
> The obscure vehicle of its light.

How one remembers plays into this structure of relationships in ways that are quite revealing of the shared yet divergent forms of Muslim and Jewish culture. Memory, we are told, is fallible: the witness who is sure of what was seen is too often wrong; the recollection of what must have been may only be the afterglow of an imagined event. Memory, we are also told, is contested, the subject of different perceptions, interpretations, and uses, a will-of-the-wisp that is both insubstantial and the subject of much obfuscation. But memory, like the belief in ghosts, may have real consequences even when it is not itself real, and the ways in which we remember can have similarly profound effects even when they seem quite indefinable. We may not all remember collectively in the same way; we may even share memories without fully sharing the mechanisms by which those memories are triggered or understood.

Indeed, one could argue that the Jews and Muslims of Morocco are ambivalent about *how* to remember, though perhaps not entirely in the same ways. We see this among Moroccan Jewish writers: Esther Benaim-Ouaknine, who emigrated to Canada, speaks about "a memory that has been prevented," Victor Malka of the "fractured memory of the Jews of North Africa," and Edmond El-Melah of "the fleshy presence of a timeless memory." Perhaps, assimilating the Muslims' sense of time and memory as having to affect current relations or lose meaning, the Jews' memories can only retain a ghostly presence: detached from ongoing relationships, memory itself dissipates. The shared sense that something *is* missing, the hazy feeling that the memory of memory should be able to conjure up the reality, begins to fail in the absence of an actual person with whom one can engage. And if, to whatever extent, Muslim and Jew rue the absence of the other, such an attitude affects ties to members of one's own group as well. And so the absence is doubled, becoming an absence that, like any memory, will itself disappear when the structure within which it must be manifest disappears along with the passing of those generations for whom it was so vital. Then it will, perhaps, turn into nostalgia instead of memory, and its structure, its place, will play a very different role for a new generation.

For the Haj and Hussein, for Yaghnik and their fellow Muslims, memory may work a bit differently than for the Jews in one other respect. For them memory largely works backward—from current relationships to those whose actions continue to inform the present. It is not that there is no sense of the future but that what lies ahead will only have meaning if it perpetuates some relationship whose continuing effects are traceable to God, people, spirits, or saints that already have some social presence. By comparison, for the Jews time and memory tend to be forward oriented, decoupled from any particular relationship of the moment; they might almost agree with Lewis Carroll's White Queen, who tells Alice that "it is a poor sort of memory that only works backwards." Or they might find resonance in Carlos Fuentes's admonition to "remember the future; imagine the past." For while the sacred text of the Muslims does not concentrate on a worldly goal, beyond keeping chaos at bay so the Community of Believers may flourish, for the Jews the realization in this world of Zion is deeply writ in holy text and in that vision of hope embodied in the high holiday avowal "Next year in Jerusalem." Anthony Gidden's suggestion—that it is a preoccupation with the future and safety that generates a concept of risk—may put matters in too unidirectional a causal relationship. Rather, it may be at least as true that knowing their goods, their well-being, their very lives were always at risk increased the Jews' emphasis on a future that may lie outside their present sphere, an emphasis that may then have played a crucial role in their willingness to leave their native land for their home in Israel.

Notwithstanding their distinctive perspectives Muslims and Jews have, as in so many other ways, also partaken to some extent of the other's orientation: the Muslims look forward to the relationships their association with Jews can make possible; the Jews look back to the mix of Muslim antipathy and support without assuming that what has been must always be so. Islam and Judaism both claim to fear admixture, yet both have survived in part by dressing up in each other's garb, being drawn into each other's ritual sphere, sampling one another's vision of time and personhood, feeling out the other through ritual reversals. It was a cultural process that worked well enough for centuries. But when the two faith communities became sufficiently separated in space and contact, the discrepancy, the loss, indeed the cognitive confusion could become acute, the one not sure how to assess relationships without the intimate stranger who stands as counter and confirmer of the mundane, the other cast into a world that does not value difference as a means to achieve authenticity. The "memory palaces of Andalusia," so tangible as to seem a force of nature, begin to crumble, the generation gap within one's own belief community yawns, and as the needed presence of the other begins to slip away, it makes sense that, as for Tahar Ben Jelloun's character, many do indeed feel as though they are losing part of themselves.

Sociologists have long struggled with the role of the stranger and the ways in which groups of different cultural orientations manage their relationships to such a figure. Thus Peter Berger and Thomas Luckmann have suggested, "As long as competing definitions of reality can be conceptually and socially segregated as appropriate to strangers, and ipso facto as irrelevant to oneself, it is possible to have fairly friendly relations with these strangers. The trouble begins whenever the 'strangeness' is broken through and the deviant universe appears as a possible habitat for one's own people. At that point, the traditional experts are likely to call for the fire and the sword—or, alternatively, particularly if fire and sword turn out to be unavailable, to enter into ecumenical negotiations with the competitors."

Barrows Dunham says: "Our experience of relations amply shows that every relation unites distinct entities. If their distinction disappears so does the relation, as having nothing any longer to unite. But if, on the other hand, the distinctness of the elements is total, then the elements cannot be related at all. What we familiarly find is that elements exist quite distinctly in their various relations with one another." Perhaps, then, one might argue that the differences between Muslims and Jews, as they came to be organized in the Moroccan experience, allowed just enough difference for each to see an aspect of himself that could be socially fulfilled in the other. Each could sample the other's life just enough in ritual to imagine it as an alternative, and each knew that when difference disappears, something goes out of one's own sense of personal creativity and collective identity. That may be why there could only be an element of sadness along with relief from the fraught ambiguity when, in time, Jews and Muslims went their separate ways. For each might now say, as did the poet Cavafy of the sudden departure of the Other: "And now, what's going to happen to us without barbarians? They were, those people, a kind of solution."

The temptation for the outsider listening to Shimon and Zohara is, then, to somehow grasp the multifaceted and seemingly contradictory aspects of the Muslim-Jewish relationship in some shorthand expression. Capturing a sense of Muslim-Jewish relations in a simple metaphor is tempting perhaps because, as Freud reminded us, we know that a metaphor cannot be completely accurate even though it can make us feel at home. It is thus not surprising that many of the analogies by which writers have sought to capture the relation of Muslims and Jews in Morocco should call forth images that are either mechanical or organic. The relationship can, therefore, be thought of as being like gears that mesh and grind. Alternatively, we could think of each as a catalyst creating a reaction in the other without itself being fundamentally altered, or as a symbiotic relation in which the economic adjustment or emotional need that is felt to be missing in the one is supplied by the other. Whatever the metaphor one uses to capture the reality, what emerges is that each confessional community managed to accommodate itself to the differences, indeed the contradictions, encountered in the other and to make some use of those features in the construction of an identity and a way of functioning within its own sphere.

Tennessee Williams once said, "In memory everything seems to happen to music." Perhaps that is why those evenings in the Moroccan café or in the auditorium a continent away may also serve as useful metaphors for the relations of Muslims and Jews more generally. It is a feature one finds underscored in a full-page article in the French newspaper *Le Monde* of March 17, 1980, entitled "When Jews and Arabs Sing Together." There the novelists Tahar Ben Jelloun and Edmond Amram El-Maleh wrote: "For centuries Jews and Muslims in Morocco had recited the same poems and sung the same songs. . . . Jews and Arabs recognized each other and exchanged differences; they shared a common history and thus left their children a common memory and cultural heritage." It is the absence of that "exchange of difference" that Jews and Muslims have felt so keenly when, as the events of Shimon's life so clearly indicate, they began to withdraw from one another.

"I'm not a learned person, my tales go in one ear and out of the other. . . . The problem is that the tale you have read is to be found in a book. All your friends can have this book and read it. But the story I tell exists only in one book, this one." . . . And he pointed to his heart.

—Ahmed Sefrioui, *La Boîte à merveilles*

The whole world is a narrow bridge, and the most important part is not to be afraid!

—Rabbi Nachman of Breslov

Throughout his life Shimon trusted his Muslim friends and chose, until the needs of his children became overwhelming, to remain among those friends, quietly tending, despite all difficulties, to the concerns of his family, his compatriots, and his faith. It was not blind trust; it was the act of a man who understood Morocco and its people well and viewed them with his eyes wide open. If making *aliyah*, "arising" to Israel, is, in the strict sense of the concept, the very opposite of the diaspora—the ultimate ingathering as one repossesses Zion and Jerusalem—and if, in the end, Shimon and his family did engage in such a return, it was not without a genuine sense that he and Zohara were leaving home. They knew that soon the Jews of Sefrou would be completely gone, as they are from their ancient places throughout most of the Middle East, and that just as their own ancestors had once emigrated from their points of origin, the next generation's attachments would lie distant from their own. Casablanca's Jewish community of about four thousand does thrive, but few of its residents lack strong ties abroad. If the remaining Jewish communities continue to live for a while in the memory of the older generation and ever more faintly in the memory of those who left at an early age, each of them may still retain the vision of a time when peace and difference were not regarded as incommensurable.

Older patterns persist: the king, like his father before him, tugs and eases, restrains and relents, imprisons and pardons while always keeping the leonine Moroccan on the end of his hair-thin chain. Thus he jails a rap star or journalist for lèse majesté and then releases him early, jails a Jewish singer for taking money out of the country and then ensures that the government will protect Jewish graveyards (including making sure visitors are asked to wear head coverings by the Muslim caretakers), requests that Jews join in rain prayers to help alleviate the drought conditions, funds the reconstruction of Jewish grave sites in Cape Verde as well as AIU schools and synagogues in Morocco, and at the same time criticizes Israel's occupation of the West Bank by delaying a visit by Israeli president Shimon Peres (who had been the guest of Hassan II in 1986 when Peres was prime minister) but retains a Jewish counselor who has close ties to Mossad. He supports the efforts of Moroccan Jews living in other countries but balances this "outside remembering" by not making too public a show of the only museum of Jewish heritage in the Arab world, located in an obscure part of Casablanca. He establishes a truth and justice commission to review his predecessor's policies concerning dissidents but allows no direct criticism of his father's actions. And when terrorist bombs killed thirty-three civilians and twelve terrorists at several places, mainly Jewish, in Casablanca on the night of May 16, 2003, the king visited the sites and had several thousand suspects arrested, resulting in numerous convictions. Like so many of his countrymen, the king has not been prepared to simply bid the Jews of Morocco adieu. Whether for purposes of practical politics or personal predilection, letting the Jews of Morocco slip entirely out of the national imaginary would come at a cost of self-regard, and not just diplomatic utility, that remains too high for Moroccans of a certain age to welcome.

For the Muslims, then, the Jews were at once in and out of category. They were set apart from society yet were for a very long time vital to its operation. They challenged the categories by which society was composed and were thus dirty, dangerous, and funny, as all things that are "out of category" may be. Because of their ambiguous status they reinforced the concept and range of ambiguity in many other domains of Muslim life. As they became embroiled in Westernized forms, their situation yielded, for some, that "final paradox" of which Mary Douglas spoke, one in which "the attempt to force experience into logical categories of non-contradiction" often means that "those who make the final attempt find themselves led into contradictions." Thus the Jews can be simultaneously denigrated and missed not just for their interstitial social position and psychological intimacy but because they are no longer part of the language play through which the Muslims probe the ambivalence with which they confront so many aspects of their life. The freedom the Jews afforded them is a felt absence, one for which no other group or way of imagining contrasting relationships has been able to find a place.

There is, I am told, a linguistic form in some languages that can be characterized as the "absent present," a way of indicating that something still exists even if it is not tangible, palpable, here. It is this sentiment that older Muslims experience as well, in their regret at the Jews' departure, their sense that some fissure has opened up that no other people are present to fill. The younger generation, of course, does not know the Jews as its parents and grandparents did. Perhaps that is why Omar Boum, revisiting his own Muslim community in the country's far south, found that it was only the elderly who recalled the proverb that "a market without Jews is like bread without salt" and that (as one ninety-year-old man said) "when the Jews settled outside Morocco the market lost its salt." By contrast a recent poll showed that 92 percent of Moroccans have a poor opinion of Jews—who now, of course, are usually equated with Israelis. A number of Moroccan youth have even engaged in hacking Israeli websites as a form of protest about the situation of the Palestinians. Yet attitudes remain mixed. As Oren Kosansky says, "Jews as flesh-and-blood neighbors are increasingly beyond the experience of Muslim Moroccans. . . . Muslim nostalgia for Jews relies partly on the sense that local Muslims and Jews shared an identity as Moroccans. . . . For Moroccans, losing Jewish neighbors has meant losing a part of oneself." Perhaps that also helps to explain why, as Rachel Newcomb learned during a recent visit to Fez, the Muslims who live beside a house owned by departed Jews have refused to take it over: It belongs to our neighbors, they said, and it is here for them if they return.

For the Jews who have left, whether for Europe, North America, or Israel, the contradictions with which Shimon and Zohara had to contend are not the same as those their children face. As Oriental Jews they seemed very strange to their European cousins when they arrived in Israel, particularly since so much of their culture was deeply affected by their lives in Arab lands. In his poem "Who Is a Jew and What Kind of Jew," Moroccan-born Sami Shalom Chetrit captures some of those new contradictions:

> Tell me, you're from Israel?
> Yes, I'm from here. . . .
> Excuse me for prying, but I just have to ask you, are you Jewish or Arab?
> I'm an Arab Jew.
> You're funny.
> No, I'm quite serious.
> Arab Jew? I've never heard of that.
> It's simple: Just the way you say you're an American Jew. Here, try to say "European Jews."
> European Jews.

Now, say "Arab Jews."

You can't make that comparison, European Jews is something else.

How come?

Because "Jew" just doesn't go with "Arab," it just doesn't go. It doesn't even sound right.

Depends on your ear.

Look, I've got nothing against Arabs. I even have friends who are Arabs, but how can you say "Arab Jew" when all the Arabs want is to destroy the Jews?

And how can you say "European Jews" when the Europeans have already destroyed the Jews?

Guy Sitbon's novel *Gagou*, about a Jewish family that moves from North Africa to France, also explores the Europeans' sense of contradiction between being at once Arab and Jew:

You have lived in an Arab country?

No, I am Arab.

Oh, I thought you were Jewish.

Just so.

Let's be clear: are you Jewish or Arab?

Both.

Half and half?

No, both, fully.

And when they fight each other, what side are you on?

On the side that cries out in grief. (*Du coté des Lamentations*)

All Moroccan Jews, wherever they may now live, have had to find the appropriate balance between memories of good and bad moments in the lives they led among their Muslim neighbors, some tipping the balance decisively to one side or the other, some teetering forever in ambivalence. Few want to forget altogether. "When we have gone, respect the traces of our passing," says the Moroccan poet. The traces are still there in Sefrou—in the shrines and the graveyards, the pictures at the back of the photographer's shop and the fading line on the wall, high above one's head, that marks the limit of the floodwaters. They are there, less tangibly, in the wistful memories of the aging and the quizzical look at the busload of Israeli tourists. They may even be there, beyond sight but vouched safe, in a remembered tale:

This is the story of the Rav Hida who saved the Jewish community [of Sefrou] when it was besieged by tribesmen in the early nineteenth century and who gave up his life in the process. "He said to his people: 'Come let me make you a charm to protect the town. What is it I shall do? I shall write a sort of scroll in which are some Divine Names and other things.' He wrote these for it and made them put it in the post of the Mellah Gate. Then he said to them: 'From now on, whoever does anything of this sort to you will not do it again.' (He was referring to the Muslims moving against the Jews, and entering the Mellah in order to despoil them.) After the scholar made them that mezuzah, whenever a tribe rose up and came on a campaign against the Jews, the latter would repel them and throw them out and they would go back empty-handed. That scholar, Rav Hida—peace be upon him—did not live out the year when he passed away. And the protective force of that talisman still surrounds the town. It is still there in the Mellah Gate as it was written." Years later when people went to remove the scroll to see what it said the gate trembled around them. Then they returned it to its place. It remains in the Mellah Gate, a hidden mezuzah in the Mellah Portal.

Much has, of course, changed since Shimon and his family departed, some of it poignant, some of it amusing. The mellah has been renamed "The Quarter of Hope," as if mimicking the name of Shimon's home in Israel, Petah Tikva, "The Gate of Hope." By 2008 there were no Jews living in the town and only one I knew of who came up from Fez to trade with some of the tribesmen. The old mellah is populated with the poorest of rural migrants, but even the density of their population is only a fraction of what it was when all of the Jews lived there. Indeed, beginning in 2014 significant portions of the mellah were being bulldozed. After their departure the street to which many of the Jews had moved in the *ville nouvelle*, the Rue du Serpent, was renamed Coffee Street, and now houses, mostly attorneys' offices, perhaps because the association with serpents would cut a little too close to home for the lawyers' self-image. The Moroccan government continues to urge Jews who grew up in the country and their children who grew up abroad to visit their ancestral home; in 2010 alone, nineteen thousand Israelis and thirty thousand Jews from other countries returned to visit the synagogues, shrines, and cemeteries the government and private groups have maintained and, in many cases, restored. Perhaps the mezuzah does indeed remain in the wall beside the gate of the mellah where a wonder-working rabbi placed it. Perhaps, too, in those moments when nostalgia and empowerment merge, when Jews and Muslims alike may recall that Sefrou, half of its residents being Jewish, was often called the "Little Jerusalem," they may all appreciate the words of a French visitor who passed by the Jewish grave sites and wrote to the son of the Pasha Si Bekkai: "Quiet witnesses to the past, the fitting inscriptions in the Jewish cemetery, at the exit to the city, seem to convey to us a message and a challenge: Tiny Jerusalem, scaled to a smile, cannot Sefrou epitomize that moment when we were still seeking to recapture the Garden of Eden?"

The Moroccans say of a man who is sensible to the ways of the world that he is *nadi*, awake, alert, looking knowingly at all around. Watchful and forbearing, Shimon and his Muslim neighbors may have possessed, as María Rosa Menocal has said of the age of *convivencia* in Moorish Spain, "the courage to cultivate a society that can live with its own flagrant contradictions." In the end, Shimon saw that his children and grandchildren would encounter contradictions quite unlike his own and that life would require of them new avenues of vigilance and resilience. He chose, with his eyes wide open, to risk those contradictions against the ones he was able to abide in Morocco and to live out his days helping guide his children through that transition. It is in that spirit of wide-awake awareness and commitment, of bearing witness to a world of difference and its varying inconsistencies, that I should like to think that when Shimon passed away several years after I saw him in Israel, the Almighty would have counted him among those righteous men who "have fulfilled their pious duties and followed hard trades," a man the Bible calls *tam*—simple, blameless, upright, complete—and has permitted him, along with friends both Jewish and Muslim, as in the words of the ancient Judeo-Arab adage, to "enter paradise with open eyes."

כי זה
אלהים אלהינו
עולם ועד הוא
ינהגנו על־מות

For such is God, our God, for ever and ever;
He will be our guide even to the end.
It is completed and fulfilled.

תָּם

Epilogue: Making a Difference

Well, now that we have seen each other, if you'll believe in me, I'll believe in you. Is that a bargain?

—Lewis Carroll, *Through the Looking-Glass*

Something happened. Something objective, but no longer verifiable. When I was a child, they used to claim all history was knowable, if you could catch up with the light emitted by the body, and traveling eternally in space. "Light prints," they talked about. An intriguing idea. But Einstein said that wasn't possible. The past is always gone, retrieved only, ultimately, in the filaments of memory.

—Scott H. Turow, *The Laws of Our Fathers*

They are gone now—the Haj and Shimon Benizri. Perhaps the Africans are right when they say that "when an old man dies, a library burns to the ground." But somehow I doubt it. For while I do not imagine, even in the sense that Pirandello meant when he spoke of the dead living still within us, that their voices have been fully captured here, or within me, I do believe that their ideas, however reframed, will suffuse their own cultures, however transformed, for a very long time to come. Indeed, is it not in the lives of ordinary men and women that the forces of cultural replication find their way into the future? And is there not a good deal of truth in Lionel Trilling's claim that "every person we meet in the course of our daily life, no matter how unlettered he may be, is groping with sentences toward a sense of his life and his position in it"?

Writing another's history is far more difficult than I had imagined. Notwithstanding that one may carry another's words for decades before grasping their meaning, it is not simply, as an Egyptian woman once told anthropologist Unni Wikan, that "it is a heavy burden to carry an unreciprocated gift." Nor is it even the uncertainties that attend those memory holes into which one slips all along the way. Rather, it is knowing to some extent how things turn out when you are struggling to recall how it felt at the time. It is knowing that the very terms for capturing the past may have undergone subtle change and that at each moment in that past you were dealing not with some steady state, some fixed way of viewing things, but, as a wise student of semantics and Islam once put it, "a surface seething with life and movement." Chronological unfolding is so appealing to Westerners that it takes an act of will to force oneself, ever susceptible to the tyranny of metaphor, to switch analogies. The dangers for the anthropologist are rife: seeking patterns that are not pinned to one's need for coherent explanation or support for one's favorite theory of culture and humankind is hard to avoid. Perhaps, then, in reviewing my friends' thoughts, I should say of the often unexpected course of my venture what one writer said of his, that "the account of my wanderings has ended up more akin to time-lapse photography than a chronological documentary."

I recall, too, hearing a talk by Prince Hassan bin Talal of Jordan in which he said that Arabs live by analogy, and in that spirit I have tried a number of analogies at times to compress my view of Arab social life into a handy frame. I have thought of Arab social life as being like an arabesque, that convoluted expanse of interwoven words and living designs that draws the believer into persistent replication and interminable moral choice, knowing, as one writer has said, that "the answer to chaos is repetition." I have thought of it, too, as being like the teased-out array of packets of energy, a sociological version of string theory, or as an organism whose simplicity belies its breathtaking adaptability, or as a fractal design whose precise details must always be abridged lest its replication be as vast as the universe it seeks to identify. And if cleaving to some analogy were not alluring enough, it is also true that in order to do their job properly anthropologists need a very high degree of tolerance for ambiguity. Here at least the analytic penchant conforms to the ethnographic impulse, for just as Arabs have a great affinity for analogy, so, too, are they greatly at home with ambiguity. They rejoice in it as a vehicle for limiting power, for testing whether proffered leadership deserves following, for maintaining the possibility of both accumulating and dispersing power by acting as an intermediary, and because—as a necessary adjunct to the constraints of religion—ambiguity places limits on the otherwise boundless personalism that could steer both leader and led to immoral ends.

If the world these Moroccans have constructed is, in that wonderful phrase of Clifford Geertz's, one in which "the real is as imagined as the imaginary," then an account of that world must be no less attentive to the symbols and concepts, the relationships and the institutions through which its adherents gain access to it. Yet it is also a world of tastes and scents, of the feel of a rough Berber cape thoughtfully cast over one's shoulders, a scrap of fatted meat set before one in the home of the poor, a moment spent under the wall of the city in the night when a broken glass filled with coffee is passed among the exhausted porters to one who has been gathered into their midst. Like the realm of dreams that can only be entered through the wakeful account of them, the memories of these men cannot be gained directly, nor can they be absorbed through my own recollections. Yet when the words through which they work the world become the words I employ as well, the melding of associations, dangerous to the investigator, becomes balm to the friend.

In the end, then, it is my memory as well as theirs. I can picture Yaghnik as he bounded out of his car that first morning and commenced his ever-gracious, enduringly humorous introduction to his country and his faith. I can still feel Hussein's hand when he took mine in his own as we walked through the marketplace—a sign of our alliance, a gesture of solidarity with a stranger, a recognition that the public place was our shared place. I can feel the Haj, as we slept on the banquettes at the home of Sheikh Driss in a notch of the Middle Atlas Mountains, reaching in the cold night to pull the cover over my shoulders, and how I caught, through sleep-hazed eyes, that smile of ineffable warmth. I can see Shimon Benizri, seated beside his son at a table in their apartment in Tel Aviv after we had spoken of our days together in Morocco, when silence enfolded us and each seemed to be thinking, his gaze cast to infinity, of a distant time, a distant place that has settled for each of us to a private level of recall and self-awareness.

The worlds in which the Haj and Shimon Benizri lived are largely gone. Few men now walk the streets of Morocco clad in bright red fez and yellow leather slippers, recalling the days before the French, the vision of a Jew mounted on a donkey's back with the child of his protector riding ahead an ever-receding image. But as their ideas reach out to their progeny, the thread of their thought, drawn to them from all that went before, spins out in turn to a world in which their offspring confront their own worlds, and one another, in ways both exemplary and new. What they make of those worlds—what the Haj and Shimon made of theirs—will be for them alone to determine, but the place from which each of their predecessors looked out will, in ways that may grow dim and indistinct, direct their vision for still some time to come.

Yaghnik, for one, stands simultaneously in the very middle of the Muslim situation and at its friable edge. He is as certain of his faith as he is open to understanding those of others. He is as comfortable with the modern world as he is connected to the traditions of an enduring past. Where others may see contradictions, he sees compatibilities; where others sense discord, he amalgamates and synthesizes. He, too, has his own understanding of God's limits, including his awareness that, as Akbar Ahmed has so perceptively noted, Muslims today are confronted by living in a world of radical doubt while their own faith, as Franz Rosenthal noted, has long equated doubt with unbelief. If that middle course Yaghnik has walked is to be a path of stability rather than one that borders on the chaotic, he and others like him will have to find a way to continue their own style of compromise without compromise and a way to convince others that such a course is both possible and authentically Islamic.

Hussein's world, by comparison, may seem on its surface to be harder to place. His may appear an ever more irrelevant backwater, particularly to those who emphasize globalization and see matters through the prism of the urban corridor that runs from Kenitra through Rabat and Casablanca to El Jedida, where 61 percent of the nation's urban population, 80 percent of its permanent jobs, and 53 percent of its tourism are to be found. But that could be a serious mistake. Not only has the rural slice of Morocco that extends from the edge of the desert through the central Atlas to Fez and Meknes been the region from which many political and government figures stem, but the connections of people in the region often run more quickly to centers of power in the capital than from the "beltway" areas of Rabat and Casablanca. For it is in this region, where groups, orientations, and attitudes toward central power are more characteristically mixed, that the success or failure of government policies and alternative political claims often meet their crucial test. Those who see the world as globalized, "flat," or ever more uniform will continue to be surprised by the constant reassertion of the local. But humanity's propulsion to fabricate categories of relatedness—of kinship and residence, religious logic and assumptions of human nature, in short, what anthropologists mean by culture—is so central to our being human that local variations of such categories will always arise and, with them, forces that cannot simply be reduced to the universal. Whether this takes place in urban slums or suburban villas, in country markets or mountain-bound huts, the history of Morocco supports the proposition that Hussein's domain will continue to be a prime generator of Moroccan ideas and associations. The nation will not be determined by his sphere alone, but it will not be determined without it.

In America, when two men meet, they commonly ask, "What do you do?" occupation being an index to many other social and political attachments and views. Moroccans, by contrast, commonly inquire as to one another's *asel*, the place of one's "origins," that supplies both the sources of one's knowledge and the conventions used to form attachments to others. Because, from their perspective, people are ultimately linked and knowable only through face-to-face contacts, rather than as rigidified categories of persons, Moroccans will then exchange the names of specific people until a set of individuals is imagined through whom one can claim some linkage and, with it, some idea of how the other might form a new relationship. This set of relations, what I have elsewhere called "a chain of consociation," does not reduce all of one's contacts to a homogenized set. Quite the contrary, it elaborates, celebrates, makes indispensable use of the very differences that render each chain at once distinctive and available for one's own points of attachment (*ribat*). Like their fellow countrymen and many Muslims beyond, the subjects of this study bear witness to the proposition that one understands men through their contradictions. For men like the Haj and Yaghnik, Hussein and Shimon these differences have worked like an electrical grid whose contrasting charges energized their lives and united their disparate networks by their shared assumptions and modes of fabrication; for Muslim and Jew it describes the very reality created by the Almighty. This sense of the world as knit together from such negotiated ties reverberates throughout the history of the region in a variety of striking ways.

In the early years of Islam there was a debate as to which game was most appropriate for Muslims to play. Some said it should be a game of chance played with dice, while others favored the game of chess. In time, chess was declared the appropriate game for Muslims to play, since it embraced the notion that God had endowed man with reason in order to better the situation of himself and his dependents as opposed to being a mere plaything in the hands of the divine. An analogy thus suggests itself. For if chess has an infinite range of moves and can thus be endlessly alluring without having to alter its basic rules, so too the Moroccan style of arranging one's bonds of indebtedness can appear to remain intensely variable within a largely unchanging frame. But the impact of the years represented in the lives of the men described here may have affected the framework of their social lives in a variety of fundamental ways. While in the past what united these men, and those like them, was not a single dramatic event under whose pressure they were fused into a single cohort—a wrenching civil war, for example, or a cataclysmic natural event—they did partake of a common core of relational models. For among the features that held these men and their compatriots together was their engagement in a set of understandings by which they could perceive and form networks of obligation with one another, a process that not only incorporated difference but thrived on it.

Moreover, when these diverse yet related modes of engagement are situated in their physical locales, a sense of common terrain, indeed of a shared "country," could morph into a broadly agreed-upon sense of nationhood. It is true, as a number of Middle Eastern historians have suggested, that in this part of the world sovereignty was often based on control over peoples rather than preservation of bounded domains. The colonial experience, however, began to disrupt that pattern not just by emphasizing geographical limits but by flattening social distinctiveness, rendering the scope and relevance of social differentiation less viable. As populations flowed into the cities and were less dependent on enduring obligations, as bureaucratic structures undercut the role of a local patron, and as increased involvement in world markets teased economic relations out of the skein of total reciprocal social obligation, the very differences an earlier generation may have relied upon may have begun to dissipate. Corruption (as the failure to share with one's network) became both a symptom and a source of diversity's decline, just as the Jew's departure signaled the loss of a vitalizing and intimate stranger, and the neighbor whose combination of physical proximity and kin-based distance began to give way to the anonymized outsider whose own network may lack any meaningful links to one's own.

The braided relationships that differentness had vitalized now appear to have slackened, allowing greater individual "freedom" in certain respects but yielding greater collective uncertainty in others. This change has not, however, been a matter of social entropy, some ineluctable force leading to social decline. The world of these men's successors may not be constructed on the same basis of diversity—certainly as it concerns the interstitial presence of the Jews—as in the past. In such a changed world the ability to live in difference may slowly dissolve while the need for the benefits it once offered may not readily find an organizational or emotional substitute. In such an environment, where the variety of knowledge and contacts that once spelled comprehension and relative security, a new generation will have to find a new way of addressing a world they still regard as contingent and vulnerable, and no less dependent than it ever was on human relationships for one's ultimate security.

The influence each man's approach to this changing world may have in the future is, notwithstanding such inklings, impossible to predict. If the worlds of the Haj and Shimon may figure less prominently in Morocco's future, those of Yaghnik and Hussein continue to endure. Or, more precisely, their worlds may represent two versions of a single alternative their successors may choose to accept. For their middle way—whether that of the urban educated man, for whom the idiom of religion is most compelling, or the rural entrepreneur, for whom the path of enterprise is felt to approximate most closely the realities and morality of everyday life—rests precariously alongside extremes to either side. Will an unemployed son grant support to those who seek more radical or reactionary change, or will it be the technocratic son who finds ways to give his brothers and sisters direction? Will the children of the countryside bear witness to the parents' skepticism and forge their own alliances accordingly, or will they, feeling uprooted from the close ties of kin and region, move inexorably to new associations that speak to needs their fathers never knew?

Yaghnik and Hussein can continue to contribute to that dialogue, but when their voices too are stilled, their ideas, however diffuse, however distant, will persist in the lives of those who walk through covered market and rock-strewn field alike. That lived-in space, those lived-through circumstances that made their voices so immediate, like all those other packets of relationship Moroccans store away when they no longer bear on current ties, may fade from memory altogether. But it is also possible that by their clarity and force, by their grasp of that reality to which those who follow also subscribe, their vision may continue to exist, through the terms they will have handed on, deep in the very being of their countrymen, though their names be long forgotten.

A Moroccan friend once told me a story about crossing the Straits of Gibraltar to Morocco. In those days there was a Soviet-built hydrofoil that had the advantage of being quick but the disadvantage of being notoriously unstable. During the crossing, the sea became very rough and the passengers got quite concerned. As if in some medieval drama, the Muslims, he said, all moved to one side of the boat, where they began to pray, while the Christians all moved to the other side for the same purpose. My friend, himself a scientist, said that it may have been that it was only because of this separation that the boat remained balanced and afloat. Once again one recalls that passage in the Quran that says, "Had God so willed He could have made us all alike," and perhaps not for the first or last time salvation lay in difference. When the chips are down, as my friend noted, it is not only for Moroccans that safety lies in diversity.

And that, ultimately, may be the collective lesson these friends have to offer to the outsider: that identities are and should be intertwined; that it is possible to live in a world in which groups that appear incommensurable in the experience of other cultures are, by the terms of the socio-logic they practice, workably compatible; that our fortunes and our futures are not built on lines of exclusivity, nor should the understanding of our place in the order of things be held hostage to the limitations of any one culture's experience. As Albert Camus said, "Indeed it is not so much identical conclusions that prove minds to be related as the contradictions that are common to them." The lives of these men and their no less extraordinary women have not been unconflicted, but neither has their belief in human society as suffused by ambiguity and indeterminacy undermined their faith in humanity's God-given reason. Through it all they have maintained a sense that they—and we—are in this together, a thought, an attitude, an act that in its own right is as wondrous and heartening as anything any one of us could ever hope for or imagine.

ACKNOWLEDGMENTS

If you come to Morocco for a week, you'll write words; for a month, you'll write phrases; for a year, you'll write a book. Longer than that, you won't be able to write at all!

—Henri Matisse, *Letters, Tangiers*, 1912

This book has been so long in the making that Matisse's admonition might well have come true. As early as my first fieldwork in the mid-1960s I conceived this project, and over the years I have purposely returned to follow up my friends' intellectual lives with this book in mind. Perhaps I was able to avoid Matisse's warning by never staying too long; as Simon Bolivar wisely said, "You must study a place close up and understand it from far back." And if, over the years, I have succeeded to some extent in maintaining that doleful separation, it has come at a cost, as it did for the patron saint of the Sefrou hinterland, Sidi Lahsen Lyoussi, for one might say, in a version of one's own, what he said so plaintively of his unnatural fractionation:

> One part of me is in Marrakech, in doubt;
> Another in Meknes with my books;
> Another in our homeland among my fellow tribesmen;
> Another among my friends of the town and countryside.
> Oh God, reunite them. No one can do it but You.
> Oh God, put them back in place.

Having taken on the Moroccan coloration of seeing things in relational terms, to the extent that I have managed to hold together my own disparate attachments, it has been due in no small part to the many students, friends, and colleagues who have, willingly or inadvertently, been drawn within the ambit of this book. From its inception Edmund (Terry) Burke III has seen me through the historical details while in his own work setting a model of balancing those aspects that are local and those that are world embracing. Sadly, Mustafa Benyaklef and Taoufik Agoumy did not live to see this book completed, but as teachers and friends their insights and concerns deeply influence all of my work. From my earliest fieldwork I was the recipient of the intellectual and personal generosity of Ernest Gellner and David Hart, and though we disagreed on details, we never parted company in our respect for and fascination with the people of Morocco. Throughout, Abdellah Hammoudi has been my touchstone for all things Moroccan, keeping me constantly aware of the richness of his thought and that of his countrymen. For help with the pictures I am indebted to the advice and skills of Mary Cross, Dale Garell, Ravi Shivanna, and most especially Jeremiah D. LaMontagne. The expert editing of George Roupe and my sister Jeanne Rosen has added significantly to whatever clarity the final manuscript attains, and I am immensely grateful to them for all their help. David Brent at the Press has been my editor since the beginning of my career, and no author could be more grateful than I for his ongoing support and sage advice. At Princeton I have been the recipient of the assistance and encouragement of Carol Zanca, Mo Lin Yee, and Gabriela Drinova, as well as my many colleagues and students. I am truly grateful to all of them.

Over the years, I have received support from the John D. and Catherine T. MacArthur Foundation, the Guggenheim Foundation, the Institute for Advanced Study in Princeton, the Woodrow Wilson International Center for Scholars, the Carnegie Corporation, the Mellon Foundation, the Center for Advanced Studies in the Behavioral Sciences of Stanford University, the William and Nettie Adams Fellowship at the School for Advanced Research in Santa Fe, and Princeton University. To each I am most grateful. Archivists and librarians at the Bibliothèque Nationale in Morocco, the British Library, the Library of Congress, the Alliance Israélite Universelle, the Gospel Missionary Union of Smithville, Missouri (now Avant Ministries), the New York Public Library, and the libraries and archives of Aix-Marseille University, Oxford University, and Cambridge University have been ever gracious in their assistance. Over the years, I have been the beneficiary of assistance from the Ministries of Interior and Justice in Morocco, the office of the mayor of the city of Sefrou, and the officials of its local courts, to all of whom I am truly grateful. A special note of thanks and affection is also in order to Si Muhammad Zwitun, former head of the courts in the Sefrou region and member of his country's highest court.

My primary debt is to Hildred and Clifford Geertz, who invited me to join them in Morocco after my initial preparation for fieldwork in Indonesia had to be abandoned as a result of that country's civil war. They were consistently generous in sharing their experience and their support. It was Hilly, who by gentle direction and unparalleled example, showed me how to do fieldwork; it was Cliff who was later to say, as he so clearly exhibited in the field, that "we had to become parochial in order to become cosmopolitan" and that "there is no ascent to truth without descent to cases." Our joint book, *Meaning and Order in Moroccan Society*, was our only collective publication, but in many respects their ideas have continued to inform all of my work. Dedicating this volume to them is hardly adequate recompense for their guidance and friendship, but I hope it may stand as partial repayment for all I am so pleased to owe them.

The literature on Morocco, Islam, and the broader issues raised in the social sciences by this study is vast. Many of the relevant works are, of course, in French, Spanish, Arabic, and Hebrew, though many of the English-language materials offer excellent summations of the works in other languages. Readers may also wish to note specific works on Sefrou related to this study, among them a joint volume by Clifford Geertz, Hildred Geertz, and Lawrence Rosen, *Meaning and Order in Moroccan Society* (Cambridge: Cambridge University Press, 1979); and several of my own publications, including *Bargaining for Reality: The Construction of Social Relations in a Muslim Community* (Chicago: University of Chicago Press, 1984). A particularly valuable book on Sefrou is that of the geographer Hassan Benhalima, *Petites villes traditionnelles et mutations socio-économiques au Maroc: Le cas de Sefrou* (Rabat: Université Mohammed V, 1987).

Haj Hamed Britel and History

Among the broad-scale histories of Morocco, each of which has a somewhat different take on the way to interpret this history, are Susan Gilson Miller, *A History of Modern Morocco* (Cambridge: Cambridge University Press, 2013); C. R. Pennell, *Morocco since 1830* (London: Hurst, 2000); Charles André Julien, *Le Maroc face aux impérialismes, 1415–1956* (Paris: Éditions J. A., 1978); Abdallah Laroui, *The History of the Maghrib: An Interpretive Essay* (Princeton, NJ: Princeton University Press, [1970] 1977), and his *L'histoire du Maghreb II: Un essai de synthèse* (Paris: Maspero, 1976).

Nineteenth-century European travelers provide important eyewitness accounts of life in the country at that time, and even when their views are deeply colored by their personal and national perspectives, they add valuable support for many of Haj Hamed's recollections. Among those most germane to his account are Dr. Louis Linares, *Voyage au Tafilalet avec S. M. le Sultan Moulay Hassan en 1893* (Rabat: Bulletin de l'Institut d'Hygiëne du Maroc, nos. 3 and 4, 1932); Mohammed Aafif, "Les harkas Hassaniennes d'après l'ouvre d'A. Ibn Zadine," *Hespéris Tamuda* 19 (1980–81): 153–68 (including an excellent map of all of Hassan I's expeditions to quell the tribes); Lawrence Harris, *With Mulai Hafid at Fez: Behind the Scenes in Morocco* (London: Smith, Elder, 1909); and Eugène Aubin, *Morocco of Today* (New York: E. P. Dutton, 1906). An overview of such accounts may be found in Roland Lebel, *Les Voyageurs Français du Maroc* (Paris: Larose, 1936).

An earlier Moroccan traveler to France who offers a view, as it were, from the other side will be found in Muḥammad Aṣ-ṣaffār, *Disorienting Encounters: Travels of a Moroccan Scholar in France in 1845–1846* (Berkeley: University of California Press, 1992). Charles de Foucauld described his visit to Morocco disguised as a rabbi in Viconte Ch. de Foucauld, *Reconnaissance au Maroc 1881–1884* (Paris: Challamel, 1888). One of the main rebels of the period is described in Mohammed Essaghir al-Khalloufi, *Bouhamara* (Rabat: Imprimerie El Maârif Al Jadida, 1993), and in the essays by Ross E. Dunn, "Bu Himara's European Connection: The Commercial Relations of a Moroccan Warlord," *Journal of African History* 21.2 (1980): 235–53; "The Bu Himara Rebellion in Northeast Morocco: Phase I," *Middle Eastern Studies* 17.1 (1981): 31-48; and "France, Spain and the Bu Himara Rebellion," in *Tribe and State: Essays in Honour of David Montgomery Hart*, edited by E. G. H. Joffé (Wisbech, UK: Minas, 1991), 145–58. The role of Muhammad al-Kittani is fleshed out by Sahar Bazzaz, *Forgotten Saints: History, Power, and Politics in the Making of Morocco* (Cambridge, MA: Harvard Middle East Studies, 2010). On slavery in this period see Mohammed Ennaji, *Serving the Master: Slavery and Society in Nineteenth-Century Morocco* (New York: St. Martin's, 1999), and Choukri El-Hamel, *Black Morocco: A History of Slavery, Race, and Islam* (Cambridge: Cambridge University Press, 2013).

For an argument that Morocco and Algeria were not simply divided into dissident and submissive regions as colonial powers often claimed, see Amira K. Bennison, *Jihad and Its Interpretations in Pre-colonial Morocco: State-Society Relations during the French Conquest of Algeria* (London: Routledge-Curzon, 2002). For an in-depth re-creation of the sociocultural life of Fez at the turn of the century, see Roger Le Tourneau, *Fès avant le Protectorat* (Casablanca: SMLE, 1949), and his *La vie quotidien à Fès en 1900* (Paris: Hachette, 1965). A very helpful comparison to Fez is provided for the twin city to Rabat in Kenneth L. Brown, *People of Salé: Tradition and Change in a Moroccan City, 1830–1930* (Manchester: Manchester University Press, 1976). The coastal city of Safi, where the Haj lived for much of the colonial era, is described in Yassir Benhima, *Safi et son territoire* (Paris: Harmattan, 2008); Allal Ragoug, ed., *Safi, regards Européens XVIIIé–XXé siècle* (Rabat, 2009); and Maurice de Périgny, *Au Maroc: Marrakech et les ports du sud* (Paris: P. Roger, 1918).

Military and civil officials who published memoirs of their time in Morocco during the transition to the Protectorate that are especially relevant to the Sefrou region include Pierre Khorat, *En colonne au Maroc* (Paris: Perrin, 1913); F. Weisgerber, *Au seuil du Maroc moderne* (Rabat: Éditions du Porte, 1947); Général Gouraud, *Au Maroc, 1911–1914: Souvenirs d'un Africain* (Paris: Plon, 1949); and Louis Arnaud, *Au temps des Mehallas, ou le Maroc de 1860 à 1912* (Casablanca: Éditions Atlantides, 1952).

The best overall analysis of the run-up to the Protectorate is provided in Edmund Burke III, *Prelude to Protectorate in Morocco: Precolonial Protest and Resistance, 1860–1912* (Chicago: University of Chicago Press, 1976), while his description of the important Middle Atlas Berber warrior mentioned in the chapter about Haj Hamed will be found in "Mohand N'Hamoucha: Middle Atlas Berber," in *Struggle and Survival in the Modern Middle East*, edited by Edmund Burke III and David N. Yaghoubian (Berkeley: University of California Press, 2006), 89–102. See also the discussion of tribal military action in the Middle Atlas in Edmund Burke III, "Tribalism and Moroccan Resistance, 1890–1914: The Role of the Aith Ndhir," in *Tribe and State: Essays in Honour of David Montgomery Hart*, edited by E. G. H. Joffé (Wisbech, UK: Middle East and North African Studies Press, 1991), 119–44.

Sociologists played a major role in developing French colonial approaches to Morocco. In addition to a long series of books describing various towns and tribes, one of the most trenchant works is surely Edmond Doutté, *En tribu* (Paris: P. Geuthner, 1914). Edmund Burke III analyzes the role played by these sociologists in *The Ethnographic State: France and the Invention of Moroccan Islam* (Berkeley: University of California Press, 2015). Particular aspects of the colonial period are covered in such works as Moshe Gershovich, *French Military Rule in Morocco: Colonialism and Its Consequences* (Portland, OR: Frank Cass, 2000); John P. Halstead, *Rebirth of a Nation: The Origins and Rise of Moroccan Nationalism, 1912–1944* (Cambridge, MA: Harvard Middle East Studies, 1967); Jacques Berque, *French North Africa: The Maghreb between Two World Wars* (London: Faber and Faber, 1967); William A. Hoisington Jr., *Lyautey and the French Conquest of Morocco* (New York: St. Martin's, 1995); Gavin Maxwell, *Lords of the Atlas: The Rise and Fall of the House of Glaoua, 1893–1956* (New York: Dutton,

1966); Douglas Porch, *The Conquest of Morocco* (New York: Farrar, Straus and Giroux, 2005); Yvonne Knibiehler et al., eds., *Des Français au Maroc: La présence et la mémoire (1912–1956)* (Paris: Éditions Denoël, 1992); Will D. Swearingen, *Moroccan Mirage: Agrarian Dreams and Deception, 1912–1986* (Princeton, NJ: Princeton University Press, 1987); Driss Maghraoui, ed., *Revisiting the Colonial Past in Morocco* (London: Routledge, 2013); and several books by Daniel Rivet: *Lyautey et l'institution du Protectorat Français au Maroc* (Paris: L'Harmattan, 1988); *Le Maroc de Lyautey à Mohammed V: Le double visage de Protectorat* (Paris: Denoël, 1999); and *Le Maghreb à l'épreuve de la colonisation* (Paris: Hachette, 2002).

For accounts by some of the French colonial administrators, see Roger Gruner, *Du Maroc traditionnel au Maroc moderne: Le contrôle civile au Maroc, 1912–1956* (Paris: Nouvelles Éditions Latine, 1984). On the service of Moroccans, like the Haj's son, in the French forces during the colonial period, see Driss Maghraoui, "Moroccan Colonial Soldiers: Between Selective Memory and Collective Memory," *Arab Studies Quarterly* 20.2 (Spring 1998): 21–41. For a vivid depiction of North Africans who served in the Second World War and were never properly acknowledged, see Rachid Bouchareb's film *Days of Glory* (in French, *Indigènes*; 2006).

The story of an American missionary in Sefrou is told in Evelyn Stenbock, *Miss Terri! The Story of Maude Cary* (Lincoln, NE: Back to the Bible, 1970). The career of the pasha of Sefrou and first prime minister of independent Morocco is presented in Achour Bekkai Lahbil, *Si Bekkai: Rendezvous avec l'histoire* (Casablanca: Imprimeries Mithaq-Almaghrib, 1999). On the role played by women in the struggle for independence, see Alison Baker, *Voices of Resistance: Oral Histories of Moroccan Women* (Albany: SUNY Press, 1998).

Yaghnik Driss and Religion

Good introductions to Islam are provided by Malise Ruthven, *Islam in the World*, 3rd ed. (Oxford: Oxford University Press, 2006); Fazlur Rahman, *Islam* (New York: Anchor Books, 1966); and Reza Aslan, *No God but God: The Origins, Evolution, and Future of Islam* (New York: Random House, 2005). My preferred translation of the Quran is Arthur J. Arberry, *The Koran Interpreted* (Oxford: Oxford University Press, 1964). For Islam in Morocco, see Dale F. Eickelman, *Moroccan Islam: Tradition and Society in a Pilgrimage Center* (Austin: University of Texas Press, 1976), and his *Knowledge and Power in Morocco: The Education of a Twentieth-Century Notable* (Princeton,

NJ: Princeton University Press, 1985); Stefania Pandolfo, *Impasse of the Angels: Scenes from a Moroccan Space of Memory* (Chicago: University of Chicago Press, 1997); Edmond Doutté, *Magie et religion dans l'Afrique du nord* (Paris: J. Maisonneuve, [1908] 1984); and the works of the Finnish ethnographer Edward Westermarck, *Ritual and Belief in Morocco* (London: Macmillan, 1926), and *Wit and Wisdom in Morocco: A Study of Native Proverbs* (New York: Liveright, 1931).

Jacques Berque has written about the patron saint of the Ait Youssi tribe, Abu Ali al-Hassan ibn Masud al-Youssi (1631–91), in *Al-Yousi: Problèmes de la culture Marocaine au 17è siècle* (The Hague: Mouton, 1958). A comparison of Indonesian and Moroccan Islam, including an analysis of the aforementioned saint, will be found in Clifford Geertz, *Islam Observed: Religious Development in Morocco and Indonesia* (New Haven, CT: Yale University Press, 1968). For an overview and assessment of the work in Sefrou by Clifford Geertz, including his work on Islam, see Susan Slyomovics, ed., *Clifford Geertz in Morocco* (London: Routledge, 2010). Approaches to such religious figures generally are collected in Jan Knappert, *Islamic Legends: History of the Heroes, Saints, and Prophets in Islam* (Leiden: Brill, 1985). A number of the essays in Ernest Gellner's *Muslim Society* (Cambridge: Cambridge University Press 1983) are very useful, while a general appraisal of his work will be found in John A. Hall, *Ernest Gellner: An Intellectual Biography* (London: Verso, 2010). Yaghnik's experience acting Shakespeare can be compared to the Bard's role in the theater of other Arab countries as described by Margaret Litvin, *Hamlet's Arab Journey: Shakespeare's Prince and Nasser's Ghost* (Princeton, NJ: Princeton University Press, 2011) and the essays in a special issue of *Critical Survey*, vol. 19, no. 1 (2007).

Among the more insightful studies of the relation of Islamic thought to broader cultural patterns are Jean-Paul Charnay, *Ambivalence dans la culture Arabe* (Paris: Éditions Anthropos, 1967), and two books by Toshihiko Izutsu, *God and Man in the Koran: Semantics of the Koranic Weltanschauung* (Tokyo: Keio Institute of Cultural and Linguistic Studies, 1964), and his *Ethico-Religious Concepts in the Qur'ān* (Montreal: McGill, 1966). My own essay, "Reading the Quran through Western Eyes," in Lawrence Rosen, *Varieties of Muslim Experience* (Chicago: University of Chicago Press, 2008), 75–92, may be useful for those first encountering the Quran in translation.

On the nature and roles of jinns, see Mohammed Maarouf, *Jinn Eviction as a Discourse of Power: A Multidisciplinary Approach to Moroccan Magical Beliefs and Practices* (Leiden: Brill, 2007), Robert Lebling, *Legends of the Fire Spirits: Jinns and Genies from Arabia to Zanzibar* (London: I. B. Tauris, 2010), and Barbara Drieskens, *Living with Djinns: Understanding and Dealing with the Invisible in Cairo* (London: Saqi, 2008). Moroccan ideas of the body, including the impact of jinns and concepts of purity, are explored in Josep Lluís Mateo Dieste, *Health and Ritual in Morocco: Conceptions of the Body and Healing Practices* (Leiden: Brill, 2013). On Islamic concepts of death and the afterlife, see Jane Idleman Smith and Yvonne Yazbeck Haddad, *The Islamic Understanding of Death and Resurrection* (Albany: SUNY Press, 1981); and Nerina Rustomji, *The Garden and the Fire: Heaven and Hell in Islamic Culture* (New York: Columbia University Press, 2009). For the impact of such views in more ecstatic theology, see Peter J. Awn, *Satan's Tragedy and Redemption: Iblis in Sufi Psychology* (Leiden: Brill, 1983).

Attempts to reconcile more traditional views of eschatology with modern science are analyzed in Rudolph Peters, "Resurrection, Revelation and Reason: Husayn Al-Jisr (d. 1909) and Islamic Eschatology," edited by J. M. Bremer, Th. P. J. van den Hout, and R. Peters, *Hidden Futures: Death and Immortality in Ancient Egypt, Anatolia, the Classical, Biblical, and Arab-Islamic World* (Amsterdam: Amsterdam University Press, 1994), 221–31. On the relation of Western medicine and science to the colonial enterprise, see Ellen J. Amster, *Medicine and the Saints: Science, Islam, and the Colonial Encounter in Morocco, 1877–1956* (Austin: University of Texas Press, 2013). The role of portraiture in Islam is discussed in my essay "Why Portraits Hold No Meaning for Arabs," in *Varieties of Muslim Experience*, 93–104. On the comparative study of the Adam and Eve story, see *Eve and Adam: Jewish, Christian, and Muslim Readings on Genesis and Gender*, edited by Kristen E. Kvam, Linda S. Schearing, and Valarie H. Ziegler (Bloomington: Indiana University Press, 1999).

Good studies of women in Morocco include Fatima Mernissi, *Le Maroc raconte par ses femmes* (Rabat: SMER, 1986); her autobiographical *Dreams of Trespass: Tales of a Harem Girlhood* (Reading, MA: Addison-Wesley, 1994); and Rachel Newcomb, *Women of Fez: Ambiguities of Urban Life in Morocco* (Philadelphia: University of Pennsylvania Press, 2010). See also the documentary *Class of 2006: Morocco's Female Religious Leaders*. http://www.pbs .org/wnet/wideangle/episodes/class-of-2006/introduction/961/.

The younger generation of Moroccans is discussed in Mounia Bennani-Chraibi and Rémy Leveau, *Soumis et rebelles: Les jeunes au Maroc* (Paris: CNRS, 1994). On the contemporary Islamist movements, see Marvine Howe, *Morocco: The Islamist Awakenings and Other Challenges* (Oxford: Oxford University Press, 2005); and Eva Wegner, *Islamist Opposition in Authoritarian Regimes: The Party of Justice and Development in Morocco* (Syracuse, NY: Syracuse University Press, 2011).

Hussein ou Muhammad Qadir: Politics and Tribes

Tribal organization in Morocco, as seen from quite different theoretical perspectives, can be found in David M. Hart, *Tribe and Society in Rural Morocco* (London: Routledge, 2000); Jacques Berque, *Structures sociales du Haut Atlas* (Paris: Presses Universitaires de France, 1955; also in English from the Human Relations Area Files); Ernest Gellner, *Saints of the Atlas* (London: Weidenfeld and Nicolson, 1969); Robert Montagne, *The Berbers: Their Social and Political Organization* (London: Cass, 1973); Amal Rassam Vinogradov, *The Ait Ndhir of Morocco* (Ann Arbor: University of Michigan Near East Studies, 1974); and my own essays "What Is a Tribe and Why Does It Matter?" 39–55, and "Ambivalence towards Power," 21–38, both in Lawrence Rosen, *The Culture of Islam: Changing Aspects of Contemporary Muslim Life* (Chicago: University of Chicago Press, 2002). For the story of a local election to which Hussein refers, see Lawrence Rosen, "Rural Political Process and National Political Structure in Morocco," in *Rural Politics and Social Change in the Middle East*, edited by Richard T. Antoun and Iliya Harik, 214–33 (Bloomington: Indiana University Press, 1972). Still quite useful are the essays in *Arabs and Berbers: From Tribe to Nation in North Africa*, edited by Ernest Gellner and Charles Micaud (Lexington, MA: Heath, 1972). The book by Marshall D. Sahlins, *Tribesmen* (New York: Prentice-Hall, 1968), though written when the author was in his cultural evolution phase, remains a good overview of the distinctive qualities of tribal forms of organization.

A general overview of the Berbers of North Africa from prehistoric times to the present is Michael Brett and Elizabeth Fentress, *The Berbers* (Oxford: Blackwell, 1996). The markets in which Hussein is involved are well presented in John Waterbury, *North for the Trade: The Life and Times of a Berber Merchant* (New York: Columbia University Press, 1972); and Deborah Kapchan, *Gender on the Market: Moroccan Women and the Revoicing of Tradition* (Philadelphia: University of Pennsylvania Press, 1996). On the broader context of the Moroccan economy during the Protectorate and early independence years, see Charles F. Stewart, *The Economy of Morocco, 1912–1962* (Cambridge, MA: Harvard University Middle East Studies, 1964). On the changing views the French entertained about the Berbers of the Middle Atlas Mountains, see Lahsen Jennan, "Le Moyen Atlas et les Français: Évolution des connaissances et du savoir sur l'espèce et sur la société rurale," in *Présences et images Franco-marocaines au temps du protectorat*, edited by Jean-Claude Allain (Paris: L'Harmattan, 2003), 53–75. The Berber Dahir and its relation to the current Berber revival is discussed in David M. Hart,

"The Berber Dahir of 1930 in Colonial Morocco: Then and Now (1930–1996)," *Journal of North African Studies* 2.1 (Autumn 1997): 11–33; and Gilles Lafuente, *La politique Berbère de la France et le nationalisme Marocain* (Paris: L'Harmattan, 1999). The training of a Berber elite is analyzed in Mohamed Benhlal, *Le collège d'Azrou: Une élite Berbère civile et militaire au Maroc, 1927–1959* (Paris: Karthala, 2005). The armed nationalist struggle is described in Nadir Bouzar, *L'Armée de Libération Nationale Marocaine: 1955–56* (Paris: Publisud, 2002); and Mohammed Zade, *Résistance et Armée de Libération au Maroc (1947–1956)* (Rabat: Imprimerie des Éditions Kawtar, 2006). The approach of the Istiqlal movement leader Allal al-Fassi is available in translation in his *The Independence Movements in Arab North Africa* (London: Octagon Books, 1970).

The central study of Moroccan political culture during the reign of Hassan II remains John Waterbury, *The Commander of the Faithful: The Moroccan Political Elite* (New York: Columbia University Press, 1970), while more current issues of King Hassan's politics and human rights record are described by Susan Slyomovics, in *The Performance of Human Rights in Morocco* (Philadelphia: University of Pennsylvania Press, 2005); and Fadoua Loudiy, *Transitional Justice and Human Rights in Morocco: Negotiating the Years of Lead* (Abingdon, UK: Routledge, 2014). The story of the imprisoned family of the general who sought to overthrow the king in the early 1970s is told in the memoir by his daughter Malika Oufkir, *Stolen Lives: Twenty Years in a Desert Jail* (London: Hyperion, 1999). On the background to the Saharan war, see Tony Hodges, *Western Sahara: The Roots of a Desert War* (Westport, CT: Lawrence Hill, 1983). On the politics of rural dwellers in the early years of independence, see Remy Leveau, *Le fellah Marocain, défenseur du Trône* (Paris: Presses de la Fondation Nationale des Sciences Politiques, 1976). The Berber revival is discussed in Bruce Maddy-Weitzman, *The Berber Identity Movement and the Challenge to North African States* (Austin: University of Texas Press, 2011).

Broader interpretations of Moroccan politics can be found in Mohammed Tozy, *Monarchie et Islam politique au Maroc* (Paris: Presses de Sciences PO, 1999); and Daoud Zakya and Maâti Monjib, *Ben Barka* (Paris: Michalon, 1996). Abdellah Hammoudi's *Master and Disciple: The Cultural Foundations of Moroccan Authoritarianism* (Chicago: University of Chicago Press, 1997) offers an interpretation of the sources of paternalistic authority in Moroccan culture more generally. On the Arab Spring in North Africa, see *L'année du Maghreb*, 8 (Paris: CNRS Éditions, 2012).

Shimon Benizri and Muslim-Jewish Relations

The history of Muslim-Jewish relations in various periods and places is available in Bernard Lewis, *The Jews of Islam* (London: Routledge and Kegan Paul, 1984); Maria Rosa Menocal, *The Ornament of the World: How Muslims, Jews, and Christians Created a Culture of Tolerance in Medieval Spain* (Boston: Little, Brown, 2002); Abdelwahab Meddeb and Benjamin Stora, eds., *A History of Jewish-Muslim Relations: From the Origins to the Present Day* (Princeton, NJ: Princeton University Press, 2013); and Norman Stillman et al., eds., *Encyclopedia of Jews in the Islamic World* (Leiden: Brill, 2010). Whether a number of the Jews of North Africa came from Palestine after the destruction of the second temple in 70 C.E. and made Berber converts along the way is considered in H. Z. (J. W.) Hirschberg, *A History of Jews in North Africa*, 2 vols. (Leiden: Brill, 1974 and 1981), while a more recent appraisal of the issue is contained in Daniel Schroeter, "On the Origins and Identity of Indigenous North African Jews," in *North African Mosaic: A Cultural Reappraisal of Ethnic and Religious Minorities*, edited by Nabil Boudraa and Joseph Krause (Newcastle, UK: Cambridge Scholars, 2007), 164–77. On the (perhaps mythical) Jewish/Berber woman warrior-queen Kahina, see Abdelmajid Hannoum, *Colonial Histories, Post-colonial Memories: The Legend of the Kahina, a North African Heroine* (London: Heinemann, 2001). Among the many accounts of early travelers to Morocco who noted the situation of the Jews are Lancelot Addison, *The Present State of the Jews* (London: William Crook, 1682); Samuel Aaron Romanelli, *Travail in an Arab Land* (Tuscaloosa: University of Alabama Press, 1989); and G. Montbard, *Among the Moors* (New York: Charles Scribner's Sons, 1894). For a study of the nineteenth-century martyrdom of Sol Hashuel, see Sharon Vance, *The Martyrdom of a Moroccan Jewish Saint* (Leiden: Brill, 2011).

An increasing number of Moroccan Muslims have been studying Muslim-Jewish relations; See, for example, Mohammed Kenbib, *Juifs et Musulmans au Maroc 1859–1948* (Rabat: Université Mohammed V, 1994). The attacks on Jews in Fez in 1912 are described in a number of documents, many of them translated into English and French, in Paul B. Fenton, *Le pogrome de Fès ou le Tritel, 17–19 avril 1912* (Jerusalem: Centre de Recherche Français à Jérusalem, 2012). On the efforts of Sir Moses Montefiore to address the Jews' situation, see David Littman, *Mission to Morocco, 1863–1864* (Oxford: Oxford University Press, 1995). Jews who served the sultans' courts at various times are discussed in Daniel J. Schroeter, *The Sultan's Jew: Morocco and the Sephardi World* (Stanford, CA: Stanford University Press,

2002); and Michel Abitbol, *Les commerçants du roi: Tujjar al-sultan: Une élite économique Judéo-marocaine au XIXè siècle* (Paris: Maisonneuve et Larose, 1998). On the protection of Jews by foreign governments, see Mohammed Kenbib, *Les protégés: Contributions à l'histoire contemporaine au Maroc* (Rabat: Publications de Faculté des Lettres et Sciences Humaines, 1996). On the colonial period generally, see Doris Bensimon, *Évolution du Judaïsme Marocain sous le Protectorat* (The Hague: Mouton, 1968); and Daniel J. Schroeter, "From Dhimmis to Colonial Subjects: Moroccan Jews and the Sharifian and French Colonial State," *Studies in Contemporary Jewry* 19 (2003): 104–23.

Pictures of the Vichy-era camps in southern Morocco, along with various Jewish settlements and shrines in the area, will be found at the website jewishmorocco.org, while a fuller analysis of the camps will be found in Jacob Oliel, *Les camps de Vichy: Maghreb-Sahara, 1939–1945* (Montreal: Éditions du Lys, 2005). More ethnographic accounts of Jewish communal life, dating from various periods, include José Bénech, *Essai d'explication d'un mellah* (Paris: Larose, 1940); Joseph Georges Arsène Goulven, *Les mellahs de Rabat-Salé* (Paris: P. Geuthner, 1927); and Shlomo Deshen, *The Mellah Society: Jewish Community Life in Sharifian Morocco* (Chicago: University of Chicago Press, 1989). An excellent analysis of the legal relations of Muslims and Jews, mainly in Meknes, will be found in Jessica M. Marglin, "In the Courts of the Nations: Jews, Muslims, and Legal Pluralism in Nineteenth-Century Morocco" (PhD diss., Princeton University, 2013). For an important comparative example, see Abraham Udovitch and Lucette Valensi, *The Last Arab Jews: The Communities of Jerba Tunisia* (New York: Harwood, 1984). The historical structure of Jewish communal organization is presented in Jane Gerber, *Jewish Society in Fez, 1450–1700* (Leiden: Brill, 1980). Saint veneration is a constant theme in studies of Moroccan Jewry: See, for example, Issachar Ben-Ami, *Saint Veneration among Jews in Morocco* (Detroit: Wayne State University Press, 1998); L. Voinot, *Pèlerinage Judéo-musulmans du Maroc* (Paris: Larose, 1948); and Elie Azoulay, *Maroc terre des saints: Histoire et origine des saints Juifs du Maroc* (Laval, QC: Jeremy, Elie et Jacob Victor Azoulay, 2000).

The establishment of Western schools in Morocco is discussed in Michael M. Laskier, *The Alliance Israélite Universelle and the Jewish Communities of Morocco 1862–1962* (Albany: SUNY, 1983); and Shalom Bar-Asher, "The Emancipation of North African Jewish Women: The *Alliance Israélite Universelle*," in *Jews and Muslims in the Islamic World*, edited by Bernard Dov Cooperman and Zvi Zohar (College Park: University Press of Maryland, 2013), 33–50. The period surrounding the Second World War and the role played by Sultan Muhammad V in protecting the Jews of Morocco is carefully analyzed in Robert Satloff, *Among the Righteous: Lost Stories from the Holocaust's Long Reach into the Arab Lands* (New York: PublicAffairs, 2006); Michel Abitbol, *The Jews of North Africa during the Second World War* (Detroit: Wayne State University Press, 1989); and Robert Assaraf, *Mohammed V et les Juifs du Maroc à l'époque de Vichy* (Paris: Plon, 1997). On the 1967 war, see Avi Raz, *The Bride and the Dowry: Israel, Jordan, and the Palestinians in the Aftermath of the June 1967 War* (New Haven, CT: Yale University Press, 2012); and William Roger Louis and Avi Shlaim, eds., *The 1967 Arab-Israeli War: Origins and Consequences* (Cambridge: Cambridge University Press, 2012).

On the festival of Mimouna as a time of ritual interaction between Muslims and Jews, see Harvey Goldberg, "The Mimuna and the Minority Status of Moroccan Jews," *Ethnology* 17.1 (January 1978): 75–87; Nessim Mohammed, *Trois énigmes* (Los Angeles: J. T. Productions, 2003); and a lecture by Abdellah Hammoudi, "Giving and Receiving Yeast; or, How to Keep Radically Different Identities Together," which can be seen at http://www.youtube.com/watch?v=XdxV274f0H8. For similar rituals see Abdellah Hammoudi, *The Victim and Its Masks: An Essay on Sacrifice and Masquerade in the Maghreb* (Chicago: University of Chicago Press, 1993). The shared music of Muslims and Jews is discussed by Joseph Chetrit, "Music and Poetry as a Shared Cultural Space for Muslims and Jews in Morocco," in *Studies in the History and Culture of North African Jewry*, edited by Moshe Bar-Asher and Steven D. Fraade (New Haven, CT: Yale Program in Judaic Studies, 2011), 65–103. The effort to get Moroccan Jews to Israel is described in Michel Meir Knafo, *Le Mossad et les secrets du réseau Juif au Maroc, 1955–1964* (Paris: Biblieurope, 2008); and Agnes Bensimon, *Hassan II et les Juifs* (Paris: Seuil, 1991).

How Jews and Muslims of different generations in the Anti-Atlas region, individually and collectively, recall their history is discussed in Aomar Boum, *Memories of Absence: How Muslims Remember Jews in Morocco* (Stanford, CA: Stanford University Press, 2013). For other recollections see Armand Lévy, *Il était une fois les Juifs Marocains* (Paris: Harmattan, 1995); Robert Assaraf and Michel Abitbol, eds., *Perception & réalités au Maroc: Relations Judéo-Musulmanes* (Rabat: CRIM, 1998); and Albert Memmi, *Jews and Arabs* (Chicago: O'Hara, 1975). There are also many memoires and novels, among them Ruth Knafo Setton, *The Road to Fez: A Novel* (Washington, DC: Counterpoint, 2001); Victor Malka, *La mémoire brisée* (Paris: Éditions Entente, 1978); Emanuela Trevisan Semi and Hanane Sekkat Hatimi, *Mémoire et représentations des Juifs au Maroc: Les voisins absents de Meknès* (Paris:

Éditions Publisud, 2011); and Paul Ohana, *Mon père au coeur du Judaïsme Marocain* (Paris: Harmattan, 2012). Abraham Serfaty, a Casablancan Jew, tortured and imprisoned for seventeen years in the 1970s and 1980s by King Hassan for his political views, discusses his experiences and those of other Jews with his coauthor Mikhaël Elbaz in *L'insoumis: Juifs, Marocains et Rebelles* (Paris: Desclée de Brouwer, 2001). For a novel whose Muslim characters express ambivalence toward Jews in the Algerian setting, see Tahir Wattar, *The Earthquake* (London: Saqi Books, 2000), especially at pages 156ff.

For more recent encounters, see André Levy, *Moroccan Voyage* (Chicago: University of Chicago Press, 2015), and several of his articles, including "Notes on Jewish-Muslim Relationships," *Cultural Anthropology* 18.3 (2003): 365–97, and "Controlling Space, Essentializing Identities: Jews in Contemporary Casablanca," *City & Society*, 1997 (1997): 175–96. Additional sources include Arlette Berdugo, *Juives et Juifs dans le Maroc contemporain* (Paris: Paul Geuthner, 2002); and Lawrence Rosen, "Contesting Sainthood," in Lawrence Rosen *The Culture of Islam*, 75–87. The role of Moroccan saint veneration in the lives of Moroccan Jews who have emigrated to Israel is discussed in Yoram Bilu and Eyal Ben-Ari, "The Making of Modern Saints: Manufactured Charisma and the Abu-Hatseiras of Israel," *American Ethnologist* 19.4 (November 1992): 672–87; and Alex Weingrod, *The Saint of Beersheba* (Albany: SUNY Press, 1990).

The lives of Moroccan Jewish émigrés are also analyzed in Shlomo A. Deshen, *The Predicament of Homecoming: Cultural and Social Life of North African Immigrants in Israel* (Ithaca, NY: Cornell University Press, 1974); and Moshe Shokeid, *The Dual Heritage: Immigrants from the Atlas Mountains in an Israeli Village* (Manchester: Manchester University Press, 1971). For a film sponsored by the American Jewish Joint Distribution Committee that follows the departure of an entire community from the Moroccan south in the 1950s entitled *The Jews of Morocco*, see http://www.youtube.com/ watch?v=TarnykO-sWI (accessed February 17, 2015). The immigrants' lives are also portrayed in such documentaries as *Routes of Exile* and *Tinghir-Jérusalem: Les échos du Mellah* (which can be viewed at http://www.youtube .com/watch?v=hYuTbuD9tfM), as well as in the fictional film *Turn Left at the End of the World*.

The archives of the Jewish community of Sefrou were taken to Israel by the chief rabbi who subsequently published many of the documents and his own commentary in a five-volume work in Hebrew, David Ovadyah, *Kehilat Tsafaru : divre yeme ha-Yehudim bi-ḳ.ḳ. Tsafaru . . . Maroḳo: meḳorot u-teʿudot le-matsevam u-maʿamadam ha-kalkali, ha-ḥevrati, ha-medini veha-*

ruḥani : ḳorotehem u-me'or'otehem, taḳanotehem u-minhagehem, mikhteve-hem, igroteh (Jerusalem: Makhon le-Heker Toldot Kehilot Yehude Maroko, 1974–). A detailed history of one Sefrou rabbinical family is to be found in Refa'el Maman, *Sefer 'Amram* (Jerusalem: Mekhon "Imre Shalom," 2006). A historical example of the role played by a key Sefrou rabbi of the late eighteenth to early nineteenth century is discussed in Moshe Amar's "The Responsa *Avnei Shayish* by Rabbi Shaul Yeshu'a Abitbol of Sefrou: A Source for the History of the Jews in Morocco in the Years 1770–1810," in *Studies in the History and Culture of North African Jewry*, edited by Moshe Bar-Asher and Steven D. Fraade (New Haven, CT: Program in Judaic Studies, Yale University, 2011), 11–34. Excellent collections of photographs and postcards depicting Morocco and Jewish life from the late nineteenth century onward can be found at the website of the Centre de la Culture Judéo-Marocain in Brussels, Belgium, and in the Collection Gérard Lévy, Paris. A number of online sources that contain (sometimes erroneous) recollections of life in the Jewish communities of Morocco, including Sefrou, can be found at Diarna Geo-Museum of Jewish Life in the Middle East and North Africa, www.Dafina.net; and http://rickgold.home.mindspring.com/links1.htm.

Committed to Memory: Haj Hamed Britel

The image that begins the chapter is the name of God written in the North African style.

A Midmost Nation: Yaghnik Driss

The image that begins the chapter is a stylized calligraphic rendition of the name of God.

The Arabic at the end of the chapter is the phrasing that begins most chapters of the Quran: *b-ismi-llāhi r-raḥmāni r-rāḥimi* (In the name of God, the most Gracious, and the most Merciful)

Courier of the Horizons: Hussein ou Muhammad Qadir

The word that begins the chapter, *Tamazight*, is the Berber word for the people of the Middle Atlas Mountains written in the Berber alphabet.

The image that concludes the chapter is the Berber ideograph that represents a man and translates as "free."

A Nation among Nations: Shimon Benizri

The image that begins the chapter is a Moroccan version of the Star of David.

The concluding passage from Psalm 48:14 is often associated with the name Shimon and may be recited by a man with that name at the conclusion of the major prayer called the *Amidah*.

INDEX